THE PANARION
OF
EPIPHANIUS OF SALAMIS

NAG HAMMADI STUDIES

EDITED BY

MARTIN KRAUSE – JAMES M. ROBINSON
FREDERIK WISSE

IN CONJUNCTION WITH

ALEXANDER BÖHLIG – JEAN DORESSE – SØREN GIVERSEN
HANS JONAS – RODOLPHE KASSER – PAHOR LABIB
GEORGE W. MACRAE† – JACQUES-É. MÉNARD –
TORGNY SÄVE-SÖDERBERGH – R. MCL. WILSON – JAN ZANDEE

XXXV

VOLUME EDITOR

JAMES M. ROBINSON

THE PANARION
OF
EPIPHANIUS OF SALAMIS

Book I (Sects 1-46)

TRANSLATED BY

FRANK WILLIAMS

E.J. BRILL
LEIDEN · NEW YORK · KØBENHAVN · KÖLN
1987

Library of Congress Cataloging-in-Publication Data

Epiphanius, Saint, Bp. of Constantia in Cyprus.
  The Panarion of Epiphanius of Salamis Book I,
Sects 1-46.

  (Nag Hammadi studies, ISSN 0169-9350; 35)
  Translation of: Panarion.   Book I, Sects 1-46.
  Includes bibliographical references and index.
  1. Heresies, Christian—History—Early church,
ca. 30-600. 2. Gnosticism. I. Title. II. Series.
BR65.E653P36   1987   273'.4   87-6375
ISBN 90-04-07926-2

ISSN 0169-9350
ISBN 90 04 07926 2

PRINTED IN THE NETHERLANDS BY E. J. BRILL

CONTENTS

(Most sections of the work are titled as in the manuscripts. Modern titles are noted with an asterisk.)

ACKNOWLEDGEMENTS

The initial work on this translation was made possible by a grant from the National Endowment for the Humanities of the United States of America, for which I am most grateful.

I am indebted to Dr. J. Dummer, for graciously making available his suggested emendations in advance of the publication of the second edition of Holl.

I owe many thanks to Professors James M. Robinson, James Brashler, and Douglas M. Parrott, of the Institute for Antiquity and Christianity, for their encouragement and fostering of this enterprise; and to Professors Richard MacNeal and Ekkehard Mühlenberg, and Dr. Jon Dechow, who read portions of the manuscript and offered valuable suggestions.

I appreciate the hard work of Mrs. Deborah DeGolyer and Mr. Clayton Jefford in typing the manuscript.

Finally, special thanks are due my wife, Charlotte, without whose patience, understanding and encouragement this work could never have been done.

INTRODUCTION

The following translation renders Book I of the *Panarion* of Epiphanius of Salamis, as edited by Karl Holl in *Die griechischen christlichen Schriftsteller der ersten drei Jahrhunderte*, and updated by Jürgen Dummer. Issued in 1915 by the J. C. Hinrichs'sche Buchhandlung, Book I includes Sects 1-46 of the *Panarion*, and is preceded by the introductory letter of Acacius and Paul, and Epiphanius' two Proems. The new edition of Holl's text, now in production under Dummer's editorship, expands the notes considerably but only occasionally makes new emendations to the text. Where these are available we translate them as updates of Holl's work, and note them with an asterisk.

An entirely new edition of the *Panarion*'s text is now in preparation under the direction of Pierre Nautin. This may differ more largely from Holl than does Dummer's text, and so require a number of alternate translations. It should be possible to issue a list of these when the new edition becomes available.

Holl's text of Book II, Sects 47-64, was published in 1922. Book III, containing Sects 65-80 and Epiphanius' concluding essay, *De Fide*, was completed after Holl's death by Hans Lietzmann and Walter Eltester, and published in 1933. A translation of these portions of the *Panarion* is in progress.

It is hoped that a modern language version of the *Panarion* will meet a need. Sixteenth and seventeenth century ecclesiastical interests gave rise to three Latin versions, but the concerns of later scholarship have been with the *Panarion*'s text itself, or with historico-theological investigation. A Russian version of the entire *Panarion* did appear in the nineteenth century. Otherwise the only modern translations of parts of Book I are: German versions of the first three Anacephalaeoses and the essay, *The Advent*, by Wolfsgruber in 1880[1] and Hörmann in 1919;[2] an English rendering of parts of Sect 26 by S. Benko in 1967;[3] an English rendering of Sect 30 in its entirety by Glen Alan Koch in 1976.[4] The present version

---

[1] C. Wolfsgruber, *Ancoratus, Anakephalaiosis und Panarion 78*, Bibliothek der Kirchenväter, 1880.

[2] J. Hörmann, *Ancoratus, Anakephalaiosis und Panarion 78*, Bibliothek der Kirchenväter, 1919.

[3] S. Benko, "The Libertine Gnostic Sect of the Phibionites according to Epiphanius," *Vigiliae Christianae* 21 (1967), pp. 103-119.

[4] Glen Alan Koch, *A Critical Investigation of Epiphanius' Knowledge of the Ebionites: A Translation and Critical Discussion of Panarion 30*, Dissertation, University of Pennsylvania, 1976, Chapter 2.

has been compared with these, although the German translators worked from the Migne text.[5]

Text

Holl presented the history of the *Panarion*'s text in *Texte und Untersuchungen* 36.2 (1910). He concluded that the *Panarion* had been the victim of poor transmission. Its eleven extant manuscripts, none complete, all descend from one carelessly copied archetype, and the text has been further contaminated by Atticizing scribes. Holl criticized the editors who preceded him for paying insufficient attention to these matters, ignoring Epiphanius' distinctive style and vocabulary, and either emending wilfully, or else allowing absurdities to stand on the assumption that Epiphanius was in any case a confused thinker.

It is easy to understand Holl's impatience on both points. The Koine of Epiphanius would certainly tempt an Atticizer to make improvements. On the other hand, while Epiphanius is a rather difficult author he is certainly not a "confused thinker" in the sense that he could not express himself intelligibly. In the *Panarion* he planned and carried through a work on a grand scale, and that in a short time. He was competent in his own field, scriptural exegesis as he understood the discipline. He does not lose his place in his complex argumentation; his digressions are rarely over-lengthy, and he unfailingly returns to the point. The difficulties in understanding the *Panarion* stem partly from Epiphanius' idiom, partly from his manner of paraphrasing sources, and partly from the rapid informality of his delivery; but Epiphanius' expression makes sense.

Holl's work has not escaped criticism. Nonetheless it is a carefully edited critical text, and a great improvement on its predecessors. Holl made rather sparing emendations. Oftener than corrections of presumedly miscopied words, Holl's emendations usually had to do with scribal omissions, most commonly, of a word or a short phrase, occasionally of a longer unit. These appear to clear up many difficulties; in context, many of Holl's restorations seem the most logical choice.

Naturally it is often possible to suggest other alternatives; moreover, the text sometimes gives a plausible sense unrestored. The *Panarion* was written—or, to judge by its manner, in part dictated—under pressure, and may not have been as smooth as Holl assumed. For consistency's sake, however, and to avoid an attempt to revise Holl piecemeal, we render Holl's text, with Dummer's updates, as it stands.

---

[5] Modern translations of other portions of the *Panarion* are, Jon Dechow, *Epiphanius, Panarion 64*, publication pending; C. Riggi, *Epifanio contro Mani*, (*Panarion 66*), Rome, 1967.

Epiphanius' Life and Writings

Our chief sources of information about Epiphanius' life are his own works and correspondence, references in Jerome, who was Epiphanius' friend, in Palladius' *Dialogue*, Basil of Caesarea, Theophilus of Alexandria, the ecclesiastical histories of Socrates and Sozomen, and the anonymous preface to the ancient editions of Epiphanius' *Ancoratus*. The legendary Life ascribed to the monks John and Polybius witnesses to the veneration in which Epiphanius was held, but is not historically valuable. In modern times Jon Dechow has prepared a careful study of Epiphanius' biography, and the anti-Origenist aspect of his thought.[6]

Early in the fourth century A.D., perhaps between 310 and 320, Epiphanius was born in Palestine at Besanduc, a village in the environs of Eleutheropolis, near Gaza. If his *Letter to Theodosius*[7] is authentic, we have his own testimony that he was brought up by Christian parents "in the faith of the fathers of Nicaea."[8] He received his early education from monks (Soz. *Hist.* VI.32) and completed his training in Egypt. An important influence on him, in Egypt and later in Palestine, was his friend and teacher the ascetic Hilarion, who in his turn had been taught by Anthony of Egypt.

This background is an aid to the understanding of Epiphanius. Indoctrinated early with Nicene Christianity, he was a monk practically from childhood. His education, Christian and scriptural rather than classical —and certainly along Nicene lines—would have amply reinforced his childhood training. A particular version of Christianity would have been part of his identity from the first. It is no surprise that alternate versions appeared as threats—Epiphanius would have termed them "poisonous snakes"—to be guarded against.

One such threat came early in the form of a sexually-oriented group which Epiphanius encountered in Egypt (*Panarion* 26,17,4-9) and identified as "Gnostics." This episode, which endangered Epiphanius' chastity as well as his faith, may help to explain his particular detestation of anything Gnostic.

Returning to Palestine at the age of twenty, Epiphanius founded a monastery at Eleutheropolis (*Ancoratus*, Praef.) and presumably served as

---

[6] Jon Dechow, *Dogma and Mysticism in Early Christianity: Epiphanius of Cyprus and the Legacy of Origen*, Dissertation, University of Pennsylvania, 1975. Available from University Microfilms International, Ann Arbor, Michigan.

[7] For a discussion of the authenticity of Epiphanius' writings against images, see Karl Holl, "Die Schriften des Epiphanius gegen die Bilderverehrung," *Gesammelte Aufsätze zur Kirchengeschichte* II, Tübingen, 1928, pp. 351-398.

[8] Cited in Nicephorus, *Adversus Epiphanium*, XV, 61, Pitra, *Spicilegium Solesmense*, p. 340, 8-10.

its abbot. His friendship with Hilarion continued; Jerome tells us (*Vita Hilarionis*, Praef.) that when Hilarion died some years later, Epiphanius composed a letter in praise of his virtues.

We know little of Epiphanius' governance of his monastery. *Panarion* 40,1,6, his only personal reminiscence of his abbacy, shows that he was diligent in keeping the community free of heresy. We know that he made efforts during this period to foster his version of Nicene Christianity. He seems to have remonstrated with Eutychius, bishop of Eleutheropolis, for supporting the rejection of the *homoousion* at the Council of Seleucia in 359; he may have had some influence upon Eutychius' later reversal of his position.[9]

Epiphanius' meeting with Eusebius of Vercelli, alluded to at *Panarion* 30,5,2, would have come some time after 355, the approximate date of Eusebius' exile from his see. It was on this occasion that Epiphanius met the Jew, Josephus of Tiberias, who told him the colorful story he relates at *Panarion* 30,6,1-12,10.

In about 367 Epiphanius was invited to Cyprus to become bishop of Salamis (Constantia) near the modern Famagusta. Hilarion, who had moved to Cyprus shortly before, may have had some influence on the election. In any case it was an instance of the growing tendency, later to become widespread in eastern Christianity, to draw bishops from the monastic ranks. Epiphanius' contemporaries, Basil of Caesarea and John Chrysostom, are other examples.

Again, we know little of the details of Epiphanius' episcopal administration. The *Panarion* speaks so highly in praise of the ascetic life that we must visualize its author, on Cyprus, as continuing his previous austerity. (However, he did not abstain from meat and wine, and did not particularly approve of those abstinences.) He fostered the monastic movement on Cyprus; Jerome's *Vita Paulae* tells us that his fame attracted novices from all over the world. *Ancoratus* 102-107 shows us that he was missionary-minded. And the interest in detail which he repeatedly manifests, in the *Panarion* and elsewhere, suggests administrative capacity.

Of his writings, and of his travels in the interest of Nicene Christianity, we are better though not fully informed. His earliest datable extant work is a fragment of a *Letter to Eusebius, Marcellus, Bibianus and Carpus*, preserved on pages 238 and 239 of Codex Ambrosianus 515, and written between 367 and 373. This contains a chronology of the week of Christ's passion, and is meant to defend the Antiochene date of Easter, the Sun-

---

[9] Dechow, *Dogma and Mysticism*, pp. 20-23.

day after Nisan 14.[10] Undatable are a detailed refutation of Marcion's canon, and an epistle to the Christians of Arabia defending the doctrine of Mary's perpetual virginity (*Panarion* 42,11-12 and 78).

Written in 374, the *Ancoratus* is Epiphanius' most acute work. Its form is that of a letter to the church of Syedra in Pamphylia. The "barque" of this church, it is said, cannot enter harbor because of contrary winds of bad doctrine, particularly the denial of divinity and personality to the Holy Spirit. Epiphanius shows it how to become "anchored", ἀγκυρωτός (*Ancoratus*, Letter of Palladius 1;3; *Ancoratus* 119,16). In addition to the Holy Spirit, the *Ancoratus* discusses the Trinity, the Incarnation and Resurrection, attacks Origen's treatment of Genesis, and includes a polemic against the Greek gods. At 12,7-13,8 it gives the outline of what was to become the *Panarion*, suggesting that Epiphanius already had this work in mind. The *Panarion* itself was begun in 375, and issued about three years later. As a comprehensive refutation of everything Epiphanius considered heresy, it can be regarded as a sequel to the *Ancoratus*. We discuss it below.

During the same period Epiphanius attempted to make peace in the Melitian schism at Antioch. The Antiochene Christian community was split into four factions, headed respectively by the Arian Euzoeus, and by three representatives of some form of Nicene Christianity, Melitius (in exile), Apollinarius and Paulinus. The situation was further complicated by Apollinarius' denial of a human mind (νοῦς) to Christ, though Epiphanius was at first unaware of Apollinarius' position.

Epiphanius found himself dealing, first with young disciples of Apollinarius who arrived at Cyprus about 370, and later with Vitalis, whom Apollinarius consecrated bishop of Antioch, perhaps late in 376.

Apollinarius' disciples apparently taught a distorted version of his doctrine, which they were brought to recant. Somewhat later, perhaps in 376, Epiphanius journeyed to Antioch in hopes of reconciling Vitalis and his congregation with Paulinus and his. Here investigation convinced Epiphanius that Vitalis and his mentor Apollinarius were teaching an inadequate Christology; he therefore entered into communion with Paulinus.[11]

From 377 on it became apparent that Apollinarius, who rejected Epiphanius and Paulinus and consecrated new bishops, intended to continue on his chosen path. Damasus of Rome, whose support he had sought, condemned him in letters to Paulinus, and to a group of Egyp-

---

[10] Karl Holl, "Ein Bruchstück aus einem bisher unbekannten Brief des Epiphanius," *Festgabe für Adolf Jülicher zum 70. Geburtstag*, 1927, pp. 159-189.

[11] For a full discussion of Epiphanius' relations with Antioch during these years, see Dechow, *Dogma and Mysticism*, pp. 39-78.

tian exiles in Diocaesarea. This condemnation was supported by synods in Alexandria and Antioch, and in 381 by the First Council of Constantinople.

Whether Epiphanius attended this Council is uncertain. In 382, however, he travelled with Jerome to Rome, to attend the synod which Damasus convened to deal with the disputes between east and west. At Rome Epiphanius boarded with the wealthy widow Paula, and was instrumental in convincing her to abandon the luxurious life of a Roman aristocrat for the cloister. As a result Paula journeyed east with Jerome and became foundress of a convent at Bethlehem (Jerome, *Vita Paulae* 20). A few years later, perhaps in 385, we find Epiphanius visiting her there on her sickbed, and laboring unsuccessfully to convince her of the propriety of drinking wine when ill (Jerome, *Vita Paulae* 20).

Seven years later, in 392, Epiphanius published *De Mensuris et Ponderibus*, a sort of manual of information for students of scripture. In 393 we find him on another visit to Palestine. It was on this journey that he discovered a curtain painted with an image in a village church, tore it down, and told the parishioners to use it as a burial shroud for the poor. His *Letter to John*, bishop of Jerusalem, written in 394 or 395 (Epiphanius/Jerome *Epistle* 51) discusses this incident and gives Epiphanius' promise to replace the curtain. The letter also tries to explain Epiphanius' ordination of Jerome's brother Paulinian to the priesthood at Bethlehem in 394—an ordination of questionable canonicity, since it was performed in John's jurisdiction but without his sanction. Most importantly, the *Letter to John* contains an attack on the teaching of Origen, with which John seems to have sympathized and to which Epiphanius was extremely hostile.

This letter thus illustrates two of Epiphanius' important concerns, his opposition to the use of images and his anti-Origenism. Dechow has suggested that Epiphanius' writings and influence were an important stimulus to the growth of anti-Origenism in the late fourth and early fifth centuries.[12] Epiphanius respected Origen's scholarship, and the *Hexapla*, but considered his doctrine Gnostic in character, the source of Arianism, and a danger to the church. Some of Epiphanius' objections to Origen's teachings were voiced in the *Ancoratus* (54-63; 87-92); they, and others, are discussed at length in *Panarion* 64. The *Letter to John*, written fourteen or fifteen years after the *Panarion*, amounts to an anti-Origenist tract. Later still Epiphanius' journey to Constantinople, the last of his life, was also motivated by his opposition to Origenism. This opposition was thus characteristic of Epiphanius throughout his career, and of major importance to him.

---

[12] Dechow, *Dogma and Mysticism*, pp. 376-378.

His writings against images appear to date from the same decade as the *Letter to John*. Again, this concern makes itself apparent in the *Panarion*. In this work Epiphanius most commonly attacks pagan images, though 27,6,9-10 shows his dislike of Christian image-making. Three writings specifically against Christian images can be partially reconstructed from conciliar *acta* and other sources.[13] These are a *Treatise Against Those Who, by Idolatrous Custom, Are Accustomed to Make Images Representative of Christ, the Mother of God and the Martyrs, and Further, of Angels and Prophets*; a *Letter to Theodosius*; and a *Testament to the Citizens* (of Salamis). It has been suggested that Epiphanius' attitude toward images is closely linked with his anti-Origenism.[14] Without denying the possibility of this, we would urge that the sort of arguments he uses against Christian images would be equally appropriate from the pen of a writer on either side of the Origenist controversy.

Another of Epiphanius' works, *De Gemmis*, also comes from the last decade of the fourth century, dating perhaps from 394 or 395. Preserved only in a Latin epitome, this is a discussion of the symbolism of the stones of the high priest's breastplate. It was written for Diodore of Tarsus, and witnesses to the close attention with which Epiphanius read scripture.

The last years of Epiphanius' life coincided with the crisis of the Origenist controversy in Egypt. Under pressure from anti-Origenists, Theophilus, the patriarch of Alexandria, abandoned his previous tolerance of Origenism and proceeded against the Origenist monks at the monasteries at Nitria. Early in 400 a synod convened at Alexandria condemned the reading and possession of works by Origen; this was followed shortly by a decree of exile for the Nitrian Origenists. Theophilus wrote to the churches of Palestine and Cyprus for support, and in particular urged Epiphanius to call a similar synod on Cyprus. Summoned by Epiphanius, the Cypriote synod condemned the reading of Origen; in a jubilant letter to Jerome (Epiphanius/Jerome *Epistle* 91) Epiphanius announced this result.

Meanwhile the exiles from Nitria had made their way to various Christian and monastic centers. Led by Isidore and the "Tall Brothers" (Ammonius, Dioscurus, Eusebius and Euthymius) about eighty came to Constantinople and appealed for help to the patriarch, John Chrysostom.

Whatever his views on Origen, Chrysostom showed sympathy for the exiles and wrote to Theophilus urging their reinstatement. Epiphanius

---

[13] John of Damascus, *De Imaginibus Oratio* I. 25; *Acts of the Council of 754*, Mansi XIII 292D; *Acts of the Council of 787*, Mansi XIII 293D; Nicephorus, *Apologia Minor*, Migne 100 837B; *Adversus Eusebium*, Pitra *Spicilegium Solesmense* IV 292-294; Theodore Studita, *Antirrhetum* II, Migne 99, 388A; 484 A/B; *Epistle 36 Ad Naucratem*, Migne 99, 1213D.

[14] Dechow, *Dogma and Mysticism*, pp. 367-370.

was moved to set out on what proved to be his last journey, a voyage to Constantinople for the defense of orthodoxy and the unmasking of Origenism.

Arriving in the spring of 402 or 403, Epiphanius declined Chrysostom's offer of hospitality and communion. He held a service himself, however, outside the city, and with dubious canonicity ordained a deacon. Socrates (*History*, VI.10; 12-14) and Sozomen (*History* VIII.14-15) give differing accounts of the subsequent events. According to the later Sozomen, Epiphanius became convinced of his own unfairness through an encounter and conversation with Ammonius. Socrates, however, says that while on his way to a public appearance in the Cathedral of the Holy Apostles, Epiphanius was confronted by Chrysostom's emissary, Serapion, who accused him of uncanonical behavior and warned him of the danger of a riot. Whatever the truth of the matter, Epiphanius left Constantinople without taking decisive action against Origenism. He died at sea on his way home to Cyprus.

The Panarion

The *Panarion*, Epiphanius' major literary effort, is an extremely long work, which its author divided into three Books totalling seven Sections; in Holl's edition, with notes and apparatus, it occupies 1500 pages. It was begun in 374 or 375 (*Panarion* Proem II 2,3) and was written in great haste, in less than three years. Book I, presented here, extends through Sect 46 and comprises somewhat more than a third of the whole work.

The *Panarion* is heresiology. This is a literary genre not uncommon in the ancient Christian world, found in Islam and some oriental religious traditions and, in the form of anti-"cult" writings, still alive in western Christendom. Heresiology may be characterized as the description and refutation of religious bodies, systems and views which the author regards as dangerous; the *Panarion* in particular might be called an historical encyclopedia of heresy and its refutation. Epiphanius undertook the monumental task of listing all pre- and post-Christian sects— a total of eighty—from Adam till his own lifetime, sketching their history and chief doctrines as he understood them, and telling the faithful, in a few words, what answer to give them.

The number eighty is based on Song of Songs 6:8-9, "There are threescore queens, and fourscore concubines, and virgins without number. My dove, my undefiled, is but one." The eighty "concubines" are sects—groups which use the name of Christ as the concubine uses the name of her master. (It is not certain what meaning Epiphanius would have seen in the "queens," though sixty of Epiphanius' "sects" are specifically Christian in outlook). The "dove," predictably, is the church, the lawful wife. The "virgins without number" are various "philosophies" which are in no way related to Christianity (*Panarion* 35,3,5 and *De Fide* 6,9).

Panarion, or "Medicine Chest," is Epiphanius' own choice for the title of his work. It expresses his purpose in writing: "...I shall be telling you the names of the sects and exposing their unlawful deeds like poisons and toxic substances, but matching the antidotes with them at the same time —cures for those who are already bitten, and preventatives for those who will have this experience..." (*Panarion* Proem I 1,2).

The *Panarion* is furnished with two Proems. The first is Epiphanius' own table of contents, the second explains his purpose and methods. The entire work ends with a "brief and accurate description of the catholic faith and apostolic church" and is commonly called *De Fide*.

Interspersed throughout the *Panarion* are seven "Anacephalaeoses," one heading each Section and summarizing the sects to be discussed in it. Unlike the Proems these are probably not authentic. Epiphanius makes no mention of them in the body of the work, though he does mention both Proems and the essay we call *De Fide*. The Anacephalaeoses are so worded as to suggest that they were written to be read as a whole. Anacephalaeosis III, for example, ends, "This will summarize the three Sections of Volume I, which includes forty-six Sects"—though Anacephalaeosis III, as it is now placed in the *Panarion*, deals only with Sects 34-46. Moreover the opening lines of Sect 34 of the *Panarion*, though this Sect follows Anacephalaeosis III, are so worded as to suggest that the reader has just finished Sect 33 and that no material intervenes.

Occasionally, moreover, the Anacephalaeoses reveal small discrepancies of content with the *Panarion*; indeed, the order of sects in Anacephalaeosis I is not the same as the *Panarion*'s order. It would seem that the Anacephalaeoses circulated independently and served as an epitome of the *Panarion*. Augustine used them as the basis of his *Contra Omnes Haereses*; whether he knew the *Panarion* itself is debatable.

For the discussion of a sect in the *Panarion* Epiphanius, consciously or unconsciously, developed a sort of four-part form. He begins, sometimes after a brief introduction, with a few remarks indicating what he thought was the sect's relationship to the groups which preceded it. He then moves to a sketch of the sect's doctrines, then to their refutation. This third part, the refutation, is normally the longest part of the essay. The usual close is a few lines comparing the sect under discussion to an unattractive animal, oftenest a snake. However Epiphanius does not invariably adhere to this form as described here; descriptive and refutatory material are sometimes mixed.

Epiphanius' refutations are in part the logical *reductio ad absurdum* of the sects' positions, in the manner of Book II of Irenaeus' *Contra Omnes Haereses*. In larger part, however, they consist of arguments from scripture, which Epiphanius saw as the supreme expression of all truth. Epiphanius' scriptural arguments of course utilize pre-modern exegetical methods and arrive at pre-determined answers; nonetheless they are often acute, and of real interest in themselves.

In dealing with individual sects Epiphanius strove for brevity, and achieved it oftener than the length of the *Panarion* would lead us to suppose. However, particularly in the latter portions of the *Panarion*, Epiphanius' deep concern with his subject—and perhaps the demands which ecclesiastical politics made upon him—led him to enlarge on his themes and add long excerpts from other writers. These practices account for the length of the book, and have preserved much otherwise unavailable material.

The many parallels which it is possible to find between material reported in the *Panarion* and material contained in ancient heterodox literature suggest that the *Panarion* is a fairly good index to some aspects of ancient "heretical" thought. As an history of men and movements its value is debatable. Epiphanius seems well informed about events in or near his own time. For earlier periods he is dependent upon the material in his documentary sources and the inferences he himself draws. The basis of these inferences, in turn, is sometimes the doctrinal similarity he perceives between the teachings of one sect and another, sometimes some other clue he has observed in his literary sources. We do not know that he had no independent knowledge of, say, the historical development of the early Gnostic schools; but it is easy to doubt that he did.

A further caution is in order. We cannot assume that, because Epiphanius refers to a given group as a "sect" and gives it a name, it was necessarily an organized body. In some cases it was; the corporate life of the Valentinians and Marcionites, for example, is well attested. On the other hand, Epiphanius says that he himself coined the names, "Alogi," "Antidicomarians," and "Collyridians," and he may have done the same in other cases. Certainly some of his "sects" are simply persons who take a particular position; Epiphanius speaks of "Origenists" but there was no "Origenist Church." An Epiphanian "sect," then, may represent anything from an organized church to a school of thought, or a tendency manifested by some exegetes. By the same token, the names Epiphanius gives to his αἱρέσεις are not necessarily ones that they would have given themselves.

The Sources of the Panarion

Epiphanius was at pains to explain the nature of his sources to the reader. "Some of my knowledge of the things I shall tell the reader about sects and schisms, I owe to my fondness for study. Certain things I learned from hearsay, though I encountered certain with my own ears and eyes. I am confident that I can give a full account, based on accurate report, of the origins and teachings of some sects, and tell something of what the others do. Of these latter, I know one through the works of ancient authors, another from the report of men who confirmed my notion precisely." (Proem II 2,4)

In Epiphanius' view, then, the three bases of the *Panarion* are observation, documentation and oral testimony. In some cases we should add a fourth to these: historical conjecture on Epiphanius' own part. As a scriptural exegete Epiphanius was used to reading documents with great attention to see what he could infer from them, and it seems likely that he did the same with documents other than scripture. Thus when he says, for example, that the Ebionites and Nazoraeans influenced each other (*Panarion* 30,2,9) it may be that he is following some tradition to this effect, but it is at least equally likely that he infers this from the fact that he associates both groups with Cocabe. Again, his reason for saying that the Gnostics are an offshoot of the Nicolaitans (*Panarion* 26,1,1) may simply be that he regarded both as sexually immoral. In other words, Epiphanius may not without further investigation be assumed to be in possession of much historical information about the origins of the sects he discusses.

Epiphanius solicited information about sects from persons he considered trustworthy (Cf. Basil *Epistle* 258) and apparently made an effort to sift such information (Cf. *Panarion* 64,3,11-13). His objectivity was hampered, however, by the fact that he apparently took the piety and orthodoxy of his informants as one of his main touchstones of credibility (Cf. *Panarion* 30,5,5-6). This devout monk was unlikely to distrust one whom he considered a firm believer in the faith of Nicaea; and in any case, he knew what he was looking for (*Panarion* Proem II 2,4 above). As a result he sometimes accepts questionable material.

Epiphanius' documentary sources are his most important fund of information. A number of documents lie behind *Panarion* I. Epiphanius cites Irenaeus, Hippolytus, Clement of Alexandria and Eusebius by name. His frequent parallels with Pseudo-Tertullian suggest that he knew Hippolytus' lost *Syntagma*, which Pseudo-Tertullian is thought by many to represent. Epiphanius refers frequently to the Pseudo-Clementines. For historical details he sometimes draws on *Jubilees*, on

Eusebius' or some other Chronicle, and on Eusebius' *Praeparatio Evangelica*. He was familiar with the *Didascalia* and the *Apostolic Constitutions*. Whether he knew Justin Martyr's lost *Contra Omnes Haereses* is uncertain but possible. Additionally, he not infrequently cites heretical works, and has certainly read some of them.

As an historical source, Epiphanius gives first place to scripture. Wherever possible he elucidates the history and beliefs of sects from scriptural sources. He also finds prophecies of the specific errors of the sects in scripture.

Of the three Sections of Book I, the first is the one whose sources are least easy to identify. This section contains a brief and not well informed treatment of certain main schools of Greek philosophy, and Epiphanius' Samaritan and Jewish material, including perhaps some sketchy reminiscences of Qumran and the Mandaeans, and references to popular astrology in its Jewish form. Some of the information in Sect 19, the Ossaeans, is from an Elkasaite work also used by Hippolytus, and there is scripture behind parts of the other Jewish Sects; but only these sources are clearly identifiable. It must be said that Epiphanius' attitude, like that of many of his Christian contemporaries, was bitterly anti-Jewish.

Sections II and III, chiefly concerned with Gnosticism and Jewish Christianity, utilize all the heresiologists and historical works previously mentioned. Here Epiphanius' most frequently quoted source is Irenaeus, whom he greatly admired (*Panarion* 31,33,1-2). Irenaeus supplies part of the material in at least sixteen of the twenty-six Sects of these two Sections. Sects 22, 23, 27, 34, 35, and 36 are entirely dependent upon him and quote or paraphrase his work extensively, thus affording a useful witness to his Greek text. Sect 31, the Valentinians, likewise reproduces a long extract from Irenaeus, though this Sect also quotes at length from an otherwise unknown Valentinian document.

But Epiphanius does not follow Irenaeus slavishly. Sect 37, the Ophites, for example, seems to ignore him in favor of an alternate source. Sect 36, the Heracleonites, takes traits Irenaeus had included under the general head of Marcus, and, for whatever reason, attributes them specifically to Heracleon. Finally, thirteen of the Sects in Sections II and III contain material not obviously from any ancient heresiologist whose work survives.

Of special interest are Epiphanius' quotations from or references to sectarian literature. Sect 21 may contain short quotations from the Simonian *Apophasis Megale*, and Sect 24, reminiscences of the *Exegetica* of Basilides. The "Gnostics" of Sect 26 introduced Epiphanius to their literature, and he may have drawn on it for some of the startling details he presents in this Sect. In Sect 30, the Ebionites, Epiphanius offers an extract from an "Hebrew Gospel;" Sect 30 also uses the same Elkasaite work as Sect 19. Sect 31 preserves portions of an otherwise unattested Gnostic work, probably Valentinian. Sects 38 and 40 are based in part on Gnostic writings, while Sect 33, the Ptolemaeans, preserves Ptolemy's *Letter to Flora* in its entirety. Finally, the long Sect 42 contains the fullest account extant of Marcion's canon of scripture.

Epiphanius and Nag Hammadi

The discovery of the Nag Hammadi Library has increased our knowledge of primary Gnostic sources, and provides material with which the early Christian heresiologists can be compared. They fare well by the comparison in some respects though not in all. The systems of thought which Nag Hammadi presents as such never tally exactly with the systems reported by the heresiologists; the Valentinians come the closest to doing so. On the other hand most of the Gnostic myths, ideas and theologumena which Epiphanius reports are found, sometimes in several versions, in Nag Hammadi. Insofar as Nag Hammadi is an indicator, Epiphanius may be termed a fairly reliable reporter of the content of certain aspects of that ancient Christian thought which the mainstream judged heterodox.

Epiphanius misrepresents the Gnostics less in his account of their content than in what he says of their spirit and motivation. No more than the other heresiologists does he appreciate their essential seriousness— or the delicate allegories which are found in some of their writings. He says repeatedly that the Gnostics are merely intent on glorifying themselves and making trouble—scarcely a fair judgment. Moreover, he assumes that most Gnostics are sexual libertines, another judgment of unlikely accuracy. While the testimony of *Panarion* 26 is not entirely to be discounted, and there is other evidence of libertinism among Gnostics, Gnostic writings often reveal a puritanical bent. In all probability libertine Gnostics were a minority.

The Panarion's Language and Its Translation

Epiphanius' language is a version of the ecclesiastical Koine of the fourth century, and by no means uncultivated. While the author of the *Ancoratus* and *Panarion* lacked a classical education, he had clearly been exposed to good spoken and written Greek. Epiphanius' vocabulary is large, and his idiom varied and flexible. Though not always gracefully constructed, his long, complex sentences are grammatically correct and consistent. Considerable use is made of such refinements as the optative mood, and even the future infinitive and participle.

The most important literary influence on Epiphanius' language is the Greek scripture; this affects not only his vocabulary, but sometimes his grammar. He is also influenced by the vocabulary and manner of his other sources, Irenaeus in particular. His language reflects the theological terminology of his time, and the terminology of exegetical debate; it may contain some liturgical tags as well. And while Epiphanius' writing is formal, it is undoubtedly affected by the spoken vernacular.

Assessments of Epiphanius' style should take account of his stated intention to write plainly, in the interest of being understood (*Panarion* Proem II 2,6; 42,12,el.13). Even had he been capable of the manner of a Greek rhetorician, Epiphanius would not have employed it. At the same time his works are serious presentations of matters of import, and as such are characterized by formality. One suspects that Epiphanius wrote much as he preached.

For the kind of presentation he intends, Epiphanius is not an inept stylist. However, the quality of his style varies from work to work, and even within one work. Epiphanius is capable of an attractive homiletic prose, characterized by clear, well-arranged sentences, graceful citations of scripture, and a certain eloquence. The opening chapter of the *Ancoratus*, or the close of its polemic against idolatry (chapter 107, for example) may serve to illustrate. At other times Epiphanius exhibits lively disputation on paper, in the manner of a diatribe—so, for example, at *Ancoratus* 14,5-15,4, and many other places. He is very good at telling a story (e.g., *Panarion* 30,6,1-12,10 et al.).

Side by side with the more attractive passages exist those that are much less so. The long series of exegeses tend to be monotonously worded. Epiphanius is fond of heaping up epithets for the eternal Divine Word, and at times does so at inordinate length. And with Epiphanius, it seems legitimate to speak of "run-on sentences;" Greek sentences are characteristically long, but Epiphanius sometimes seems to be going on because he does not know how to stop. This is particularly likely to occur when elaborate typologies are being developed (so *Panarion* 29,3,7-9; 46,6-8); or when Epiphanius is simply in a hurry (see below); or both.

Relatively, the *Panarion* is not as well written as the *Ancoratus*. This is in part due to the number of literary sources which underlie the *Panarion*, and Epiphanius' manner of using such sources. While he sometimes simply quotes verbatim, he is as likely to adapt his sources' sentences, augmenting them with material of his own. The result is often a somewhat intractable sentence, overcrowded with information. At *Panarion* 27,2,1-3, for example, which is based on Irenaeus' account of the Carpocratians as Hippolytus' Greek preserves it, characteristically Epiphanian words and expressions double the length of Hippolytus' text. And yet Epiphanius adds almost nothing other than repetition of the same information, and invective.

The *Panarion*'s style also suffers from the haste of its author. One sign of this may be the proliferation of genitive absolutes—occurring with normal frequency in the *Ancoratus* but used to an extreme in the *Panarion*. Epiphanius appears to employ this construction as the handiest way of conveying information rapidly, the better to hurry on to his next block of material. (In this connection, one wonders how thoroughly the *Panarion* was revised.)

Some of Epiphanius' sentences appear to be crafted—though even here his periods may be harmed by the last-minute impulse to introduce a metaphor. One suspects this happened at *Panarion* 21,1,1, where Epiphanius thought of saying that Simon Magus mixed "hellebore with honey." Other sentences, however, appear not to be crafted at all, but simply set down as the author thought of the words. These sentences may be of the "run-on" variety as when, at *Panarion* 30,18,3, Epiphanius tries to tell us everything he knows about Ebionite marriage customs in one breath.

Such cases suggest that Epiphanius frequently dictated his work rather than writing it. If so, it is easy to understand why short, exclamatory interjections sometimes interrupt the course of an Epiphanian sentence. At times one observes other phenomena for which dictation might account. So at *Panarion* 39,8,7, where Epiphanius finds himself going on too long about Near Eastern geography, he backtracks with a rapid genitive absolute, and starts over. All these phenomena pose difficulties for the translator. Others are occasioned by the technical nature of some of the discussion, and by certain of Epiphanius' mannerisms. He makes much use of periphrastic expressions involving verbs such as ἔχειν, λαμβάνειν, ἀναδέχεσθαι; he is also fond of rather wordy noun locutions in places where another author might have preferred a simple preposition: ἐν τῇ περί ... περιτομῆς σχέσει, meaning "in relation to circumcision." One encounters redundancies on the order of μαχόμενοι θάτερον εἰς θάτερον πρός ... meaning simply, "inconsistent with." Perhaps these are instances of the influence on Epiphanius of spoken Greek. Occasional "literary" expressions might actually be survivals in the spoken language: ἀμιλλᾶσθαι, reminiscent of Homer: τὶ δῆτα, common in Plato; σφῶν αὐτῶν (also in Irenaeus), used for "their own" when a very specific expression is needed to avoid confusion.

Otherwise, the main difficulty of Epiphanius' Greek arises from words and phrases which are unexampled elsewhere, unusual, or ambiguous. Only Epiphanius uses σχέσις for "(religious) position." τὸ πᾶν μέρος, followed by a genitive, means "the whole of." φθοριμαῖος, in context, appears to mean not "corrupt" or "corrupting," but "doomed to perish" (*Panarion* 26,2,4; 39,8,5). γεννάδας is probably not "noble," but "natural-born", i.e., true to type (*Panarion* 30,12,4; *Ancoratus*105,3). ἰοβολία, a typical pejorative epithet for heretical doctrine, appears to mean the venom emitted by a poisonous snake. ξενολεκτεῖς for doctrines foreign to the faith, μοχθηρίαι for bad arguments, ideas or teachings, and many others, require difficult translation choices.

The present version attempts to render the sense of the *Panarion* closely in dignified, readable modern English. The unit of translation is the word, phrase or idiom. However, we have not felt it necessary to reproduce the structure of every individual Greek idiom with complete literalness. We prefer "his dupes" to "the persons deceived by him," "some people do this for a living in the gymnasia" to "in the gymnasia this work is an occupation for some people for their daily livelihood," and the like. For convenience we sometimes substitute the English active voice for the Greek passive, treat certain of the ever-recurring genitive absolutes as independent sentences, and break the lengthier Greek sentences into more manageable English units. The translator apologizes for flaws of accuracy and style which no amount of care can entirely eliminate from a translation, particularly one of this length.

Insofar as Epiphanius' text and his understanding of them permit, the frequent scriptural quotations are rendered in the style of the King James Version—of the Great Bible, in the case of Psalms. This device is intended to set the quotations off from Epiphanius himself, and also emphasize their solemn character in his mind. Other quotations are translated in the same manner as the words of Epiphanius, unless they seem themselves to be imitative of Biblical style.

The question whether αἵρεσις should be rendered "heresy" or "sect" has been sufficiently vexed to give rise to a literature.[15] In fact Epiphanius seems to employ the word in both senses. With Montsoulas we believe that "sect" is the more common. Epiphanius says that an αἵρεσις has "teachings" and "does" things (*Panarion* Proem II 2,4), expressions appropriate to a body of people; and more often than not the word gives a good sense on the assumption that it refers to people rather than ideas. We render "heresy" where the context seems to call for it. Thus, when Epiphanius says that the Basilideans' αἵρεσις is a μῦθος, "heresy" is clearly the better choice.[16]

---

[15] E. Montsoulas, "Der Begriff 'Häresis' bei Epiphanius von Salamis, *Texte und Untersuchungen 92*, pp. 362-371; C. Riggi, "Il termine hairesis di Epifanio di Salamina," *Salesianum* 29 (1967), pp. 3-37.

[16] It can be urged that "sect," which implies an organized body, is not the optimal translation choice. "Faction" would in fact be more accurate; we reject this because it lacks ecclesiastical connotation.

The rendering of αἵρεσις is further complicated by the fact that Epiphanius uses this word for each of the eighty divisions of the *Panarion*, where we might say "section" or "chapter." Where this is the meaning we render "Sect" with a capital rather than "sect."

The usual title of a Sect is in the form of the preposition κατά followed by the name of a group in the genitive plural with no article. We take κατά in this context to mean "against" rather than "concerning." Epiphanius employs the preposition in both senses, and either translation could be defended. However, we choose "against" because of Epiphanius' manner of titling certain Sects in which he merely describes without attempting to refute: Πυθαγόρειοι, Πλατώνικοι, Ἐπικούρειοι. When, in the same series of Sects, he both describes and attacks the Stoics, he says κατὰ Στωικῶν. It would seem then, that Epiphanius employs κατά to show that his purpose is to refute a given sect.[17]

Epiphanius has come in for severe criticism. Much of this is justified, though the strictures drawn oftenest are not the most important. Epiphanius' weaknesses as an historian are shared by many ancient historiographers. His habit of name-calling, though he carried it to an extreme, was a common one in the controversial literature of his day; so was the retailing of scurrilous stories about opponents. Epiphanius tells us in Proem I that the intent of his abusive language was pedagogical (*Panarion* Proem I 2,3-4). He firmly believed that sharp polemic, supported by an exemplary life on the polemicist's part, was an effective missionary method (Cf. *Ancoratus* 102-107).

And in polemic Epiphanius was not unskilled. He was not a creative theologian; but he handles Biblical exegesis of the literal, "Antiochene" type with ingenuity. Biased or not, Epiphanius' criticisms of opposing views are often shrewd. Good examples of his ability are his treatment of Ptolemy's *Letter to Flora*, beginning at *Panarion* 33,9; and his attack on Marcion's canon in Sect 42.

It is Epiphanius' inflated self-esteem which renders him least attractive. It is clear that he considered his own scholarship superior to most, and his own word on any question of importance decisive; once he had pronounced, nothing need be added. Nor was he given to regarding opponents with respect. His world, as he saw it, was divided into orthodox Christians on the one side, and everyone else on the other; there was no question as to who were the heroes, and who the villains (Cf. *Panarion*

---

[17] Note also the (perhaps not Epiphanian) title of the anti-iconic work, "Against Those Who ... Are Accustomed to Make Images ..." κατά in this context seems clearly to mean "against."

30,24,4). He thus reveals the militant attitude—underlain, perhaps, by a degree of insecurity—which is common among deeply devout persons of all kinds and in all periods.

Yet the impression often conveyed, that Epiphanius did nothing but hunt heresy, is incorrect. The conversion of the heathen and the lost was a serious concern of his; so was the fostering of the monastic movement. *De Mensuris et Ponderibus* and *De Gemmis* show that he could write with verve on primarily scholarly subjects. As a scholar he could render sincere tribute even to such a *bête-noire* as Origen.

An author such as Epiphanius should be seen against the background of his century. It was a time of intellectual ferment when the church, newly recognized by the state, needed to define its identity more clearly; when the man on the street took an interest in ecclesiastical issues; and when the state was deeply involved in ecclesiastical affairs. In such an atmosphere the appearance of heresiology is understandable, and surprised no one. The tradition of Christian heresiology was already ancient when Epiphanius wrote, and can be traced back as far as Justin. Augustine, who by request produced an heresiology of his own, speaks of Epiphanius with respect. Epiphanius was merely trying to do, systematically and comprehensively, a work which others before him had done, and for which a demand existed.

Despite the criticisms to which he is open, Epiphanius should not be viewed as essentially negative. There is an element of hostility in his writings, but also an element of loyalty and love. Epiphanius writes not so much to attack heresy as to defend an ideal, eloquently set forth in the *Ancoratus* and parts of the *Panarion*. He is totally committed to the inculcation and defense of a faith in a triune God who has sent an incarnate Savior, foretold by an infallible scripture, preaching a stern moral code, dying for human transgressions of that code, risen and ascended, and promising a bodily resurrection at the last. This is the real subject of Epiphanius' work.

Notes

Notes are sometimes explanatory, but most are references to passages from other relevant ancient literatures which parallel Epiphanius in some manner. We are indebted to Holl's excellent collection of Patristic references. These have been amplified chiefly from the numerous documents, of the Nag Hammadi Library and others, which were unavailable to Holl.

Citations of Mandaean and other Gnostic literature are by page and line of the following editions:

Mark Lidzbarski, *Ginza*, Göttingen, Vandenhoeck und Ruprecht; Leipzig, J. C. Hinrichs, 1925.

Mark Lidzbarski, *Das Johannesbuch der Mandäer*, Giessen, A. Töpelmann, 1966.

Ethel Stefana Drower, *The Canonical Prayer Book of the Mandaeans*, Leiden, E. J. Brill, 1959.

Violet MacDermot, *The Books of Jeu and the Untitled Text in the Bruce Codex*, text edited by Carl Schmidt, Leiden, E. J. Brill, 1978.

Violet MacDermot, *Pistis Sophia*, text edited by Carl Schmidt, Leiden, E. J. Brill, 1978.

Sigla

† Obelus marks a presumably miscopied word or phrase corrected by Holl.

< > Pointed brackets enclose words restored by Holl.

() Parentheses enclosing a word or two indicate words supplied by the translator. When parentheses enclose a sentence they indicate that the material is parenthetic to Epiphanius' argument.

* Asterisk marks an emendation suggested by Dummer.

Frank Williams
The University of Texas at El Paso
January 26, 1985

ABBREVIATIONS

Allog.	*Allogenes*
Anc.	Epiphanius, *Ancoratus*
ap Gen	*Genesis Apocryphon*
Apoc. Adam	*The Apocalypse of Adam*
Apoc. Jas.	*The Apocalypse of James*
Apoc. Pet.	*The Apocalypse of Peter*
Apoc. Paul	*The Apocalypse of Paul*
Apocry. Jas.	*The Apocryphon of James*
Apocry. Jn.	*The Apocryphon of John*
Ascl.	*Asclepius*
Aug.	Augustine
Ath. De Decret. Nic. Syn.	Athanasius, *De Decretis Nicaeae Synodi*
Auth. Teach.	*Authoritative Teaching*
BG	*Berlin Gnostic Codex 8502*
Adam. Rect. Fid.	Adamantius, *De Recta Fide*
CD	*Covenant of Damascus*
CG	*Cairo Gnostic Codex*
Clem. Alex. Strom.	Clement of Alexandria, *Stromateis*
Clem. Hom.	*Pseudo-Clementine Homilies*
Clem. Recog.	*Pseudo-Clementine Recognitions*
Const. Ap.	*Apostolic Constitutions*
Corp. Herm.	*Corpus Hermeticum*
Cyr. Jerus. Cat.	Cyril of Jerusalem, *Catecheses*
Dia. Sav.	*The Dialogue of the Savior*
Did.	*Didache*
Ep. Clem. Ad Jac.	The (Pseudo-Clementine) *Epistle of Clement to James*
Epist. Apost.	*Epistula Apostolorum*
Eug.	*Eugnostus the Blessed*
Eus.	Eusebius
Chron.	*Chronicle*
H.E.	*Ecclesiastical History*
Onom.	*Onomasticon*
Praep. Ev.	*Praeparatio Evangelica*
Exc. Theod.	*Excerpta Ex Theodoto*
Exeg. Soul	*The Exegesis on the Soul*
G. Egypt.	*The Gospel of the Egyptians*
GL	*Left Ginza*
GR	*Right Ginza*
GT	*The Gospel of Thomas*
Georg. Syncel.	Georgius Syncellus
Gos. Mary	*The Gospel of Mary*
Gos. Phil.	*The Gospel of Philip*
Gos. Tr.	*The Gospel of Truth*
Gr. Pow.	*The Concept of Our Great Power*
Gr. Seth	*The Second Treatise of the Great Seth*
H	*Thanksgiving Psalms (Hodayyoth)*
Haeret. Fab.	*Haereticorum Fabulae*
Hippol. Haer.	Hippolytus, *Contra Omnes Haereses*
Hyps.	*Hypsiphrone*
Interp. Know.	*The Interpretation of Knowledge*
Iren.	Irenaeus, *Contra Omnes Haereses*

Jer.	Jerome
Adv. Jov.	*Adversus Jovinianum*
Adv. Lucif.	*Adversus Luciferum*
C. Pelag.	*Contra Pelagium*
Chron.	*Chronicle*
Doct. Pat.	*Doctrina Patrum*
Vir. Ill.	*De Viris Illustribus*
Vit. Paul.	*Vita Paulae*
Jos.	Josephus
Ant.	*Antiquities of the Jews*
Bel.	*Bella Judaica*
Jub.	*Jubilees*
Justin Dial.	Justin Martyr, *Dialogue with Trypho*
Justin Apol.	Justin Martyr, *Apologia*
Keph.	Manichaean *Kephalaia*
Let. Pet.	*The Letter of Peter to Philip*
Man. Ps.	*Manichaean Psalms*
Mand. PB	*The Mandaean Prayer Book*
Mars.	*Marsanes*
Melch.	*Melchizedek*
Method. Conviv.	Methodius, *Convivium*
NHL	James M. Robinson ed., *The Nag Hammadi Library in English*, Harper and Row, 1977
Nat. Arc.	*The Nature of the Archons*
On Bapt.	*On Baptism*
On Res.	*The Treatise on the Resurrection*
Orig.	Origen
C. Cels.	*Contra Celsum*
De Princ.	*De Principiis*
Orig. Wld.	*On the Origin of the World*
p Hos	*pesher Hosea*
PS	*Pistis Sophia*
Pr. Thank.	*The Prayer of Thanksgiving*
Pap. Oxyr.	*Papyrus Oxyrynchus*
Para. Shem	*The Paraphrase of Shem*
Ps.-Cypr. De Rebapt.	Pseudo-Cyprian, *De Rebaptismo*
Ps.-Tert.	Pseudo-Tertullian, *Contra Omnes Haereses*
S	*Manual of Discipline (Serekh)*
SJC	*The Sophia of Jesus Christ*
Silv.	*The Teachings of Silvanus*
Tac. Hist.	Tacitus, *Historiae*
Tert.	Tertullian
Adv. Val.	*Adversus Valentinum*
De Carn. Christ.	*De Carne Christi*
De Virg. Vel.	*De Virginibus Velandis*
Praescr.	*Haereticorum Praescriptio*
Test. Tr.	*The Testimony of the Truth*
Theoph. Ad Autol.	Theophilus, *Ad Autolycum*
Tri. Prot.	*The Trimorphic Protennoia*
Tri. Trac.	*The Tripartite Tractate*
U	The Untitled Document of the Codex Brucianus
Val. Exp.	*A Valentinian Exposition*
Zost.	*Zostrianus*

LETTER OF ACACIUS AND PAUL

A letter written in the ninety-second year of the Diocletian era, the twelfth of the reign of Valentinian and Valens and the eighth of Gratian,[1] to Epiphanius of Palestine and Eleutheropolis, < some time > abbot in the district of Eleutheropolis, now bishop of the city of Constantia in the province of Cyprus, from the presbyters Acacius and Paul, archimandrites, or abbots, in Chalcis and Beroea in Coelesyria. < They inquired about his > writing a complete heresiology, and not only they, but many < others > as well had urged him to do so, and practically compelled him to.

Greetings in the Lord from the archimandrites, Acacius, presbyter, and Paul, presbyter, to the Most Reverend Father, the bishop Epiphanius, our master and most highly esteemed in all respects!

1,1 A glimpse of Your Reverence would suffice us, Father, since it would fill us with spiritual utterances, and produce, in our own case, the same degree of affection that has arisen in < those > who have the sight of you. (2) But with its report of the good repute of his words and deeds, fame, which precedes a disciple of the Savior, makes one desperate to take his fill of words and sense. We ought to have come in person then, for our share of the benefit which God has given to you, as to an apostle.

1,3 But since bodily infirmity and distress prevent the journey, we are unable to come < to you > ourselves, fall prostrate at your feet, and hear and understand the sacred, spiritual words from your (own) lips. (4) (For we are confident that by coming and hearing them, were we worthy to, we would set our chosen way of life on a firmer footing—provided that we are fit to attain its goal.)

1,5 Since infirmity has overtaken us, therefore, we beseech Your Reverence in all your greatness not to begrudge us a share of the gifts the Savior has truly given you. (6) For not we alone, but all who hear of you, confess that the Savior has raised you up for us in this generation as a new apostle and herald, a new John, to proclaim what ought to be observed by those who resolve on this course.

1,7 As our brother in common, Marcellus, is troubled at such great fame and drawn by longing for Your Reverence—and he belongs to our community, and despite his recent instruction he can help us by making such a long journey—we have entrusted < him > with the very daring venture of us sinners towards you, the Savior's disciple. (8) And our re-

---

[1] 376 A.D.

quest is that you share with us the words you have spoken to certain brethren for their instruction. For you, the righteous, this can be no trouble; but it will be rejoicing in the Lord for us sinners when we partake of them. For the load of our transgressions is lifted when we are filled with your spiritual utterances. (9) We have heard names assigned by Your Honor to the sects, and we ask Your Reverence to tell us explicitly the sect belonging to these names for each religion. For everyone's gift is <not> the same. (10) We likewise ask you—you, the righteous—to pray to the Lord for all who long for you and await your gift. (11) We are in fasting and prayer that the brother of us all may be received gladly by Your Honor and obtain the gift of your bestowing, and so offer the accustomed prayers to Father, Son and Holy Spirit.

1,12 All the brethren hope to be established by your prayer on their behalf. Since yours is a benefit given by God to apostles, we urge you to share it without compunction. (13) All the little ones in the cloisters make their prayer to God that they may share a spiritual gift from Your Reverence. May you remain well in the Lord, and happy in Christ and the Holy Spirit, <as you administer> the throne that has been granted you and your divine gift, till (you receive) the crown that awaits you!

PROEM I

Epiphanius' reply to the presbyters Acacius and Paul, with regard to their letter about his writing an heresiology. (Proem I)

Greetings in the Lord from Epiphanius to his highly esteemed brothers and fellow-presbyters, Masters Acacius and Paul!

1,1   By drawing up a preface, or set of remarks, as a sort of title, ancient authors would give a glimpse of the whole work following through their riddle. Hence, beloved, since I am the same sort, I am writing you a preface to give the gist of my †<treatise> against sects. (2) Since I shall be telling you the names of the sects and exposing their unlawful deeds like poisons and toxic substances, matching the antidotes with them at the same time—cures for those who are already bitten, and preventatives for those who will have this experience—I am drafting this Preface here for the scholarly, to explain the "Panarion," or chest of remedies for the victims of wild beasts' bites. It is a work in three Volumes and †contains eighty Sects, which stand symbolically for wild animals or snakes.

1,3   But "one after the eighty"[1] is at once the foundation of the truth, the teaching and the saving treatment of it, and Christ's "holy bride," The Church. The church has always been, but was revealed in due course by Christ's incarnation, during the period of these sects. (4) I mention it in connection with the preaching of Christ. And again, after all the iniquities of these sects, I give a concise, clear account of it in accordance with the apostles' teaching, to refresh those who have read through all of the laborious work on the Sects.

2,1   Please, all you scholarly readers of the Preface, the Sects that follow it, and the Defense of the Truth, Exposition of the Truth, and Faith of the Holy Catholic Church, I am only human, and am trying my best to defend true religion, with hard work and zeal from God. (2) I beg your pardon if I <attempt> too much in my desire to make the best defense I can in the all-holy, all-august Name itself. For God allows me this, though I am investigating matters too difficult for me, since my discussion is for the truth's sake, and my work is for the sake of piety.

2,3   And further, if you should find—it is surely not my way to mock people or make fun of them. But please <pardon me> if, from anger over the sects and for the reader's protection, I should speak under provocation, or call certain persons "frauds," or "scum" or "pathetic." (4)

---

[1] Song of Songs 6:8-9.

It is the very necessity for the words of the debate that puts me in such a sweat—to protect the reader and show that their practices, mysteries and teachings are the furthest thing from my mind. Also to prove my independence of them by those words and the intensity of my opposition, and wean some people away from them, precisely by the words that appear too harsh.

3,1   And here are the contents of the entire work which includes the three Volumes, Volumes One, Two, and Three. These three Volumes I have divided into seven Sections with a certain number of Sects and Schisms in each, making eighty in all.

The names of these sects, and the occasions for them, are as follows: (2) 1. Barbarism. 2. Scythianism. 3. Hellenism. 4. Judaism. 5. Samaritanism. (3) Derived from these are the following. Before Christ's incarnation, but after Barbarism and the Scythian superstition, the outgrowths of Hellenism are: 6. Pythagoreans or Peripatetics, a sect divided (from Hellenism) by Aristotle. 7. Platonists. 8. Stoics. 9. Epicureans.

3,4   Next the Samaritan sect, an offshoot of Judaism, and its four breeds: 10. Gorothenes. 11. Sebuaeans. 12. Essenes. 13. Dositheans.

3,5   Next the afore-mentioned Judaism, which took its characteristic features from Abraham, was amplified through the Law given to Moses, and got its ancestral name, "Judaism," from Judah the son of Jacob or Israel, through David, the king from Judah's tribe. (6) And derived from Judaism itself are the following seven sects: 14. Scribes. 15. Pharisees. 16. Sadducees. 17. Hemerobaptists. 18. Ossaeans. 19. Nasaraeans. 20. Herodians.

4,1   From these sects, and later in time, there appeared the saving dispensation of our Lord Jesus Christ—that is to say, his incarnation, preaching of the Gospel, and proclamation of a kingdom. This alone is the fount of salvation, and the faith in the truth of the catholic, apostolic, and orthodox church.

4,2   From this the following sects, which have Christ's name only but not his faith, have been broken away and split off: (3) 1. Simonians. 2. Menandrians. 3. Satornilians. 4. Basilideans. 5. Nicolaitans. 6. Gnostics, who are also known as Stratiotics and are the same as the Phibionites. But some call them Secundians, others, Socratists, others, Zacchaeans, and by some they are called Coddians, Borborites, and Barbelists. 7. Carpocratians. 8. Cerinthians, also called Merinthians. 9. Nazoraeans. 10. Ebionites. 11. Valentinians. 12. Secundians, with whom Epiphanes and Isidore are associated. 13. Ptolemaeans.

4,4   14. Marcosians. 15. Colorbasians. 16. Heracleonites. 17. Ophites. 18. Cainites. 19. Sethians. 20. Archontics. 21. Cerdonians. 22. Marcionites. 23. Lucianists. 24. Apelleans. 25. Severians. 26. Tatianists.

4,5 27. Encratites. 28. Phrygians, also known as Montanists and Tascodrugians. But again, the Tascodrugians are differentiated as a group in themselves. 29. Pepuzians, also known as Priscillianists and Quintillianists, with whom Artotyrites are associated. 30. Quartodecimans, who celebrate one day of the year as Passover. 31. Alogi, who do not accept the Gospel and Revelation of John. 32. Adamians. 33. Sampsaeans, also known as Elkasaites. 34. Theodotianists. 35. Melchizedekians. 36. Bardesianists. 37. Noetianists. 38. Valesians. 39. Catharists, also known as Navatians. 40. Angelics. 41. Apostolics, also known as Apotactics. 42. Sabellians. 43. Origenists who are immoral as well. 44. Origenists, also known as Followers of Adamantius.

4,6 45. Disciples of Paul of Samosata. 46. Manichaeans, also known as Acuanites. 47. Hierakites. 48. Melitians, an Egyptian schism. 49. Arians, also known as Ariomanites.

4,7 50. The Audian schism. 51. Photinians. 52. Marcellians. 53. Semi-Arians. 54. Pneumatomachi, also called Macedonians and Disciples of Eleusius, who blaspheme the Holy Spirit of God. 55. Aerians. 56. Aetians, also called Anhomoeans, with whom Eunomius, or rather, "Anomus," is associated.

4,8 57. Dimoirites, who do not confess Christ's incarnation in the full sense, also called Apollinarians. Sect number 58, or those who say that St. Mary, the ever-virgin, had intercourse with Joseph after giving birth to the Savior. Such people I call "Antidicomarians." Sect number 59, or those who offer a loaf in the name of the Virgin Mary; they are called Collyridians. 60. Massalians, with whom the Greek Martyrians, and the Euphemites and Satanists, are associated.

5,1 Now I give another list of them divided into Volumes, and in this summary of mine indicate how many of these eighty Sects are in Volume One, and so on in Volumes Two through Three—for each of the seven Sections in the three Volumes, moreover, which portion of the Sects it contains. Thus:

5,2 There are three Sections and forty-six Sects in Volume One, including < their mothers and the original > names of these, I mean Barbarism, Scythianism, Hellenism, Judaism and Samaritanism. In Volume Two there are two Sections and twenty-three Sects. And there are two Sections, and eleven Sects, in Volume Three.

5,3 In the first Section of Volume One there are twenty Sects, as follows: Barbarism, Scythianism, Hellenism and Judaism. Varieties of Hellenes: Pythagoreans or Peripatetics, Platonists, Stoics, Epicureans. The Samaritan sect, which stems from Judaism. Four Samaritan peoples, as follows: Gorothenes, Sebuaeans, Essenes, Dositheans. Seven Jewish sects as follows: Scribes, Pharisees, Sadducees, Hemerobaptists, Ossaeans, Nasaraeans, Herodians.

5,4   There are likewise thirteen Sects in the second Section of Volume
One, as follows: Simonians; Menandrians; Satornilians; Basilideans;
Nicolaitans; Gnostics, also called Stratiotics and Phibionites, but Secundians by some, Socratists by others, Zacchaeans, Coddians, Borborites
and Barbelists by others; Carpocratians; Cerinthians, also called Merinthians; Nazoraeans; Ebionites; Valentinians; Secundians, with whom
Epiphanes and Isidore are associated; Ptolemaeans.

5,5   In the third Section of this first Volume there are thirteen Sects
as follows: Marcosians; Colorbasians; Heracleonites; Ophites; Cainites;
Sethians; Archontics; Cerdonians; Marcionites; Lucianists; Apelleans;
Severians; Tatianists. This is the summary of the first Volume with its
three Sections.

5,6   There are two Sections in Volume Two. And in the first Section
of Volume Two—the fourth in numerical order from the beginning—
there are eighteen Sects as follows: Encratites; Phrygians, also known as
Montanists and Tascodrugians. But the Tascodrugians are differentiated
from the (two) preceding. Pepuzians, < also known as Priscillianists >
and Quintillianists, with whom Artotyrites are associated. Quartodecimans, who celebrate one day in the year as Passover; Alogi, who
do not accept the Gospel and Revelation of John; Adamians; Sampsaeans, also known as Elkasaites: Theodotianists; Melchizedekians;
Bardesianists; Noetians; Valesians; Catharists; Angelics; Apostolics, also
known as Apotactics, with whom the so-called Saccophori are associated;
Sabellians; Origenists who are immoral as well; the Origenists who
follow Adamantius.

5,7   In the second Section of this second Volume—counting as
before, it is the fifth—there are five Sects, as follows: Disciples of Paul
of Samosata; Manichaeans, also known as Acuanites; Hierakites; Melitians, an Egyptian schism; Arians. And this is the summary of the second
Volume, with its < two > Sections.

5,8   Similarly, there are also two Sections in Volume Three. In the
first Section of the third Volume—the sixth according to the previous
numbering—there are seven Sects, as follows: Audians, a schism; Photinians; Marcellians; Semi-Arians; Pneumatomachi, who blaspheme the
Holy Spirit of God; Aerians; Disciples of Aetius the Anhomoean, with
whom Eunomius, also known as Anomus, is associated.

5,9   In the second Section of this Volume Three—seventh by the
previous enumeration of the Sections—which is a seventh Section and
closes the treatise—there are four Sects as follows: Dimoirites, who do
not confess Christ's incarnation in the full sense, also known as
Apollinarians. Those who say that St. Mary, the ever-virgin, had intercourse with Joseph after giving birth to the Savior—I call them "An-

tidicomarians.'' Those who offer a loaf in the name of Mary, and are called Collyridians. Massalians. And the brief defense of the orthodox faith and the truth, ''The Holy, Catholic and Apostolic Church.''

This is the summary and superscription of the entire Treatise Against Eighty Sects, and one (further treatise), the Defense of the Truth of the Sole Church, that is the Catholic and Orthodox. It is arranged in three Volumes below, but divided into seven Sections.

ANACEPHALAEOSIS I

The following are in the first Section of Volume One of the Refutation of the† Eighty Sects. <This includes twenty Sects> as follows:

First, the mothers of all the sects, and their original names. From these five mothers the others sprang. And these are the first four:

1,1 <1.> First is Barbarism, a sect which is by itself. It lasted for ten generations, from Adam's time till Noah. (2) It was called Barbarism because the people of that time had no leader or common agreement. Everyone followed his own lead instead and served as a law for himself, to suit his personal preference.

2,1 <2.> A second is Scythianism, from the time of Noah, and after that until the building of the tower and Babylon; and for a few years after the time of the tower, that is until Peleg and Reu. (2) Since they were on the border of the region of Europe, these people were joined with Scythia and its peoples from the time of Terah, the ancestor of the Thracians, and afterwards.

3,1 <3.> A third is Hellenism. This began in Serug's time[1] with idolatry and the submission to it by the people of the era—each in accordance with some superstition—for the sake of a higher civilization and fixed customs and laws.

3,2 However, when idols were first instituted the various peoples made gods for <the leaders> whose rule they <were> then accepting, originally by painting pictures and portraying the autocrats or sorcerers they had always honored, or persons who had done something that appeared memorable in their lifetimes, <and stood out> for their courage and physical strength. (3) But then, from the time of Terah[2] the father of Abraham, they also introduced the imposture of idolatry by way of statuary. They honored their forefathers, and those who had died before them, with images, at first with the potter's art, then by depicting them with every technique—builders by carving stone, silversmiths and goldsmiths by making them with their media, and so with woodcarvers and the rest. (4) (Egyptians, together with Babylonians, Phrygians and Phoenicians, were the first to introduce this religion, which consisted of image-manufacture and mystery rites.[3] Most of these rites were brought

---

[1] Cf. Jub. 11.1-4.
[2] Cf. Jub. 11.16; 12.2.
[3] Cf. Eus. Praep. Ev. I.6.

to Greece from Cecrops'[4] time and onwards.) (5) Afterwards, and much later, they designated Cronus, Rhea, Zeus, Apollo and the rest as gods.

3,6   Hellenes are named for a Hellen, who was one of the settlers of Hellas, and gives the country its name. But as others tell it, it is named for the olive that grew at Athens. (7) Actually the Ionians were the first of the Hellenes, <and are named for> Iovan, one of the builders of the tower at the time of the division of men's languages. Thus they are all called "Meropes" as well, because of the "divided" speech. (8) But afterwards, at a later period, Hellenism was made into sects—I mean Pythagoreans, Stoics, Platonists, Epicureans and the rest.

3,9   But a type of the worship of God existed together with the natural law, and was customary from the time of these peoples. It set itself apart from the foundation of the world, and existed during the period of Barbarism, Scythianism and Hellenism, till it was combined with Abraham's worship of God.

4,1   <4.> And afterwards came Judaism. From the time of Abraham it had received its characteristic feature through circumcision, and it was amplified during the lifetime of Moses, the seventh from Abraham, by the Law which was given through him by God. But it finally got the name, "Judaism," from Judah, the fourth son of Jacob surnamed Israel, through David, the first king from Judah's tribe.

4,2   For (it was) about these four sects that the apostle clearly said, in reproof, "In Christ Jesus there is neither Barbarian, Scythian, Hellene nor Jew, but a new creation."[5]

Varieties of Hellenes:

5,1   <5.> Pythagoreans, or Peripatetics. Pythagoras' doctrines were the monad, providence, and the prohibition of sacrifice to the beings <considered> gods, if you please, as well as the refusal to eat meat and abstention from wine. (2) At the same time he distinguished between what is above the moon, which he called immortal, and what is below it, which he called mortal. And he taught the transmigrations of souls from body to body, even of beasts and vermin, as well as the keeping of a five-year period of silence. Lastly he pronounced himself divine.

6,1   6. The doctrines of the Platonists were: God; matter and form; that the world is begotten and perishable, while the soul is unbegotten, immortal and divine; that the soul has three parts, the rational, the emotional, and the appetitive; (2) that wives are common to all and that no one has one spouse of his own, but that anyone who wishes may have in-

---

[4] Cecrops is mentioned at Eus. Praep. Ev. X.9; Eus. Chron. p. 159 (Karst); Jer. Chron. 21.24 (Helm).
[5] Col. 3:11.

tercourse with any women who are willing; likewise the transmigration of souls into various bodies, even vermin's, but at the same time, also, the origin of many gods from the one.

7,1   7. Stoics, who held that the universe is a body, and believed that this visible world is God; and some declared that it originates from the substance of fire. (2) They also defined God as "mind," and like a soul of the whole vault of heaven and earth. And the universe is his body, as I said, and the luminaries are his eyes. The flesh of all things perishes, and the soul transfers from body to body.

8,1   8. Epicureans supposed that indivisible and simple bodies, homogeneous and infinite in number, are the first principle of all things. And they held that pleasure is the goal of well-being, and that neither God nor providence directs affairs.

9,1   9. Samaritanism and the Samaritans who belong to it, which is derived from Judaism. The occasion for it came at the time of Nebuchadnezzar and the captivity of the Jews, before the establishment of sects among Greeks and the rise of their doctrines, but after there was a Greek religion and during the period of Judaism. (2) Samaritans were immigrants from Assyria to Judaea and had received Moses' Pentateuch only, since the king had sent it to them from Babylon by a priest named Ezra. (3) All their opinions are the same as the Jews', except that they detest gentiles and will not touch certain persons, and that they deny the resurrection of the dead and the other prophecies, the ones after Moses.

Four Samaritan peoples:

10,1   10. Gorothenes, who celebrate the festivals at different times of year than the Sebuaeans.

11,1   11. Sebuaeans, who differ from the Gorothenes for the same reason, the festivals.

12,1   12. Essenes, who are not opposed to either party; they make no distinction, and celebrate with whoever happens to be there.

13,1   13. Dositheans, who follow the same customs as the Samaritans—circumcision, the Sabbath and the rest—and use the Pentateuch; but over and beyond the others, they observe abstinence from meat and keep very frequent fasts. (2) And some are celibates as well, while others practice continence. And they believe in the resurrection of the dead, which is strange to Samaritans.

Seven Jewish Sects:

14,1   14. Scribes, who were lawyers and repeaters of the traditions of their elders. Because of their further, self-chosen religion they observed customs which they had not learned through the Law but had formulated for themselves—ways of showing reverence to the ordinance of the legislation.

15,1   15. Pharisees, meaning "men set apart," whose life was the most extreme, and who, if you please, were more highly regarded than the others. They believed in the resurrection of the dead as the Scribes did, and agreed that there are such things as angels and the Holy Ghost. And they had a different way of life: periods of continence, and celibacy; fasting twice a week; and cleansings of vessels, platters and goblets, (as the Scribes did); (2) payment of tithes and first-fruits; constant prayer; the styles of dress which were characteristic of a self-chosen religion and consisted of the shawl, the robes or rather tunics, the width of the "phylacteries," or borders of purple material, fringes, and tassels on the corners of the shawl. Things of this sort were signs of their periods of continence. And they also introduced the ideas of destiny and fate.

16,1   16. Sadducees, meaning "most righteous," who were descended from the Samaritans, as well as from a priest named Zadok. They denied the resurrection of the dead and did not recognize the existence of angels or spirits. In all other respects they were Jews.

17,1   17. Hemerobaptists. These were Jews in all respects, but claimed that no one can obtain eternal life without being baptized every day.

18,1   18. Ossenes, meaning "boldest." They kept all the observances as the Law directs. But they also made use of other scriptures after the Law, though rejecting most of the prophets that came after it.

19,1   19. Nasaraeans, meaning, "rebels," who forbid all flesh-eating, and do not eat living things at all. They have the holy names of patriarchs which are in the Pentateuch, up through Moses and Joshua the son of Nun, and they believe in them—(2) I mean Abraham, Isaac, Jacob, and the earliest ones, and Moses himself, and Aaron, and Joshua. But they hold that the scriptures of the Pentateuch were not written by Moses, and maintain that they have others.

20,1   20. Herodians, who were Jews in all respects, but thought that Herod was Christ, and awarded the honor and name of Christ to him.

This is the first Section, containing refutations of all of these twenty sects. The subject of Christ's advent is in it as well, and the confession of the truth.

The Heresiology of Epiphanius, Bishop, Entitled "Panarion," or "Medicine Chest" (Proem II)

1,1   To start my account and discussion of faith and unbelief, of orthodoxy and heresy, reminds me of the beginning of the world's creation and course. Not that I begin on the strength of my own ability or on the basis of my own reasonings. I do it as God, the Lord of all and the merciful, has revealed the knowledge of the entire subject to his prophets, and vouchsafed it to me through them, so far as human nature allows.

1,2   And I feel quite anxious at the outset, as soon as I begin to consider the subject. Indeed I am extremely frightened at undertaking a task of no small importance, and I call on the holy God himself, on his only-begotten Son Jesus Christ, and on his Holy Spirit, to give my poor mind light, and thus illumine it with the knowledge of these things.

1,3   For the Greek authors, the poets and chroniclers, would invoke a Muse when they undertook some work of mythology. A Muse, not God—their wisdom was demonic, "earthly, and not descended from above,"[1] as scripture says. (4) I, however, call upon the holy Lord of all to come to the aid of my poverty and inspire me with his Holy Spirit, that I may include no falsehood in my treatment of the subject. (5) And having made this very petition—for "according to the measure of faith and in proportion,"[2] I know my inadequacy—I beseech him to grant it.

2,1   When a person reads a work on any question the <treatise's> aim should be <clear> to him—the discoveries training enables my small mind to grasp lie in the temporal realm, and I certainly do not promise <to teach> everything in the world. (2) There are things which cannot be uttered, and things which can. There are things untold, beyond counting, inaccessible so far as man is concerned, and known only to the Lord of all. (3) But we are dealing with variance of opinions and kinds of knowledge, with faith in God and unbelief, with sects, and with heretical human opinion which misguided persons have been propagating in the world from man's formation on earth till our own day, the eleventh year of the reigns of Valentinian and Valens and the eighth of Gratian's.[3]

2,4   Some of the things which I shall tell the reader <about> sects and schisms, I owe to my fondness for study. Certain things I learned from hearsay, though I experienced some with my own ears and eyes. I am confident that I can give an account of some sects' origins and teachings from accurate report, and of part of the things which others do. Of these things, I know one from the works of ancient authors, another from the report of men who confirmed my notion precisely.

2,5   I did not gather all this reflection together on my own initiative, or from familiarity with further subjects, too extensive for my brief style of expression. In fact <I have also written> this work—which, by God's will, I have consented to compose—<at the request> of scholarly per-

---

[1] Jam. 3:15.
[2] Cf. Rom. 12:6.
[3] 375 A.D.

sons who goaded my weakness at various times in various ways, and practically forced me to do it. Such a request Your Honors made in writing, my most esteemed brothers and scholarly fellow presbyters, Acacius and Paul, in a letter of recommendation. (6) Now since I have considered the number of the requests, by no means without God's help, and from extreme love of the servants of God have consented, I shall begin—not with eloquence of language or polished phrases, but with simplicity of dialect and speech, though with accuracy in the content of what I say.

3,1 Nicander too, the investigator of beasts and reptiles, imparted the knowledge of their natures. And others, who studied roots and plants, <described> what they were made of—Dioscurides the Wood-Cutter, Pamphilus, King Mithridates, Callisthenes, Philo, Iolaus of Bithynia, Heraclidas of Taranto, Cratenus the Root-Collector, Andrew, Bassus the Tulian, Niceratus, Petronius, Niger, Diodotus, and certain others. (2) And no more than they do I, in my similar attempt to reveal the roots and origins of the sects, <describe them> to harm those who care to read (my description).

2,3 Those authors made a diligent effort, not to point evil out, but to frighten men and ensure their safety, so that they would recognize the dreadful, dangerous beasts and be secure, and escape them, by God's power, by taking care not to engage with such deadly creatures if they encountered them, and were menaced by their breath or bite, or the sight of them. And <meanwhile>, from the same concern, these authors prescribed medicines made from roots and plants, to cure the illness caused by these serpents. (4) Thus, dearest, my work too <has been compiled> as a defense against them and for your <safety>, to expose the appearance of the dreadful serpents and beasts, and their poisons and deadly bites. (5) And to correspond with these I shall give as many arguments, like antidotes, as I can in short compass—one or two at most—to counteract their poison and, after the Lord, to save anyone who cares <to be>, when he has willingly or inadvertently fallen into these snakelike teachings of the sects.

1.

<1. Barbarism>

1,1 For at the beginning Adam was brought to life on the sixth day, after being formed from earth and infused with (God's breath). He was not begun on the fifth day, as some think, and finished on the sixth; the notion of those who say this is mistaken. He was unspoiled and innocent of evil and had no other name, for he had no surname referring to an

opinion, a belief, or a distinction of his mode of life. He was simply called
"Adam," which means "man." (2) A wife like him was formed for him
out of himself—out of the same body, <by> the same breath. Adam
had male and female children. And after 930 years of life he died.

1,3   The child of Adam was Seth, the son of Seth was Enosh, and his
descendants were Cainan, Mahalaleel and Jared. And the tradition
which I have learned says that mischief first appeared in the world at this
point.[1] It also had at the beginning, through Adam's disobedience, and
then through Cain's fratricide. But now, in the lifetime of Jared and
afterward, came sorcery, witchcraft, licentiousness, adultery and iniquity. (4) <However> there was no different opinion, no changed belief;
there was one language, and one stock which had been planted on earth
at that time. (5) This Jared had a son named Enoch, who "pleased God
and was not; for god took him away" and he "did not see death."[2]
Enoch was the father of Methuselah, Methuselah of Lamech, and
Lamech of Noah.[3]

1,6   God's righteous judgment brought a flood on the world and
wiped all humanity out, and all other <living things>. But by his decree
he preserved Noah in the ark, since he had pleased God and found
favor—Noah himself; his three sons, Shem, Ham and Japheth; Noah's
own wife; and his three sons' wives. (7) So eight human beings were preserved in the ark then from the water of the flood. And some of every
kind of animal and living thing, cattle and everything else on earth, were
preserved—by twos in some cases, by sevens in others—to renew the existence of every kind of thing in the world. (8) And thus a tenth generation had passed making 2262 years.[4] And the flood came to an end, and
Noah and his household provided the world with a surviving stock.

1,9   But there was no difference of opinion yet, no people that was at
all different, no name for a sect, and no idolatry either. Since everyone
followed his own opinion, however, the name, "Barbarism," was given
to the era then, during the ten generations. (For there was not one law.
Everyone served as his own law, and followed his own opinion. Hence
the apostle's usage, not only of "Barbarism" but of the other terms as
well; for he says, "In Christ Jesus there is neither Barbarian, Scythian,
Hellene nor Jew.")[5]

---

[1] Cf. Jub. 4.15;22.
[2] Gen. 5:24; Heb. 11:5.
[3] The genealogy is taken from Gen. 5:21-29.
[4] This is the reckoning of Julius Africanus. Cf. Georg. Syncel. 83; Jer. Ep. 51.6.7 (=
Epiphanius to John of Jerusalem).
[5] Col. 3:11; Gal. 3:28.

2.

< 2. Scythianism >

2,1   After the flood Noah's ark came to rest in the highlands of Ararat between Armenia and Cardyaei,[6] on the mountain called Lubar. Thus the first human settlement after the flood was made there, and there the prophet Noah planted a vineyard and became the pioneer settler of the area. (2) His children—there is no indication that he had more—had children and children's children down to a fifth generation, 659 years in all. This omits Shem. But I shall list the descendants of the one son in succession. Shem was the father of Arphachshad; Arphachshad, of Kenah; Kenah, of Shelah. Shelah was the father of Eber, the pious and godfearing. Eber was the father of Peleg.[7]

2,3   And there was nothing on earth yet, no sect, no divided opinion. There were only "men," "of one speech and one language."[8] There were only ungodliness and godliness, the natural law and the natural error, not learned from teaching or books, of each individual's will. There was no Judaism, no Hellenism, no other sect at all. But in a way, the faith now native to God's present day holy catholic church existed, for it existed at the first, and was revealed again later. (4) Anyone willing < to make an > impartial < investigation can > see, from the very object of it, < that > the holy catholic church is the start of everything. Adam, < the > man formed first, was not formed with a circumcised body, but an uncircumcised one. But he was no idolater, and he knew Father, Son, and Holy Spirit as God, for he was a prophet.

2,5   Without circumcision he was no Jew. As he did not worship carved images or anything else, he was no idolater. For Adam < was > a prophet, and knew that the Father had said, "Let us make man,"[9] to the Son. What was this, then, if he was neither circumcised nor an idolater—what but that he showed some signs of the characteristics of Christianity? (6) And we must believe this of Abel, Seth, Enosh, Enoch, Methuselah, Noah and Eber, down to Abraham.

2,7   Godliness and ungodliness, faith and unbelief, were in actual existence then. Faith was in the image of Christianity, while unbelief, contrary to the natural law, had the characteristics of ungodliness and transgression, until the time I have indicated.[10]

---

[6] Jub. 5.28.
[7] The genealogy is taken from Gen. 11:10-17.
[8] Gen. 11:1.
[9] Gen. 1:26.
[10] I.e., the time of Abraham.

2,8   In the fifth generation after the flood, now that men were multiplying from Noah's three sons, the children and their children, who had been born successively, became a world-population of seventy-two chief men and patricians. (9) And as they expanded and moved far away from Mt. Lubar and the Armenian highlands, or region of Ararat, they reached the plain of Shinar[11] where they presumably chose <to live>. (Shinar is now in Persia, but anciently it belonged to the Assyrians.) (10) In Shinar they joined together and consulted about building a tower and city. From the region near Europe which borders[12] on Asia they were all called "Scythians," which corresponds to the name of the era.

2,11   They began the erection of their tower and built Babylon. But God was displeased with their foolish work, for he dispersed their languages, and divided them from one into seventy-two, to correspond with the number of the men then living. This is why they were called "Meropes," because of the "divided" language. A blast of wind blew the tower over.[13]

2,12   So they were dispersed right and left over the whole earth, with some going back where they came from and others further east, while others reached Libya. (13) Anyone who wants the facts about them can discover how each one who went further obtained his allotment in each particular country. For example, Egypt fell to Mistrem, Ethiopia to Cush, Axomitia to Phut. Regman, Sabakatha and †Ludan, also known as †Judad, obtained the land near Garamitia. But to avoid composing this preface in great detail, I shall return to the subject, and resume the series in order.

3.

<3. Hellenism>

3,1   And now came the first taking of counsel and the first autocracy, in the time between Eber and Peleg, and the building of the tower and the first city after the flood,[14] which was founded in the very building. (2) For Nimrod[15] the son of Cush the Ethiopian, the father of Asshur, ruled as a king. His kingdom arose in Orech, Arphal and Chalana, and he also founded Theiras, Thobel and Lobon in Assyria. The Greeks say that he is Zoroaster and that he went on further east and became the pioneer settler of Bactria.

---

[11] Jub. 10.19.

[12] We adopt Holl's conjecture of κεχλικότος for κεχλικότες.

[13] Jub. 10.26.

[14] Gen 10:25 implies that Peleg was contemporary with the tower.

[15] For Nimrod as a magician, identified with Zoroaster, cf. Clem. Hom. IX. 4-5.

3,3   Every transgression in the world was disseminated at this time, for Nimrod was an originator of wrong teaching, astrology and magic—which is what some say of Zoroaster.[16] But in actual fact this was the time of Nimrod the giant; the two, Nimrod and Zoroaster, are far apart in time.

3,4   Peleg was the father of Reu, and Reu was the father of Serug, which means "provocation;" and, as I was taught, idolatry and Hellenism began among men with him.[17] The human reason originated its own evil, and invented transgression instead of goodness with its freedom, reason and intellect, but only with paintings and portraits. Not with carved images yet, or reliefs in stone, wood, or silver-plated substances, or made <of> gold or any other material.

3,5   Nahor was born as a son to Serug and was the father of Terah. Image-making with clay and pottery began at this point, with the craft of this person, Terah.[18] And by now the world had reached its twentieth generation, comprising 3332 years.

3,6   And no one of the previous generations ever died before his father;[19] fathers died before their children and left their sons to succeed them. (Never mind Abel—he did not die a natural death.) (7) But since Terah had set up a rival to God by making one with his own sculpture he was rightly repaid with the equivalent and provoked to jealousy himself, through his own son. (8) Hence sacred scripture remarked with astonishment, "And Haran died before his father, Terah, in the land of his nativity."[20]

3,9   A kind of succession of Scythianism, and its name, remained until this time. But there was no such thing as a sect yet, no device other than simply a "<first> fornication, thinking on idols."[21] And after that people made gods of unfortunate despots, or sorcerers who had deceived the world, and paid homage to their tombs. (10) And much later they deified Cronus, and Zeus, Rhea, Hera and the rest of them. And then they worshipped Acinaces—and the Scythian Sauromatians worshipped Odrysus and the ancestor of the Thracians, from whom the Phrygian people are derived. This is why Thracians are named for the person called Theras, who was born during the building of the tower.

3,11   Now when error began it was the point in history which I have indicated. <Hellenism originated with Egyptians, Babylonians and

---

[16] "Zoroaster the magus" is ruler of Bactria at Eus. Praep. Ev. X.9, cf. Eus. Chron. 29,1 (Karst); Jer. Chron. 20,13.

[17] Idolatry begins with Serug at Jub. 11.4-6.

[18] Jub. 11.16 ascribes the first idolatry to Terah.

[19] Clem. Recog. I.31.3; but the crime is incest, not idolatry.

[20] Gen. 11:28.

[21] Cf. Wisd. Sol. 14:12.

Phrygians >, and it now confused < men's > ways. After that historians
and chroniclers borrowed from the imposture of the Egyptians' heathen
mythology < and conveyed it to the other nations >, thus giving rise to
sorcery and witchcraft. (12) But from the time of Cecrops these things
were brought to Greece. And this was the time of the Assyrians Ninus
and Semiramis who were contemporary with Abraham, and the †six-
teenth Egyptian dynasty. But the only kings then were the kings of Si-
cyon,[22] the kingdom founded by Europs.

4.

< 4. Judaism >

1,1   And God made choice of Abraham, who was faithful in
uncircumcision—again, characteristically of the holy catholic church—
and was perfection itself in godliness, a prophet in knowledge, a follower
of the Gospel in life. (2) For he had lived at home honoring his father;
< but > like Peter, Andrew, James and John he parted from his family
when summoned by (God's) bidding, in obedience to his Summoner.

1,3   And to avoid another prolongation, I shall summarize. Circumcision was enjoined on this patriarch by God when he was ninety-nine,
and thus the characteristic feature of Judaism originated, after
Hellenism. And it was the twenty-first generation < from > the foundation of the world, the year 3431. (4) For Scythianism extended from the
flood till the tower and Serug, and Hellenism from Serug till Abraham, and till now. But after Abraham there was no (new) name for
a sect yet, other than simply the name of his godly self. So those derived
from Abraham were called Abramians.

1,5   For Abraham had eight sons. Isaac was the sole heir, however,
both because he adhered to devotion to God as his father wished, and
because he had been given to his father by God's promise. (6) Before him
Abraham had Ishmael by the maidservant, Hagar, and Khetura bore
him six children. They were distributed over the land called Arabia
Felix—Zimran, Jokshan, Ishbak, Shuah, Medan and Midian. (7) And
the ''son of the bondmaid''—as I said, his name was Ishmael—also seized < the wilderness >, and founded the city called Phara in the
wilderness. He had twelve children altogether; these were the ancestors
of the tribes of the Hagarenes, or Ishmaelites, though today they are
called Saracens.

---

[22] This chronological information comes from Eus. Chron. 42,28; 81,30 (Karst), cf.
Jer. Chron. 16,2-17 (Helm).

1,8   Isaac had two sons, Esau and Jacob, and then the stock of the godfearing were called both Abramians and Isaacites. After Esau's banishment to Idumaea, which lies to the southeast of Canaan, he became the first settler of Mount Seir, and for a city founded Edom,[23] known as Rokom and Petra. (9) He had children, who were also called "princes of Edom," and each in turn ruled in Idumaea. The fifth in succession from Esau—omitting Abraham but counting from Isaac—was Job. (10) For Isaac was the father of Esau, Esau of Raguel, Raguel of Zara, and Zara of Job. His name was Jobab earlier, but later he was named Job, shortly before his trial. The custom of circumcision was maintained (by these people).

1,11   By his father's and mother's advice Jacob fled from his brother, Esau, to Mesopotamian Padan beyond Souba in Mesopotamia, because of Esau's anger. He took wives of his own kindred from there, four of them in all, and they bore him twelve children, also known as "patriarchs." (12) During his flight back to Canaan, to his own father, Isaac, and his mother, Rebekah, he had a vision from God near the gorges of the Jordan—the stream is called the Jabbok—perhaps where he had seen encampments of angels. (13) "And lo," we are told, "(there appeared) a man at even and wrestled with him until the breaking of the day."[24] The passage indicated that this man was an angel. As a blessing he gave Jacob an honorific name, "Israel." (14) On leaving Jacob named the place "Sight of God." < Now > since the angel who blessed him with the words, "Thy name shall be called no more Jacob, but Israel shall it be called," < had named him Israel >, and since he had distinguished him by saying, "Thou hast had power with God, and with men thou shalt be mighty,"[25] they have been called Israelites since this time.

2,1   And after Joseph had gone down to Egypt Israel went too, with his entire household of sons and grandchildren, their wives and others, seventy persons in all. (2) Israel's people lived in Egypt for five generations. For Jacob was the father of Levi and Judah, and the other ten patriarchs; Levi was the father of Kohath; Judah of Perez. Kohath was the father of Amram; Amram of Moses. Perez was the father of Esrom; Esrom of Aram; Aram of Aminadab, and Aminadab of Nahshon.

2,3   During the lifetime of Moses and Nahshon, in the fifth generation reckoned from Levi, Israel departed from Egypt miraculously through the Red Sea, and encamped in the wilderness of Sinai. (4) And when God directed his servant, Moses, to make a count of men between

---

[23] Eus. Onom. 142,7 (Klostermann).
[24] Gen. 32:25.
[25] Gen. 32:29.

twenty and fifty who could draw a sword and bear arms, he found as many as 628,500.

2,5   Inachus was becoming known in Greece at that time. His daughter was Io or Atthis, for whom the modern Attica is named. Her son was Bosporus, and there is a city named Bosporus for him on the Black Sea. Egyptians call her Isis, and worship her as a goddess besides. There is also a river with his name, for its name is Inachus.

2,6   That was the origin of the Greek mysteries and initiatory rites. Their evil invention had come earlier, in Egypt, and in Phrygia, Phoenicia and Babylonia, but they were brought to Greece from Egypt by Cadmus, and Inachus himself—who had formerly been named Apis, and had built Memphis. But they also originated with Orpheus and certain others, (7) and were organized into sects later, during the lifetimes of Epicurus, Zeno the Stoic, Pythagoras and Plato. They gained strength from the time of their origin until the period of the Macedonians and Xerxes, king of Persia—this was after the first fall of Jerusalem, and the captivity under Nebuchadnezzar and Darius—and the career of Alexander of Macedon. (8) For Plato was becoming known at that time, and his predecessors, Pythagoras and the later Epicurus. As I said, this occasioned the rise of Greek literature, (9) and later of the celebrated sects of the philosophers. These agree in error, and join in fabricating a similar knowledge of idolatry, impiety and godlessness; but they conflict with each other because of the same error.

5.

Against Stoics, < Sect > three from Hellenism, but five of the series

1,1   And the Stoic notion of deity is as follows. They claim that God is mind, or a mind of the whole visible vault—I mean the vault of heaven, earth and the rest—like a soul in a body. (2) But they also divide the one Godhead into many individual beings: sun, moon and stars, soul, air and the rest. (3) And < they have a doctrine of > reincarnations of souls and transmigrations from body to body, with < souls > being removed < from > bodies, entering (others) in turn, and being born over again—with their great deceit they finish off with this impiety. And they think that the soul is a part of God, and immortal.

1,4   Zeno was the founder of their Stoa, and there is much confused chatter about him. Some have said that he was < a son > of a Cleanthes of Tyre. But others claim that he was a Citean, a Cypriote islander, and that he lived at Rome for a while, but later offered this doctrine at Athens, at the Stoa as it is called. Some, however, say that there are two Zenos, Zeno of Elis and the one just mentioned. Both taught the same doctrine anyhow, even though there might be two of them. (5) And so like the other sects, this (other) Zeno also maintains that matter is contemporaneous with God, and that there is a fate and fortune by which all things are directed and influenced.

1,6   Now then, I shall <administer> a remedy for Zeno's condition, as far as this brief discussion of mine can do it. For rather than overload the content of the treatise, <I need only> give <the main points>. However, skimming the surface so as not to digress, I shall address Zeno:

2,1   Mister, where did you get the guidance for your teaching? Or which Holy Spirit has spoken to you from heaven about your imposture? For you have to say that there are two contemporaries, matter and God. Your count will be wrong and prove untenable. (2) For you admit that there is some sort of creator whom you also call "almighty," though you divide him into a plurality of gods. But what can he be creator of, if matter is contemporaneous with him? Matter in itself must be in control of itself, if it did not originate from any cause and is not subject to one. (3) And if the creator took his material from it, and acquired it on loan, there must be a weakness (in him). And this must be an interest-free loan to a bankrupt, who provided for his own creation's existence, not from his own resources, but from property mortgaged to someone else.

2,4   And there is plenty wrong with your false notion of transmigration, you self-appointed sage who promises men knowledge! For if the soul is a part of God and immortal, and yet you associate wretched bodies with the fashioning of it—though you claim that its essence is from God! Not just <human> bodies—bodies of four-footed beasts too, and things that crawl, and vermin of foul origin! And what could be worse?

3,1   You further introduce fate as the cause of whatever happens to man and other beings. But I shall expose your invention succinctly with one argument. If cleverness, understanding, the generation of the rational and irrational, and everything else, is a matter of fate, then no more laws! Fate is in control of adulterers and the rest. Rather than the man, who does the deed under necessity, the stars, which have imposed necessity, must pay the penalty.

3,2   Moreover, I shall say some more on this subject, in a different way. No more diatribes! No more sophists, rhetoricians and grammarians, no more doctors and the other professions, and the countless manual trades! No one should give instruction any more, if people's acquisition of the sciences depends on fate, not education. For if fate has made him educated and erudite, one should not learn from a teacher. Let the thread-spinning Fates † weave knowledge into him naturally, as your imposture with its boastful oratory says.

6.

Platonists, Sect four from Hellenism, but six of the series

1,1   But so much for Zeno and the Stoics. Plato tended in the same
direction, <in his adherence to> reincarnation, the transmigration of
souls, polytheism, and the other idolatries and superstitions. But perhaps
he did not entirely agree with Zeno and the Stoics about matter. (2) For
he himself knows God, and that whatever has been produced is a product
of the God who is.[1] But (he says) that there is a first, a second, and a third
cause. And the first cause is God, but the second arises from God,
<together with> certain powers. Through it and the powers matter has
come into being.

1,3   For Plato says as follows: "Heaven came into being with time,
and hence will be destroyed with it as well."[2] This is a revision of his own
previous statements about matter. For at one time he had said that matter is indeed contemporaneous with God.[3]

7.

Pythagoreans, Sect five from Hellenism, but seven of the series

1,1   Pythagoras and the Peripatetics indicated that God is one before
Plato. However, they adhered <both> to other philosophies and to the
principles <of the philosophers I have been mentioning>. Like them,
Pythagoras and his school once more gave expression to the teachings
characteristic of their unlawful, extremely impious outlook, the deifica-
tion and transmigration of souls and the destruction of bodies.

1,2   Pythagoras finally died in Media. He said that God is a body,
meaning heaven, and that sun and moon, the other stars, and the planets
in heaven are God's eyes and other features, as in a man.[4]

8.

Epicureans, Sect six from Hellenism, but eight of the series

1,1   Coming after them, Epicurus first taught the world that there is
no providence. He said that all things are composed of atoms and revert
back to atoms. Everything, and the world, exists by chance, since nature
constantly generates, is used up again, and is renewed out of itself once

---

[1] Plato Ep. II 312E.
[2] Plato Tim. 38B.
[3] Cf. Hippol. Haer. I.19.4.
[4] Cf. Corp. Herm. XVI.19; Ascl. 2.

more—but it never comes to a halt, since it arises out of itself and is worn down into itself.

1,2   Originally the whole was like an egg; but the spirit was then coiled snakewise round the egg, and bound nature tightly all round like a wreath or girdle. (3) At some time it had a strong impulse to squeeze the whole matter, or nature, of all things harder. It thus split all existent things into the two hemispheres, and from this the separation of the atoms resulted. (4) For the light, finer parts of all nature—light, aether, and the finest parts of the spirit—floated up on top. But the parts which were heaviest and like dregs have sunk downwards. This means earth—anything dry, in other words—and the moist substance of the waters. (5) The whole moves of itself and by its own momentum with the revolution of pole and stars, since all things are still driven by the snakelike spirit.[5]

I have spoken of these things if only in part; in the same way, these four sects ought to be refuted. <But> for brevity of reading's sake <I shall not undertake it.> .

(Judaism continued)

2,1   At this point—as I said just now—poets, prose authors, historians, astronomers, and those who introduced the other kinds of error accustomed their minds to any number of bad causes and lines of argument, and made men's notions giddy and confused. And this "first error" and teaching's first mishap, "thinking on idols"[1] arose.

2,2   And everything was divided into Hellenism and Judaism—though it was not called Judaism till it had had <five> leaders in succession. (In addition, however, it had acquired the ancestral name of the godly religion through Israel.) (3) For Nahshon, born in the wilderness as head of the tribe of Judah, was the father of Salmon. Salmon was the father of Boaz; Boaz, of Obed; Obed of Jesse—and meanwhile the godly were still called Israelites. Jesse was the father of King David, the first of the tribe of Judah to reign as king. From him now came the successive kings of his line, each in turn, with son succeeding father.

2,4   In fact, however, the first king in Israel, before David himself, was Saul the son of Kish, of the tribe of Benjamin. <But he was rejected>, and no son succeeded him; his kingship passed to David, and through David, the first, to the tribe of Judah. (5) For the first child of Jacob was Reuben, the second was Simeon, the third was Levi, the fourth was Judah. Thus they are called Jews for the tribe of Judah, as

---

[5] Cf. Ascl. 17.

[1] Cf. Wisd. Sol. 14:12.

this is what the godly people's name was changed to. So they were called Israelites and Jews.

3,1   The earth's four generations formed a continuity until this time, though up to the time I have mentioned here and beyond, we have distinguished the following four divisions, corresponding with the early periods. (2) That is: from Adam till Noah there was Barbarism. From Noah till the tower, and until Serug, two generations after the tower, came the Scythian superstition. After that, from the tower, Serug and †Terah until Abraham, Hellenism. From Abraham on, a fear of God ascribed to Abraham—Judaism, (named) for Judah, Abraham's lineal descendant. (3) God's Spirit-inspired, holy apostle Paul bears me out in this with some such words as, "In Christ Jesus there is neither barbarian, Scythian, Hellene nor Jew but a new creation."[2] (For originally, when creation had been brought into being, it was new and had not been given any more distinctive name.) (4) And again, Paul says something consonant in another passage: "I am debtor both to the Hellenes and to the barbarians; both to the wise and to the unwise."[3] (This is to show that the Jews are "wise," but the Scythians "unwise". And he says, "I am debtor," < to indicate that "salvation is of the Jews." >)[4]

3,5   For this reason the whole people of Israel were called Jews from the time of David. And all Israel continued to be called by their ancestral name of "Israelites," and to have the additional name of "Jews," from the time of David, of his son Solomon, and of Solomon's son—I mean Rehoboam, who ruled in Jerusalem after Solomon.

3,6   But to avoid getting side-tracked, bypassing the topic of the Jews' religion, and failing to touch on the subject of their beliefs, I shall give a few examples. For the facts about the Jews are obvious to practically everyone. Hence I shall certainly not take the trouble to deal with this subject in great detail; but I still need to give a few examples here.

4,1   Now Jews, who are Abraham's lineal descendants and the heirs of his fear of God, have Abraham's circumcision, which he received by God's command at the age of ninety-nine, for the reason I gave earlier. It was to keep his descendants from repudiating the name of God when they became strangers in a foreign land. They would bear a mark on their bodies instead to remind and confound them, to keep them true to their father's fear of God. (2) And Abraham's son, Isaac, was circumcised the eighth day as God's oracle commanded. It is acknowledged that circumcision was by God's ordinance at that time. But it had been ordained for a type then; I shall prove this of it later, as I proceed in order.

---

[2] Col. 3:11; Gal. 6:15.
[3] Rom. 1:14.
[4] John 4:22.

4,3   So Abraham's own children in succession—I mean beginning
with himself, and Isaac and Jacob, and Jacob's children after him—
continued to be circumcised and adhere to the fear of God in the land
of Canaan, (Judaea and Philistia as it was called then, though its name
is now Palestine.) And they did so in Egypt as well. (4) For Jacob, or
Israel, went down to Egypt with his eleven children in his hundred and
thirtieth year. (Joseph, his other son, was already in Egypt reigning as
king, though he had been sold by his brothers from envy. God's provision, which serves the righteous well, had turned the plot against this
Joseph into a marvel.)

4,5   So Jacob went down to Egypt as I said, and his sons, wives and
grandchildren, seventy-five persons in all—as the first book of Moses'
Pentateuch tells us, and clearly indicates of all of them. (6) And they remained there for five generations—as I have said often enough, but must
now repeat. For the posterity of Jacob were the generations which are
reckoned through Levi, the ancestor of the priests; and the ones which
are reckoned through Judah, from whom in time came David, the first
king. (7) And Levi was the father of Kohath and the others; Kohath was
the father of Amram; Amram was the father of Moses, and of Aaron the
high priest. Moses brought the children of Israel out of Egypt by the
power of God, as the second book of the legislation says.

5,1   Still, it is obviously impossible to say distinctly what the regimen
of the children of Israel was until this time, other than simply that they
had the fear of God and circumcision. (Though scripture does say, "The
children of Israel multiplied in the land of Egypt and became abun-
dant."[5] It must surely have been due to laxity that the period of their sojourn and intercourse (with gentiles) produced this "abundance.") (2)
But it had not yet been really clearly indicated what they should eat, what
they should forbid, or the other things they were commanded to observe
by the Law's injunction. (3) However, on their departure from Egypt,
in the second year of their exodus, they were vouchsafed God's legislation at the hands of Moses himself.

5,4   The legislation God gave them taught them like a guardian—
indeed the Law was a guardian in giving its commandments physically,
though with a spiritual object. Its teachings were, circumcision; Sabbath
observance; the tithing of all their produce and any human or animal offspring born among them; the presentation of firstfruits both on the fiftieth and on the thirtieth days; and to know God alone and serve him.
(5) Thus the Name <was> preached under the aspect of Unity; but the
Trinity was always proclaimed in the Unity, and was believed in by the

---

[5] Exod. 1:7.

most outstanding of them, the prophets and the consecrated. In the wilderness Israel offered sacrifices and various kinds of worship to the all-sovereign God in the service of the holy tabernacle, which Moses had constructed from patterns God had shown him.

5,6   In addition, these Jews at least received prophetic oracles regarding the Christ to come. He was called "prophet," though he was God; and "angel," though he was the son of God, who yet would become man and be reckoned with his brethren. So say all the sacred scriptures, especially the fifth book of the legislation, Deuteronomy, and <the ones> that follow.

6,1   By the time of the captives' return from Babylon these Jews had acquired the following books and prophets, and the following books of the prophets: (2) 1. Genesis. 2. Exodus. 3. Leviticus. 4. Numbers. 5. Deuteronomy. 6. The Book of Joshua the son of Nun. 7. The Book of the Judges. 8. Ruth. 9. Job. 10. The Psalter. 11. The Proverbs of Solomon. 12. Ecclesiastes. 13. The Song of Songs. 14. The First Book of Kings. 15. The Second Book of Kings. 16. The Third book of Kings. 17. The Fourth Book of Kings. 18. The First Book of Chronicles. 19. The Second Book of Chronicles. 20. The Book of the Twelve Prophets. 21. The Prophet Isaiah. 22. The Prophet Jeremiah, with the Lamentations and the Epistles of Jeremiah and Baruch. 23. The Prophet Ezekiel. 24. The Prophet Daniel. 25. I Ezra. 26. II Ezra 27. Esther. (3) These are the twenty-seven books given the Jews by God. They are counted as twenty-two, however, like the letters of their Hebrew alphabet, because ten books which (Jews) reckon as five are double. But I have explained this clearly elsewhere. (4) And they have two more books of disputed canonicity, the Wisdom of Sirach and the Wisdom of Solomon, apart from certain other apocrypha.

6,5   All these sacred books taught (them) Judaism and Law's observances till the coming of our Lord Jesus Christ. (6) And they would have been all right under the Law's guardianship, had they accepted the Christ whom their guardian, I mean the Law, foretold to them and prophesied—so as to learn of the Law's fulfillment, not its destruction, by accepting Christ's divinity and incarnation. For the types were in the Law, but the truth is in the Gospel.

6,7   The Law provides for physical circumcision. This did temporary duty until the great circumcision, baptism, which cuts us off from our sins and has marked us in the name of God. (8) The Law had a Sabbath to restrain us until the great Sabbath, the rest of Christ, so that in Christ we might enjoy a Sabbath-rest from sin. (9) And in the Law a lamb, a dumb animal, was sacrificed to guide us to the great, heavenly Lamb, slain for our sins and "for the whole world."[6] (10) And the Law ensured tithing, to keep us from overlooking the "iota," ten, the initial letter of the name of Jesus.

7,1 Now since the Jews were led by the type, and failed to reach the fulfillment which the Law, the prophets and others, and every book (in scripture) proclaims, they were put off the estate. And the gentiles came in, since Jews can no longer be saved unless they return to the grace of the Gospel. For they have broken all the ordinances—so each witness says, as it stands in every passage. (2) But in a few words, using one text, I shall state the impossibility of postponing their sentence or altering it. The precise decree against them is plain to see. Scripture says, "Whatsoever soul will not hearken unto that prophet shall be cut off from his tribe, and from Israel, and from under the heavens,"[7] (3) meaning that the Lord will give a final, saving confirmation of the truths he has transmitted mystically through the Law, but a person who does not listen to him and refuses to, cannot be saved even though he keeps the Law. For the Law cannot perfect the man, since its ordinances are (only) written words and their real fulfillment is in Christ.

7,4 So much for Judaism—I did mention a few points, so as not to omit all the facts about them, but to intimate them in part. For the subject of the Jews, and their refutation, is known beforehand to practically everyone. (5) Also, at the outset, I indicated their origin. Originally, because of their descent from him, <the> godly people were named <Abramians> after the patriarch Abraham's godly self, but Israelites after his grandson, I mean Jacob or Israel. (6) But all twelve tribes were called both Jews and Israelites from the time of David, the king from the tribe of Judah, and until David's son Solomon, and Rehoboam, who was Solomon's son but David's grandson.

7,7 And because of God's chastisement and Rehoboam's unworthiness, the twelve tribes were divided, and became two and a half with Judah—that is, with Rehoboam—and nine and a half with Jeroboam. (8) The nine and a half were called both Israelites and Israel, and were ruled by Jeroboam, the son of Nebat, in Samaria. But the two and a half at Jerusalem were called Jews, and were ruled by Solomon's son, Rehoboam. (9) And in turn there was a succession of kings. Rehoboam was the father of Abijah; Abijah, of Asa; Asa, of Jehoshaphat; Jehoshaphat, of Jehoram; Jehoram, of Ahaziah; Ahaziah, of Joash; Joash, of Amaziah; Amaziah, of Azariah or Uzziah; Azariah or Uzziah, of Jotham; Jotham, of Ahaz; Ahaz, of Hezekiah. At the time of Hezekiah

---

[6] John 2:2.
[7] Deut. 18:19; Exod. 12:15;19.

and Ahaz, tribes from Israel were taken as captives to the mountains of Media. (10) After this, Hezekiah became the father of Manasseh. Manasseh was the father of Amon; Amon, of Josiah. Josiah was the father of Jeconiah, or Shallum, also called Amasiah. This Jeconiah was the father of the Jeconiah who is known as Zedekiah and Jehoiakim.

8,1 And no reader need have any doubt about him. Instead, he should admire the precision of the information I have set down here for the benefit of the worthy persons who, from their desire for learning, would like to grasp the finer points of scripture. They cannot fail to be enthused directly on receiving the benefit. For they will have regained the exact words in the Gospel which certain ignorant persons have removed because of an ambiguity, as though to make an improvement.

8,2 For St. Matthew enumerated the generations (of Christ's genealogy) in three paragraphs,[8] and said that there were fourteen generations from Abraham till David, fourteen from David till the captivity, and fourteen from the captivity until Christ. The two first counts are accurate and do not fall short, for they cover the times previous to Jeconiah. (3) But the third, we find, no longer has the full count of fourteen generations as indicated by a succession of names; it has thirteen instead.[9] This is because certain persons found a Jeconiah next to another Jeconiah, and thought that the item had been duplicated. (4) It was not a duplication though, but a distinct item. The son had been named "Jeconiah the son of Jeconiah" for his father. By removing the one name as a correction, certain persons ignorantly made the promise to give all fourteen names fail of its purpose, and eliminated the frequency of the correspondence between them.

8,5 So the Babylonian captivity began then, from the time of Jeconiah. During this time of the captivity, the elders approached Nebuchadnezzar in Babylon and begged that some of his own subjects be sent to Israel as settlers, to keep the country from becoming an uninhabited woodland. (6) He accepted their appeal—he did not put them off—and sent four nations of his own people, known as the Cuthaeans, Cudaeans, Seppharuraeans and Anagogavaeans. Taking their idols they then migrated to Samaria and settled it, choosing this land because of its richness and extreme fertility.

8,7 But in time, when they were mauled by the wild beasts—lions, leopards, bears and the other predators—they sent to Babylon, asking with extreme astonishment what sort of life <the> former settlers had lived to be able to withstand the rapine and violence of the beasts. (8) The

---

[8] Matt. 1:1-17.
[9] Cf. Matt. 1:12-17.

king sent for the elders and asked how they had conducted themselves
<when> they held Judaea, and how they had escaped the rapine of the
beasts, since there were so many onslaughts and maimings by animals
in that country.

8,9   They told him about God's legislation and wisely let him know
the sensible conclusion. They said that no nation could settle there unless
it kept the Law of the God of heaven, given through Moses. For God is
the protector of the land, and will not have sins of idolatry and the rest
committed in it by gentile nations.

8,10   The king paid attention, listened to his informants' entirely true
explanation, and asked for a copy of the Law. They gave him one without demur, and with the Law also sent a priest named Ezra, a teacher
of the Law, from Babylon, to instruct the Assyrian settlers in Samaria—
the Cuthaeans and <the> others—in the Law of Moses. (11) This took
place in about the thirtieth year of the captivity of Israel and Jerusalem.

So Ezra and his successors taught the nation in Samaria; and those
who had received the Law through Ezra, who came from Babylon, were
called Samaritans. After another forty years the captivity was called off,
and Israel returned from Babylon.

9,1   It is an amazing coincidence that, to correspond with the four nations, four sects have also arisen in that very nation—I mean first, the
Essenes, second, the Gorothenes, third, the Sebuaeans, and fourth, the
Dositheans. Here I can begin my treatment of the subject of sects, and
shall briefly explain how this <came about>. (2) How else but <in the
same way that> tribes arose from the proliferation of the different
languages, various nations emerged to correspond with each tribe and
clan, every nation chose its own king, and the outbreak of wars, and con-
flicts between clashing nations, resulted. For each used force to get its
own way and, from the insatiable greed that we all have, to take its
neighbors' property. (3) So too at this time. Since there had been a
change in Israel's one religion, and the scripture of the Law <had been
brought> to other nations—I mean to Assyrians, the ancestors of the
colonist Samaritans—the division of Israel's opinion also resulted. (4)
And now error began, and discord began to sow many false opinions
from the one fear of God just as each individual thought best, and meant
to acquire proficiency in the letter (of scripture) and expound it to suit
himself.

9.

Against Samaritans, Sect seven from Hellenism, but nine of the series

1,1   "Samaritans" begins the series of heresies which were based on
sacred scripture after the Greek ones I have mentioned. Those were

<invented† by men of their† own stupid notion, without sacred scripture.

Thus the whole nation were called Samaritans. (2) "Samaritans" means "watchmen"—because of their stationing in the land as watchmen, or because they are keepers of Moses' commandment in the Law. (3) Also, the mountain where they settled was named Somoron—and Somer too for one of the ancients, Somoron the son of Somer was his name. (4) Somoron was a son of one of the Perizzites and Girgashites who lived in the country at that time. They were descendants of Canaan, who had seized this land, the one now called Judaea or Samaria. It belonged to the sons of Shem, not to them, since Canaan himself was the son of Ham, Shem's uncle (sic). (5) And thus they are called Samaritans for various reasons—Somer, Somoron, their guardianship of the land, and their keeping of the Law's precepts.

2,1   The first difference between them and Jews is that they were given no text of the prophets after Moses, but simply the Pentateuch—(which was given to Israel's descendants through Moses, at the close of their exodus from Egypt. By "Pentateuch" I mean Genesis, Exodus, Leviticus, Numbers and Deuteronomy; in Hebrew their names are B'reshith, Elleh sh'moth, Vayyiqra, Vayidabber and Elleh ha d'varim.) (2) There are intimations of the resurrection of the dead in these five books, but of course no obvious proclamation of it. There also hints of God's only-begotten Son, of the Holy Spirit, and of the attack on idols. But more clearly, the subject of <the> Unity is introduced in them, while the Trinity is proclaimed spiritually in the Unity.

2,3   Those who had received the Law were eager to abandon idolatry and learn to know the one God, but not interested in more precise information. Since they had gone wrong and not clearly understood the whole of the faith and the precise nature of our salvation, they knew nothing of the resurrection of the dead and do not believe in it. And they do not recognize the Holy Ghost, since they did not know about him.

2,4   And yet this sect, which denies resurrection but rejects idolatry, <is continually> idolatrous in itself with knowing it, because the idols of the four nations are hidden in the mountain[1] they quibblingly call Gerizim. (5) Whoever cares to make an accurate investigation of Mount Gerizim, should be told that the two mountains, Gerizim and Ebal, are near Jericho. They are across the Jordan east of Jericho, as Deuteronomy and the Book of Joshua the son of Nun say.[2] (6) They are unwitting idolaters then, because, wherever they are, they face the

---

[1] The Treasure Scroll, 3Q 15,61, makes Mt. Gerizim a repository of treasure.
[2] Cf. Deut. 11:29-30; Eus. Onom. 64.18-20 (Klostermann).

mountain for prayer; <they think>, if you please, that it is sacred! For scripture cannot be telling a lie when it says, "They continued even to this day keeping the Law and worshipping their idols,"[3] as we learn in the Fourth Book of Kings.

3,1   But they are altogether refuted on the subject of resurrection. First because of Abel, since his blood conversed with the Lord after death. But blood is not soul; the soul is in the blood. And God did not say, "The soul crieth unto me," but, "The blood crieth unto me,"[4] proving that there is hope for a resurrection of bodies.

3,2   Moreover Enoch was taken away so as not to see death, and was nowhere to be found. Moreover, Sarah was brought to life again for impregnation, after her womb was dead and her menstrual flow had dried up; and she bore a child by promise in her old age, because of the hope of the resurrection.

3,3   And this is not all. Moreover, when Jacob saw to (the disposal of) his own bones, he gave directions about them as though they were imperishable. And not only he, but in giving his orders on the same analogy, Joseph too hinted at the form of the resurrection. (4) And this is not all. Moreover Aaron's rod, which budded when dry, bore fruit again in hope of life, indicating that our dead bodies will arise, and referring to resurrection. And Moses' wooden rod was a similar indication of resurrection, since it was brought to life by God's will and became a serpent.

3,5   And moreover, when Moses blessed Reuben he said, "Let Reuben live, and let him not die,"[5] though he <meant> a person who had been long dead. This was to show that there is life after death, but a sentence of second death, for damnation. So he gave him two blessings, and said "Let him live," at the resurrection, and "Let him not die," at the judgment—not meaning death by departure from the body, but death by damnation.

3,6   These few points will suffice against the Samaritans. But they have some other customs too, which are entirely stupid. They wash with urine on returning from a foreign land, <as though> they had been contaminated, if you please! Whenever they touch someone else, who is a gentile, they immerse themselves in water with their clothes on.[6] For they think it is pollution to take hold of one person, or touch another,[7] if he is of another persuasion. But they have a bad case of insanity.

---

[3] Cf. 4 Kings 17:32-34.
[4] Gen. 4:10.
[5] Deut. 33:6.
[6] Cf. Hippol. Haer. IX.15.3-6.
[7] Cf. the Essene attitude toward outsiders, as shown, e.g., at 1Q S 5,11-20; CD 12,6-11; 13,14-15.

4,1 But pay attention, Mister, and you will know how their foolishness can be refuted in a minute. They abhor a dead body at sight, though they are dead in their works themselves. Not one but many witnesses testify that a corpse is not unclean, but that the Law was speaking in riddles. (2) For no "two or three witnesses," but 620,000, bear me out in this, the ones which were numbered in the wilderness, <and buried the people that lusted in the wilderness.> And as many others and more, and many more still—the ones which followed Joseph's burial urn. It was carried with them for forty years, during the entire period of the sojourn, and it was not considered unclean or a source of pollution.

4,3 However, the Law truthfully said, "He that toucheth the corpse remaineth unclean until even, and shall wash himself with water and be purified."[8] But† it said this to hint at the dying of our Lord Jesus Christ during his suffering in the flesh. (4) This is shown by "the," the so-called "definite article." Wherever the article appears, it is the confirmation of some one thing which is specified and is very easy to recognize, because of the article. But without the article we must understand the word indeterminately, of anything. (5) If we say "king," for example, we have indicated a noun, but not shown clearly which king is specified; we speak both of a "king" of Persians, and a "king" of Medes and Elamites. But if we add the article and say "the king," what we mean is beyond doubt. The king in question, someone called king, someone known to be king, or the ruler of this or that kingdom is implied by the article.

4,6 And if we say "god" without the article, we have spoken either of any heathen god, or of the actual God. But if we say "the God," it is clear that because of the article we mean the actual God, who is the true God and is known to be. And so with "man" and "the man."

4,7 And if the Law said, "If ye touch a corpse," the sentence would be pronounced on everyone, and the word in question would apply generally <to> any dead body. But since it says, "If one touch *the* corpse," it is referring to one particular corpse—I mean the Lord, as I indicated above. (8) So the Law said this as a riddle, of those who would lay hands on Christ and crucify him; these had a need for purification till their sun should set, and another light dawn on them through the baptism of water, the "laver of regeneration."[9] (9) Peter bears me out here in speaking to the Israelites at Jerusalem who asked him, "Men and brethren, what shall we do?"[10] For he had said "this Jesus whom ye have crucified,"[11] to them. And when they were pricked to the heart he said,

---

8 Cf. Lev. 11:24-25.
9 Titus 3:5.
10 Acts 2:37.
11 Acts 2:36.

"Repent, men and brethren, and let every one of you be baptized in the name of our Lord Jesus Christ, and your sins will be forgiven, and ye shall receive the gift of the Holy Ghost."[12]

4,10 So the law is not speaking of a corpse—or, though the Law speaks of a corpse, it is a specific one. <Regarding an unspecified corpse> its decree is different, for it says, "If a corpse pass by, shut your doors and windows, lest the house be defiled." This is as though it were saying, with reference to hearing of sin, "If you hear a sound of sin, or (see) a sight of transgression, shut your eye to lust, your mouth to evil-speaking, and your ear to wicked rumor, lest the whole house—meaning soul and body—be killed." (11) This is why the prophet says, "Death is come up through the windows,"[13] and surely does not mean actual windows—otherwise we could shut our windows and never die. But the bodily senses—sight, hearing and so on—are windows to us, and death enters us through them if we sin with them.

4,12 So Joseph buried Israel and was not rendered unclean, even though he fell on his face and kissed him after he was dead. And scripture does not say that he washed for purification. (13) The tradition I have been taught says that the angels buried the body of the holy man, Moses,[14] and they did not wash; and neither were the angels profaned by the saint's body. (5,1) And again, I am afraid of prolonging the solution of the problem. But one argument, or a second, will give a wise man skill in the Lord against the opposition.

5,2 And even though I shall have to speak with brevity of the Spirit, I do not mind doing it. For example, the Lord expressly says to Moses, "Bring up unto me seventy elders into the mount, and I shall take of the Spirit that is upon thee, and will pour it out upon them, and they shall give thee assistance."[15]

5,3 And to let us know about the Son, <the> Father says, "Let us make man in our image and after our likeness."[16] "Let us make," does not mean one person (alone), and neither does, "The Lord rained upon Sodom and Gomorrah fire and brimstone from the Lord out of heaven."[17]

5,4 And <there is no point in arguing with Samaritans> about prophets. They were given <only> the Pentateuch at first and no further scriptures, <and> they were satisfied with just the Pentateuch and

---

[12] Acts 2:38.
[13] Jerem. 9:20.
[14] Cf. Aug. Ep. 158.6 (= Evodius to Augustine).
[15] Num. 11:16-17.
[16] Gen. 1:26.
[17] Gen. 19:24.

not the rest. Today, of course, even if someone speaks of the others to
them—I mean David, Isaiah and the prophets after them—Samaritans
do not receive them. They are hindered from that by the tradition they
have carried down from their own ancestors.

5,5   And let this conclude my sketch of the Samaritans. I have
deliberately given it in brief, because of the danger I foresee of making
the subject of the treatise too inclusive.

10.

Against Essenes, Sect one after Samaritans,[1] but ten of the series

1,1   The Samaritans were divided into four sects. These agreed
<on> circumcision, the Sabbath, and the <other matters> in the
Law. But each of the three differed from its fellows—unimportantly, with
the sole exception of the Dositheans, and to a limited extent.

1,2   The Essenes continued the conduct they had started with and
never went beyond it.[2] After them, Gorothenes disagreed over a certain
small point. For a dispute has arisen among them, I mean among
Sebuaeans, Essenes and Gorothenes. (3) The nature of the dispute is this.
The Law directed the Jews to gather at Jerusalem from all quarters—
often, <and> at three times of year, Unleavened Bread, Pentecost and
Tabernacles. (4) Jews lived here and there both in Judaea and Samaria,
and therefore used to travel across Samaria to Jerusalem. (5) Since (Jews
and Samaritans) would meet at one season, (each) with their gathering
for the festival, this caused fighting. Besides when Ezra was building
Jerusalem after the return from Babylon, and the Samaritans asked if
they could contribute aid to the Jews and take part in the building, and
were refused by Ezra himself, and Nehemiah,

11.

Against Sebuaeans, Sect two from Samaritans, but eleven of the series

1,1   then in anger and rage the Sebuaeans changed the dates of the
feasts. Primarily this was because of their anger with Ezra, but in the second place it was for the reason I mentioned, which incited them to battle
because of the people who went across their land. (2) They put the new
moon of the Feast of Unleavened Bread after the new year, which falls

---

[1] The surprising tradition which locates the Essenes in Samaria might find some
justification from Josephus' remark that they were widely dispersed, Jos. Bel. II.8.4.
[2] Essene strictness as to the dates of their feasts is witnessed at 1Q S 1,14-15; 1Q H
4,11-12; 1Q D 1,8; 4Q pHos 2,15-17.

in the autumn—that is, after the month of Tishri, which is called August
by the Romans but Mesori by the Egyptians, Gorpiaeus by the Macedonians, and Apellaeus by the Greeks. (3) They begin the year at that point
and celebrate the Days of Unleavened Bread immediately, but they
celebrate Pentecost in the autumn, and observe their Feast of Tabernacles at the time of the Jewish Days of Unleavened Bread and Passover.

12.

Against Gorothenes,[3] *Sect three from Samaritans, but twelve of the series*

1,1 But the Gorothenes and the others did not listen to the
Sebuaeans. When Essenes are in the neighborhood of the others they do
the same as they;[4] only Gorothenes and Dositheans have the contention
with Sebuaeans. (2) And they, I mean Gorothenes and Dositheans, keep
the Feasts of Unleavened Bread, Passover, Pentecost and Tabernacles,
and their one fast-day, when the Jews observe them. The others, though,
(i.e., the Sebuaeans) do not keep them then but in the months I mentioned, following their own custom.

13.

Against Dositheans,[5] *Sect four from Samaritans, but thirteen of the series*

1,1 Dositheans differ from these (others) in many ways. They
acknowledge resurrection and have ascetic disciplines. They abstain from
meat; moreover, some abstain from matrimony† after having been married, while others are even virgins. (2) Likewise they have the customs
of circumcision, the Sabbath, and not touching one person or another out
of loathing for all humanity. It is said that they keep fasts and have a
rigorous discipline.

1,3 Dositheus' reason for holding these views was as follows. He was
a mixture, because he turned from the Jews to the Samaritan peoples.
He was a leading student of the Law and the Jewish repetitions of it,[6] and
ambitious for the highest rank. But as he failed to achieve it and was not
considered worthy of any special respect among the Jews, he defected to
the Samaritans and founded this sect.

---

[3] Gorothenes are mentioned at Eus. H. E. IV.22.5.
[4] This is most improbable; cf. Note 2 above.
[5] Dositheans are mentioned or discussed at Eus. H. E. IV.22.5; Ps.-Tert. 1.1; Jer.
Vit. Paul. 13; Clem. Hom. II.24; Recog. I.54; Const. Ap.VI.8.1.
[6] Origen ascribes a rigorist position to Dositheus at De Princ. IV.3.2.

1,4   From an excess of self-chosen wisdom he retired to some cave. We are told that he persisted in futile, hypocritical fasting, and so died[7] from lack of bread and water—willingly, if you please! After a while people came to visit him, and found his body reeking with decay and breeding worms, and a cloud of flies swarming on it. By ending his own life with such futility he became the cause of their sect, and his imitators are named Dositheans, or Dosithenes, after him.

2,1   And as far as I have learned, these are the differences between these four sects; they will be refuted by what I have said about them. (2) But I shall return to the successive infiltrations (into our ranks), connect the prey of imposture with each other, and give the argument against them—by the exposure of their vile practices, and a brief refutation of the vicious, deadly serpents' emission of poison.

This concludes the four Samaritan sects. Judaism remains to be dealt with. Judaism was divided into seven sects:[1]

14.

Against Sadducees, Sect one from Judaism, but fourteen of the series

1,1   Again, after these Samaritan sects and <the> Greek ones I mentioned earlier, seven in all arose in Judaea and Jerusalem among the Jews, before Christ's incarnation.

2,1   First are the Sadducees, who branched off from Dositheus.[2] These give themselves the name of "Sadducees," and the title is derived from "righteousness," if you please; "zedek" means "righteousness." (But anciently there was also a priest named Zadok.)[3]

2,2   However, these did not abide by their master's teaching. They rejected the resurrection of the dead[4] and held an opinion like the Samaritans'. But they do not admit the existence of angels, though Samaritans do not deny this. And they do not know the Holy Ghost,[5] for they are not deemed worthy of him. All their observances are just like

---

[7] In contrast, Origen notes that the Samaritans believed Dositheus had not died, Orig. In Joh. XIII.27.

[1] Gnostic sources accuse the Jews of spawning sects at Tri. Trac. 112, 18-22; GR 25,20-21; 26,3-4; 43,26-27; 215,11-12; Book of John 193,4-5.

[2] The Sadducees are traced to Dositheus at Clem. Recog. I.54.4; Ps.-Tert. 1.1. Hippol. Haer. IX.29 links them with Samaria. Christian sources refer to them as a "sect" at Eus. H. E. IV.22.7; Justin Dial. 80; Const. Ap. VI.6.2.

[3] Cf. Ezek. 40:46; 43:19; 44:15; 48:11; Matt. 1:14. For "sons of Zadok" see 1Q S 5,1;8; 1Q S 2,22; CD 4,3-4; 5,4.

[4] Cf. Matt. 22:23.

[5] Cf. Acts 23:8.

the Samaritans'. (3) But they were Jews, not Samaritans; for they offered sacrifice in Jerusalem, and cooperated with Jews in everything else.

3,1   But they too will be silenced by the Lord's faithful saying, which they brought on themselves through his solution to their problem when they came to him and said, "Can there be resurrection?

"There were seven brothers,[6] and the first took a wife and died childless. And the second took her—Moses commands a man to perform the levirate for his brother's wife if he has died childless, and marry her for his brother's sake, to beget offspring in the name of the deceased. So the first took her, and the second," they said, "and died, and so with all seven. But at the resurrection of the dead whose wife will she be, since all seven knew her?"

3,2   But the Lord replied, "Ye do err, not knowing the scriptures nor the power of God. In the resurrection of the dead they neither marry nor are given in marriage, but are equal unto the angels. But that the dead will be raised Moses will teach you, as God declared to him and said, 'I am the God of Abraham, and the God of Isaac, and the God of Jacob.' And he is a God of the living, not of the dead." And he "put them to silence."[7] For they are easily cured and cannot hold out even briefly against the truth.

15.

Against Scribes, <Sect> two from Judaism, but fifteen of the series

1,1   After these Sadducees came Scribes—during their time or even at exactly the same time. Scribes were men who repeated the Law by teaching it as a kind of grammar. They followed the other Jewish customs but introduced a kind of extra, quibbling instruction, if you please. (2) They did not live merely by the Law; in addition, they observed "washing of pots, cups, platters"[1] and other vessels for table service as though, if you please, they were served for purity and holiness' sake! They "washed their hands diligently,"[2] and also diligently cleansed themselves of certain types of pollution in natural water and baths.

1,3   And they had certain "fringes" indicative of their way of life, to vaunt their boast and win the praise of the onlookers. And at home they would put "phylacteries"—that is, broad borders of purple cloth—on their clothes.

---

[6] Cf. Mark 12:18-27 parr.
[7] Matt. 22:34.

[1] Mark 7:4.
[2] Mark 7:3. It seems best to keep the traditional translation of πυγμῇ, since Epiphanius gives no clue as to what he means by the word.

1,4   One would think—for this is in the Gospel too—that it is speaking of amulets, since some people used to call their amulets "phylacteries." (5) But the saying has nothing to do with this. People like the Scribes would wear dresses or shawls, and robes or tunics[3] made of broad strips of cloth, and made "purple woven"[4] with purple fabric; and precise speakers used to give the purple strips the new name of "phylacteries." Thus the Lord has called them "phylacteries" as they did. (6) But the sequel, "and the craspeda of their outer garments," also explains the idiom of their language; <it says> "the craspeda" for fringes, and "the phylacteries" for the purple strips. <For it says,> "Ye make broad the phylacteries, and enlarge the craspeda of your outer garments."[5]

1,7   But during his time of continence or celibacy, each Scribe had certain tassels at the four corners of his cloak, tied to the warp itself. For each Scribe would assign and designate a time for chastity or continence,[6] and they had these tassels principally to give public notice of their undertaking, so that no one would lay a hand on the pretendedly sanctified.

2,1   Scribes had four repetitions of the Law. One <was in circulation> in the name of the prophet Moses, a second in that of their teacher who is either named Aqiba or Bar Aqiba, another in the name Addan or Annan, also called Judas, and another in the name of the sons of Hasmonaeus. (2) Whatever customs they derive from these four repetitions on the notion of their being wisdom—they are mostly folly— are boasted of and praised, and celebrated and talked about as the foremost teaching.

                                    16.

Against Pharisees,[1] <*Sect*> *three from Judaism, but sixteen of the series*

1,1   Another sect, the Pharisees, is next after these two. They had the same ideas—I mean as the Scribes whose name means "teachers of the Law," for the Lawyers were also associated with them. (2) But again, the Pharisees also thought differently, since their disciplines were more am-

---

[3] Cf. Ep. Aristeas 158; Justin Dial. 46.

[4] This is a folk etymology. Epiphanius derives φυλακτήριον from ἀλουργοῦφείς, "purple woven," by rearrangement.

[5] Matt. 23:5.

[6] Is this a vague reminiscence of the Essene novitiate? Cf. Jos. Bel. II.119, Hippol. Haer. IX.23.2.

---

[1] Pharisees are discussed as a "sect" at Eus. H. E. IV.22.7; Hippol. Haer. IX.28; Ps.-Tert. 1.1; Clem. Recog. I.54.6; Const. Ap. VI.6.3; Justin Dial. 80.

bitious. When some Pharisees practiced asceticism and marked off a ten-, eight-, or four-year period of chastity or continence like the Scribes, they, oftener than the Scribes, instituted the following trial of strength accompanied by constant prayer—to avoid having an accident or wet dream, if you please! (3) To live as much as possible without sleep, they would make their beds on benches only a span wide and stretch out on these at evening, so that, if they went to sleep and fell to the floor, they could get up again for prayer. (4) Others would gather pebbles and scatter them under their bedclothes, so that they would be pricked and not fall fast asleep, but be forced to keep themselves awake. Others, for the same reason, even had thorns for a mattress.

1,5[2]　　They fasted twice a week, on the second and fifth days. They paid tithes, gave the firstfruits—those of the thirtieth and those of the fiftieth days—and rendered the sacrifices and prayers without fail.

1,6　　They had the style of dress I spoke of before the Scribes, with the shawl, the other fashions, and women's cloaks, and they anticipated the Scribes in their wide boots, and the wide tongues on their sandals. (7) But they were called "Pharisees" because they were separated from the others by the extra voluntary ritual they believed in;[3] "pharesh" is Hebrew for "separation."

2,1　　They acknowledged resurrection of the dead and believed in angels and a Spirit,[4] but like the others knew nothing of the Son of God. (2) Moreover fate and astrology[5] meant much to them. To begin with, they replaced the Greek names from the astrology in which the misguided believe with other names in Hebrew.[6] (3) For example, Helius is renamed Chammah and Shemesh.[7] Selene is Jareach, or Ha'l'banah, and hence is called Mene—the "month" is called "jareach," but the moon is called "mene," as it also is in Greek because of the month.

Ares is Kokhabh Okbol; Hermes is Kokhabh Chochmah; Zeus, Kokhabh Ba'al; Aphrodite, Zerva or Lilith.[8] Cronus is Kokhabh Shabb'tai. (They have other terms for him too, but I cannot give the names of these things exactly.)

---

[2] Cf. Luke 18:12; Matt. 23:23 par. For the "second" and "fifth" days see Did. 8.1; Const. Ap. VII.23.1.

[3] Cf. Ps.-Tert. 1.1; Clem. Hom. XI.28.4; Orig. In Matt. 23:23.

[4] Cf. Acts 23:8.

[5] Cf. Jos. Bel. II.8.14; Ant. XIII.5.9; Hippol. Haer. IX.28.5; Const. Ap. VI.6.3. There are occasional references to "fate" (i.e., גורל) in the Qumran literature; see S 6.18; 21; 9.7; CD B 13,4.

[6] The list which follows gives the Hebrew names for the planets, but uses Epiphanius' transliteration only where the underlying Hebrew is not clear. There are similar lists at GR 28,25-20; 176,15-17 et al; PS 356 et al; Keph. 168,1-16.

[7] Shamish is mentioned at Keph. 168,2.

[8] Libath, Dlibath and Estra are mentioned at GR 28,26-27; 46,31-32 et al.

2,4   Moreover, here again are their Hebrew names for what the
misguided futilely regard as planets, though <the Greeks, who>
wrongfully misled the world into impiety, call them the signs of the
zodiac:[9] Tela', Sor, T'omin, Zar'tan, Ari, Bethulah, Moznaim,
'Akrabh, Qesheth, G'di, Dalli, Daggim. (5) Following the Greeks to no
purpose, they, I mean the Pharisees, translated the same terms into
Hebrew as follows. Aries is what they call Tela'; Taurus is Sor; Gemini,
T'omim; Cancer, Zar'tan; Leo, Ari; Virgo, Bethulah; Libra, Moznaim;
Scorpio, Akrabh; Sagittarius, Qesheth; Capricorn, G'di; Aquarius,
Dalli; Pisces, Daggim.

3,1   I have not made this list to confuse the reader, or endorse the
vulgar chatter of those who introduced the untenable, insane nonsense
of astrology to the world. The truth convicts this of untenability and error. (2) In other treatises I have said a great deal in refutation of those
who believe in fortune and fate; furthermore, I have written briefly
against them in the preface to this work. But lest it be thought that I make
vexatious attacks on anyone, rather than finding the exact truth from
traditional accounts and giving it, I have even given names in saying
these things.

3,3   But the Pharisees are in the worst possible quandary, and un-
commonly silly, since they both acknowledge resurrection and declare
judgment just. (4) How can there be (both) judgment and fate? It must
be one way or the other. Either there is such a thing as fate, and then
there is no judgment, since the (human) agent does not act for himself,
but acts under the sway of the rule of fate. (5) Or else there is a judgment
which really threatens, laws do decide our case, and evildoers do stand
trial—with law acknowledged to be just, and God's judgment absolutely
trustworthy. Then fate means nothing, and there is no proof whatever
of its existence.

4,1   The determination that one person must be brought to book for
his offenses while another is commended for his good behavior, is made
because of their ability to sin or not, in keeping with the difference
betwen them. (2) This is † proved concisely with one saying, <the>
truth uttered by the prophet Isaiah in the person of the Lord, "If ye be
willing and hearken to me, ye shall eat the good of the land; but if ye are
not willing and do not hearken to me, a sword shall devour you. (3) For
the mouth of the Lord hath spoken it."[10] Thus it is clear and obvious to
everyone, and no one can doubt, that the God <who> said, "If ye be

---

[9] For the zodiac as a synagogue floor decoration, with the signs often labelled in
Hebrew, see Goodenough, *Jewish Symbols in the Graeco-Roman Period*, vols. 1;9.
[10] Isa. 1:19-20.

willing and if ye are not willing," in his own person, has provided us with free agency—so that whether he does right or aims at evil is up to the man.

4,4   Thus the notion of those who believe in fate is mistaken, the Pharisees' especially. What the Savior told them not once but often, must be said of them even many times oftener: "Woe unto you, Scribes and Pharisees, hypocrites! For ye have abandoned the weightier matters of the Law, judgment and mercy, and pay tithes of dill and mint and rue.[11] And ye make clean the outside of the cup and of the trencher, but their interior is full of uncleanness and excess.[12]

4,5   "And ye sanction swearing by that which is upon the altar, but with you the oath sworn by the altar itself is void. And ye say that to swear by heaven is nothing, but if one swear by that which is above heaven, this is demanded of him. Doth not the altar bear that which lieth upon it, and is not heaven the throne of him that sitteth upon it?[13]

4,6   "Ye say, if a man shall say to his father and mother, It is Corban, that is to say, a gift, by which thou mightest be profited by me, he shall no longer honor his father, and ye have made the commandment of God of none effect through the tradition of your elders.[14] (7) And ye compass sea and land to make one proselyte, and when he is made ye make him twofold more the child of hell than yourselves."[15]

4,8   What more could one cite against them than the sacred sayings? Indeed, I would rather rest content with the wise, true words of the Savior, which the Pharisees cannot face for even an instant.

17.

Against Hemerobaptists,[1] Sect four from Judaism, but seventeen of the series

1,1   A sect of Hemerobaptists, as they are called, accompanies these. It is no different from the others, but has the same ideas as the Scribes and Pharisees. It is unlike the Sadducees, however, in their denial of resurrection, though like them in the unbelief which is found in the others.

1,2   But this sect had this added characteristic, that they were always baptized every day in spring, fall, winter, and summer, and thus came

---

[11] Matt. 23:23.
[12] Cf. Matt. 23:25.
[13] Cf. Matt. 23:18-22.
[14] Mark 7:11;9.
[15] Matt. 23:15.

[1] Hemerobaptists are mentioned at Eus. H. E. IV.22.7; Const. Ap. VI.5; Justin Dial. 80. Clem. Hom. II.23.1 uses the term of John the Baptist. The resemblance to the Essenes is obvious. Ἡμεροβαπτισταί translates the Hebrew term טובלי יוק.

to be called Hemerobaptists. (3) For this sect made the claim that there is no life for a man unless he is baptized daily with water, and washed and purified from every fault.[2]

2,1   But this sect too I can refute with one argument, since the words are expressions of unbelief on their part rather than faith. If they are baptized every day their conscience convicts them, since their hope of yesterday is dead, their faith and purification. (2) For if they were satisfied with one baptism they would have confidence in this, as though it would live and be immortal forever. But they must think it has been nullified since they bathed today, not to cleanse the body or for dirt, but because of sins. Again, by taking another bath the next day, they have served notice that yesterday's baptism is dead. For unless yesterday's had died they would not need another the next day for the purification of sins.

2,3   And if they do not avoid sin altogether, and expect the water to cleanse them when they keep sinning every day, there is nothing to their opinion, and what they do is undone and out of date. (4) Not Ocean, not all the rivers and seas, the perennial streams and brooks, and all the water in the world together, can wash away sin—this is not reasonable and is not God's ordinance. Repentance cleanses, and the one baptism, through the name in the mysteries.

2,5   But I shall pass this sect by also. I feel I have said enough to indicate the quick-acting remedy for their lunacy, as it has been set down here for the reader's benefit.

18.

Against Nasaraeans,[1] Sect five from Judaism but eighteen of the series

1,1   I shall next undertake to describe the sect after the Hemerobaptists, called the Nasaraeans. They were Jews by nationality—originally from Gileaditis, Bashanitis and the Transjordan I am told, but descended from Israel himself. They practiced Judaism in all respects, and scarcely had any beliefs beyond those of the Jewish sects I have mentioned. (2) They too had acquired circumcision, and they kept the same Sabbath and were attached to the same feasts, but they did not introduce fate or astrology.

---

[2] Purification and sanctification by water are mentioned at 1Q S 3,4-5:8-9; 4,21; 5,13-14.

[1] This group may possibly represent the Mandaeans, whose usual name for themselves is "Nazoraeans," and whose origin is thought to be Semitic. However, Mandaeans do not practice Judaism.

1,3   They too recognized the fathers in the Pentateuch from Adam to Moses, who had been conspicuous for excellence of piety. I mean Adam, Seth, Enoch, Methuselah, Noah, Abraham, Isaac, Jacob, Levi and Aaron, Moses and Joshua the son of Nun. But they would not accept the Pentateuch itself. They acknowledged Moses and believed that he had received legislation—not this legislation, however, but some other.[2] (4) And so, though they were Jews who kept all the Jewish observances, they would not offer sacrifice or eat meat.[3] They considered it unlawful to eat meat or make sacrifices with it. They claimed that these books are fictions,[4] and that none of these customs were instituted by the fathers. (5) This was the difference between the Nasaraeans and the others; and their refutation is to be seen in many places, not just one.

2,1   First, <in> their acknowledgement of the fathers and patriarchs, and Moses. Since no other writing speaks of them, how do they know the fathers' names and excellence if not from the Pentateuchal writings themselves? (2) And how can there be truth and falsehood in the same place with scripture telling the truth in part but lying in part, (3) when the Savior says, "Either make the tree good and his fruits good; or else make the tree corrupt and his fruits corrupt. For a good tree cannot bring forth evil fruit, neither can a corrupt tree bring forth good fruit?"[5]

2,4   Hence their notion and advice are worthless, and there are many grounds for its refutation. Not only, for example, are the events recorded in scripture famous to this day, but even the sites of the wonders are preserved. (5) First there is the spot where Abraham offered the ram to God, Mount Zion as it is called still. Moreover, the site of the oak of Mamre, where the calf was served to the angels. But if Abraham served a meat-dish to angels, he would not have failed to eat it himself.

3,1   Moreover, the tradition of the lamb <which> was slaughtered in Egypt is still famous among the Egyptians, even the idolatrous ones. (2) At the time when the Passover was kept there—this is the beginning of spring, at the first equinox—all Egyptians take red earth, though without knowing why, and smear their lambs with it. And they also smear the trees, the fig-trees and the rest, and spread the report that fire once

---

[2] Jews are said to falsify the Law and the works of Abraham at GR 43,21-23. 1Q CD A 5,11-12 says this of persons unspecified.

[3] Mandaeans are not vegetarians. Animal sacrifice is deprecated at 1Q S. 59,4-5; CD A 6,11-14, and in Gnostic sources at Gos. Phil. 54,34-55,1 and perhaps 62,35-63,4; Melch. 6,28-7,1. Manichaean elect are said to be vegetarians at Keph. 129,11-13; Man. Ps. 33,20-21. See also Ascl. 41.

[4] The Pentateuch is called a forgery at the Book of John 81,7; 19-21; 124,6-7; 192,15-193,2.

[5] Matt. 12:33 and 7:18.

burned up the world on this day. But the fiery-red appearance of the blood is a protection against a calamity of that magnitude and character.

3,3   But where can I not find proof of the series (of miracles)? For example, even today the remains of Noah's ark are still pointed out in Cardyaei.[6] (4) And if one were to make a search and discover them—this stands to reason—he would surely also find the ruins of the altar at the foot of the mountain. That was where Noah stayed after leaving the ark; and when he had offered some of the clean beasts, and their fat, to the Lord God, he was told, "Behold, I have given thee all things even as herbs of the field. Slay and eat!"[7]

3,5   But again, I shall also pass the alienness and foolishness of this sect by. I am content with the few things I have said, and inserted here with my limited ability, against the error of this sect.

19.

Against Ossaeans, Sect six from Judaism, but nineteen of the series

1,1   After this sect in turn, comes another closely connected with them, called the Ossaeans. These are Jews like the former, hypocritical and ingeniously inventive. (2) I have been told that they originally came from Nabataea, Ituraea, Moabitis and Arielis, the lands beyond the basin of what sacred scripture called the "Salt Sea"; this is the one known as the "Dead Sea." (3) And from the translation of the name, this "People of the Ossaeans" means "sturdy people."

· 1,4   The man called Elxai[1] joined them later, in the reign of the emperor Trajan, after the Savior's incarnation; Elxai was a false prophet. He wrote a book[2] by prophecy, if you please, or as though by inspired wisdom. But they say that another person, Iexaeus, was Elxai's brother. (5) Elxai was personally misguided and a deliberate fraud. Originally he was a Jew with Jewish beliefs, but he did not live by the Law. He introduced substitutes, and formed his own sect (6) by designating salt, water, earth, bread, heaven, aether, and wind as objects for them to swear by in worship. But again, he designated seven other witnesses at some time or other—I mean the sky, water, "holy spirits" <as> he says, the

---

[6] Hippol. Haer. X.30.7; Eus. Onom. 2,21-23; Theoph. Ad Autol. III.19.16-17.
[7] Gen. 9:3 and Acts 10:13.

[1] Cf. Hippol. Haer. IX.13.2-4.
[2] This book is mentioned at Hippol. Haer. IX.13.1; Eus. H. E. VI.38. Epiphanius appears to have read it.

angels of prayer, the olive, salt, and the earth.[3] (7) He has no use for celibacy, detests continence and insists on matrimony.[4]

As though <by> revelation, if you please, he introduced some further figments of his imagination. (8) But the taught hypocrisy, by saying that even though <one> should happen to worship idols at a time when persecution threatens, it is not a sin[5]—just so long as he does not worship them in his conscience and, whatever confession he may make with his mouth, he does not make it in his heart.

1,9   In addition, the fraud ventured to produce a witness. He said that a Phineas, a priest of the stock of Levi, Aaron, and the ancient Phineas, escaped death in Babylon during the captivity by bowing down to the image of Artemis at Susa in the reign of King Darius. It thus follows that everything he says is false, and of no value.

2,1   <As has been said> earlier, Elxai was connected with the sect I have mentioned, called the Ossaean. Even today there are still remnants of it in Nabataea, which is also called Peraea near Moabitis; this people is now known as the Sampsaean. They appear to call Elxai a power revealed, if you please, since "el" means "power," but "xai" is "hidden." (2) But the whole custom was exposed as insolence, and badly discredited with those who could perceive the truth and be sure of it, in our own time. (<The sect was> still <in existence> even in our day, during the reigns of Constantius and the present emperors.) (3) For until Constantius' time a Marthus and a Marthana, two sisters descended from Elxai himself, were worshipped as goddesses in the Ossaean territory—because they were Elxai's descendants, if you please! Yet Marthus has recently died, (though Marthana is still alive)! (4) The misguided sectarians in that country would take even the sisters' spittle away with them, and the other dirt from their bodies, as a protection against diseases, if you please! They did not work. But whatever has gone astray is always proud and ready to be fooled—evil is a blind thing, and error a stupid one.

3,1   And how much time shall I spend in uttering all the lies this charlatan has told against the truth—(2) first, by teaching the denial of God and hypocrisy, with his claim that one can partake of the abominable sacrifices of idolatry, deceive the listeners, and deny his own faith with his lips without sinning? It follows that their condition is incurable and cannot be corrected. (3) For if the mouth that confesses the truth is prepared to lie, who can trust them not to have deceived hearts?

---

[3] Cf. Hippol. Haer. IX.15.2;5.
[4] Cf. the Mandaean polemic against celibacy, e.g., at GR 50,3-6; 53,2-5; 61,16-67,18; Book of John 60,18-61,9.
[5] Mandaeans permit dissimulation when persecuted by Christians, GR 29,24-26.

The divine oracle expressly declares, and teaches in the Holy Spirit, "With the heart man believeth unto righteousness, and with the mouth confession is made unto salvation?"[6]

3,4   Again, moreover, he confesses Christ by name, if you please, and says "Christ is the great king."[7] But from the deceitful, false composition of the book of his foolishness, I am not quite sure whether he gave this description of our Lord Jesus Christ. For he does not specify this either. He simply says "Christ," as though—from what I can gather—he means someone else, or expects someone else.

3,5   For he forbids prayer facing east. He claims that it is not right to face in that direction, but that Jerusalem must be faced from all quarters. Some must face Jerusalem from east to west, some from west to east, some from north to south and south to north, so that Jerusalem is faced from wherever one is. (6) And mark the fraud's insanity! He bans burnt offerings and sacrifices, as something foreign to God and never offered to him on the authority of the fathers and Law, and yet he says we must pray towards Jerusalem, precisely where the altar and sacrifices were—though < he > rejects the Jewish custom of eating meat and the rest, and the altar, and fire as being foreign to God! (7) In the following words he makes the claim that water is fortunate while fire is inimical: "Children, go not unto the sight of fire, since ye are deceived; for such is deceit. Thou seest it as very nigh, and yet it is far away. Go not unto the sight of it, but go rather unto the sound of water."[8] And his mythological descriptions are numerous.

4,1   Then he describes Christ as a kind of power, and even gives his dimensions—about ninety-six miles, twenty-four schoena tall, and twenty-four miles, six schoena wide, and similar prodigies about his thickness and feet, and the other mythological descriptions. (2) And the Holy Ghost—a feminine one at that—is like Christ too, and stands like an image, under a cloud and in between two mountains.[9] And the rest I shall skip, so as not to leave an impression of mythology in the reader's ears.

4,3   Later in the book he deceives with certain words and empty phrases by saying, "Let none seek the interpretation. Let him say these things only in prayer." These too he has taken from the Hebrew, if you please—as I understand in part—though Elxai's imaginings are not worth anything. He claims to say, "Abhar anid moibh nochile daasim

---

[6] Rom. 10:10.

[7] Cf. Hippol. Haer. IX.15.1.

[8] Fire is contrasted unfavorably with water at GR 29,30-34; 200,10-28 et al; Mandaean Prayer Book 21; 70.

[9] Cf. Hippol. Haer. IX.13.2-3.

ane daasim nochile moibh anid abhar selam." In translation this can be understood as follows: (4) "Let the humiliation <which> is from my fathers pass, (the humiliation) of their condemnation, degradation and toil, by degradation in condemnation through my fathers. (Let it pass) from bygone humiliation by an apostleship of perfection."[10] (5) But all this is fulfilled in Elxai; his power and imposture have come to nothing.

But if anyone cares to hear one word painfully rendered by one word, I do not mind doing even this. In just the right manner for those who want a pedantic version, I shall give his very words, and their translations opposite, thus: (6) "Abhar": "Let it pass away. "Anid": "humiliation." "Moibh": "which is from my fathers." "Nochile": "of their condemnation." "Daasim": "and of their degradation." "Ane": "and of their toil." "Daasim": "by degradation." "Nochile": "in condemnation." "Moibh": "through my fathers." "Anid": "from humiliation." "Abhar": "bygone." "Selam": "in apostleship of perfection."

5,1 This, then, is the Ossene sect, which lives the Jewish life in Sabbath observance, circumcision, and the keeping of the whole Law. Though it is different from the other six of these seven sects, it causes schism only by forbidding the books <of Moses> like the Nasaraeans.

5,2 <One text> will be enough to expose its foreignness to God, since the Lord plainly says, "The priests in the temple profane the Sabbath."[11] (3) But what can this profanation of the Sabbath be except that no one did work on the Sabbath, but the priests broke it in the temple by offering sacrifice, and profaned it for the sake of the continual sacrifice of animals?

5,4 And I shall also pass this sect by. For again, Elxai is associated with those who came later, the Ebionites after Christ, as well as the Nazoraeans. (5) And four sects are bewitched by his imposture, and have made use of him. Of those <that came> after him, <the> Ebionites <and> Nazoraeans. Of those before his time and during it the Ossaeans, and the Nasaraeans whom I mentioned earlier.

5,6 This is the <sixth> sect of the seven in Jerusalem. They persisted till the coming of Christ, and after Christ's incarnation until the capture of Jerusalem by the Emperor Titus, Domitian's brother but Vespasian's son, in the second year of his father Vespasian's reign. (7)

---

[10] Epiphanius has misread this as Hebrew, presumably from Greek transliteration, and given a forced translation. Holl, following Levy, suggested that the words were the Aramaic formula, אנא מסעד עליכין ביק דינא רבא, "I am your help in the day of the great judgment," written as a palindrome. Does the word, σελάμ or (?), have a force equivalent to "Amen?"

[11] Matt. 12:5.

And after Jerusalem's fall this, and the other sects which enjoyed a brief
period of celebrity—I mean the Sadducees, Scribes, Pharisees,
Hemerobaptists, Ossaeans, Nasaraeans and Herodians—lingered on till,
when its time came, each was dispersed and dissolved.

6,1   Once he has observed their vulgar teaching and chatter, all a sensible person need do is prepare his own remedy from their lunacy itself,
and the terms of the preaching of the deadly poison. (2) Especially when
the Lord says straight off, in the Law and the Gospel, "Thou shalt have
none other gods,"[12] and, "Thou shalt not swear by the name of any
other god."[13] And again he says in the Gospel, "Swear not, neither by
heaven, nor by earth, neither any other oath. But let your Yea be Yea,
and your Nay, Nay; whatsoever is more that these cometh of the evil
one."[14] (3) It is my belief that the Lord prophesied about this because
certain persons would tell us to swear by other names—in the first place,
because it is wrong to swear, by the Lord himself or anything else; swearing is <of> the evil one. (4) Hence the one who spoke in Elxai was evil
too—he who compelled him not only to swear by God, but also by salt,
water, <bread>, aether, wind, earth, and heaven. Anyone willing to be
cured need only take an antidote, in passing as it were, through the two
arguments against Elxai's imposture.

6,5   Next, passing Elxai's nonsense and this sect's deceitfulness by,
I shall compose the rebuttal of the seventh sect current among the Jews
of that period. And the sect is,

20.

Against Herodians,[1] Sect seven from Judaism, but twenty of the series

1,1   And again, after this sect and the others there was a seventh,
known as the Herodians. These had gotten nothing different (from the
others), but <were> altogether Jews, good for nothing and hypocrites.
They believed, however, that Herod was Christ, thought that the Christ
awaited in all scriptures of the Law and prophets was Herod himself, (2)
and were proud of Herod because they were deceived in him. This was
because, (besides holding the vain opinion to gratify the reigning king),
they were won to it by the literal wording of the text, "There shall not
fail a leader from Judah, nor a ruler out of his loins, till he come for

---

[12] Exod. 20:3.
[13] Cf. Exod. 23:13.
[14] Jas. 5:12 and Matt. 5:37.

[1] Herodians are mentioned at Ps.-Tert. 1.1; Jer. Adv. Lucif. 23.

whom it is prepared."[2]—or, "for whom are the things prepared," as the other copies say.

1,3   This was because Herod was the son of an Antipater of Ashkelon, a priest of the idol of Apollo.[3] This Antipater's father was named Herod, and he too was the son of an Antipater.

Antipater was taken prisoner by Idumaeans and fathered Herod during his stay in Idumaea. (4) Since his father was poor and could not ransom his son—I mean Antipater—he remained there for a long time as a slave. But later, with his young son, Herod, he was ransomed by public subscription and returned home. This is why some call him an Idumaean, though others know he was from Ashkelon.

1,5   Afterwards he made friends with † Demetrius,[4] was appointed governor of Judaea, and became acquainted with the Emperor Augustus. Because of his governorship he became a proselyte, was circumcised himself, and circumcised his son, Herod. The kingship of the Jews fell to Herod, but he was king in Judaea as a tributary ruler, under the Emperor Augustus.[5]

1,6   So Herod, a gentile, was reigning as king. Now the crown had been handed down in succession from Judah and David and the rulers or patriarchs of Judah's line <had failed>, but the crown had gone to a gentile. Thus, to the notion of misguided persons, the mistaken belief that he was Christ seemed reasonable (7) in consequence of the wording I have quoted, "There shall not fail a ruler from Judah till he come for whom it is prepared"[6]—as though they had to take this <to mean>, "It was 'prepared' for this ruler. The rulers from Judah have 'failed,' and this one is not descended from Judah—indeed not a descendant of Israel at all. But <the> role of Christ was 'prepared' for someone like this."[7]

2,1   But the next sentence refutes them by saying, "He is the expectation of the nations, and in him shall the peoples hope."[8] Which of the nations hoped in Herod? Which "expectation of the nations" awaits Herod? How did they think "He slept as a lion, and as a lion's cub; who shall raise him up?" applied? (2) Where did Herod "wash his garment in blood," or "his covering in the blood of the cluster,"[9] as our Lord Jesus Christ did in sprinkling his body with his own blood, and his covering

---

[2] Gen. 49:10.

[3] A version of this story appears at Eus. H. E. I.6.2-4; I.7.11-12.

[4] In Eusebius' version Herod makes friends with Hyrcanus.

[5] Cf. Eus. Chron. 61,25-27 (Karst); Jer. Chron. 160,1-3 (Helm).

[6] Gen. 49:10.

[7] The text is applied to "The Messiah of righteousness... the Branch of David" at 4Q Patriarchal Blessings 3-4.

[8] Gen. 49:10.

[9] Gen. 49:11.

with the blood of the cluster? (3) No, "Consider what I say, for the Lord will give thee understanding in all things."[10] For the purification of the state of the Lord's people, he came to cleanse their teeth of human teaching with his own blood—teeth stained in the blood of fat and unlawful sacrifice. (4) And why should I say the multitudes of things (that suggest themselves)? There are many, and the time I have for each of these sects does not permit me to extend the discussion.

3,1   At all events, these were the seven sects in Israel, in Jerusalem and Judaea, while the four I mentioned in "Samaritans" were in Samaria. But most of them have been eliminated. There are no more Scribes, Pharisees, Sadducees, Hemerobaptists or Herodians. (2) There are only a handful of Nasarenes, perhaps one or two, beyond the Upper Thebaid and beyond Arabia; and the remnant of Ossaeans, no longer practicing Judaism but joined with the Sampsites, who in turn <live> in the territory beyond the Dead Sea—now, though, they are joined with the Ebionite sect. (3) And so they have lapsed from Judaism—as though a snake's tail or body had been cut off and a snake with two heads and no tail had sprouted from it, grown on a half of a body and attached to it.

3,4   So much for my discussion of the four Samaritan and seven Jewish sects. With the sole exception of three Samaritan ones, <the> Gorothenes, Dositheans and Sebuaeans, none of them exist any longer. There are no Essenes at all; it is as though they have been buried in darkness. And there are no more sects among the Jews except the Ossaeans, and a few isolated Nasaraeans. But Ossaeans have abandoned Judaism for the sect of the Sampsaeans, who are no longer either Jews or Christians. That will do for these.

Christ's sojourn here, and true advent in the flesh in person; the one and only Faith of God (De Incarnatione)

1,1   Right on their heels came the arrival in the flesh of our Lord Jesus Christ, which overtook these seven sects at Jerusalem; his power snuffed them out and scattered them. But then, after his sojourn, all of the later sects arose. I mean after Mary had been given the good tidings at Nazareth by Gabriel and in a word, after the entire period of the Lord's visit in the flesh—in other words, after his ascension.

1,2   For God consented, for man's salvation, that his own Son should descend and be conceived in a virgin womb, though he was the Word from heaven, begotten, not in time and without beginning, in the bosom of the Father; of one essence with the Father and in no way different from

---

[10] 2 Tim. 2:7.

the Father, but immutable and unalterable, impassible and entirely without suffering, though he shared the suffering of our race.

1,3   He came down from heaven and was conceived, not of man's seed but by the Holy Ghost. He truly had a body from Mary, since he had fashioned his own flesh from the holy Virgin's womb, and had taken the human soul and mind and everything human apart from sin, and united it with himself by his own Godhead. (4) He was born in Bethlehem, circumcised in the cavern, presented in Jerusalem, embraced by Simeon, openly confessed by Anna the prophetess, the daughter of Phanuel, and taken away to Nazareth.

The following year he came to appear before the Lord in Jerusalem, (5) and came to Bethlehem to visit his family, borne in the arms of his mother. Once more he was taken back to Nazareth, and after a second year came to Jerusalem and Bethlehem, borne by his own mother as before. But in Bethlehem he came to a house with his own mother and Joseph, who was old but accompanied Mary. And there, in his second year, he was visited by the magi, was worshipped, received gifts, (6) and was taken to Egypt the same night because of an angel's warning to Joseph. Again he returned from Egypt two years later, since Herod had died and Archelaus had succeeded him.

2,1   The Savior was born at Bethlehem of Judaea in the thirty-third year of Herod,[1] but the forty-second of the Emperor Augustus. He went down into Egypt in the thirty-fifth year of Herod, and returned from Egypt after Herod's death. (2) Hence in the thirty-seventh year of that same reign of Herod, the child was four years old—when Herod died after a reign of thirty-seven years.

2,3   Archelaus was king for nine years. Joseph left Egypt with Mary and the child at the beginning of his reign, and, on hearing that Archelaus was king went back to Galilee, and at this time settled in Nazareth. (4) Archelaus had a son, Herod the Younger, and this Herod succeeded him as king in the ninth year of the reign of his father, Archelaus; and the years of Christ's visit in the flesh totalled thirteen.

2,5   In the eighteenth year of Herod also called Agrippa, Jesus began to preach, and at that time received the baptism of John. He preached an "acceptable year," with no opposition from anyone, Jews, Greeks, Samaritans or anyone else. (6) Then he preached a second year, in the face of opposition; and this Herod had reigned for nineteen years, but the Savior had lived for thirty-two.

---

[1] The chronology of Herod's dynasty comes from Eusebius H. E. I.7.11-12, cf. Jer. Chron. 160,1; 170,5; 171,11 (Helm). Epiphanius has identified Herod the Younger with Herod Agrippa, and made him Archelaus' son.

2,7   But in the twentieth year of Herod called the tetrarch came the
saving passion, (and yet the impassibility); the tasting of death—and
even the death of a cross—by One who truly suffered, yet remained impassible in his divine nature. ("Forasmuch as Christ hath suffered for us
in the flesh,"[2] says the sacred scripture, and again, "being put to death
in the flesh, but quickened by the Spirit,"[3] and what follows.) (8) He was
crucified and buried, descended to the underworld in Godhead and soul,
led captivity captive, and rose again the third day with his sacred body
itself.

For he had united the body with his Godhead, a body no longer subject
to dissolution, no longer subject to suffering, no longer under death's
dominion—as the apostle says, "Death hath no more dominion over
him?[4]—(3,1) truly the body itself, the flesh itself, the entire humanity
itself. He had quickened the actual body, not something else, and joined
it to a single unity, a single divinity, the fleshly (made) imperishable, the
bodily (made) spiritual, the gross ethereal, the mortal immortal—having
seen no corruption, for the soul had not been left in hell, (2) its instrument had not been severed from it on sin's account, its mind had not
been defiled by change. He had taken all the attributes of man and preserved them all in their fullness, since <the> Godhead had granted
them to the true Manhood for its proper needs. By these I mean the
needs <that arise> from a body, soul and human mind, and guarantee
the fullness of <the true humanity>—that is, by hunger and thirst,
weeping and discouragement, tears and sleep, weariness and repose.
(3) For these are no sort of sin, but a token of truest humanity, since the
Godhead truly dwells with the Manhood, not undergoing human experience, but consenting to what is proper, and free from sin and forbidden change.

3,4   Moreover, he arose, and entered where doors were shut to prove
that his body was ethereal, the actual body itself with flesh and bones.
For after his entry he exhibited hands and feet, side pierced, bones,
sinews and the rest, so that the sight was no illusion. Since he had fulfilled
all things himself, he was giving the promise of our faith and hope.

3,5   And he met with them in reality, not appearance, and by his instruction taught them to proclaim the kingdom of heaven in truth. He
indicated the greatest and supreme <mystery> to his disciples and said,
"Make disciples of the nations"—that is, convert the nations from
wickedness to truth, from sects to one unity—(6) "baptizing them in the

---

[2] 1 Pet. 4:1.
[3] 1 Pet. 3:18.
[4] Rom. 6:9.

name of Father, Son and Holy Spirit.''[5] In the Lord's term for the Trinity, the sacred, kingly seal, to prove, by the word, ''name,''[6] that there has been no alteration of the one Unity. (7) For since he commands the candidates < to be sealed > ''in the name of Father...'' the praise of God is assured. Since he commands this ''in the name of ...Son,'' the (divine) surname[7] is no less assured. Since he commands it ''in the name of ...Holy Spirit,'' the tie[8] has not been cut or moved and bears the seal of the one Godhead.

4,1 And he was taken up to heaven in his body itself and his soul and mind, having conjoined these as one unity and one supernatural entity and made them divine. He sat down at the Father's right hand, and sent messengers into all the world: (2) Simon Peter, his brother Andrew, James and John the sons of Zebedee, his original choices—Philip and Bartholomew, Matthew, Thomas and Judas and Thaddeus, Simon the Zealot. For though Judas Iscariot had originally belonged to the twelve, he turned traitor and was stricken from the sacred roll of the apostles.

4,3 But he also sent seventy-two others to preach, including the seven who were placed in charge of the widows, Stephen, Philip, Prochorus, Nicanor, Timon, Parmenas and Nicolaus—(4) but before them was Matthias, who was included among the apostles in Judas' place. After these seven, and Matthias who preceded them, he sent Mark and Luke, Justus, Barnabas and Apelles, Rufus, Niger and < the > rest of the seventy-two. (5) After them all, and together with them, he chose the holy apostle Paul with his own voice from heaven to be both apostle and herald of the gentiles, and the one to complete the apostles' teaching. (6) It was Paul who found St. Luke, one of the seventy-two who had been scattered, brought him to repentance, and < made him > his own follower, both a co-worker in the Gospel and an apostle. And thus the entire work of preaching the Gospel was completed up to this point.

4,7 So much for my dicussion of the twenty sects, and the world's enlightenment with the Gospel by Christ and his disciples, which I have mentioned briefly by way of a sequel. (8) Similarly, it would be possible to gather and cite oracles and prophecies from the Law and Psalms, observe the agreements and proofs of the other scriptures, and see exactly how Christ's visit in the flesh and his teaching of the Gospel are not spurious, but are true, were announced beforehand by the Old Testament, and are open to no doubt. But not to extend the work of composition to a burdensome length, I shall rest content with the above.

---

[5] Matt. 28:19.

[6] I.e., the word ὄνομα is used only once in the baptismal formula, meaning that only one God is spoken of.

[7] υἱός is here treated as an ἐπίκλησις, or surname, for πατήρ.

[8] ''Tie,'' σύνδεσμος, means simply the unity of the three Persons, cf. Anc. 4,5 et al.

4,9 And next I shall move ahead and similarly describe the opinions which, for a wrong reason, grew on the world later. By now I have made a sufficiently good inventory of the eleven sects with Jewish and Samaritan backgrounds, and the nine before them with Greek, barbarian and other origins before the Lord's advent and until his time.

ANACEPHALAEOSIS II

Here in turn are the contents of this second Section of Volume One. It includes thirteen Sects as follows:

21,1   21. Simonians, derived from Simon, the magician from the Samaritan village of Gitthon at the time of the apostle Peter. He was originally a Samaritan, but he assumed Christ's name though only that. (2) But he taught that an unnatural act, sexual congress for the purpose of polluting women, is a matter of moral indifference. He rejected the resurrection of bodies, and claimed that the world is not God's. (3) He gave his disciples an image of himself in the form of Zeus to worship, and one <in the> form of Athena of the whore who accompanied him, whose name was Helen. He said that he was the Father to Samaritans, but Christ to Jews.

22,1   22. Menandrians, who originated from this Simon through a Menander, but were somewhat different from the Simonians. Menander said that the world was made by angels.

23,1   23. Satornilians, who lent strength to the Simonians' filthy talk in Syria. But to cause further consternation they preached differently from the Simonians. Their founder was Satornilus. (2) Like Menander, he said that the world was made by angels—though only seven—against the wishes of the Father on high.

24,1   24. Basilideans, initiates into the same obscenity, derived from Basilides, who was trained along with Satornilus by Simonians and Menandrians. He had similar ideas but was somewhat different. (2) He said that there are 365 heavens, and gave angels' names for them. Thus the year too has the same number of days, and the name, Abrasax, has the same value and totals 365. And this is the holy name.

25,1   25. Nicolaitans, derived from Nicolaus, whom the apostles placed in charge of the widows. Out of envy of his own wife he taught his disciples to perform the obscenity along with the others, (2) and instructed them about Kaulakau, Prunicus, and other outlandish names.

26,1   26. Gnostics are the successors of these sects, but insanely perform the obscenity more than all of them. In Egypt they are called Stratiotics and Phibionites; in Upper Egypt, Secundians; in other places, Socratists, and Zacchaeans in others. (2) But others call them Coddians, others, Borborites. They boast of Barbelo, also known as Barbero.

27,1   27. Carpocratians, derived from a native of Asia, Carpocrates, who taught his followers to perform every obscenity and every sinful act. And unless one proceeds through all of them, he said, and fulfils the will of all demons and angels, he cannot mount to the highest heaven or get by the principalities and authorities.

27,2   He said that Jesus had an intellectual soul, knew what is on high, and made it known here, and that if one does the sorts of things that Jesus did, he is like Jesus. (3) Like the sects from Simon on, Carpocrates repudiated the Law together with the resurrection of the dead. (4) Marcellina at Rome was one of his followers. He secretly made images of Jesus, Paul, Homer and Pythagoras, and offered them incense and worship.

28   28. Cerinthians, also known as Merinthians. These are a type of Jew derived from Cerinthus and Merinthus, who boast of circumcision, but say that the world was made by angels and that Jesus was named Christ as an advancement to a higher rank.

29   29. Nazoraeans, who confess that Christ Jesus is Son of God, but all of whose customs are in accordance with the Law.

30,1   30. Ebionites are very like the Cerinthians and Nazoraeans; the sect of the Sampsaeans and Elkasaites was associated with them to a degree.

30,2   They say that Christ has been created in heaven, also the Holy Spirit. But Christ lodged in Adam at first, and from time to time takes Adam himself off and puts him back on—for this is what they say he did during his visit in the flesh.

30,3   Although they are Jews they have Gospels, abhor the eating of flesh, take water for God, and, as I said, hold that Christ clothed himself with a man when he became incarnate. (4) They continually immerse themselves in water, summer and winter, if you please for purification like the Samaritans.

31,1   31. Valentinians, who deny the resurrection of the flesh and reject the Old Testament, though they read the prophets and accept whatever can be interpreted allegorically to resemble their own sect. (2) They also introduce some other fictions and give the names of thirty aeons, which are male and female and were begotten all together by the Father of all, and which they hold to be both gods and aeons. (3) But Christ has brought a body from heaven, and passed through Mary as though through a conduit.

32,1   32. Secundians, with whom Epiphanes and Isidore are associated, are familiar with the same pairs of aeons; for their ideas are like Valentinus', though to a certain extent they describe different things. (2) In addition, they teach the performance of the obscenity. They too repudiate the flesh.

33   33. Ptolemaeans, also disciples of Valentinus, with whom Flora is associated. They say the same things as Valentinus and the Secundians about the pairs of aeons, but in a way they too are different.

This, in turn, is the summary of the thirteen Sects of the Second Section of Volume One.

21.

Against Simonians,[1] first after the single Faith in Christ, but twenty-one of the series

1,1 Simon Magus's makes the first sect to begin in the time since Christ. It is composed of persons who do not <believe> in Christ's name in a right or lawful way, but who do their dreadful deeds in keeping with the false corruption that is in them.

1,2 Simon was a sorcerer, and came from the city of Gitthon[2] in Samaria—though it is a village now. He impressed the Samaritan people by deceiving them and catching them with his magic,[3] (3) and he said that he was the supreme power of God, and had come down from on high.[4] To the Samaritans he called himself the Father; but to Jews he said he was the Son, though he had suffered without actually suffering, suffering only in appearance.[5]

1,4 Simon mimicked the apostles and in company with many he too, like the others, was baptized by Philip. All except Simon waited for the arrival of the chief apostles, and received the Holy Spirit through the laying on of their hands. (Philip, a deacon, was not authorized to give the imposition of hands for the conferral of the Holy Spirit.)[6] (5) For since Simon's heart was not right or his reason either, but he was devoted to a sordid covetousness and avarice and never deviated from his evil pursuit, he offered to pay the apostle Peter to give him authority to convey the Holy Spirit through the laying on of hands. For he had counted on spending a little money, and amassing a huge fortune and more in return for a small investment, by giving the Holy Spirit to others.

2,1 His mind was deranged and hallucinated from the devilish deceit in magic, and he was always ready to display the barbarous deeds of his own wickedness, and the wickedness of demons, through his trickery. He

---

[1] The main sources for this Sect are: The Acts of the Apostles; Iren. I.23.1-3; perhaps Hippol. Haer. VI.7.1; 18.1; and a further source, perhaps the Simonian Apophasis Megale, perhaps an orthodox Christian attack on Simonianism. Simon is further mentioned or discussed at Ps.-Tert. 1.2; Const. Ap. VI.7-9; Eus. H. E. IV.22.5; Justin Apol. I.26.2-3; 56.1-2; Dial. 120; Test. Truth 58,2-6, et al.
[2] Cf. Hippol. Haer. VI.7.1; Clem. Hom. I.15.2; II.22.2; Recog. II.7.1; Justin Apol. I.26.2.
[3] Cf. Acts 8:9.
[4] Acts 8:10.
[5] Iren. I.23.1;3; Hippol. Haer. VI.10.4; 6; Ps.-Tert. 1.2.
[6] Cf. Acts 8:12-19.

therefore came forward, and under the name of Christ—as though he were mixing hellebore with honey—he poisoned the dignity of Christ's name for those whom he had caught in his baneful error, and induced death in his converts.

2,2 Since he was naturally lecherous, and was spurred on by the respect that was shown for his professions, the scum created a false impression for his dupes. He had gotten hold of a female vagabond from Tyre named Helen, and he took her without letting his relationship with her be known.[7] (3) And while privately having an unnatural relationship with his paramour, the charlatan was teaching his disciples stories for their amusement and calling himself the supreme power of God, if you please! And he had the nerve to call the whore who was his partner the Holy Ghost, and said that he had come down on her account.[8] (4) He said, "I was transformed in each heaven to correspond with the appearance of the inhabitants of each, so as to pass my angelic powers[9] by unnoticed and descend to Ennoia[10]—to this woman, likewise called Prunicus and Holy Spirit,[11] through whom I created the angels.[12] But the angels created the world[13] and men. But this woman is the ancient Helen on whose account the Trojans and Greeks went to war."[14]

2,5 Simon told a fairy tale about this, and said that the power kept transforming her appearance on her way down from on high,[15] but that the poets had spoken of this in allegories. For these angels went to war over the power from on high—they call her Prunicus, but she is called Barbero[16] or Barbelo by other sects—[17] because she displayed her beauty

---

[7] Cf. Iren. I.23.1; Hippol. Haer. VI.18.3; Clem. Hom. II.23.3; Recog. II.8-9; Justin Apol. I.26.3; Tert. De Anima 34.2.

[8] "He said...on her account." Iren. I.23.2; Hippol. Haer. VI.18.3; 19.2; Justin Apol. I.26.3; Tert. De Anima 34.3. For the power's descent to find the lost Wisdom, see Iren. I.23.3; Hippol. Haer. VI.19.4; Ps.-Tert. 1.2; Tri. Prot. 40.12-18.

[9] The redeemer changes form, or becomes invisible, during his descent: Iren. I.23.3; Hippol. Haer. VI.19.6; Ps.-Tert. 6.5; Tert. De Anima 34.4; Epist. Apost. 13; Gos. Phil. 57,28-58,2; Gr. Seth 56,21-33; Zost. 4,29-30; PS 12; 99; GR 152, 30-33; 154, 7-8 et al; GL 465,14-17; Mandaean Prayer Book 214; Keph. 61,22-23. The passage quoted presumably comes from the "further source," see note 1.

[10] For Gnostic uses of the name, Ennoia, and variations on it, see the Index to *The Nag Hammadi Library in English*.

[11] The Holy Spirit is equated with Prunicus at Iren. I.29.4. Epiphanius has here equated the Holy Spirit and Prunicus with Simon's Ennoia.

[12] Sophia or Prunicus is the creatress at Clem. Hom. II.25.2; Recog. II.12.1-2; cf. Tert. De Anima 34.3. Ennoia serves as a kind of mediatress, calling for further Aeons, at Apocry. John 4,27-6,2.

[13] Cf. Acts of Paul VII.1.15.

[14] Iren. I.23.3; Hippol. Haer. VI.19.2; Tert. De Anima 34.5.

[15] There is a descent of a specifically female emanation at Hyps. 70,14-24; Keph. 71,19-23.

[16] Cf. Keph. 35,15-17.

[17] For the very common Gnostic figure, Barbelo, see Index to *Nag Hammadi Library*.

< and > drove them wild, and was sent for this purpose, to despoil the archons who had made this world. She has suffered no harm, but she brought them to the point of slaughtering each other from the lust for her that she aroused in them.[18] (6) And detaining her so that she should not go back up,[19] they all had relations with her[20] in each of her womanly and female bodies—for she kept migrating[21] from female bodies into various bodies of human beings, cattle and the rest—so that, by the deeds they were doing in killing and being killed, they would cause their own diminution through the shedding of blood. Then, by gathering the power[22] again, she would be able to ascend to heaven once more.

3,1 "This woman was then, she who by her unseen powers has made replicas of herself[23] in Greek and Trojan times and immemorially, before the world and after. (2) She is the one who is with me now, and for her sake I am come down. But she herself awaited my arrival; for this is Ennoia, she whom Homer calls Helen.[24] And this is why Homer has to describe her as standing on a tower, signalling the Greeks her plot against the Phrygians with a lamp.[25] But with its brightness, as I said, he indicated the display of the light from on high."

3,3 Thus again, the charlatan said that the wooden horse, the device in Homer which Greeks believe was made for a ruse, is the ignorance of the gentiles.[26] And "as the Phrygians, in drawing it, unwittingly invited their own destruction, so the gentiles—the persons outside the sphere of my knowledge—[27]draw destruction on themselves through ignorance."[28]

3,4 In turn, moreover, the impostor would say that this same woman whom he called Ennoia was Athena, using the words of the holy apostle Paul if you please, and turning the truth into his falsehood—the words, "Put on the breastplate of faith and the helmet of salvation, the greaves, the sword and the shield."[29] In Philistion's style of mime the cheat now

---

[18] Hippol. Haer. VI.19.2. Cf. Clem. Recog. II.12.1; Exeg. Soul 127,22-128,1 and perhaps Thunder 18,23-25; Keph. 35,15-17; 80,25-29.

[19] Cf. PS 37; 43-44; 137-138; GR 393, 30-37; GL 459,31-35 et al; Man. Ps. 10,10-14; Orig. World 116,15-18 and perhaps Thunder 15,4-14.

[20] Cf. Orig. World 116,15-21. Something comparable is said of the soul at Exeg. Soul 127,25-128,1.

[21] Iren. I.23.2; Tert. De Anima 34. The Trimorphic Protennoia "transforms the forms" of all things "into (other) forms" at Tri. Prot. 45,21-27.

[22] Sophia's power is stolen at Tri. Prot. 39,28-32; PS 44-45. It is recovered or gathered at PS 129-131; Keph. 29,1-7; 54,15-55,1; 76,29-77,3; 80,25-29.

[23] This paragraph may come from the "further source."

[24] Iren. I.23.2; Hippol. Haer. VI.19.1-3.

[25] Hippol. Haer. VI.19.1; Clem. Recog. II.12.4.

[26] Cf. Hippol. Haer. VI.19.1.

[27] The angels reduce man to slavery at Iren. I.23.3; cf. Hippol. Haer. VI.19.5.

[28] Perhaps from the "further source."

[29] Cf. Eph. 6:14-17.

turned all these things, which the apostle had said with reference to firm reason, the faith of a chaste life, and the power of sacred, heavenly speech, into a mere joke. "What does this mean?" he said. "Paul was using all these figures mystically, as types of Athena." (5) Thus again, as I said, to indicate the female companion he had taken from Tyre, the ancient Helen's namesake, he would call her by all these names—Ennoia, Athena, Helen and the rest—and say, "For her sake I am come down. For this is that which is written in the Gospel, the sheep that was lost."[30]

3,6   Furthermore, he has given his followers an image—as one of himself, if you please!—and they worship this in the form of Zeus. He has likewise given them another, an image of Helen in the form of Athena—and his dupes worship these.

4,1   He instituted mysteries consisting of dirt[31] and—to put it more politely—the fluids generated from men's bodies through the seminal emission and women's through the menstrual flux, which are collected for mysteries by a most indecent method. (2) And he said that these are mysteries of life <and> the most perfect knowledge. But for one with understanding from God, knowledge is first of all a matter of regarding these things as abomination instead, and as death rather than life.

4,3   Simon also offers certain names of principalities and authorities, and he speaks of various heavens, describes powers to correspond with each firmament and heaven, and gives outlandish names for these.[32] He says that there is no way to be saved but by learning this mystical doctrine, and offering sacrifices of this kind to the Father of all, through these principalities and authorities. (4) This world has been defectively[33] constructed by wicked principalities and authorities, he says. But he teaches that there is a death and destruction of flesh, and a purification of souls only—and (only) if these are initiated through his erroneous knowledge. And thus the † imposture of the so-called Gnostics begins.

4,5   He claimed that the Law is not God's,[34] but belongs to the power on the left,[35] and that prophets are not from a good God either, but from

---

[30] From the "further source"? Cf. Iren. I.23.2; Hippol. Haer. VI.19.2; Tert. De Anima 34.5. The scriptural quotation is from Matt. 18:12.

[31] Cf. Pan. 26,4,5-7. Epiphanius might have made this assumption of the Simonians on the basis of the accusation of lewdness at Iren. I.23.3, cf. also Hippol. Haer. VI.19.5. The closest parallel to Epiphanius' accusation occurs at Test. Tr. 58,2-6.

[32] Tert. Praescr. 33.

[33] For "in defect" see Tri. Trac. 78,5; SJC 107,21.

[34] Clem. Hom. III.2.2.

[35] The characterization of good and evil as "right and left" is common in Gnostic literature. See, e.g., PS 361; 362; U 261; Tri. Trac. 98,12-20; 104,9-11; 106,2-6; 18-21; Gos. Phil. 60,26-28; Nat. Arc. 95,35-96,3; Orig. World 106,11-18; Test. Tr. 43,10-13; Val. Exp. 38,27-33; Corp. Herm. XI.8.

one power or another. And he decides on a power for each as he chooses—the Law belongs to one, David to another, Isaiah to another, Ezekiel again to someone else, and he attributes each particular prophet to one principality.[36] But all of these are from the power on the left, and outside of the Pleroma;[37] and whoever believes the Old Testament must die.

5,1   But this doctrine is refuted by the truth itself. If Simon is God's supreme power, and the tart who is with him is the Holy Ghost as he says himself, then he should give the name of the (supreme) power—or else say why there is a title for the woman, but none at all for him! (2) And how does it happen that Simon died at Rome one day when his turn came—when the wretched man fell down and died right in the middle of Rome![38]

5,3   <And> why did Peter declare that Simon has no part or share in the heritage of true religion? (4) And how can the world not belong to a good God, when all the good were chosen from it?

5,5   And how can the power which spoke in the Law and the prophets be "on the left," when it has given tidings beforehand of Christ's coming <from the> good God, and when it forbids all wrongdoing? (6) And since the Lord has said, "I am not come to destroy the Law, but to fulfil,"[39] how can there not be one Godhead and the same Spirit, of the New Testament and the Old? And to show that the Law was proclaimed by himself and given through Moses, while the grace of the Gospel has been preached by himself and his presence in the flesh, he told the Jews, "Had ye believed Moses, ye would have believed me also, for he wrote of me."[40]

5,7   And many other arguments against the charlatan's drivel <can be found>. How can unnatural acts be productive of life, unless perhaps by the will of demons, when, in the Gospel, the Lord himself gave the answer, "All men cannot receive this, for there be eunuchs which have made themselves eunuchs for the kingdom of heaven's sake,"[41] to those who told him, "If the case of the man and wife be so, it is not good to marry"[42]—thus proving that real celibacy is the gift of the kingdom of heaven? (8) And again, of the lawful wedlock which Simon corrupts to

---

[36] The archons speak to the prophets at PS 351.
[37] No prophet has entered the light, PS 351.
[38] Cf. Didascalia p. 101,6-8 (Lagarde); Const. Ap. VI.9.3-4; Vercelli Acts of Peter 32.
[39] Matt. 5:17.
[40] John 5:46.
[41] Matt. 19:12.
[42] Matt. 19:10.

make shameful provision for his own lust, the Lord says elsewhere, "Them that God hath joined together, let not man put asunder."[43]

6,1   Again, why does the swindler refute himself by overlooking his own nonsense, as though he does not know what he has said? After saying that he himself created the angels through his Ennoia he went on to say that he was transformed at each heaven, to escape their notice on his way down. In other words he evaded them from fear; and why is the driveller afraid of the angels he made himself?

6,2   And how can the basis of his imposture not be entirely easy for the wise to refute at once, when the scripture says, "In the beginning God created the heaven and earth?"[44] And in agreement with this, the Lord says, "Father, Lord of heaven and the earth?"[45] in the Gospel, as though to his own God and Father. (3) Now if God the Father of our Lord Jesus Christ is maker of heaven and earth, there is nothing to any of the humbug Simon's statements—that the world was produced defectively by angels, and everything else the impostor madly told the world at random to deceive certain persons, the victims of his deceit.

7,1   And these brief remarks of mine regarding his sect will give the reader sufficient occasion for truth and healing, and a sufficient refutation of those who try to harm the ignorant with such beastly filth. (2) But I have given thrashing enough to Simon's stream of poison, and shall pass it by and proceed in turn to the refutation of another sect. For there is inconstancy and uncertainty in him, since he is an impostor but has assumed an appearance of the name of Christ—like the snake-like filth hatched out of season from the infertile eggs of asps and other vipers. (3) As the prophet says, "They have broken the eggs of asps, and he who would eat of their eggs hath found an egg infertile, and in it a basilisk."[46]

But as I said, beloved, by Christ's power we have struck Simon with the words of the truth, and have done away with his corruption. Let us go on to the next.

22.

Against Menander,[1] *Sect two from Christ's Advent, but twenty-two of the series*

1,1   A Menander follows the Simonians. He was originally a Samaritan,[2] but at some time became a pupil of Simon's. He likewise

---

[43] Matt. 19:6.
[44] Gen. 1:1.
[45] Matt. 11:25 par.
[46] Isa. 59:5.

[1] The probable source of Sect 22 is Iren. I.23.5. See also Ps.-Tert. 1.2; Justin Apol. 1.26; Tert. De Anima 50.
[2] Cf. Justin Apol. I.26.4.

said that the world is the product of angels,[3] but that he himself had been sent from on high as a power of God.[4] (2) To perpetrate worse trickery than his predecessor for man's deception, he said he had been sent ''for salvation''—to gather certain persons in his own mystery, if you please, so that they would not be subject to the angels, principalities and authorities who have made the world.[5]

1,3 He put everything together like his own teacher, and was unflagging in his < devotion to > spells and the other magic arts. But in his teaching he was no different, only that he called himself greater than his teacher before him.

2,1 He met with the same defeat as his teacher, however; and he too will be convicted and overthrown by the same words of refutation of the truth. For † he has died, and his sect has mostly come to an end. (2) But I shall pass it by, again proceed with my instruction, and come to another.

In fact, the ancients tell the story that when a number of asps were put in a single earthen jar and buried in the foundations of the four corners of each temple of the idols which were erected in Egypt, the strongest would attack the others and eat them. (3) But when it was left by itself and could find no food, it would bend round and eat < its entire > body, from its tail up to a certain part. And so it remained, no longer whole, but half of a snake. (4) Hence the ancients called it an ''aspidogorgon,'' which tells us that, though anciently this was the case, it is no longer so; the practice has been ended. In the same way, while this entirely defunct sect is open to contradiction by myself, its existence has been ended by the power of Christ. Let us pass it by too, beloved, and go to the next.

23.

Against Satornilus,[1] number three from The Lord's Advent but twenty-three of the series

1,1 A Satornilus arose after him from the same origins, I mean Menander and his immediate predecessors. Satornilus lived near Syria—that is, near Antioch by Daphne—and brought the world a great deal more experience and skill in imposture.

---

[3] Iren. I.23.5; Hippol. Haer. VII.4.
[4] Cf. Iren. I.23.5; Tert. De Anima 50.2.
[5] Cf. Iren. I.23.5; Acts of Paul. VII.1.5.

[1] The source for Sect 23 is Iren. I.24.1-2. Cf. Hippol. Haer. VII.3; 28; Const. Ap. VI.8.1; Eus. H. E. IV.22.5; Justin Dial. 35; Tert. De Anima 23.1.

1,2   For these two, Basilides and Satornilus,[2] were fellow students. Basilides went to Egypt, and there preached the dark recesses of the very depth of imposture. But Satornilus spent his life in the place I indicated, and like Menander declared that the world was produced by angels.[3]

1,3   He said that an unknowable Father is one, and that he has made powers, principalities and authorities. But the angels rebelled against the power on high, and a certain seven of them have made the world and everything in it.[4] The world, however, has been parcelled out by lot to each of the angels.[5]

1,4   These angels met and deliberated, and created the man together, in the form of the luminous image that had peeped down from on high—[6]for because of its immediate withdrawal they could not detain it when it peeped down, and they wanted to reproduce it. (5) And it is they who have fashioned the man, for no other reason. For the light had induced a sort of itch in the angels when it peeped down from on high, and in longing for the heavenly likeness they undertook to fashion the man. (6) For since they had fallen in love with the light from on high, and were held spellbound with desire for it and enjoyment of it when it appeared and disappeared from them—and they loved it, yet could not sate themselves with its loveliness, because of the light's immediate withdrawal—the charlatan dramatically represents the angels as saying, "Let us make man in an image and after a likeness."[7]

1,7   To give his imposture plausibility he falsified the word, "our," spoken in Genesis by the holy God, <but> retained "in an image"—as though other persons were making an image, if you please, and <were showing> that it was someone else's image <by> saying, "Let us make a man in an image and after a likeness."[8]

1,8   But when the man was made, he says, they could not finish him[9]

---

[2] "Satorninus" and Basilides are mentioned together at Iren. I.24.1.

[3] As above. Cf. also Acts of Paul VII.1.15.

[4] Creation is performed by potentially or actively dissident powers at Tri. Trac. 70,20-36; GR 67,8-30.

[5] Creation is divided among ruling powers at Tri. Trac. 99,19-100,18; G. Egypt. 58,1-6; GR 107,5-8; 408,9-23. The entire paragraph is modelled on Iren. I.24.1, cf. Hippol. Haer. VII.28.1.

[6] Iren. I.24.1; Hippol. Haer. VII.28.2. Versions of this legend are found at Apocry. John 14,25-15,6; Nat Arc. 87,11-88,3; 94,26-34; Orig. World 100,21-22; 103,28-32; Gr. Pow. 38,5-9; GR 174,1-6 et al; Keph. 133,12-15; 133,31-134,4; 136,1-11; Corp. Herm. I.14.

[7] Cf. Gen. 1:26. "Our" is also omitted at Iren. I.24.1; Hippol. Haer. VII.28.2.

[8] Cf. Gen. 1:26.

[9] Cf. Iren. I.24.1; Hippol. Haer. VII.28.3. Versions of this legend are found at Apocry. John 19,18-20,5; Nat. Arc. 87,33-88,15; Orig. World 115,3-116,8; GR 108, 14-113,16; 242,25-243,1; 245,1-11; GL 465,18-23; 505,24-509,21 et al.

because of their weakness. He lay quivering, flat on the ground like a worm with no legs, and could not stand or do anything else,[10] till the power on high peeped down, felt sorry for its own image and semblance, and sent a spark of its power out of pity. It raised the man up with this and brought him to life; Satornilus claims, if you please, that the spark is the human soul.[11]

1,9   And thus the spark will surely be preserved, but all of the man must perish. What came down from on high will sooner or later be received back on high, but what is from below, anything fashioned by the angels, is left here for them.[12]

1,10   But the trickster claims that Christ himself has come only in the form and semblance of man, and has done everything—being born, living, being visible, suffering—in appearance.[13]

2,1   With this the thing that is falsely termed ''knowledge'' begins again to add to the depth of its wickedness. It had had its inception and cause in Simon, but (now) it is augmented with other, further nonsense, whose refutation I shall give later.

2,2   For in speaking of the angels Satornilus claims that the God of the Jews is one of them too, and that he and they have rebelled against the power on high. But the Savior has been sent from the Father against the powers' wishes, to destroy the God of the Jews and preserve those who trust in <himself>. But they, the members of this sect, are the ones with the spark[14] of the Father on high.

2,3   For Satornilus claims that originally two men were fashioned, one good and one evil. By descent from these two breeds of men, the good and the evil, exist. (4) But since the demons were on the side of the evil, the Savior came in the last days as I said, to assist the good men and destroy the evil and the demons.[15]

2,5   But the scum also says that marriage and procreation are of Satan. Thus most Satornilians abstain from meat, to attract certain persons to their deceit, if you please, with this pretended discipline.[16] (6)

---

[10] Cf. GR 100,1-11; 168,11-12; 454, 16-23.

[11] Apocry. John 20,9-28. ''The righteous Spark'' is important in Para. Shem 31,23;29-30; 33,30-35; 46,13-15; 17-18. Neither Irenaeus nor Hippolytus explicitly equates the spark with the soul.

[12] Cr. Auth. Teach. 32,16-23; GL 430,35-38.

[13] Cf. Iren. I.24.2; Hippol. Haer. VII.28.5. These ideas are voiced at Man. Ps. 191,4-8; 196,22-25; Acts of John 87-97. There is a polemic against them at Melch. 5,1-11.

[14] Cf. Iren. I.24.2; Hippol. Haer. VII.28.5. There is a polemic against the God of the Old Testament at Test. Truth 47,14-48,27.

[15] Cf. Iren. I.14.2; Hippol. Haer. VII.28.6. A struggle of this type is reported or implied at G. Egypt. 61,16-22; Gr. Seth 52,11-53,26; Val. Exp. 38,24-33.

[16] Cf. Iren. I.24.2; Hippol. Haer. VII.28.7.

Again, the charlatan claims that some of the prophecies were given by
the angels who made the world, but some by Satan. For Satan is an angel
too, he claims, the opponent of the angels who made the world, but
especially of the God of the Jews.[17]

3,1   But by the very act of claiming these things the oaf can be shown
to confess the unity of God, and to refer all things back to a single unity
of governance. For if the angels have made < the man >, but angels in
turn owe the reason for their being to the power on high, they are not
the cause of the fashioning of the man. The cause is the power on high—
which made the angels by whom the fashioning of the man has been accomplished. (2) For the tool is not the cause of the things it makes. The
cause is the man who uses the tool to perform the operation by which the
product is made. As scripture says, "Shall the axe boast itself without
him who wieldeth it?"[18] and so on. (3) Thus, the sword is plainly not the
cause of the murder, but the man who committed the murder with the
sword. And the mould cannot make its products itself, but the man who
made the mould and the product can.

3,4   Hence not the angels, but the angels' maker is the cause, even
though he gave them < no > orders to make a man. (5) Satornilus may
be finding the power on high guilty of ignorance, and of not knowing
what would happen, since it was being done against its will. Or < he may
mean > that the angels have done the work of preparing the man with
the power's consent, for a useful purpose, and that it made the angels
with the intent of preparing him, though it did not order them to finish
the project—which, according to Satornilus' mythological art-work, was
the figure of the man.

4,1   Or why not reply to the fabulist with the question, "Did the
power on high know what they would do?"

"Yes," says Satornilus.

"Very well, if it knew, it has made the man, not they. Yet if it knew
but did not want it done, and they still undertook the project themselves
against its wishes, why has it not prevented them? (2) But if it was unable
to prevent them, this is its first weak point. It prepared the angels it has
made to its own disadvantage, in opposition to itself and for its own provocation; and in the second place, it could have prevented them, but did
not. Instead, it lent its assistance to the evil work the angels have performed.

4,3   "But if it did not assist the work, and could not prevent it even
though it wanted to, there is a great deal of weakness in this power that

---

[17] Cf. Iren. I.24.2; Hippol. Haer. VII.28.7.
[18] Isa. 10:15.

wanted to prevent, yet could not. And the band of the angels that the power made must be more powerful than the power, though it is the cause of the angels it has made.'' Hence the sect's case is condemned on every count by incurring (a verdict of) untenability, not of truth.

4,4 ''But if it knew, and yet it had to make these angels who <would> do a wrong thing against its will, it will find itself with one more deficiency.'' To hear Satornilus tell it, nothing in the power on high will turn out to be up to the mark.

4,5 But let us go on questioning him. ''Tell us, Mister, since you squinted through a window—to ridicule your nonsense—and in taking your squint watched while the angels were created, and then observed their artistic <undertaking> aimed at the fashioning of the man, and tracked down the manufacturing operation of the power on high! Did the angels know what they were going to fashion, or were they unaware? But if they were unaware, was anyone making them finish the thing <they had done> in ignorance?''

''No,'' says Satornilus, ''they were not unaware. They knew what they would do.''

4,6 ''Well, did the power on high know that they would attempt this, or was it unaware?''

''It was not unaware.''

''Then did it, or did it not, make them for the purpose of doing this?''

''No,'' says Satornilus, ''it merely made them. But they set out to fashion something against the wishes of the power on high.''

4,7 ''Then, you supreme fool, on your terms the angels knew, but the power on high was unaware. And the preparation of men must (also) be their origin, and the angels who caused this are in the know, but the power that made the angels is in ignorance! (8) But this would be foolish and absurd, that the work is more perfect than the workman, and the workman weaker than the angels he made, since they are responsible for the origin of man. Hence you are altogether obliged to admit that the universe <must> be attributed to the same creator, who is one, and to the single governing principle.

5,1 For in fact it was God the Father, not the angels, who made man and all things by his own consent. Nor has anything come into being by the counsel of the angels. For when God said, ''Let us make man,'' He said, ''in our image,'' not merely ''in an image.''[19] (2) He was inviting his Word and Only-begotten to be co-artificer in his work—as the faithful truthfully conceive, and as the exact truth is. In other, longer works on the subject I have confessed, distinctly and at length, that the Father in-

---

[19] Gen. 1:26.

vited the Son, through whom he made all other things as well, to join him in making the man. (3) And not just the Son—the Holy Spirit too. "By the Word of the Lord were the heavens established, and all the host of them by the Spirit of his mouth."[20] (4) Willingly or even unwillingly, he will be altogether forced to confess—I mean Satornilus will, the founder of this sect—that God is one, God and Lord, creator and artificer of all that is, and of man as well.

5,5   But both in what he says about prophets, and in his cheap accusation against lawful wedlock, he will be altogether exposed as a humbug. Our Lord Jesus Christ himself makes the express pronouncement in the Gospel, and says, with the prophet, "Lo here am I, that speak in the prophets"—and again, "My Father worketh hitherto, and I work."[21] (6) But to show what his Father's work, and his own work, is, he declared it by telling those who asked him if a wife may be divorced for every cause, "How is it written? When God made man, he made them male and female."[22] And again he said, later in the passage, "For this cause shall a man leave his father and his mother and cleave unto his wife, and they twain shall be one flesh,"[23] and immediately added, "That which God hath joined together, let not man put asunder."[24] So the Savior unquestionably teaches that the maker of men is the God of all, but his Father.

5,7   And as to marriage's not being of Satan, but of God. In the first place, the Lord says, "That which God hath joined together, let not man put asunder."[25] Then the holy apostle: "Marriage is honorable and the bed undefiled."[26] And he gives a similar commandment to the real widows, and says through Timothy, "Younger widows refuse; for after they have waxed wanton against Christ, they will marry." And later, "Let them marry, bear children, guide the house"[27]—giving a law which may not be transgressed, since it is from God and has been granted to men with all solemnity.

6,1   And there are any number of things to say about the unfounded suspicions he has raised against God's prophecies, as though they are not from God. As the Only-begotten himself says † when he proclaims that the world is his, first, "Our father Abraham desired to see my day, and

---

[20] Ps. 32:6.
[21] John 5:17.
[22] Matt. 19:4.
[23] Matt. 19:5.
[24] Matt. 19:6.
[25] Matt. 19:6.
[26] Heb. 13:4.
[27] 1 Tim. 5:11;14.

he saw it, and was glad.''[28] And again he says, "Had ye believed Moses, ye would have believed me, for he wrote of me.''[29]

6,2   And what persons of sound mind, and with understanding from God, can fail to fault the cheat, Satornilus, since they know that, when the Savior was revealed in glory in proof of the truth, he showed his glory only between Moses and Elijah—who also appeared with him in their own glory?

6,3   But any number of other things like these, said by the Lord himself and throughout the New Testament, unite Law, prophets, and the whole Old Testament with the New—since they both belong to one God, as he says, "They shall come and recline on the bosoms of Abraham, Isaac and Jacob in the kingdom of heaven, and shall find rest from the east and west,''[30] and so on. (4) And again, the prophecy of him which is given as David's, "The Lord said unto my Lord, sit thou on my right hand.''[31] And again, his own remark to the Pharisees, "Did ye never read, the stone which the builders rejected?''[32] (5) And Luke's affirmation that the Savior himself appeared to Nathanael and Cleopas on the road after the resurrection, and admonished them from the psalms and the prophets that "Thus it behooved Christ to suffer and to rise from the dead the third day.''[33] And there is no discrepancy whatever between Christ's presence in the flesh and the oracles of the prophets.

7,1   But that will do for Satornilus' sect—not to waste time by becoming involved in his foolish controversies and their refutations. (2) Next, moving on from this one, I shall describe the sect of Basilides, Satornilus' fellow-student and fellow-dupe also. These men share < the same doctrines > as though they had borrowed their poison from each other, as in the familiar proverb of "an asp borrowing poison from a viper." For they each belong to the other's school and council, though each stands by himself as founder of his own sect. And they borrowed the wickedness from each other, but initiated the disagreement between them.

7,3   So whether Satornilus obtained venom from the ancients like a viper and has imparted it to Basilides, or whether Basilides imparted it to Satornilus, let us leave their poison behind us, deadly as it is, and coming from such serpents as these—for with the Lord's teaching, as with an antidote, we have weakened it and deprived it of its strength. But let us call on God, beloved, and go on to the next.

---

[28] John 8:56.
[29] John 5:46.
[30] Matt. 8:11.
[31] Ps. 109:1.
[32] Matt. 21:42.
[33] Cf. Luke 24:26.

24.

Against Basilides.[1] *Number four, but twenty-four of the series*

1,1   As I mentioned earlier, Basilides journeyed to Egypt and pursued his studies there. He then went to Prosopitis and Athribitis, and further, to the environs, or "nome," of Saites and Alexandria.

1,2   Egyptians call the neighborhood or environs of each city a "nome." If you have intellectual interests, you may find even this of use to you for love of learning and clarity's sake, as a pious confirmation and explanation of the points in sacred scripture that baffle some because of their inexperience. (3) Whenever you find something about "nomes" of Egyptian cities in the holy prophet Isaiah—such as the "nomes" of Tanis or Memphis, or the "nome" of Bubastis—it means the area around one city or another. And this, for love of learning's sake, is what "nome" means.

1,4   So this scum spent his entire life in these places. They were the original home of his sect which flourishes even today, and which took occasion from his teaching. (5) And he began to preach at far greater length than the charlatan who had been his fellow-student, and whom he had left in Syria—to convince himself that he was making a greater impression on his audience by telling greater things, if you please, and was pleasing and gathering more of a crowd than his colleague, Satornilus. (6) And now, to fob certain imaginary inventions off on us, he begins as follows—though in fact, he did not begin the shocking, deadly things on his own notion; he took occasion from Satornilus, and from Simon whom we refuted earlier. He did handle them differently, though, and gave the mythological descriptions in greater bulk.

1,7[2]   The Unbegotten was one, he says, and it is the only Father of all. Mind has been emitted from this, Reason from Mind, Prudence from Reason, and Power and Wisdom from Prudence. From Power and Wisdom principalities, authorities and angels have been emitted. (8) By these powers and angels a highest first heaven has been made, and other angels[3] have been made by them. Again, the angels they made have created a second heaven, and made angels themselves in their turn. (9) And again, their angels have made a third heaven. And thus, by preparing another heaven and other angels in turn, the angels which go with

---

[1] The source for Sect 24 is clearly Iren. I.24.3-6. There may be some data from Basilidean writings, and Epiphanius' personal knowledge of Egypt contributes to the picture. Other discussions or mentions of the Basilideans occur at Hippol. Haer. VII.28.7; Ps.-Tert. 1.5; Test. Tr. 57,8.

[2] For the paragraph that follows see Iren. Haer. I.24.3. Cf. Ps-Tert. 1.5.

[3] Angels in each firmament are mentioned at GR 11,23.

each heaven have produced a total of 365⁴ heavens, from the highest to ours.

2,1 This might afford fools the temptation to believe his insane nonsense. But for the wise, the way his speech and judgment have perverted his own judgment into something extremely, immeasurably bad, is easy to expose and an absurdity. (2) As though struck with a poetic frenzy, the pathetic excuse for a man decides on names for every archon in the heavens, and to the ruin of his dupes' souls he makes these names known, to win credence from the weak-minded through the names of his fabrication. What is more, the cheat never flagged in his devotion to conjuror's devices and mumbo-jumbo.⁵

2,3 He says that this creation was produced later by the angels of our heaven and the power in it. One of these angels he calls God. And he distinguished him by saying that he alone is God of the Jews, though he counted him in with the angels whose names he coined in the style of mime. By him the man was fashioned.⁶

2,4 The angels, himself included, have parcelled the world out by lot to the angelic host;⁷ but this God of the Jews has drawn the Jewish people. To insult this same almighty Lord however, who alone, and no other, is the true God—for we confess that it is he who is the Father of our Lord Jesus Christ—Basilides, as I have shown, denies him and represents him as one of his so-called angels.

2,5 The Jews have fallen to his lot, and he defends them.⁸ But he is the most self-willed⁹ of all the angels, and he led the children of Israel out of Egypt by the self-will of his own arm,¹⁰ since he was more reckless and self-willed than the others. (6) Hence this God of theirs has decided—because of his willfullness, the charlatan blasphemously says—to subject all the other nations to the stock of Israel, and has instigated wars for this purpose.

Though Basilides is utterly pathetic himself, he does not hesitate to give free rein to his tongue, speak up, and say many other things against the holy God. (7) He says that this is the reason the other nations made war on this one and inflicted many evils on it, the rivalry of the other

---

⁴ The idea is common in Gnostic literature, though the number may be either 365 or 360. Cf. Apocry. John 11,23-25; Eug. 84,1-85,9; Val. Exp. 30,29-38; U 230; 236; 240; 245.

⁵ The Basilideans are accused of employing magic at Iren. I.24.5.

⁶ Cf. Iren. Haer. I.24.4; Ps.-Tert. 1.5.

⁷ Sec Sect 23, note 5.

⁸ For this paragraph and the next cf. Iren. Haer. I.24.4; Ps.-Tert. 1.5. But neither of these sources employs the term αὐθάδης.

⁹ αὐθάδης or αὐθάδεια occur occasionally in Gnostic literature in connection with the wicked archon. Cf. Apocry. John 13,26-28; Let. Pet. 135,21; 136,5; PS 42; 44.

¹⁰ This is a play on βραχίονι ὑψηλῷ at Exod. 6:6.

angels. In provocation—since they felt despised by the God of the Jews—they stirred their own nations up against the nation of Israel, which was under his control.[11] And this is why wars and disorders constantly broke out against them.

3,1   This is the fraud's specious argument. And his opinion of Christ is similarly that he was manifest in appearance (only). He says that since he "appears," he is an "appearance"; but he is not man and has not taken flesh.[12]

3,2   The second author of mime[13] gives us another dramatic piece in his account of the cross of Christ; for he claims that not Jesus, but Simon of Cyrene, has suffered. When the Lord was taken from Jerusalem, as we must conclude from the Gospel, one Simon of Cyrene[14] was compelled to bear the cross. (3) Here he found <an occasion> for his trickery, a way to compose his drama, and he says as follows. As he bore the cross Jesus changed Simon into his own form and himself into Simon, and delivered Simon to crucifixion in his place. (4) During Simon's crucifixion Jesus stood opposite him unseen, laughing at those who were crucifying Simon. But he himself flew off on high once he had delivered Simon to crucifixion, and returned to heaven without suffering. (5) It was Simon himself who was crucified, not Jesus. Jesus, Basilides says, passed through all the powers on his flight to heaven, till he was restored to his own Father. (6) For he is the Father's Son of whom we have spoken, sent to men's aid because of the disorder that the Father saw both in men and in angels.[15] And he is our salvation, he says, who came and revealed this truth to us alone.

3,7   Such are the recitals of the scum's invention. And here moreover—since the uncleanness which began with Simon makes further progress—Basilides allows his pupils the full performance of every kind of base art and licentiousness, and gives his converts thorough instruction in promiscuous intercourse of men with women for an evil purpose.[16] (8) Of them and their kind the apostle says, "The wrath and righteous judgment of God is revealed against those who hold the truth in

---

[11] Each archon has his γένος and ἄξια at Tri. Trac. 100,3-4.

[12] Cf. Ps.-Tert. 1-5.

[13] This renders μιμολόγος; the "first" would be Satornilus. The suggestion that this is a sly allusion to the Second Logos of the Great Seth (CG VII,3) appears improbable, since Epiphanius characteristically emphasizes his humor.

[14] This story appears at Gr. Seth 55,15-56,19, cf., 53,23-26; Iren. I.24.4; Ps.-Tert. 1.5. Other docetic views of the crucifixion appear at I Apoc. Jas. 31,14-22; perhaps at Apoc. Adam 77,9-18; Apoc. Pet. 81,6-83,15; perhaps at Let. Pet. 139,15-25; Man. Ps. 191,4-8; 196,22-26; Acts of John 97-99; 101; 102. Melch. 5,7-8 disputes the docetic view.

[15] The creatures of the demiurge quarrel at Tri. Trac. 80,4-19; 83,34-84,24.

[16] This accusation is probably deduced from Irenaeus' universae libidinis, Iren. I.24.5. The Basilideans are accused of immorality at Clem. Alex. Strom. III.3.3-4.

unrighteousness.''[17] For many fall into the heresy for this reason, luxury—through the unnatural acts they find it possible to do what they please with impunity.

4,1   Again, he gives the permissive teaching that martyrdom is not necessary.[18] There will be no reward for a martyr, since he does not bear witness to the creator of man; he is testifying for the crucified, Simon. (2) Now, how can he have a reward when he dies for Simon, the one who was crucified, while avowing that it is for Christ—of whom he is ignorant—and dying for a person he does not know he is dying for? One must deny then, and not die rashly.

5,1   But Basilides plainly leads a host of devils against souls by teaching them the denial of God, for the Lord himself says, ''Whosoever denieth me before men, him will I deny before my Father which is in heaven.''[19] (2) But the scum says, ''We are the 'men.'[20] The others are all swine and dogs. And this is why he said, 'Cast not thy pearls before swine, neither give that which is holy unto dogs.' ''[21] (3) For he hides his wickedness from people with sense, but discloses it to his own coterie, and to the people he hoodwinks. Since it is in fact a ''shame even to speak''[22] of the things they say and do, Basilides says that the truth must be confessed ''before 'men'—for we are the 'men', but the others are swine and dogs,'' as I said.

5,4   Basilides claims that < they may > not reveal anything at all to anyone about the Father, and about his own mystery, but < must > keep it secret within themselves[23] and reveal it[24] to one out of thousands and two out of ten thousands.[25] He advises his disciples, ''Know all yourself, but let none know you.''[26] (5) When questioned, he and his followers claim that they are no longer Jews and have not yet become Christians, but that they always deny, keep the faith secret within themselves, and tell it to no one. For he suspects his own dishonor because of the unspeakable nature of his obscenity and bad teaching.

---

[17] Rom. 1:18.

[18] Cf. Iren. I.24.4; Clem. Alex. Strom. IV.81.1-3; Eus. H. E. IV.7.7; Orig. Comment. In Matt. 25 Ser. 38. In Nag Hammadi martyrdom is deprecated at Test. Tr. 33,24-34,26; Apoc. Pet. 78,31-79,21; and perhaps at Gr. Seth 49,26-27. But it is strongly urged at Apocry. Jas. 5,9-6,20.

[19] Matt. 10:33.

[20] Cf. Gos. Phil. 80,23-81,14.

[21] Matt. 7:6.

[22] Eph. 5:12.

[23] Cf. Iren. I.24.6; IQ S 9,16-18; Apocry. Jas. 1,18-25; Apocry. John 31,27-31; I Apoc. Jas. 36,13-16; perhaps Allog. 68,31-34; Corp. Herm. XIII.16; Ascl. 32.

[24] The proverb that follows is common in Gnostic literature: so at GT 23; PS 350; GR 304,7-8; 306,33-34; GL 548,6-7; Book of John 49,5-6; 103,2-5.

[25] Iren. I.24.6.

[26] Iren. I.24.6.

6,1   Underlying his poor reason for it was his search for the origin of evil and his statement of what it is. But what anyone is will be shown by his business. Hence these people who love evil and not good are merchants of evil, as the scripture said: "They that seek mischief, it shall come unto them."[27] (2) There never was such a thing as "evil," there has never been a "root of evil," and evil is not a thing. At one time there was no evil, but in anyone who does it, evil exists for a reason, as something extraneous to him. In one who does not do it it does not exist, as stated above. (3) For after making all things the Lord says, "Behold, all things are very good,"[28] proving that evil is not primordial, and did not exist at the beginning before it was begun by men. It comes into being through us, and fails to come into being through us. (4) Therefore, since everyone has the power not to do evil and the power to do it, evil exists when he does, but is non-existent when he does not. So what becomes of the "root of evil," or the substantiality of wickedness?

7,1   Basilides has reached the point of extreme folly with his claim that the power <on high> emitted Mind, that Mind emitted Reason, Reason emitted Prudence, Prudence emitted Power and Wisdom, and that authorities, powers and angels spring from Power and Wisdom.[29] (2) Yet he says that the power and first principle above these is Abrasax,[30] because the sum of the letters of Abrasax is 365—as though he is trying to contrive the evidence for his invention of the 365 heavens from this figure. (3) He even develops topographical descriptions for these heavens with great care, by his practice of dividing and combining them like the mathematicians. For he and his underlings have taken their futile speculations and re-used them in their own style, for the sake of their own delusive, false teaching.

7,4   And they constitute the following of the same figures— "Abrasax" makes 365, as I said—and indicate, if you please, that this is why each year has 365 days. (5) But his silly argument is no good; a year in fact consists of 365 days and three hours. (6) Then, he says, man also has 365 members for this reason, as though one member were assigned to each of the powers.[31] Thus his contrived, spurious teaching

---

[27] Prov. 11:27.

[28] Gen. 1:31.

[29] With the following passage cf. Iren. I.24.7; Hippol. Haer. VIII.26.6; Ps.-Tert. 1.5; Jer. In Amos 3:9-10.

[30] Abrasax occurs at G. Egyp. 52,26; 53,9; 65,1; Apoc. Adam 65,22. The name is common on amulets of the Graeco-Roman period, see Preisendanz, *Papyri Magici Graeci*, Vol. 3.

[31] The members of man are in the image of various powers at U 267-268. The "365 leitourgoi" build man's members at PS 342. Something comparable is found at Apocry. John 15,13-19,10.

fails in this as well; there are 364 members in a man. (8,1) But the blessed Irenaeus, the successor of the apostles, has gone into this in depth and given a marvelous refutation of his stupidity.

8,2 Even so, I intend to refute the nonsense of this Basilides, who has descended from on high after having a good look at what is up there—or rather, who has fallen down, wide of the mark of the truth. (3) For if this heaven was produced by its angels, but they by higher ones and the higher ones by higher still, then the power on high, or Abrasax, will be maker of everything and cause of all that is. And nothing can have been produced apart from it, (4) since they declare it to be the cause and first archetype. And their so-called ''deficiency'' of this world can have been produced by nothing but the first principle and cause of the things that came later.

8,5 But Basilides should be asked, ''Why refer us to such a vast number, Mister, instead of to the first principle—that is, the one God, the almighty?'' For it is altogether certain, either that this is what he means, or that (on his principles), he must admit that the one Cause of all is the Master of all.

8,6 ''And moreover, since you fabricated this work of fiction, give us an answer about Christ! If Simon of Cyrene was crucified, then our salvation has not been secured by Jesus but by Simon. And the world can no longer hope to be saved through Jesus Christ, since he did not suffer for us. For Simon cannot save us either; he is nothing but a man. (7) But meanwhile you also find God's only-begotten Son guilty of false prosecution, if the good God delivered someone else by force to be murdered in his place. (8) And for the rest, a story like this must be a dream—that < the > Lord concealed himself by some trickery and delivered someone else in his place. Or rather, it must be a product of malignity and trickery. And your foolish chatter amounts to a false prosecution of the truth, though it cannot succeed; it stands convicted by the truth itself of the introduction of this fiction without proof.''

9,1 For the truth altogether refutes this heresiarch in the Old and New Testaments. Anyone can see that Christ went to his passion freely, and that he took flesh and became man in our midst by his own will and his Father's, with the Holy Ghost's consent. This though he was perfect God from the first, (2) begotten of the Father without beginning and not in time. But in the last days he consented to enter a Virgin's womb, patterned a body after himself, was truly born and assuredly made man, to suffer for us in the flesh itself, and lay down his life for his own sheep. (3) He refutes the Basilideans by saying, ''Behold, we go up to Jerusalem, and the Son of Man shall be betrayed and put to death, and the third day he shall rise again.''[32] And to the sons of Zebedee he said, ''Are ye able to drink the cup that I shall drink of''[33]—(4) as the apostle Peter also says, ''being put to death in the flesh but quickened by the Spirit,''[34] and again, ''who suffered for us in the flesh.''[35] (5) Again, John says, ''Whoso denieth that Christ is come in the flesh, the same is Antichrist;''[36] but St. Paul says, ''having tasted of death, even the death of the cross''[37]—as Moses also foretold, ''Ye shall see your life hanging on a tree.''[38]

9,6   But Simon is not our life. The Lord is our life, who has suffered for us to end our sufferings, who by dying in the flesh has become the death of death to break death's sting, who descended to the underworld to shatter the unbreakable bars. And having done so, he led the captive souls upwards, and emptied Hades.

10,1   Thus Christ is not responsible for Simon's death—not when he surrendered himself! What do you mean, you utter lunatic? If Christ had not willed to be crucified, could he not have said so frankly and left them? (2) Would the < Son > of God, the divine Word, play a treacherous trick and hand someone else over in his place for death by crucifixion, when he said, ''I am the truth?'' For he says, ''I am the truth and the life.''[39] (3) The life would not prepare a death for someone else, and the truth would not conceal what it was really doing and misrepresent. For the truth cannot be truth if it practices imposture and conceals its own act, but does its business through a device which is the opposite.

10,4   And to say it all practically in a word so as not to prolong the discussion, ''Woe to the world because of offenses'' and ''them that work iniquity!''[40] How many are their own darkness, and darkness for the others after them who trust in their darkness! But the truth will be evident to the wise, while the business of Basilides and his kind will be exposed as a product of imposture.

10,5   And so much for this sect, and this myth; I shall now go on to another heresy. (6) For who can fail to realize that this sort of heresy is a myth and like a horned asp lies buried in sand, but pokes up into the air with its horn, and inflicts death on those who happen on it? (7) However, ''The Lord hath broken the horn of sinners, and the horn of the

---

[32] Matt. 20:18-19.
[33] Matt. 20:22.
[34] 1 Pet. 3:18.
[35] 1 Pet. 4:1.
[36] Cf. 1 John 4:2-3.
[37] Phil. 2:8.
[38] Cf. Deut. 28:66.
[39] John 14:6.
[40] Matt. 18:7 and 7:23.

righteous alone''—which means trust in truth—''shall be exalted.''[41] (8) Therefore, since we have broken Basilides too with the teaching of the truth, let us go on to the sects following, calling on God as our help. To him be glory, honor and worship, forever and ever. Amen.

25.

Against Nicolaitans,[1] number five, but twenty-five of the series

1,1 Nicolaus was one of the seven deacons chosen by the apostles,[2] along with Stephen, the saint and first martyr, Prochorus, Parmenas and the others. (2) Originally from Antioch, he became a proselyte. But after that he got word of the preaching of Christ, joined the disciples himself, and < was > at first ranked among the foremost. He was thus included among the persons chosen at that time to care for the widows. (3) Later, however, the devil entered him and deceived his heart with the same imposture of the ancients whom we have been discussing, so that he was wounded more severely than his immediate predecessors had been.

1,4 He had an attractive wife, and had refrained from intercourse[3] as though in imitation of those whom he saw to be devoted to God. He endured this for a while but in the end could not bear to control his incontinence. Instead, since he wished to return to it like a dog to its vomit, he looked for poor excuses, and invented them in defence of his own state of intemperance. (< Being ashamed and repenting > would have done him more good!) Then, failing of his purpose, he simply began having relations with his wife. (5) But because he was ashamed of his defeat and suspected that he had been found out, he ventured to say, ''Unless one copulates every day, he cannot have eternal life.''

1,6 For he went from one pretense to another. He saw that his wife was unusually beautiful and yet behaved with humility, and he envied her. And because he thought that everyone else was as wanton as he, he began by being offensive to his wife on all occasions, and making slanderous charges against her in speeches.[4] And at length he not only

---

[41] Ps. 74:11.

[1] Sect 25 appears to be based on a variety of sources, though parts of it are traceable to Irenaeus and Eusebius. For discussions of Nicolaus see Iren. I.26.3; Hippol. Haer. VIII.36.3; Ps.-Tert. 1.6; Clem. Alex. Strom. II.25.5-7; Eus. H. E. III.29.2-4; Tert. Praescr. 33.

[2] Cf. Acts 6:5.

[3] A milder form of this story is found at Clem. Alex. Strom. III.26.6 = Eus. H. E. III.29.2. Epiphanius' version might simply be deduced from this.

[4] This would refer to Nicolaus' speech about his wife, mentioned in the passages cited above.

degraded himself to natural sexual activity, but to blasphemous opinion, to the harm that comes of bad habits, and to the imposture of the covert entry of wickedness.

2,1   And then the < founders > of the falsely termed "Knowledge" began their evil growth in the world—I mean the ones called Gnostics and Phibionites, the so-called disciples of Epiphanes, the Stratiotics, Levitics, Borborites and the rest. For to attract his own sect with his own passions, each of these people invented countless ways of doing evil.

2,2   For some of them glorify a Barbelo[5] who they claim is on high in an eighth heaven,[6] and say she has been emitted by the Father. Some say she is the mother of Ialdabaoth,[7] others, the mother of Sabaoth. (3) But her son has ruled the seventh heaven, with a sort of insolence and autocratically. To those beneath him he says, "I am the first and I am the last, and there is none other God beside me."[8] (4) But Barbelo has heard this said, and weeps.[9] And she continually appears to the archons in some beautiful form and, through their climax and ejaculation, takes their seed—to recover her power,[10] if you please, which has been sown in various of them.

2,5   And in this way, for this reason, he slyly brought the world the mystery concealed in his smutty talk. And some of the previous heretics, as I said, used many base arts to teach their followers to engage in promiscuous intercourse with women and unnatural acts of incurable viciousness, it is not right to say how. As the holy apostle says at one point, "It is a shame even to speak of the things that are done of them in secret."[11] (3,1) But if anyone would like to see the Holy Spirit's refutation which corresponds with Nicolaus' sect, he must learn it from the Revelation of St. John. John writes in the Lord's name to one of the churches—that is, to the bishop appointed there with the power of the holy angel at the altar—and says, "One good thing thou hast, that thou hatest the deeds of the Nicolaitans, which I also hate."[12]

---

[5] For Barbelo see Index, *Nag Hammadi Library*.

[6] Cf. Iren. I.30.4.

[7] For the very common Ialdabaoth see Index, *Nag Hammadi Library*.

[8] Cf. Iren. I.30.6. This is one of the commonest Gnostic motifs. Versions of it which include a quotation of Isa. 44:6 or 45:5 occur at Apocry. John 11.18-21; 13.5-9; Nat. Arc. 86,29-31; 94,19-22; Orig. World 103,2-13 cf. 100,29-33; Gos. Egypt. 58,23-59,1; II Apoc. Jas. 56,23-57,1; Gr. Seth 53,27-31; 64,18-31; Tri. Prot. 44,1-2; GR 81,25-82,12; Book of John 28,26-39; Man. Ps. 57,10. Passages whose idea is similar are found at Tri. Trac. 79,12-16; 84,3-6; 100,36-101,5; SJC 118,16-22; I Apoc. Jas. 35,13-17; Para. Shem 2,15-17.

[9] Sophia weeps at the imperfection of her creation Apocry. John 13,30-14,1.

[10] See Sect 21 Note 22.

[11] Eph. 5:12.

[12] Rev. 2:6.

3,2   But others honor a Prunicus;[13] and in turn, to gratify their own passions, they too say in mythological language of this attitude toward disgusting behavior, "We gather the power of Prunicus from our bodies, and through their emissions." That is, <they think they gather> the power of semen and menses. (3) A little later, whenever I undertake to speak of them in particular, I shall describe this precisely—not to dirty the ears of the listeners or readers, but to arouse enmity against these persons in the wise, and prevent the evil deeds from being done. I shall not accuse the guilty parties falsely, but make factual public disclosure of the things they do.

3,4   Others glorify the Ialdabaoth we spoke of and claim, as I said, that he is Barbelo's eldest son. And they say he is to be honored for making many revelations. (5) Hence they fabricate certain books in Ialdabaoth's name, and make up any number of outlandish names for archons—<as> they say—and authorities, which oppose the human soul in every heaven.[14] And in a word, the plot their imposture has evolved against mankind is a sizeable one.

3,6   Others likewise glorify Kaulakau,[15] giving an archon this name, and try hard to make an impression on the innocent through their consternation at the names, and at the pretended foreignness of Kaulakau's. But how can the teachings of their myth and imposture not be exposed at once as <un>warranted by those who have experience, and have received grace from God about every name and subject of his true knowledge?

4,1   For if they say, "Prunicus,"[16] this is just a belch of luxury and incontinence. Anything called "prunicus" suggests something named for copulation, and the enterprise of seduction. (2) For there is a Greek expression which is used of men who deflower slave women, "He wantoned so-and-so." And the Greek swindlers who compose erotica also record the word in myths by saying that beauty is "wanton."

4,3   Furthermore, how can anyone who knows about Kaulakau fail to laugh at it? To sow their imposture in the simple through something imaginary, they transform the good Hebrew expressions, correctly rendered in Greek, <still> clear to those who read Hebrew, and containing nothing obscure, into images, shapes, real principles, practically statuary, on the model of the things their disgraceful, phony craft sows. (4) The word, "Kaulakau," is in Isaiah, and is an expression in the

---

[13] Prunicus appears at Apocry. John BG 2:51,3; Thunder 12,18;19; Gr. Seth 50,25-28, et al.

[14] Cf. Iren. I.24.5-6.

[15] Iren. I.24.6; Hippol. Haer. V.8.4.

[16] I.e., "lewd."

twelfth vision, where it says, "Expect tribulation upon tribulation, hope upon hope, a little more a little more."[17] (5) I shall give the actual Hebrew here in full, word for word as they are written. "Tsav l'tsav, tsav l'tsav," means "tribulation upon tribulation." "Qav l'qav, qav l'qav" means "hope upon hope." "Z'eir sham, z'eir sham" means, "Expect a little more a little more."

4,6   Where does this leave their mythology? Their craving for fantasy? How did the world get these tares? Who made men bring destruction on themselves? (7) For if they knowingly changed the terms into an imaginary thing, they are obviously responsible for their own ruin. But if they ignorantly said what they did not know, nothing is more pathetic than they. For these things are in fact foolish, <as> anyone inspired with understanding can see. (8) For luxury's sake they have destroyed, and are destroying, both themselves and those who trust them.

4,9   For there is a spirit of imposture which moves every fool against the truth with various motions, like breath in a flute. Indeed, the flute itself is a copy of the serpent through which the evil one spoke and deceived Eve. (10) For the flute was prepared for men's deception, on the serpent's model and in imitation of it. And see what the flute-player himself represents; he throws his head back as he plays and bends it forward, he leans right and left like the serpent. (11) For the devil makes these gestures too, in blasphemy of the heavenly host and to destroy earth's creatures utterly while getting the world into his toils, by wreaking havoc right and left on those who trust the imposture, and are charmed by it as by the notes of an instrument.

5,1   Certain others of them imagine new names, and say that there were Darkness, Depth and Water, but that the Spirit in between them formed their boundary.[18] But Darkness was angry and enraged at Spirit, and it sprang up, embraced it,[19] and sired something called Womb.[20] After Womb was born it wanted the Spirit itself. (2) A certain four aeons were emitted from Womb,[21] but fourteen others from the four, and this produced "right" and "left,"[22] darkness and light. (3) Later, after all these, came the emission of an ignoble aeon. It had intercourse with the Womb we spoke of, and by this ignoble aeon and Womb, gods, angels, demons and seven spirits were produced.

---

[17] Isa. 28:10.

[18] Cf. Para. Shem 1,25-28. With this paragraph cf. Ps.-Tert. 1.6.

[19] Cf. Para. Shem 3,4-29; 4,27-31.

[20] Cf. the genesis of Womb at Para. Shem 3,30-4,27. A "womb" is mentioned at Apocry. John 5,5; Prayer of Thanksgiving 64,25-28, and elsewhere in Nag Hammadi.

[21] Cf. Para. Shem 5,6-21.

[22] "Light and darkness, life and death, right and left," Gos. Phil. 53,14-15. "My remaining garments, those on the left and those on the right," Para. Shem 39,12-14.

5,4 But their imposture's mimes are easily detected. After first saying definitely that a "Father" is "one," they later suggested that there are many gods, proving that error itself arms its falsehoods against itself and destroys itself, while the truth always proves completely <consistent>.

6,1 Well, what should I say to you, Nicolaus? What shall I discuss with you? Where have you come from, Mister, with an ignoble aeon for us, a root of wickedness, a fertile Womb, and many gods and demons? (2) In saying, "Though there be so-called gods,"[23] the apostle implies that there are no such things. With the words, "so-called," he showed that they exist in name only—not in reality, but on certain people's notion. (3) "But to us," he says, obviously meaning, "us who are acquainted with the knowledge of the truth," "there is one God."[24] And he did not say, "so-called god," but actual "God." But if there is one God for us, there cannot be many gods.

6,4 And the Lord in the Gospel says, "that they might know thee, the only true God,"[25] to refute the notion of those who say mythical things and believe in polytheism. For our God is one—Father, Son and Holy Spirit, three subsistences, one Lordship, one Godhead, one Praise—and not many gods.

6,5 And on your terms, Nicolaus, where is the fulfillment of the Savior's saying, "There are some eunuchs which were made eunuchs of men, and there are some which were eunuchs from birth, and there be eunuchs which have made themselves eunuchs for the kingdom of heaven's sake?"[26] (6) If there are eunuchs for the kingdom of heaven's sake, why have you deceived yourself and those who trust you, by holding God's truth in unrighteousness with your copulation and unnatural vice, and teaching <licentiousness>?

6,7 And where do you see the fulfillment of, "Concerning virgins I have no commandment of the Lord; but I give my judgment, as one that hath attained mercy, that it is good so to be"?[27] And again, "The virgin careth for the things of the Lord, how she may please the Lord, that she may be holy in body and in spirit."[28] (8) And how much there is to say about purity, continence and celibacy—for you brazenly define the whole of the filth of uncleanness! But by these two or three texts <which I offer> the reader in refutation of the absurd sect, my purpose here is served.

---

[23] 1 Cor. 8:5.
[24] 1 Cor. 8:6.
[25] John 17:3.
[26] Matt. 19:12.
[27] Cf. 1 Cor. 7:25-26.
[28] Cf. 1 Cor. 7:32;34.

7,1   But next I shall proceed to indicate the sect which is closely associated with Nicolaus, like a wood overgrown with grass, a thicket of thorns intertwined in every direction, or a pile of dead trees and scrub in a field, ready for burning—because of <its combination> with this sect of the wretched Nicolaus. (2) <For> as bodies contract infection from other bodies through inoculation, a malignant itch, or leprosy, so the so-called <Gnostics> are partially united with <the Nicolaitans>, since they took their cue from Nicolaus himself and his predecessors—I mean Simon and the others. They are called "Enlightened," but they are entirely despised for the wickedness and obscene behavior in the business of their unclean trade.

7,3   For with the reed that was placed in Christ's hand we have truly struck and destroyed this person as well, who practiced continence for a short while and then abandoned it—like the reptile known as the hydrops, which comes from water to land and returns to water again. Let us move on to the sects following.

26.

Against Gnostics, or Borborites.[1] *Number six, but twenty-six of the series*

1,1   In turn these Gnostics have emerged in the world. They are persons under a different delusion, and they sprout from Nicolaus like fruit from a dunghill, as anyone can see—not merely believers but perhaps unbelievers as well—and observe for a test of truth. For how can speaking of a "Womb" and dirt and the rest not appear ridiculous to everyone, "Greeks and barbarians, wise and unwise?"[2] (2) It is a great misfortune, and practically the worst of hardships, that these despicable, erring founders of the sects come at us and assault us like a swarm of insects, infecting us with diseases, smelly eruptions, and sores through a storyteller's imposture.

1,3   The Gnostics, who are closely associated with this Nicolaus, and in turn are hatched by him like scorpions from an infertile snake's egg or <basilisks> from asps, propose some further names for nonsense to us, and forge books of nonsense. One they call "Noria,"[3] and mix falsehood with truth by their alteration of the Greeks' legendary recital and imagining from the meaning the Greek superstition really has. (4)

---

[1] The literary sources of Sect 26 are unknown; there may be some points of contact with Irenaeus. Epiphanius claims personal experience as his source of information, but also indicates that what he says is in part based on reading.

[2] Rom. 1:14.

[3] CG IX,2 is entitled The Thought of Norea.

For they say that this Noria is Noah's wife.[4] But their aim in calling her Noria is to make their own alteration, with foreign names, of what the Greeks recited in Greek, and thus make an impression on their dupes so that they will translate Pyrrha's name too, and name her Noria. (5) Now since *"nura"* means "fire" in Aramaic, not ancient Hebrew—the ancient Hebrew for "fire" is *"'esh"*—it follows that they are making an ignorant, unskilled use of this name.[5] (6) Noah's wife was neither the Greeks' Pyrrha nor the Gnostics' mythical Noria, but Barthenos.[6] (And for that matter, the Greeks say that the wife of Deucalion was named Pyrrha.)

1,7   Then, once again presenting us with mime like Philistion's, they suggest the reason why Noria was not allowed to join Noah in the ark, though she would often have liked to. The archon who made the world,[7] they say, wanted to destroy her in the flood with all the rest. (8) But they say that she laid siege to the ark and burned it,[8] a first and a second time, and a third. And this is why Noah's own ark took many years to build[9]—it was burned often by Noria.

1,9   For Noah was obedient to the archon, they say, but Noria revealed the powers on high and Barbelo, the scion of the powers—the opposite of the archon, as the other powers are. And she intimated that what has been taken from the Mother on high by the archon who made the world, and the others with him—gods, demons and angels—must be gathered from the power in bodies, through the male and female emissions. (2,1) It is just my miserable luck to report all the blindness of their ignorance. For I could spend a great deal of time if I decide here to put the details into the treatise I have written about them, and describe the strange teachings of their falsely termed "knowledge" one by one.

2,2   Others—these in turn are beaten in various ways, because they strike their faces and receive blows on every side—introduce a Barkabbas[10] as a prophet. And he is worthy of just that name! (3) *"Qabba"* means "fornication" in Aramaic but "murder" in Hebrew—and again, "a quarter of a measure." And to those who know this name in their own languages, a thing like this is matter for jeers and laughter—or

---

[4] Norea or Orea is Seth's sister at Nat. Arc. 91,34 and passim. She is Seth's sister and wife at Iren. I.30.9; Noah's wife at GR 46,4; Dinanukht's at GR 211,36.

[5] Epiphanius apparently connects Norea with "nura" because of the burning of the ark, see below at 1,8.

[6] See Jub. 4.28. At IQ apGn 2,3; 8,12 she is Lamech's wife.

[7] There is a "first archon" at Apocry. John 10,19-20.

[8] This story is found at Nat. Arc. 92,14-17.

[9] The building of the ark takes 100 years at Apocalypse of Paul (James, *Apocryphal New Testament*, p. 553); 300 at GR 409,4-5.

[10] Cf. Eus. H. E. IV.7.7.

rather, it merits anger. (4) But to persuade us to have congress with bodies that perish and lose our heavenly hope, they present us with a shameful narrative by this wonderful "prophet"; and in turn, they are not above reciting the amatory exploits of Aphrodite's whoredom in so many words.

2,5   Others in turn introduce a fictitious, trivial work, a fabrication they have named and claim is a "Gospel of Perfection." And it is a true dirge for perfection, but not a Gospel of it; all the perfection of death is in such devil's sowing.

2,6   Others are not ashamed to speak of a "Gospel of Eve." For they sow <their stunted> crop in her name because, if you please, she got the food of knowledge by a revelation from the serpent which spoke to her. And as, in his inconstant mood, the utterances of a man who is drunk and babbling at random cannot be alike—some are made with laughter but others tearfully—so the cheats' sowing has come up to correspond with every form of evil.

3,1   They base their teachings on foolish visions and testimonies in what they maintain is a Gospel. For they make the following allegation: "I stood upon a lofty mount, and saw a man who was tall, and another, little of stature.[11] And I heard as it were the sound of thunder and drew nigh to hear, and he spake with me and said, I am thou and thou art I, and wheresoever thou art, there am I;[12] and I am sown in all things. And from wheresoever thou wilt gatherest thou me, but in gathering me, thou gatherest thyself."[13] (2) What devil's sowing! How has he managed to divert men's minds, and distract them from the speech of the truth to things that are foolish and untenable? A person with good sense hardly needs to give their refutation from scripture, illustrations or anything else. The villainy of their foolish talk, and their adulterer's trade, are easy for sound reason to see and detect.

3,3   Now in telling these stories and similar ones, those who associate with the Nicolaitans for "knowledge" have lost the truth and have not merely perverted their converts' minds. They have also enslaved their bodies and souls to fornication and promiscuity. They even foul their assembly, if you please, with dirt from promiscuous fornication; and they eat and handle both human flesh and uncleanness. (4) I would not dare to utter the whole of this if I were not under a kind of compulsion, from the excess of my spirit of grief at the futile things they do. For I am ap-

---

[11] Two spirits, a little one and a big one, appear at Dia. Sav. 136,17-23.

[12] Variations of this formula appear at GT 108; PS 231; 232; 233; pap. Oxyr. 1; Acts of John 100; Corp. Herm. V.11. See also Marcus' speech to the woman at Iren. I.13.3.

[13] For this sort of "gathering" see Tri. Trac. 66,24-25; Thunder 16,19-20; Keph. 228,1-14; Man. Ps. 175,19.

palled at the magnitude and depth of evils into which man's enemy, the devil, leads those who put their trust in him, defiling the minds, hearts, hands, mouths, bodies and souls of these persons whom he has trapped in such deep darkness.

3,5 But I am afraid of revealing the whole of this potent poison—like the face of a serpent's basilisk—to the reader's harm rather than his correction. For it does pollute the ears, the blasphemous assembly with its great audacity, its gathering and description of its dirt, the filthy (βορ-βορώδης) ill-will of its scummy obscenity. (6) Thus some actually call them "Borborians." But others call them Koddians—"*qodda*" means "dish" or "bowl" in Aramaic—because no one can eat with them. Food is served to them separately in their defilement, and no one can eat even bread with them because of the pollution. (7) And this is why their fellow alien residents, who consider them distinct from themselves, have named them Kodians. But in Egypt the same people are known as Stratiotics and Phibionites, as I said in part earlier. But some call them Zacchaeans, others, Barbelites.

3,8 In any case, neither will I be able to pass them by; I am forced to speak out. <For> since the sacred Moses writes by the Holy Spirit's inspiration, "Whoso seeth a murder and proclaimeth it not, let such a one be accursed," I cannot pass this great murder, and this great traffic in murder, by without a full disclosure of it. (9) For perhaps, if I reveal this pitfall, like the "pit of destruction,"[14] to the wise, I shall create fear and horror in them, so that they will not only avoid this crooked serpent and basilisk that is in the pit, but stone it too, so that no one will even dare to associate with it. And there is my partial account of them so far, a certain few remarks.

4,1 But I shall pass to the substance of their deadly story—they vary in their wicked teaching of what they please—because in the first place, they hold their wives in common. (2) And if a guest who is of their persuasion arrives, they have a sign that men give women and women give men, the tickling of the palm as they clasp hands in pretended greeting, to show that the visitor is of their religion.

4,3 And now that they know each other from this, the next thing they do is feast—and though they may be poor, they set the table with lavish provisions for eating meat and drinking wine. But then, after a drinking bout and practically filling the boy's veins, they next go crazy for each other. (4) And the husband will withdraw from his wife and tell her—speaking to his own wife!—"Get up, perform the Agape with the brother." And when the wretched couple has made love—and I am truly

---

[14] Cf. Ps. 54:24.

ashamed to mention the vile things they do, for as the holy apostle says, "It is a shame even to speak"[15] of what goes on among them. Still, I shall not be ashamed to say what they are not ashamed to do, to arouse horror by every method in those who hear what obscenities they are prepared to perform. (5) For besides, to extend their blasphemy to heaven after making love in a state of fornication, the woman and man receive the male emission on their own hands. And they stand with their eyes raised heavenward but the filth on their hands, and pray, if you please—(6) the ones called Stratiotics and Gnostics—and offer that stuff on their hands to the actual Father of all, and say, "We offer thee this gift, the body of Christ." (7) And then they eat it[16] and partake of their own dirt, and they say, "This is the body of Christ; and this is the Pascha, because of which our bodies suffer and are made to acknowledge the passion of Christ."

4,8   And so with the woman's emission when she happens to be having her period—they likewise take the unclean menstrual blood they gather from her, and eat it in common. And "This," they say, "is the blood of Christ." (5,1) And thus, when they read, "I saw a tree bearing twelve manner of fruits every year, and he said unto me, This is the tree of life," in apocryphal writings,[17] they interpret this allegorically of the menses.

5,2   But though they copulate they forbid procreation.[18] Their eager pursuit of seduction is for enjoyment, not procreation, since the devil mocks people like these, and makes fun of the creature fashioned by God. (3) They come to climax but absorb the seeds in their dirt—not by implanting them for procreation, but by eating the dirt themselves.

5,4   But even though one of them gets caught and implants the start of the normal emission, and the woman becomes pregnant, let me tell you what more dreadful thing such people venture to do. (5) They extract the fetus at the stage appropriate for their enterprise, take this aborted infant, and cut it up in a trough shaped like a pestle. And they mix honey, pepper, and certain other perfumes and spices with it to keep from getting sick, and then all the revellers in this < herd > of swine and dogs assemble, and each eats a piece of the child with his fingers.[19] (6) And now, after this cannibalism, they pray to God and say, "We were

---

[15] Eph. 5:12.

[16] This practice is mentioned, and sharply condemned at PS 381; 2 Jeu 100. Christians are accused of it by Mandaeans at GR 229,20-22.

[17] Cf. Rev. 22:1-2. Holl argues that Epiphanius here means the Book of Revelation, but Epiphanius does not elsewhere call this an apocryphon. He might, of course, have misunderstood the source of the quotation.

[18] There is a polemic against procreation at Test. Tr. 30,2-4.

[19] Mandaeans accuse Christians of this at GR 228,14-27.

not mocked by the archon of lust, but have gathered the brother's blunder up!'' And this, if you please, is their idea of the ''perfect Passover.''

5,7   And they will do any number of other dreadful things. Again, whenever they go wild for themselves, they soil their own hands with their own ejaculated dirt, get up, and pray stark naked with their hands defiled. The idea is that they <can> obtain ready access to God through such a practice.

5,8   Man and woman, they pamper their bodies night and day, anointing themselves, bathing, feasting, spending their time in whoring and drunkenness. And they curse whoever fasts[20] and say, ''Fasting is wrong; fasting belongs to this archon who made the world. We must take nourishment to make our bodies strong, and able to render their fruit in its season.''

6,1   They use both Old and New Testaments, but renounce the Speaker in the Old Testament.[21] And whenever they find a saying which might be intended against them, they say this is an utterance of the spirit of the world. (2) But if a statement can be given a form resembling their lust—not as the matter is, but in accordance with their deluded minds— they give this a new twist and claim it is spoken of their lust by the Spirit of truth. (3) And this, they claim, is what the Lord said of John, ''What went ye out into the wilderness for to see? A reed shaken with the wind?''[22] John was not perfect, they say; he was inspired by many spirits,[23] like a reed stirred by every wind. (4) And when the spirit of the archon came he would preach Judaism; but when the Holy Spirit came, he would speak of Christ. This also explains, ''He that is least in the Kingdom''[24] <and so on>. ''He said this of us,'' they say, ''because the least of us is greater than John.''

7,1   Such persons are silenced at once by the truth itself. For by the context of each saying the truth will be demonstrated openly, and security will be given for the explanation. (2) If John had worn soft clothing and lived in kings' houses, the saying would be correct of him, and a direct refutation of him. But if <it says>, ''What went ye out for to see? A man clothed in soft raiment?''[25] and John was not such a man, then the accusation in the saying cannot apply to John, who did not wear soft

---

[20] There are polemics against fasting at GT 14; 104; GR 136,12-13; 325,14-17; 34-39 et al.

[21] There is an indictment of the God of the Law at Test. Tr. 45,23-48,26.

[22] Matt. 11:7.

[23] There appear to be two sources, one good and one bad, of Jewish teachings at Tri. Trac. 110,23-113,1.

[24] Matt. 11:11.

[25] Matt. 11:8.

clothing. The reference is to those who expected to find him like that, and who were often flattered insincerely by those who lived indoors, in kings' houses. (3) They thought that when they "went out" they would be praised and congratulated by John as well, for their daily transgressions. (4) But as they had not got (what they expected), they were told the opposite by the Savior: "What did you expect to find? A man borne hither and yon with you by your passions, like people in soft clothing? John is no reed shaken by men's opinions, like a reed swayed at the behest of every wind."

7,5   The Savior did say, "Among them that are born of woman there is none greater than John."[26] And thus as a safeguard for us, lest any should think that John was greater than even the Savior himself—who was also born of woman, of the ever-virgin Mary through the Holy Ghost—he said that he who is "less" than John, meaning in the length of his incarnate life, is greater in the kingdom of heaven. (6) For since the Savior was born six months after John, he clearly < appeared younger > —though he was older than John, for he was always, and is. But who is not clear about this? Thus everything they say is worthless fabrication, good material turned into bad.

8,1   And they too have many books. They exhibit certain "Questions of Mary;" but others proffer many books about the Ialdabaoth we spoke of, and in the name of Seth.[27] They call others "Apocalypses of Adam".[28] And they have ventured to compose other Gospels in the names of the disciples, and are not ashamed to say that our Savior and Lord himself, Jesus Christ, revealed this obscenity. (2) For in the so-called "Greater Questions of Mary"—they have forged "Lesser" ones too—they suggest that he revealed it to her after taking her aside on the mountain, praying, producing a woman from his side, beginning to have intercourse with her, and then partaking of his emission, if you please, to show that "Thus we must do, that we may live." (3) And when Mary was alarmed and fell to the ground, he raised her up and said to her, "O thou of little faith, wherefore didst thou doubt?"[29]

8,4   And they say that this is the meaning of the saying in the Gospel, "If I have told you earthly things and ye believe not, how shall ye believe the heavenly things?"[30] and so with, "When ye see the Son of Man ascending up where he was before"[31]—in other words, when you see the

---

[26] Matt. 11:11.
[27] Cf. the title of CG VII,2, The Second Treatise of the Great Seth, and of CG VII,5, The Three Steles of Seth.
[28] Cf. the title of CG V,5, The Apocalypse of Adam.
[29] Matt. 14:31.
[30] Cf. John 3:12.
[31] John 6:62.

emission partaken of where it came from. (5) And when Christ said, "Except ye eat my flesh and drink my blood,"[32] and the disciples were disturbed and replied, "Who can hear this?"[33] they say the statement was about the dirt. (6) And this is why they were disturbed and fell away; they were not entirely stable yet, they say.

8,7   And by the words, "He shall be like a tree planted by the outgoings of water that will bring forth its fruit in due season,"[34] David means the man's dirt. "By the outgoing of water," and, "that will bring forth his fruit," means the emission at climax. And "Its leaf shall not fall off" means, "We do not allow it to fall to the ground, but eat it ourselves."

9,1   And I am going to omit most of their proof-texts, lest I do more harm than good by making them public—otherwise I would give all their misstatements here in explicit detail. (2) When it says that Rahab put a scarlet thread in her window, this was not scarlet thread, they tell us, but the female organs. And the scarlet thread means the menstrual blood, and "Drink water from your cisterns"[35] means the same.

9,3   They say that the flesh must perish and cannot be raised, but belongs to the archon. (4) But the power in the menses and semen, they say, is soul "which we gather and eat. And whatever we eat—meat, vegetables, bread or anything else—we do creatures a favor by gathering the soul[36] from them all and taking it to the heavens with us." Hence they eat meat of all kinds and say that this is "to show mercy to our race." (5) But they claim that soul is the same, and has been implanted in animals, vermin, fish, snakes, men—and in vegetation, trees, and the products of the soil.[37]

9,6   Those of them who are called Phibionites offer their vile sacrifices of fornication, which I have already mentioned here, in 365[38] names which they themselves have invented for archons, if you please. They thus make fools of their female partners and say, "Lie with me, that I may offer you to the archon." (7) And at each sexual act they pronounce an outlandish name[39] of one of their fictitious archons, and pray, if you please, and say, "I offer this to thee, So-and-so, that thou mayest offer it to So-and-so." But at the next he again proposes a similar offering to another archon, so that he too may offer it to a different one. (8) And

---

[32] John 6:53.

[33] John 6:60.

[34] Ps. 1:3.

[35] Prov. 5:15.

[36] This is a Manichaean idea. Cf. Keph. 191,16-17; 212,10-17; 236,24-27.

[37] A comparable idea occurs at PS 33; 34-35; 336; Keph. 124,3-6; 210,24-25; Man. Hom. 27,11-16; Corp. Herm. X.7.

[38] See Sect 24, note 4.

[39] The powers "each in its own name" Clem. Alex. Strom. III.29.2, cf. Iren. I.31.2.

until he progresses, or rather, regresses, through 365 instances of copulation, he calls on some name at each, and does the same sort of thing.
Then he starts back down through the same series, by performing the
same obscenities and making fools of his female victims. (9) Now when
he reaches a total as great as 730 instances—I mean of unnatural unions
and the names they make up—then, after that, a man of this sort has the
courage to say, ''I am Christ, for I have descended from on high through
the names of the 365 archons!''

10,1   They say that the following are the names of the archons they
consider greatest, though there are many:[40] The archon Iao is in the first
heaven. They say that Saklas,[41] the archon of fornication, is in the second, the archon Seth in the third, and Davides in the fourth. (2) For they
suppose that there is a fourth heaven, and a third—and a fifth, another
heaven, where they locate Eloaeus, also called Adonaeus. Some of them
say that Ialdabaoth is in the sixth heaven, some say Elilaeus. (3) But they
suppose that there is another, seventh heaven, and say that Sabaoth is
in that. But others disagree, and say that Ialdabaoth is in the seventh.

10,4   But in the eighth heaven they put the so-called Barbelo; and the
''Father and Lord of all,'' the same Self-begetter; and another Christ, a
self-engendered one;[42] and our Christ,[43] who descended and revealed this
knowledge to men, and whom they also identify as Jesus. (5) But he is
not ''born of Mary,'' he is ''revealed through Mary.'' And he has not
taken flesh; he is merely an apparition.

10,6   Some say Sabaoth looks like an ass,[44] others, like a pig.[45] This,
they say, is why is why he forbade the Jews to eat pork. But he is the
maker of heaven, earth, the heavens after him, and his own angels. (7)
In departing this world the soul makes its way through these archons, but
no <one> can get through them unless he is perfect in this
''knowledge''—or rather, this contemptibility—and escapes the archons
and authorities because he is ''filled.''[46]

10,8   The archon who holds this world captive looks like a dragon.[47]
He swallows[48] souls that are not in the know, and returns them to the

[40] Similar lists occur at Iren. I.30.5; Orig. C. Cels. VI.31; Apoc. John 11,19-12,33.
[41] For Sakla or Saklas, see Index, *Nag Hammadi Library.*
[42] Christ, the divine Autogenes'' appears at Apocry. John 7,10-11.
[43] ''Jesus the Christ'' is ''like the Savior who is above the eighth'' at Orig. World
105,26-27.
[44] The ass-faced archon occurs, e.g., at Jeu 141; Apocry. John 11,27-28; Orig. C.
Cels. VI.30.
[45] A pig-faced archon occurs at 2 Jeu 101.
[46] ''Filled'' is one of the commonest terms in Gnostic literature. Cf. e.g., Apocry. Jas.
2,19-36; 3,34-37.
[47] The dragon-shaped archon is a Gnostic commonplace Cf. e.g., Apocry. John
11,31-32; Keph. 33,33; 77,33-34; Man. Ps. 57,18.
[48] Cf. GL. 433,36; Book of John 191,4-5; GR 419,17-25; PS 317-319; Dia. Sav.
122,19. Matter is swallowed by the archons at PS 36-38 et al.

world through his phallus, here <to be implanted>⁴⁹ in pigs and other animals, and brought up again by those.

10,9   But, say they, if one becomes privy to this knowledge and gathers himself from the world through the menses and semen, he is detained here no longer; he gets up above these archons. (10) They say that he passes Sabaoth by and—with impudent blasphemy—that he treads on his head. And thus he mounts above him to the height, where the Mother of all living, Barbero or Barbelo, is; and thus the soul is saved.

10,11   The pathetic people also say that Sabaoth has hair like a woman's.[50] They think that the word, Sabaoth, is a sort of archon, not realizing that where scripture says, "Thus saith Lord Sabaoth," it has not given anyone's name, but a term of praise for the Godhead. (12) Translated from Hebrew, "Sabaoth" means "Lord of hosts." Wherever "Sabaoth" occurs in the Old Testament, it means a host; hence Aquila everywhere renders "Adonai Sabaoth" "Lord of armies." (13) But since Gnostics are utterly frantic against their Master they go looking for the one who does not exist, and have lost the one who does. Or rather, they have lost themselves.

11,1   <They perform> countless other actions, and it is a misfortune to speak of their madness in them. Some have nothing to do with women, if you please, but bring themselves to climax with their own hands, receive their own dirt on their hands, and then eat it. (2) For this they cite a quibblingly interpreted text, "These hands sufficed, not only for me, but also for them that were with me"[51]—and again, "Working with your hands, that ye may have to give also to them that need."[52] (3) Thus I believe that the Holy Spirit was moved to anger over these persons in the apostle Jude , I mean in the General Epistle he wrote. ("Jude" is our Jude, the brother of James, and known as the Lord's brother.) For with Jude's voice the Holy Spirit intimated that they are debauched, and debauch like cattle, as he says, "Insofar as they know not, they are guilty of ignorance, and insofar as they know they are debauched, even as brute beasts."[53] (4) For they dispose of their corruption like dogs and pigs. Dogs and pigs, and other animals as well, come to climax in this way and eat the discharge of their bodies.

11,5   For in fact they actually do "defile the flesh while dreaming, despise dominion, and speak evil of dignities. But Michael the archangel, when contending with the devil he disputed about the body of Moses,

---

⁴⁹ Cf. Apocry. John 27,20-21.
⁵⁰ Cf. PS 359.
⁵¹ Acts 20:34.
⁵² Eph. 4:28.
⁵³ Cf. Jude 10.

brought not a railing accusation, but said, The Lord rebuke thee. (6) But these speak evil of things which they naturally know not.''[54] For they blaspheme the holiest of holy things, bestowed on us with sanctification, by turning them into dirt.

11,7   And these are the things they have ventured to say against the apostles, as the blessed Paul also remarks, ''So that some dare <blasphemously to report> of us that we say, Let us do evil that good may come upon us; whose damnation is just.''[55] (8) And how many other texts I could cite against the blasphemers! For these persons who debauch themselves with their own hands—and not just they, but the ones who consort with women too—finally get their fill of promiscuous relations with women and grow ardent for each other, men for men, to correspond with the scripture, ''receiving in themselves the recompense of their error.''[56] For they congratulate each other, once they are completely ruined, on having received the preferred status.[57]

11,9   Moreover they deceive the womenfolk, ''laden with sins and led away with divers lusts,''[58] who put their trust in them, and tell their female victims, ''So-and-so is a virgin.'' And she has been debauched for years, and is being debauched daily! For they never have their fill of copulation; the more indecent one of their men is, the more praiseworthy they consider him. (10) They say that virgins are women who have never gone on to the point of insemination in normal marital relations of the customary kind. They are always having intercourse and committing fornication, but before the pleasure of their union is consummated they push their villainous seducer away and take the dirt we spoke of for food—(11) as though in resemblance to Shelah's wrongful behavior towards Tamar. <They boast of virginity>, but instead of virginity have adopted this profession of being seduced without accepting the union of seduction, and the seminal discharge.

11,12   They blaspheme not only Abraham, Moses, Elijah and the whole choir of prophets, but the God who chose them as well.[59] (12,1) And they have ventured countless other forgeries. They call one book a ''Birth of Mary,'' and make certain dreadful, baneful suggestions in it and say that this is where they find them. (2) On its authority they say that Zacharias was killed in the temple, since he had seen a vision, and though he wanted to report it his mouth was stopped from fright. For at

[54] Jude 8-10.
[55] Rom. 3:8.
[56] Rom. 1:27.
[57] Cf. Hippol. Haer. VI.19.5.
[58] 2 Tim. 3:6.
[59] Cf. Iren. I.30.10-11.

the hour of incense, while he was burning it, he saw a man standing there with the appearance of an ass.[60] (3) And when he emerged intending to say "Woe to you, what are you worshipping?" the man he had seen inside in the temple stopped his mouth, to make him unable to speak. But when his mouth was opened so that he could, he divulged this to them and they killed him; and that is how Zacharias died. (4) This, they say, is why the priest was ordered to wear bells by the law-giver himself.[61] Whenever he went in to officiate, the object of his worship would hear them jangle and hide, so that no one would spy his face, which reflected his form.

12,5 But all their silliness is an easy business to refute, and full of absurdity. If the object of their service were really visible, he could not have been hidden. But if he could really have been hidden, he could not have been visible. (6) And again, we must put it to them differently: If he was visible he was a body, and could not be a spirit. But if he was spirit, he cannot be a visible thing. And since he was not a visible thing, how could he provide for the reduction of his size at the jangling of bells? For since he was by nature invisible, he would not have been seen unless he chose. (7) But even though he was, he could not have appeared of necessity because his nature was conducive to it; it must have been as a favor. He could not have been startled and surprised into manifesting the vision of himself unexpectedly, for want of the sound of bells. And thus their false, spurious story falls apart altogether.

12,8 And they make many other silly statements. <They say Zacharias was killed—and they are right>, though Zacharias was surely not killed immediately. Even after John's birth he was still alive, and prophesied the Lord's advent, and his birth in the flesh of the holy Virgin Mary, through the Holy Spirit. (9) As he says, "And thou, child, shalt be called the prophet of the highest; for thou shalt go before the face of the Lord to prepare his ways.[62] . . . To turn the hearts of the fathers unto the children, and the disobedient to wisdom,"[63] and so on. And how much more there is to say about their lies and pollution!

13,1 The ones they call "Levites" have nothing to do with women, but with each other. And these are their persons of distinction, if you please, and the objects of their praise! But after that they make fun of those who practice asceticism, chastity and celibacy, as having taken the trouble for nothing.

---

[60] Cf. Tac. Hist. V.3-4; Tert. Apol. 16; and see note 44 above.
[61] Cf. Exod. 28:33-34.
[62] Luke 1:76.
[63] Luke 1:17.

13,2   They cite a fictitious Gospel in the name of the holy disciple, Philip,[64] as follows. "The Lord hath shown me what my soul must say on its ascent to heaven, and how it must answer each of the powers on high.[65] 'I have recognized myself,' it saith, 'and gathered myself from every quarter, and have sown no children for the archon. But I have pulled up his roots, and gathered my scattered members, and I know who thou art. For I,' it saith, 'am of those on high.'" And so, they say, it is set free. (3) But if it turns out to have fathered a son, it is detained below until it can take its own children up and restore them to itself.

13,4   And their † silly fictions are so <crude> that they even dare to blaspheme the holy Elijah, and say he was cast back down into the world when he was taken up. (5) For they say that one she-demon came and caught hold of him[66] and said, "Whither goest thou? For I have children of thee, and thou canst not ascend and leave thy children here." And he replied, "Whence hast thou children of me, seeing I lived in continence?" And she answered, "Yea, for when oft, in dreaming dreams, thou wert voided by the discharge usual to bodies, it was I that received the seeds of thee and bare thee sons."[67]

13,6   Those who say this sort of thing are very silly. How can a demon, an invisible spirit with no body, receive anything <from> bodies? But even though she does, and becomes pregnant, she cannot be a spirit, but must be a body. But since she is a body, how can she be invisible and a spirit?

13,7   And their drivel is very illogical. If you please, they cite the text against them, the one from Epistle of Jude, in their own favor instead— where he says, "And they that dream defile the flesh, despise dominion and speak evil of dignities."[68] But blessed Jude, the Lord's brother, did not say this of persons dreaming in body. He goes right on to show that he means persons dreaming <in mind>, who say their words as though they were dreaming, and have not regained the wakefulness of their reasoning powers. (8) (Even of the teachers at Jerusalem in fact, Isaiah says, "They are all dumb dogs, they cannot bark, dreaming on their couches,"[69] and so on.) And here in the Epistle of Jude, Jude shows (that

---

[64] The quotation which follows does not occur in the Nag Hammadi Gospel of Philip.

[65] There are speeches to be made by the soul to the archons at Iren. I.21.5; Orig. C. Cels. VI.31; Apoc. Paul 23,1-28; I Apoc. Jas. 33:11-36,1; Gos. Mary 15,1-17,7. At PS 286-291 the soul says mysteries to the archons, and there is a speech for it at 289; cf. 1 Jeu 84; 2 Jeu 127 et al. See also Apocry. Jas. 8,35-36.

[66] Cf. Gos. Phil. 65,1-66,4.

[67] This folk belief is witnessed to at GR 29,2-4; 50,8-11. Corp. Herm. IX.3 uses it as an image of the mind and its ideas.

[68] Jude 8.

[69] Isa. 56:10.

he means this) by saying, "speaking of that they know not."[70] And he proved that he was not speaking of dreaming while asleep, but was saying of their fictitious bombast and nonsense that it was spoken in their sleep, not with a sound mind.

14,1   It is a real misfortune for me to tell all this; only God can close the abyss of this stench. And I shall leave the spot, praying the all-sovereign God that no one has been trapped in the mud, and no one's mind has absorbed any of the reeking filth. (2) For in the first place the apostle Paul grubs up the entire root of their wickedness with his injunction about younger widows: "Younger widows refuse, for after they have waxed wanton against Christ they will marry; having damnation, because they have cast off their first faith. . . But let them marry, bear children, guide the house."[71] (3) But if the apostle says to have children, while they decline procreation, this is the enterprise of a serpent and of bad teaching. Mastered by the pleasure of fornication they invent excuses for their uncleanness, to tell themselves that their licentiousness fulfills (Paul's commandment.)

14,4   Really these things should not be said, or considered worth recording. They ought to be buried like a foul corpse exuding a pestilent vapor, to protect people from injury even through their sense of hearing. (5) And if a sect like this were a thing of the past and no longer existed, it would be better to bury it and say nothing about it at all. But since it does exist and has practitioners, and your Honors have urged me to speak of all sects, I have had to describe parts of it, in order, in all frankness, not to pass them over, but describe them for the protection of the hearers but the practitioners' banishment. (6) For where can I not find proof of their murders and monstrous deeds, and the devil's rites the idiots have been given by the † inspiration of that same devil?

15,1   For example, they are convicted in the imaginary claim they make about the tree the First Psalm says will "bring forth his fruit in due season, and his leaf shall not fall." For earlier it says, "His delight is in the Law of the Lord, and in his Law will he exercise himself day and night."[72] But Gnostics deny Law and prophets. (2) And if they deny the Lord's Law, together with the Law they also carp at the Speaker in it. They are in covert error and have lost the truth, and neither believe in judgment nor acknowledge resurrection.

15,3   Whatever bodily things they do to glut themselves with pleasure, they reap their fruit through being driven wild by the devil's

---

[70] Cf. Jude 10.
[71] 1 Tim. 5:11;14.
[72] Ps. 1:3;2.

pleasures and lusts—something of which they are altogether and everywhere convicted by the speech of the truth. (4) John says, "If there come any unto you, and bring not this doctrine."[73] Which? "If any confess not that Christ is come in the flesh, this is an antichrist. Even now there are many antichrists"[74]—since those who do not confess that Christ has come in flesh are antichrists.

15,5   Moreover the Savior himself says, "They which shall be accounted worthy of the kingdom of heaven neither marry nor are given in marriage, but are equal unto the angels."[75] (6) And not only that, but to portray plain chastity, and the sanctification of the solitary life, he tells Mary, "Touch me not, for I am not yet ascended to my Father"[76]—proving that chastity has no congress with bodies and no sexual relations.

15,7   And furthermore, in another passage the Holy Spirit says prophetically, both for the ancients and for <the> future generations, "Blessed is the barren that is undefiled, which hath not known the bed sinfully; and the eunuch which with his hand hath wrought no iniquity."[77] That disposes of the indecencies with the hands which are sanctioned by their myth.

16,1   And how much else there is to say! In one passage the apostle says, "He that is unmarried, and the virgin, careth for the things of the Lord, how he may please the Lord"[78]—but he says this to show the real chastity, at the Holy Spirit's direct command. But he then says, of the lawfully married, "Marriage is honorable, and the bed undefiled; but whoremongers and adulterers God will judge."[79] (2) Furthermore he cries out against them in his letter to the Romans, and exposes the obscenities of those who commit the misdeeds by saying, "For even their women did change the natural use into that which is against nature"[80]—and of the males, "men with men working that which is unseemly."[81] (3) Moreover in the Epistle to Timothy he says of them, "In the last days perilous times shall come, for men shall be lovers of pleasure;"[82] and again, "forbidding to marry, havig their consciences seared with an hot iron."[83] (4) For they prevent chaste wedlock and the

---

[73] 2 John 10.
[74] 2 John 7; 1 John 2:18.
[75] Luke 20:35-36.
[76] John 20:17.
[77] Wisd. Sol. 3:13-14.
[78] 1 Cor. 7:32;34.
[79] Heb. 13:4.
[80] Rom. 1:26.
[81] Rom. 1:27.
[82] 2 Tim. 3:1;2;4.
[83] 1 Tim. 4:2-3.

procreation of children, but are on fire in their consciences because they have sexual relations and come to climax, and yet hinder procreation.

16,5 In fact it is already intimated by the prophet, even from the first, that their so-called sacrifice itself, filthy as it is, is snake's flesh and not, heaven forbid, the Lord's—for he says, "Thou brakest the head of the dragon, and gavest him to be meat for the peoples of Ethiopia."[84] (6) For their loathsome worship is truly snake's food, and those who celebrate this rite of Zeus, who is now a daemon but was once a sorcerer, (7) and whom some futilely take for a god, are Ethiopians blackened by sin.

For all the sects have gathered their imposture from Greek mythology, and altered it for themselves by revising it for another and worse purpose. (8) The poets introduce Zeus as having swallowed Wisdom, his own daughter. But no one could swallow a baby—and to poke fun at the disgusting behavior of the Greek gods St. Clement said that Zeus could not have swallowed the baby if he swallowed Wisdom; <the myth of Zeus appears> to mean its own child.[85]

17,1 But what else should I say? Or how shall I get free of this dirty task, when I am both willing and unwilling to speak; when I must speak, lest it appear that I am concealing any of the facts, and yet am afraid that by the awful disclosure I may soil or wound those who are given to pleasures and lusts, or incite them to take too much interest in this? (2) In any case may I, and the whole of the holy catholic church, and any reader of this book, remain unharmed by this sort of devil's sowing and mischief! (3) For if I should start again on their other statements and actions which are like these and as numerous, and still more shocking and † worse—and if I should also decide, for a curative drug, to match a remedy, antidote-fashion, with everything they say—I would make the work of composition very onerous.

17,4 For I happened on this sect myself, beloved, and was actually taught these things in person, out of the mouths of practicing Gnostics. Not only did women under this delusion offer me this line of talk, and divulge this sort of thing to me. With impudent boldness moreover, they tried to seduce me themselves—like that murderous, villainous Egyptian wife of the chief cook—because they wanted me in my youth. (5) But he who stood by the holy Joseph then, stood by me as well. And when, in my unworthiness and inadequacy, I had called on the One who rescued Joseph then, and had been shown mercy and escaped their murderous clutches, I too could sing the hymn to God the all-holy, "Let us sing to

---

[84] Ps. 73:13-14.

[85] Cf. Clem. Hom. IV.16.2. But Epiphanius appears to be using an edition of the Clementine Homilies which differs from the one we know.

the Lord for he is gloriously magnified; horse and rider hath he thrown into the sea.''[86]

17,6   For I was pitied and rescued by my groaning to God, not by a power like that of Joseph's righteousness. Though I was reproached by the baneful women themselves, I for my part laughed to hear women like that whispering to each other, scornfully if you please, ''We cannot save the youngster; we leave him in the hands of the archon to perish!''[87] (7) (For whichever is prettiest displays herself as bait, so that they claim they ''save''—instead of destroy—the suckers through her. And then the plain one gets blamed by the more attractive ones, and they say, ''I am an elect vessel[88] since I am able to save the suckers[89] while you could not!'')

17,8   Now the women who taught this trivial myth were very lovely to look at, but in their wicked minds they had all the devil's ugliness. But the merciful God rescued me from their wickedness, and thus—after reading them and their books, understanding their true intent and not being carried away with them, and after escaping without taking the bait—(9) I lost no time reporting them to the bishops there, and finding out which ones were hidden in the church. < Thus > they were expelled from the city, about eighty persons, and the city was cleared of their tare-like, thorny growth.

18,1   Perhaps someone will commend me if he remembers my earlier promise. I have already indicated that I have met with some of the sects—though I know others from documentary sources, and some from the instruction and testimony of men who were trustworthy and could tell me the truth. So here too, in all frankness, I have not let the opportunity pass, but have shown what this one of the sects which came my way is like. (2) And I can speak plainly of it because of things which I did not do—heaven forbid!—but of which < my knowledge is > accurate because I learned them from people who tried to convert me to this and could not. They lost their hope of my destruction instead, and failed in the plot that they and the devil in them attempted against my poor soul, (3) so that, with the most holy David, I may say that ''Their blows were weapons of babes,''[90] and so on, and, ''Their travail shall return upon their own head, and their wickedness shall fall upon their own pate.''[91]

18,4   As I was preserved and passed them by after my encounter and escape, and after reading, finding out, and observing what they were—

---

[86] Exod. 15:1.

[87] Cf. 1 Jeu 40;42.

[88] ''Precious'' or ''elect'' vessel is found at GR 151,18; 332,6.

[89] ἀπατώμενοι. Epiphanius' ordinary usage is ἠπατημένοι, ''dupes.''

[90] Ps. 63:8.

[91] Ps. 7:17.

so, reader, I urge you in your turn to read, observe <their pernicious preaching>, and pass by, to avoid the poison of these serpents' wickedness. (5) But if you should ever happen on any of this school of snake-like people, may you pick the cudgel the Lord has readied for us right up, the one on which our Lord Christ was nailed. <And> may you hurl it at the serpent's head at once, and say, "Christ has been crucified for us, 'leaving us an example'[92] of salvation. (6) For he would not have been crucified if he had not had flesh. But since he had flesh and was crucified, he crucified our sins. I am held fast by faith in the truth, not carried off by the serpent's false imposture and the seductive whisper of his teaching."

19,1 Now, beloved, after passing this sect by, I shall next tread the other rough tracks—not to walk on them (myself), but to stand off and teach such as are willing to recognize the roughest spots and flee by the narrow, beaten path to eternal life, leaving the road which is broad and roomy, and yet thorny and full of stumbling-blocks—which is miry, and choked with licentiousness and fornication. (2) Something like this fornication and licentiousness may be seen in the particularly dreadful snake the ancients called the "viper with no pangs."

19,3 For the birth of this kind of viper resembles the Gnostics' wickedness. Whether they perform their filthy act with men or women, they still forbid insemination, thus doing away with the procreation God has given his creatures—as the apostle says, "receiving in themselves the recompense of their error which was meet,"[93] and so on. (4) So, we are told, when the viper with no pangs grew amorous, female for male and male for female, they would twine together, and the male would thrust his head in the jaws of the gaping female. But she would bite the male's head of, in passion and so swallow the poison that dripped from its mouth, and conceive a similar pair of snakes, a male and a female, within her. (5) When this pair had come to maturity in her belly and had no way to be born, they would lacerate their mother's side to come to birth—so that both their father and mother perished. This is why they called it the "viper with no pangs;" it has no experience of the pangs of birth. (6) Now this is the most dreadful and fearsome of snakes, since it achieves its own extermination within itself, and receives its dirt by mouth; and this crack-brained sect is like it. And now that we have beaten its head, its body and its offspring here with the wood of life, let us go on to examine the others, calling, for aid, on God, to whom be honor and might forever and ever. Amen.

---

[92] 1 Pet. 2:21.
[93] Rom. 1:27.

27.

Against Carpocratians.[1] *Number seven, but twenty-seven of the series*

1,1 Carpocrates makes another, for he founded his own unlawful school of his falsely named opinion; and his character is the worst of all. (2) (For the sect of what is falsely termed "Knowledge," which called its members Gnostics, arose from all of these—Simon and Menander, Satornilus, Basilides and Nicolaus, Carpocrates himself, and further, because of Valentinus. I have already exhibited one branch, the "Knowledgeable"—though in their behavior they are despicable.)

2,1 Carpocrates says in his turn that there is one first principle on high, and he introduces an unknowable, unnameable Father of all, like the others. But he says that the world, and everything in the world, were produced by angels far inferior to the unknowable Father.[2] For he says they rebelled against the power on high, and hence have made the world.

2,2[3] But he says that Jesus our Lord is begotten of Joseph, just as all men were generated from a man's seed and a woman.[4] He is like anyone else, but is different in life—in prudence, virtue and a life of righteousness. (3) Because he received a more vigorous soul than other men's, and he remembered what it had seen on high when he was on the unknowable Father's carousel,[5] powers were sent to his soul by the Father.[6] (4) These enabled it to recall what it had seen, and gain the power to escape the angels who made the world by progressing through every act there is and everything man can do, even strange, unlawful deeds done in secret. (5) And once Jesus' soul was freed by all the acts, its powers allowed its ascent to the unknowable Father—who had sent it powers from above, enabling it to win through to him on high after progressing through all the acts and being released.

2,6 And what is more, the souls like his < which > pursue the same ends can be freed in the same way and soar aloft to the unknowable Father, once they are finally freed by performing all the acts,[7] < and > similarly finishing with them all.

---

[1] Sect 27 is dependent upon Iren. I.25.1-5, and perhaps upon Hippol. Haer. VII.32, and Eus. H. E. IV.22.5. Cf. Ps-Tert. 3.1; Orig. C. Cels. V.62; Tert. De Anima 23.2; 35.

[2] Iren. I.25.1; Ps.-Tert. 3.1.

[3] The material from this point through 2,11 is taken almost word for word from Iren. I.25.1-2 = Hippol. Haer. VII.32.1-3.

[4] Perhaps cf. Melch. 5,2-3, "they will say of him that he is unbegotten though he has been begotten."

[5] Cf. Plato Phaedrus 347B;D; 348.

[6] Perhaps cf. Gospel of Peter 19, "My power, my power, thou hast forsaken me!"

[7] A comparable viewpoint is taken throughout Pistis Sophia towards the "mysteries" whose learning that document recommends. Cf. PS 239-241; 277-278 et al.

2,7   But though it had been reared in Jewish customs Jesus' soul despised them[8]—and so has received powers enabling it to † overcome the passions which accrue to man as punishments, and rise above the creators of the world. (8) But not only Jesus' soul itself has this capacity; the soul that can progress through † <all> the acts can get past these angels who made the world. It too will <soar aloft>—like Jesus' soul, as I said—if it receives powers and does the same sort of thing.

2,9[9]   Hence these victims of this fraud's deception have become so extremely arrogant that they consider themselves superior even to Jesus. (10) Some say they are better, not than Jesus, but than Peter, Andrew, Paul and the other apostles, because of their superior knowledge and greater progress in the achievement of various ends. Others, however, claim they are no different from our Lord Jesus Christ.[10] (11) For their souls are from the same carousel,[11] have learned to despise everything like Jesus' soul,[12] <and will turn out the same.> <In fact>, they say, all souls have been vouchsafed the same power that Jesus' soul has. And thus, they say, † they too must progress through all activity, as Jesus' soul surely has. Again, if one can despise more fully than Jesus, he will be better than Jesus.

3,1[13]   The members of this unlawful school undertake all sorts of dreadful, pernicious things. They devise magic, and have invented various incantations—love charms and spells—for every purpose. What is more, they summon familiar spirits, to <gain> great power over everyone through the employment of much magic. <Hence>, they say, each of them can be master of anyone he wishes to master, and in any action he ventures to undertake. (2) This is the way they deceive themselves, if you please, to convince their blinded reason that <souls> which have undertaken such things, have prevailed through acts like these, and have despised the angels who made the world, and the things in the world, can escape the jurisdiction of these angelic fabricators—not "creators"—to embrace the freedom on high and gain the flight aloft.[14]

3,3[15]   But they have been prepared by Satan, and put forward as a reproach and stumbling-block for God's holy church. For they have

---

[8] Cf. Test. Tr. 29,26-27, "the defilement of the Law is manifest."

[9] With this paragraph cf. also Tert. De Anima 23.

[10] Cf. Apocry. Jas. 5,1-3; 6,19-20. These passages may, however, refer to likeness to Jesus in martyrdom.

[11] Cf. Apocry. Jas. 10,34-38; Gos. Tr. 41,3-7; Nat. Arc. 96,19-22; GT 49; GR 176,38-177,2 and passim; Keph. 63,14-15.

[12] Cf. Gos. Phil. 64,25-75,2; Corp. Herm. IV.5.

[13] With this paragraph cf. Iren. I.25.2 = Hippol. Haer. VII.32.5.

[14] Cf. Corp. Herm. I.32.

[15] With the next paragraph cf. Iren. I.25.2-3.

adopted the name of "Christian"—but Satan has arranged this so that
the heathen will be scandalized by them, and ignore the benefit of God's
holy church, and its real message, because of their lawlessness and in-
curably wicked deeds. (4) Thus, when the heathen see the things the law-
breakers keep doing, and think the members of God's holy church are
the same, they will ignore God's actual teaching, as I said. Or they may
even see certain (of us) <behaving with such impiety>, and blaspheme
<us> all alike. (5) And so, from fright at the lawlessness of the
wrongdoers, most heathen, wherever they see such people, will not come
near us for conversation, an exchange of views, or to listen to sacred
discourse, and will not give us a hearing.

4,1[16] The constant occupation of these people is dissipation, and doing everything they can for bodily comfort. They never come near us,
except perhaps to catch wavering souls with their bad teaching. They
resemble us only in being proud of a name—to obtain the cover for their
own wickedness by the use of it!

4,2 But in the words of scripture, "Their damnation is just,"[17] as the
holy apostle Paul has said. They will be given the due return for their
evil deeds. (3) By their reckless abandonment of their minds to frenzy
they have surrendered themselves to the sensations of countless
pleasures. For they say that the various things men consider evil are not
evil. They are good by nature—[18] nothing is naturally evil—but they are
regarded as evil by men. (4) And if one does all of these in his one current
incarnation, his soul is not embodied again to make another payment.
By doing every act in one round it will get off scot free, with no more
debt of actions to be performed in the world.

4,5 Again, I am afraid to say what sort of actions, or I might uncover
a trench like a hidden sewer, and some might think that I am to blame
for the surfeit of foul odor. Still, since truth compels me to expose the
deeds of the deluded, I shall make myself speak, with some delicacy and
yet without overstepping the bounds of the truth. (6) The plain fact is
that these people perform everything unspeakable and unlawful, which
is not right to mention, and every kind of homosexual act and carnal intercourse with women, with every member of the body.[19] (7) They perform all magic, sorcery and idolatry, and say that this is the discharge
of their debts in the body, so that they will not be charged with anything
further or required to do anything else—and thus the soul will not be

---

[16] With the next two paragraphs cf. Iren. I.25.3.

[17] Rom. 3:8.

[18] The distinction between worldly "good" and "evil" is deprecated at Gos. Phil.
53,14-23; 66,10-16.

[19] This appears to be deduced from Iren. I.25.4.

turned back after its departure, and come for another incarnation and embodiment.

5,1[20]   The nature of their literature will astound and shock the intelligent reader, and make him doubt that human beings can do such things—not only civilized people like ourselves, but even those who <live with> wild beasts and bestial, brutish men, and all but venture to behave like dogs and swine. (2)[21] For they say they absolutely must make every use of these things, or their souls may depart shy some work, and so be returned to bodies, once more to do what they have failed to. (3) And they say that this is what Jesus meant in the Gospel by the parable, "Agree with thine adversary whiles thou art in the way with him, and do thy diligence to be quit of him, lest at any time the adversary deliver thee to the judge, and the judge deliver thee to the officer, and the officer cast thee into prison. Verily I say unto thee, thou shalt by no means come out thence till thou hast paid the uttermost farthing."[22]

5,4   But they make up a story to explain this parable. They say that the "adversary" in it is one of the angels who have made the world, and that he has been prepared for this very purpose—to bring the souls before the judge when they quit their bodies here and are put on trial there. But if they have not done all their work they are given by the archon to the "officer." (5) The officer is a ministering angel whose service to the judge who made the world is to bring the souls back and bottle them up in different bodies.[23] But they identify the "adversary," whom I said the Lord has mentioned in the Gospel, as one of the angels who made the world, and his name is "Devil."

5,6   For they say that the "prison" is the body, but interpret the "uttermost farthing" as transmigration. <Now> (the soul) <must> finish its "last act" in every incarnation, and not be left behind any more to do some unlawful deed. For they say, as I have indicated, that it must † progress through all, perform them one by one and be liberated, and thus ascend to the Unknowable on high, passing the world's makers and maker by.[24] (7) Again, they say that after doing them all, even if in one incarnation, souls must be set free and go to the heights. But if they do not do them in one, they work gradually through the performance of every unlawful deed in each incarnation, and are then freed.[25]

---

[20] With 5,1 cf. Iren. I.25.4-5.

[21] With 5,2-7 cf. Iren. I.25.4; Tert. De Anima 35.1. With 6-7 cf. Hippol. Haer. VII.32.7.

[22] Matt. 5:25-26. A similar interpretation of this verse appears at Test. Tr. 30,15-17; PS. 294-296.

[23] Reincarnation is treated as a penalty at Apoc. Paul 21,19-21 et al.

[24] The motif is common in Gnosticism, and appears, e.g., at Apocry. John 26,32-27,11; Orig. World 114,23; Interp. Know. 6,30-34; GR 42,18-19.

[25] Cf. Hippol. Haer. VII.32.7.

5,8 They say in turn, "We deign to tell this to the deserving,[26] that they may do the seemingly evil, though it is not evil by nature, and thus learn and be freed." (9) And this school of Carpocrates mark their dupes' right ear-lobes with a burning iron,[27] or using a razor or needle.

6,1 I have now heard in some connection of a dupe of theirs, a Marcellina,[28] who corrupted many people in the time of Anicetus, Bishop of Rome, successor of Pius and the bishops before him. (2)[29] For the bishops at Rome were, first, Peter and Paul, the apostles themselves who were also bishops—then Linus, then Cletus, then Clement, a contemporary of Peter and Paul whom Paul mentions in the Epistle to the Romans. (3) And no one need be surprised that others succeeded the apostles in the episcopate before him, even though he was contemporary with Peter and Paul. (For he too, as their contemporary, belongs to the apostles.) (4) I am not quite clear whether Peter appointed him bishop while they were still alive, and he declined and would not exercise the office—as a piece of advice to someone he says, "I withdraw, I depart, let the people of God be tranquil"[30] in one of his Epistles, as I have found in certain historical works—or whether he was appointed by the bishop, Cletus, after the death of the apostles.

6,5 But even so, others could have been made bishop while the apostles were still alive, I mean Peter and Paul. They often journeyed abroad to preach Christ, but Rome could not be without a bishop. (6) Paul even reached Spain, while Peter made frequent visits to Pontus and Bithynia. But after Clement had been appointed and declined, if this is what happened—I suspect so, but cannot say for certain—he could have been made to resume the episcopate later, after Linus and Cletus had died. (Linus and Cletus were bishops for twelve years each after the death of Saints Peter and Paul in the twelfth year of Nero.).[31]

6,7 In any case, the order of the succession of bishops at Rome[32] is Peter and Paul, Linus and Cletus, Clement, Evaristus, Alexander, Xystus, Telesphorus, Hyginus, Pius, and Anicetus, whom I mentioned above, on the list. And no one need be surprised at my listing the several items with such exactitude; precise information is always given in this way. (8) During Anicetus' episcopate then, as I said, Marcellina appeared at Rome spewing forth the corruption of Carpocrates' teaching,

---

[26] Iren. I.25.5.
[27] Cf. Iren. I.25.6; Hippol. Haer. VII.32.8.
[28] Cf. Iren. I.25.6.
[29] Cf. Iren. III. 3.3; Eus. H. E. V.6.1-2.
[30] 1 Clem. 54.2.
[31] Eus. H. E. II.26.1.
[32] Cf. Iren. III.3.3; Eus. H. E. V.6.1-3.

and destroyed many there by her corruption of them. And that made a beginning of the so-called Gnostics.

6,9[33]   They possess paintings—some, moreover, have images made of gold, silver and other materials—and say that such things are portraits in relief of Jesus, and made by Pontius Pilate! That is, the reliefs are portraits of the actual Jesus during his sojourn among men! (10) They possess images like these in secret, and of certain philosophers besides—Pythagoras, Plato, Aristotle, and the rest—and also place other reliefs of Jesus with these philosophers. And having erected them, they worship them and celebrate heathen mysteries. For once they have set these images up, they then follow the customs of heathen; yet what are < the > customs of the heathen but sacrifices and the rest? (11) They say that salvation is of the soul only, and not of bodies.

7,1   Hence we must refute them with all our might; let no one make light of argument, especially against cheats! But someone might say "Are (these things) not easy to detect, and foolish through and through?" Yes, but even foolish things have a way of convincing the foolish and subverting the wise, failing a mind trained in the truth. Now since Carpocrates too has fallen into the magic of Simon and the others, I shall refute him with the same arguments.

7,2   For if the unknowable, unnameable power was the cause of other angels, either it was ignorant—that is, the Father of all was ignorant—if he did not know what the angels he was preparing would do and was unaware that they would rebel and create things which he did not want created. Or he made them knowing that they would create, but they created what he did not want—and by knowledge and consent he must be maker of the things they have ventured to make. (3) Now if, as I said, he knew what they would make but did not want them to, why would he make the makers to do what he did not want done?

7,4   But if he has made the angels himself, to make what they have, then he wanted it made—this is why he prepared the angelic makers beforehand. And if he prepared them beforehand to create, but forbids what they created, this must be a plain quibble. (5) If, however, he consented to their creating, but chooses to repossess their creation, meaning men and souls, against their wishes, this must be just plain covetousness—if the men < made > by the angels are seized by the One above, against the angels' wishes. Furthermore it must be weakness, since he seizes his creatures' creations because he cannot create for himself.

7,6   And for the rest it is myth and nonsense, the way the ones below can rise above the ones in the middle, while the ones in the middle are

---

[33] Cf. Iren. I.25.6.

punished for being the causes of the ones below—and the ones below, the souls of those in this creation, are brought safely past the ones in the middle to the One above, and set free. And the One above must be adjudged feeble, since he cannot create; but his creatures must be adjudged <powerful>, since they could create the things he did not want created, or wanted to make yet could not.

7,7   For what he desires cannot be bad for him or be produced by bad individuals. If it were bad, it should perish. But if any portion of the product is preserved, the product cannot be bad—even if (only) part of it is worth preserving. Nor can its makers, <those who> executed the part worth preserving, be bad. (8) But if the soul really comes from angels, and receives power from on high after its entry by stealth, then all the more will angels attain salvation—since the soul they produced is saved, though it comes from bad producers! But if it is saved, then neither the soul itself which came from the angels, nor the angels from whom the soul itself came, can be bad. (8,1) But anyone in his right mind must see that this is all (from) folly's scummy workshop.

8,2   But they shall be put to shame again, from their other words as well. For if Jesus is not born of a virgin, Mary, but is begotten of Joseph's seed and the same woman, Mary, and yet Jesus is saved, then those who produced him will also be saved. And if Mary and Joseph are of the demiurge, then they have said that the demiurge is <also> the creator <of Jesus>. And the maker of Mary and Joseph, by whose agency Jesus came from the unknowable Father on high, cannot be defective. (3) But if Jesus too is the product of the angels, and the demiurge is one of the angels, then they will surely all fall foul of the same sort of anomaly that the angels have. And there can be no proof of their dramatic piece, which is full of poison, and crammed with every kind of virulent teaching.

8,4   But since we have repelled this sect once more—like splitting a serpent's head when it is (already lying) on the ground, with a cudgel of faith and truth—let us approach the other beast-like sects <that have appeared in the world> for its ruin. And because of our promise, let us force ourselves to begin <their refutation>.

28.

Against Cerinthians,[1] or Merinthians, Number eight, but twenty-eight of the series

1,1   Cerinthus, the founder of the so-called Cerinthians, has come in turn from this savage stock to present the world with his venom. But al-

---

[1] Sect 28 appears to be drawn from Iren. I.26.1; Acts; 1 Corinthians; and oral sources. Cf. Hippol. Haer, VII.33; Ps.-Tert. 3.2.

most nothing different from Carpocrates gushes forth (from him), just the same poisons to harm mankind.

1,2[2]   For he gives the same libellous account of Christ as Carpocrates, that he originated from Mary and the seed of Joseph; and similarly, that the world was made by angels. (3) In the introduction to his teaching he was no different from Carpocrates before him except in this one point, his partial adherence to Judaism. He, however, claims that the Law and prophets have been given by angels though the law-giver is one of the angels who have made the world.

1,4   Cerinthus moved to Asia and began his preaching there. (5) I have already said how he too preached that the world is not created by the first, supernal power. Also that when "Jesus," the product of Mary and the seed of Joseph, had grown up, "Christ," meaning the Holy Spirit in the form of a dove, came down to him in the Jordan[3] from the God on high, revealing the unknowable Father to him, and to his companions through him.

1,6   And this is the reason he performed works of power; a power had come to him from on high. And yet, at his passion, what had come from above flew away from Jesus to the realms on high.[4] (7) Jesus suffered and was raised again, but the Christ who had come to him from above flew away without suffering. That is, the thing which had descended in the form of a dove; Jesus is not Christ.

2,1   But he too has come to grief, as all you lovers of the truth can see. He claims that the law-giver is not good, but sees fit to obey his Law—obviously because it is a good one. (2) How can the evil one have given the good Law? If it is good not to commit adultery and not to murder, how much more likely that the giver of these commandments is better—if it be granted that he who does not do these things is good! And how can someone who advises what is good, and gives a good Law, be accused of doing evil? The man is crazy, arguing like that!

2,3   But Cerinthus was one of the rabble-rousers in the apostles' time, beloved, when James wrote to Antioch and said, "We know that certain which went out from us have come unto you and troubled you with words, to whom we gave no such commandment."[5] (4) He is also one of those who opposed St. Peter because of his visit to the holy Cornelius, when Cornelius was vouchsafed a vision of an angel and sent for Peter. And Peter was dubious and saw the vision of the sheet and what it held,

---

[2]   With 1,2-3 cf. Ps.-Tert. 3.2; Iren. 1.26.1; Hippol. Haer. VII.33.

[3]   So at PS 129. Comparable ideas occur at Tri. Trac. 125,5-9; Gr. Seth 51,20-34; Tri. Prot. 50,12-15.

[4]   Cf. Apoc. Ad. 77,9-18.

[5]   Acts 15:24.

and was told by the Lord to call nothing common or unclean. (5) And
so, on Peter's return to Jerusalem, Cerinthus stirred the circumcised
public up over him by saying, "He went in to men uncircumcised."[6] (6)
But Cerinthus did this before preaching his message in Asia and falling
into the further pit of his destruction. For, being circumcised himself, he
used circumcision, if you please, as his excuse for contention against the
uncircumcised believers.

3,1   But since the Lord's care for mankind is continual—and since he
safeguards the plain truth in the sons of the truth, and granted the holy
apostle Peter to give the refutation of Cerinthus and his party—
Cerinthus' stupidity became evident. (2) St. Peter said, "I was in the city
of Joppa, and at midday, about the sixth hour, I saw a sheet let down,
knit at the four corners, wherein were all manner of four-footed beasts
and creeping things. And he said unto me, Slay and eat. And I said, Not
so, Lord; for nothing common or unclean hath at any time entered into
my mouth. But the voice answered me again from heaven, What God
hath cleansed, that call not thou common. And, behold, immediately
there were two men already come unto the house, and the Spirit said unto me, Go with them, nothing doubting."[7]

3,3   And, for the rest, he explained how this had been said to him as
a parable and how he had been dubious at the time, till the Lord showed
him concretely what he was teaching him by the words and (visible)
forms. (4) For when Peter reached Caesarea, the instant he opened his
mouth, the Holy Spirit fell upon Cornelius. And seeing that, Peter said,
"Can any man forbid water to these, which have been counted worthy
to receive the Holy Ghost as we were at the beginning?"[8] (5) But this was
wholly a mystery and an act of God's lovingkindness, so that St. Peter,
and everyone, would realize that the salvation of the gentiles is of God,
now of man. God had granted the gift of the Holy Spirit, the vision of
the angel, and the acceptance of Cornelius' prayer, fasting and alms
beforehand, so that the apostles—St. Peter especially, and the other
apostles—would deprive no one truly called by God of what had been entrusted to them.

4,1   But this trouble then was instigated by the false apostle, Cerinthus. Another time too, he and his friends caused an uproar at Jerusalem
itself, when Paul arrived with Titus, and Cerinthus said, "He hath
brought in men uncircumcised with him"—speaking now of Titus—
"and polluted the holy place."[9] (2) And so Paul says, "But neither

---

[6] Acts 11:3.
[7] Acts 11:4-12.
[8] Acts 10:47.
[9] Cf. Acts 21:28.

Titus, who was with me, being a Greek, was compelled to be circumcised. But because of the false brethren, unawares brought in, who came
in privily to spy out our liberty which we have in Christ, to whom we
gave place by subjection not even temporarily."[10] And as a command to
the uncircumcised he said, "Be not circumcised. For if ye be circumcised, Christ shall profit you nothing."[11] (3) Circumcision was a temporary
expedient till the coming of the greater circumcision, the laver of
regeneration. This is plain to everyone, and is shown more clearly by the
words
of the apostles, especially the holy apostle Paul. For he makes the asser-
tion, "To them we gave place by subjection, not even temporarily."[12]

4,4   But to anyone willing to observe the apostles' trouble at that
time, it is amazing how the behavior a spirit of imposture inspired in this
faction betrays the character of those who caused the commotion among
the apostles with these factions. (5) For, as I said, no little disturbance
arose then, when they had rebelled, become false apostles, <and> sent
other false apostles—first to Antioch, as I have said already, and other
places—to say, "Except ye be circumcised and keep the Law of Moses,
ye cannot be saved."[13] (6) And these are the ones the apostle Paul calls
"false apostles, deceitful workers, transforming themselves into apostles
of Christ."[14]

5,1   For they use the Gospel according to Matthew—in part, not in
its entirety, but for the sake of the physical genealogy they do use
it[15]—and they cite the following as a proof-text, arguing from the Gospel,
"'It is enough for the disciple that he be as his master.'[16] (2) What does
this mean? Christ was circumcised; you be circumcised too! Christ lived
by the Law; you do the same." And therefore some of them, as though
succumbing to deadly drugs, are won over by the specious arguments,
for Christ was circumcised. (3) They discount Paul, however, because he
did not obey the circumcised.[17] Moreover they reject him for saying,
"Whosoever of you are justified by the Law, ye are fallen from grace,"[18]
and, "If ye be circumcised, Christ will profit you nothing."[19]

---

[10] Gal. 2:3-5.
[11] Gal. 5:2.
[12] Gal. 2:5.
[13] Acts 15:1.
[14] 2 Cor. 11:13.
[15] Iren. I.26.2 says this of the Ebionites; however, Cerinthus is mentioned in the passage.
[16] Matt. 10:25.
[17] Iren. I.26.2.
[18] Gal. 5:4.
[19] Gal. 5:2.

6,1   Again, fool and teacher of fools that he is, this Cerinthus ventures to maintain that Christ has suffered and been crucified but is not
yet risen,[20] though he will rise at the general resurrection. (2) Now this
position of theirs is untenable—both the words and the thoughts. And
hence, in astonishment at those who did not believe in the coming resurrection, the apostle said, "If the dead rise not, then is Christ not
raised,"[21] "Let us eat and drink, for tomorrow we die,"[22] and, "Be not
deceived; evil communications corrupt good manners."[23] (3) Again, for
those who say that Christ is not risen yet, he similarly adds the refutation,
"If Christ be not raised, our preaching is vain and our faith is vain. And
we also are found false witnesses against God, <because we testified
against God> that he raised up Christ, if so be that he raised him not
up."[24] <For in Corinth too certain persons had emerged to say there is
no resurrection>, as though the apostles were preaching that Christ was
not risen <yet>, while the dead are not raised (at all.)

6,4   For their school was at its very peak in this country, Asia, and
in Galatia moreover. And in these localities I even heard a piece of tradition which said that when some of their people died early without baptism, others would be baptized for them, in their names, to keep them
from being punished for rising unbaptized at the general resurrection,
and becoming subject to the authority that made the world. (5) And the
tradition I heard says that this is why the holy apostle said, "If the dead
rise not at all, why are they baptized for them?"[25] But others explain the
text well by saying that, so long as they are catechumens, the dying are
allowed baptism before the end with this hope, to show that he who has
died will also arise, and therefore needs the baptismal forgiveness of sins.

6,6   Some of these people have preached that Christ is not risen yet,
but will rise with everyone; others, that the dead will not rise at all.[26] (7)
Hence the apostle came forward and gave the refutation of them both,
and the other sects, † about resurrection, with one effort and with the
texts he recited in full to give the sure proof of the resurrection, salvation
and hope of the dead. (8) He said, "This corruptible must put on incorruption, and this mortal must put on immortality,"[27] and again, "Christ
is risen, the first fruits of them that slept,"[28] to refute both sectarian posi-

---

[20] Cf. Melch. 5,9-11.
[21] 1 Cor. 15:16.
[22] 1 Cor. 15:32.
[23] 1 Cor. 15:33.
[24] 1 Cor. 15:14-15.
[25] 1 Cor. 15:29.
[26] Cf. Acts of Paul VII.1.12.
[27] 1 Cor. 15:53.
[28] 1 Cor. 15:20.

tions and thus truly give the uncontaminated message of his teaching to anyone willing to know God's truth and saving doctrine.

7,1   Hence it is perfectly obvious that Cerinthus, with his supporters, is pathetically mistaken and responsible for the ruin of others—the sacred scriptures give us a clear explanation of all this, in detail. (2) For Christ is not the product of Joseph's seed either—how can the child be a "sign" in that case, and what proof can there be of Isaiah's oracle, "The Lord himself shall give you a sign. Behold, the Virgin shall conceive, and bear a son,"[29] and so on? (3) Further, how can the holy Virgin's words to Gabriel, "How shall this be, seeing I know not a man?" be fulfilled—and his answer, "The Holy Ghost shall come upon thee, and the power of the highest shall overshadow thee,"[30] and so on? (4) And once more, how can their stupidity not be exposed when the Gospel plainly says, "Before they came together she was found with child?"[31]

7,5   But it is plain that they did not come together at all. Heaven preserve us from saying so! Otherwise, he would not have arranged to give her to the holy virgin John after the crucifixion, as he says, "Behold thy mother"—and to her, "Behold thy son."[32] (6) He should have entrusted her to her relatives, or to Joseph's sons, if they were his sons by her—I mean James, Joses, Jude and Simon, Joseph's sons by another wife. Joseph had no relations with the Virgin, heaven forbid—after childbearing the Virgin is found inviolate. (7) However, this matter has been treated plainly already, and will be treated (further), in my other discussions. Here I speak of this subject in its turn as though in passing; otherwise, though my aim is to cure other bites and <prepare> a remedy and preventative for other poisons, I may divert the reader to different ones. (8) In any case, to a person of understanding their contemptible teaching will be proved altogether worthless; it is exposed by the apostles, seen for what is by the wise, and rejected by God and his proclamation of the truth.

8,1   But they are called Merinthians too, I am told. I am not sure whether the same Cerinthus was also called Merinthus, or whether someone else named Merinthus was a colleague of his. God knows! (2) I have already said that he was not the only one at Jerusalem who often opposed the apostles; his supporters did too, and in Asia. But it makes no difference whether it was he or whether it was another colleague who supported him, whose views were similar, and who acted with him for the same ends. The badness of their teaching is all of this sort, although they are called both Cerinthians and Merinthians.

---

[29] Isa. 7:14.
[30] Luke 1:34-35.
[31] Matt. 1:18.
[32] John 19:26-27.

8,3   And again we move to the rest, after saying all this about this
dreadful, snake-like wickedness. We give thanks for our safe passage
across the sea of these evil doctrines. But when we encounter the rest—as
though venturing into rough, beast-infested shallows—we pray that we
may not be hurt, but may reach the safe haven of the truth which I shall
present in outline, by contrasting it with the nonsense which is talked
about it.

8,4   For to anyone willing to examine and record the likenesses of
these sects, this one too, from its two names, will seem just like a snake
with two heads—and the viper called the "rot viper." Its whole body is
covered with long red hair, but it has neither the nature nor the hide of
a goat or sheep, but of a snake; and to those who happen on it, it does
a snake's damage with its bite. (5) For the sect sometimes destroys its
adherents by nullifying the New Testament with the old religion; and
sometimes by airing its slanders of the apostles—who were converts from
circumcision to faith in Christ—through false charges supposedly from
the New Testament. But we have struck its rot, poison and fangs, and
thrashed them with the cudgel of the truth; as I said, by the power of God
let us hasten to go on to the rest.

29.

Against Nazoraeans.[1] Number nine, but twenty-nine of the series

1,1   After these come Nazoraeans, who originated at the same time
or even before, or in conjunction with them or after them. In any case
they were their contemporaries. I cannot say more precisely who succeeded whom. For, as I said, these were contemporary with each other,
and had similar notions.

1,2[2]   For this group did not name themselves after Christ or with
Jesus' own name, but "Nazoraeans." (3) However, at that time all
Christians were called Nazoraeans in the same way. They also came to
be called "Jessaeans"[3] for a short while, before the disciples began to be
called Christians at Antioch. (4) But they were called Jessaeans because

---

[1] Sect 29 appears to be Epiphanius' own reconstruction, and at 7,7 he states that this
group was contemporary with himself. However, he certainly made use of Eus. H. E.
II.17.1-24, which reports Philo's account of the Therapeutai. Other discussions or men-
tions of the Nazoraeans occur at Iren. I.26.2; Hippol. Haer. VII.34; Ps.-Tert. 3; Jer.
In Isa.1:12; In Ezek. 16:16; Ep. 112.13.2; Vir. Ill. 3; Orig. C. Cels. II.1; V.61; In
Matt. XVI.12.
[2] With 1,2-3 cf. Eus. H. E. II.17.4.
[3] Perhaps vaguely comparable is the title or invocation, "Ieseus Nazareus
Yessedekeus" which occurs at G. Egypt. 64,10-11, Zost. 46,5-6, and elsewhere in Nag
Hammadi.

of Jesse, I suppose, since David was descended from Jesse, but Mary from David's line. This was in fulfillment of sacred scripture, for in the Old Testament the Lord tells David, "Of the fruit of thy belly shall I set upon thy throne."[4]

2,1   At each topic of discussion I am afraid <of making its treatment very long>. I <therefore> give this †sketch† in brief—though the truth makes me anxious to give some indication of the subjects (that arise) in the discussion itself—so as not to cover too much ground in composing the narrative. (2) Since the Lord has told David, "Of the fruit of thy belly shall I set upon the throne," and, "The Lord sware unto David and will not repent,"[5] it is plain that God's promise is an irreversible one. (3) In the first place, what does God have to swear by but "By myself have I sworn, saith the Lord?"[6]—for "God hath no oath by a greater."[7] What is divine does not even swear; yet the statement has the function of providing confirmation.

For God swore with an oath to David that he would set the fruit of his belly upon his throne. (4) And the apostles bear witness that Christ had to be born of David's seed, as our Lord and Savior Jesus Christ indeed was. As I said, I shall pass over most of the testimonies, to avoid a very burdensome discussion.

2,5   But someone will probably say, "Since Christ was physically born of David's seed, that is, of the Holy Virgin Mary, why is he not sitting on David's throne? For the Gospel says, 'They came that they might anoint him king, and when Jesus perceived this he departed…and hid himself in Ephraim, a city of the wilderness.'"[8] (6) But now that I reach the place for this, and I am asked about this text, and why it is that the prophecy about sitting on David's throne has not been fulfilled physically in the Savior's case—for some have thought that it has not—I shall still say that it is a fact. Not a word of God's holy scripture can come to nothing.

3,1   David's throne and kingly seat is the priesthood in the holy church. The Lord has combined this rank, which is both that of king and high priest, and conferred it on his holy church by transferring David's throne to it, never to fail. (2) Formerly David's throne continued by succession until Christ himself, since the rulers from Judah did not fail until he came "for whom are the things prepared, and he is the expectation of the nations,"[9] <as> scripture says.

---

[4] Ps. 131:11.
[5] Ps. 109:4.
[6] Gen. 22:16.
[7] Cf. Heb. 6:13.
[8] Cf. John 6:15; 11:54.
[9] Gen. 49:10.

3,3   For at Christ's arrival the rulers in succession from Judah came
to an end. Until his time <the> rulers <were anointed priests>,[10] but
after his birth in Bethlehem of Judaea the order ended and †changed with
Alexander, a ruler of priestly and kingly stock.[11] (4) After Alexander this
heritage from the time of Salina—also known as Alexandra—died out
under King Herod and the Roman Emperor Augustus.[12] (Though Alexander was crowned also, since he was one of the anointed priests and
rulers.[13] (5) For with the union of the two tribes, the kingly and
priestly—I mean Judah's and Aaron's and the whole tribe of Levi—kings
also became priests; nothing based on a hint in holy scripture can be
wrong.) (6) But then finally a gentile, King Herod, was crowned, and not
David's descendants any more.

3,7   But because of the change in the royal throne, the rank of king
passed, in Christ, from the physical house of David and Israel to the
church. The throne is established in God's holy church forever, and has
both the ranks of king and high-priest for two reasons. (8) The rank of
king from our Lord Jesus Christ, also in two ways: because he is descended from King David physically, and because, in Godhead, he is in fact
a greater king from all eternity. But the rank of priest because Christ is
high priest and chief of high priests—(9) since James, called the brother
and apostle of the Lord, was made the first bishop immediately. Actually
he was Joseph's son, but was said to be in the position of the Lord's
brother because they were reared together.

4,1   For James was Joseph's son by Joseph's <first> wife, not
Mary, as I have said, and discussed with greater clarity, in many other
places. (2) And moreover I find that he was of Davidic descent because
he was Joseph's son, <and> that he was born a nazirite—for he was
Joseph's first-born, and hence consecrated.[14] But I find further that he
also functioned as a priest in the ancient priesthood. (3) For this reason
he was permitted to enter the Holy of Holies once a year, as scripture
says the Law commanded the high priests. For many before me—
Eusebius, Clement and others—have reported this of him. (4) He was allowed to wear the priestly mitre[15] besides, as the trustworthy persons
mentioned have testified in the same historical writings.

4,5   Now as I said, our Lord Jesus Christ is "priest forever after the
order of Melchizedek,"[16] and at the same time king after the order on

---

[10] Cf. Jer. Chron. 160,16-17 (Helm).
[11] Cf. Eus. Chron. 61,12-14 (Karst); Jer. Chron. 148,6-8 (Helm).
[12] Cf. Eus. Chron. 61,17 (Karst); Jer. Chron. 152,11-12 (Helm).
[13] Another version of this occurs at Jer. Chron. 148,11-14 (Helm).
[14] Eus. H. E. II.23.4-6. Eusebius mentions the Clementine report of James' death at
H. E. II.23.3.
[15] This is said of John at Eus. H. E. III.31.3.
[16] Heb. 5:6.

high, and so may transfer the priesthood with its legal charter. (6) But since David's seed through Mary is seated on a throne, <his throne endures> forever, and of his kingdom there will be no end. He would need now to reposition the former crown; for his kingdom is not earthly, as he said to Pontius Pilate in the Gospel, "My Kingdom is not of this world."[17] (7) For since Christ fulfills all that was said in riddles, the beginnings have reached a limit.

For he who is always king did not come to achieve sovereignty. Lest it be thought that he advanced from a lower estate to a higher, he granted the crown to those whom he appointed. (8) For his throne endures, and there will be no end of his kingdom. And he sits on the throne of David, and has transferred David's crown and granted it, with the high priesthood, to his own servants, the high priests of the catholic church.

4,9   And there is much to say about this. However, since I have come to the reason why those who came to faith in Christ were called Jessaeans before they were called Christians, I have said that Jesse was the father of David. And they had been named Jessaeans, either because of this Jesse; or from the name or our Lord Jesus since, as his disciples, they were derived from Jesus; or because of the etymology of the Lord's name. For in Hebrew Jesus means "healer" or "physician," and "savior." (10) In any case, they had acquired this additional name before they were called Christians. But at Antioch, as I have mentioned before and as is the essence of the truth, the disciples and the whole church of God began to be called Christians.

5,1[18]   If you enjoy study and have read about them in Philo's historical writings, in his book entitled "Jessaeans," you may discover that, in his account of their way of life and hymns, and his description of their monasteries in the vicinity of the Marean marsh, Philo described none other than Christians. (2) For he was edified by his visit to the area—the place is called Mareotis—and his entertainment at their monasteries in the region. (3)[19] He arrived during Passover and observed their customs, and how some of them kept the holy week of Passover (only) after a postponement of it, but others by eating every other day—though others, indeed, ate each evening. But Philo wrote all this of the faith and regimen of the Christians.

5,4   So in that brief period when they were called Jessaeans—after the Savior's ascension, and after Mark had preached in Egypt—certain other persons seceded,[20] though they were followers of the apostles if you

---

[17] John 18:36.
[18] 5,1-2 is based on Eus. H. E. II.17.1-24.
[19] 5,3 is based on Eus. H. E. II.17.16-18, combined with II.17.21-22.
[20] Eus. H. E. II.16.1; 17.2.

please. I mean the Nazoraeans, whom I am presenting here. They were Jewish, were attached to the Law, and had circumcision. (5) But it was as though people had seen fire under a misapprehension. Not understanding why, or for <what> use, the ones who had kindled this fire were doing it—either to cook their rations with the fire, or burn some dead trees and brush, which are ordinarily destroyed by fire—they kindled fire too, in imitation, and set themselves ablaze.

5,6   For by hearing just the name of Jesus, and seeing the miracles the apostles performed, they came to faith in Jesus themselves. But they found that he had been conceived at Nazareth and brought up in Joseph's home, and for this reason is called "Jesus the Nazoraean"[21] in the Gospel as the apostles say, "Jesus the Nazoraean, a man approved by signs and wonders,"[22] and so on. Hence they adopted this name, so as to be called Nazoreans.

5,7   Not "nazirites"—that means "consecrated persons." Anciently this rank belonged to firstborn sons and men dedicated to God. Samson was one, and others after him, and many before. Moreover, John the Baptist too was one of these persons consecrated to God, for "He drank neither wine nor strong drink."[23] (This regimen, befitting their rank, was prescribed for persons of that sort.) (6,1) They did not call themselves Nasaraeans either; the Nasaraean sect was before Christ, and did not know Christ.

6,2   But besides, as I indicated, everyone called the Christians Nazoraeans, as they say in accusing the apostle Paul, "We have found this man a pestilent fellow and a perverter of the people, a ring-leader of the sect of the Nazoraeans."[24] (3) And the holy apostle did not disclaim the name—not to profess the Nazoraean sect, but he was glad to own the name his adversaries' malice had applied to him for Christ's sake. (4) For he says in court, "They neither found me in the temple disputing with any man, neither raising up the people, nor have I done any of those things whereof they accuse me. But this I confess unto thee, that after the way which they call heresy, so worship I, believing all things in the Law and the prophets."[25]

6,5   And no wonder the apostle admitted to being a Nazoraean! In those days everyone called Christians this because of the city of

---

[21] At Gos. Phil. 62,7-17 "Nazarene" is explained as Jesus' middle name, meaning, "the truth." A different explanation occurs at Gos. Phil. 56,12-13, "The Nazarene is he who reveals what is hidden."

[22] Acts 2:22.

[23] Luke 1:15.

[24] Acts 24:5.

[25] Acts 24:12-14.

Nazareth—there was no other usage of the name then. People thus gave the name of < "Nazoraeans" > to believers in Christ, of whom it is written, "He shall be called a Nazoraean." [26] (6) Even today in fact, people call all the sects, I mean Manichaeans, Marcionites, Gnostics and others, by the common name of "Christians," though they are not Christians. However, although each sect has another name, it still allows this one with pleasure, since it is honored by the name. For they think they can preen themselves on Christ's name; not on faith and works!

6,7 Thus Christ's holy disciples called themselves "disciples of Jesus" then, as indeed they were. But they were not rude when others called them Nazoraeans, since they saw the intent of those who called them this. They did it because of Christ, since our Lord Jesus was called " <the> Nazoraean" himself—so say the Gospels and the Acts of the Apostles—(8) because of his upbringing in Joseph's home in the city of Nazareth, which is now a village. (Though he was born in the flesh at Bethlehem, of the ever-virgin Mary, Joseph's betrothed. Joseph had settled in Nazareth after leaving Bethlehem and taking up residence in Galilee.)

7,1 But these sectarians whom I am now sketching disregarded the name of Jesus, and did not call themselves Jessaeans, keep the name of Jews, or term themselves Christians—but "Nazoraeans," from the place-name, "Nazareth," if you please! However they are simply complete Jews.

7,2 They use not only the New Testament but the Old Testament as well, as the Jews do. For unlike the previous sectarians, they do not repudiate the legislation, the prophets, and the books Jews call "Writings." They have no different ideas, but confess everything exactly as the Law proclaims it and in the Jewish fashion—except for their belief in Christ, if you please! (3) For they acknowledge both the resurrection of the dead and the divine creation of all things,[27] and declare that God is one, and that his Son is Jesus Christ.

7,4 They are trained to a nicety in Hebrew. For among them the entire Law, the prophets, and the so-called Writings—I mean the poetic books, Kings, Chronicles, Esther and all the rest—are read in Hebrew, as they surely are by Jews. (5) They are different from Jews, and different from Christians, only in the following. They disagree with Jews because they have come to faith in Christ; but since they are still fettered by the Law—circumcision, the Sabbath, and the rest[28]—they are not in

---

[26] Matt. 2:23.

[27] This is said of the Ebionites at Iren. I.26.2. Cf. Hippol. Haer. VII.34.1; Ps.-Tert. 3.

[28] Cf. Iren. I.26.2 (of the Ebionites); Eus. H. E. III.27.5.

accord with Christians. (6)[29] As to Christ, I cannot say whether they too are captives of the wickedness of Cerinthus and Merinthus, and regard him as a mere man—or whether, as the truth is, they affirm his birth of Mary by the Holy Spirit.

7,7   Today this sect of the Nazoraeans is found in Beroea[30] near Coelesyria, in the Decapolis near Pella, and in Bashanitis at the place called Cocabe[31]—Khokhabe in Hebrew. (8) For that was its place of origin, since all the disciples had settled in Pella after they left Jerusalem—Christ told them to abandon Jerusalem and withdraw from it[32] because of its coming siege. And they settled in Peraea for this reason and, as I said, spent their lives there. That was where the Nazoraean sect began.

8,1   But they too are wrong to boast of circumcision, and persons like themselves are still "under a curse,"[33] since they cannot fulfil the Law. For how can they fulfil the Law's provision, "Thrice a year thou shalt appear before the Lord thy God, at the feasts of Unleavened Bread, Tabernacles and Pentecost,"[34] on the site of Jerusalem? (2) As the site is closed off,[35] and the Law's provisions cannot be fulfilled, anyone with sense can see that Christ came to be the Law's fulfiller—not to destroy the Law, but to fulfill the Law—and to lift the curse that had been put on transgression of the Law. (3) For after Moses had given every commandment he came to the point of the book and "included the whole in a curse"[36] with the words, "Cursed is he that continueth not in all the words that are written in this book to do them."[37]

8,4   Hence Christ came to free what had been fettered with the bonds of the curse. In place of the lesser commandments which cannot be fulfilled, he granted us the greater, which are not inconsistent with the completion of the task as the earlier ones were. (5) For I have discussed this many times before, in every Sect, in connection with the Sabbath, circumcision and the rest—how the Lord has granted something more perfect to us.

---

[29] Iren. I.26.1-2 differentiates Ebionite Christology from Cerinthian, but in Harvey's opinion the Latin text here has been faultily transmitted. This raises the question of Epiphanius' text of Irenaeus. With Irenaeus' reading compare and contrast Hippol. Haer. VII.34.1; Eus. H. E. III.27.3; Jer. Ep. 112.13.2; Orig. C. Cels. V.61; In Matt. XVI.12.
[30] Cf. Jer. Vir. I11.3.
[31] Cf. Eus. H. E. I.7.14; Onom. 172,1-3.
[32] Cf. Eus. H. E. III.5.3.
[33] Gal. 3:10.
[34] Cf. Exod. 23:14-17.
[35] Cf. Justin Apol. I.47.
[36] Cf. Ga. 3:22.
[37] Gal. 3:10 and Deut. 27:26.

8,6   But how can people like these defend their disobedience of the Holy Spirit, who has told gentile converts, through the apostles, "Assume no burden save the necessary things, that ye abstain from blood, and from things strangled, and fornication, and from meats offered to idols?"[38] (7) And how can they fail to lose the grace of God, when the holy apostle Paul says, "If ye be circumcised, Christ shall profit you nothing...whosoever of you do glory in the Law are fallen from grace?"[39]

9,1   In this Sect too, my brief discussion will be enough. People like these are refutable at once and easy to cure—or rather, they are nothing but Jews themselves. (2) Yet these are very much the Jews' enemies. Not only do Jewish people have a hatred of them; they even stand up at dawn, at midday, and toward evening, three times a day when they recite their prayers in the synagogues, and curse and anathematize them. Three times a day they say, "God curse the Nazoraeans."[40] (3) For they harbor an extra grudge against them, if you please, because despite their Jewishness, they preach that Jesus is <the> Christ—the opposite of those who are still Jews, for they have not accepted Jesus.

9,4   They have the Gospel according to Matthew in its entirety in Hebrew.[41] For it is clear that they still preserve this, in the Hebrew alphabet, as it was originally written. But I do not know whether they have removed just the genealogies from Abraham to Christ.

9,5   But now that we have also detected this sect—like an insect that is small, yet still causes pain with its poison—and have squashed it with the words of the truth, let us pray for help from God, beloved, and go to the next.

30.

Against Ebionites.[1] Number ten, but thirty of the series

1,1   Following these and holding the same views, Ebion,[2] the Ebionites' founder, emerged in his turn—a monstrosity with many

---

[38] Acts 15:28-29.

[39] Gal. 5:2-4.

[40] This is an old variant of the birkhath ha-minim in the Jewish liturgical Eighteen Benediction. Cf. Justin Dial. 16;47; Jer. in Isa. 5:18-19.

[41] Cf. Eus. H. E. III.24.6; 39.16; V.10.3; Theophania IV.12; Jer. Vir. I11. 3; C. Pelag. III.2. The Ebionites are said to use the Gospel according to Matthew and none other at Iren. I.26.2; Eus. H. E. III.27.4.

[1] Sect 30 has points of contact with Eusebius, the pseudo-Clementines, and other literature, but its literary sources are not apparent. It may be based on oral sources, and contain some of Epiphanius' personal reminiscences. Certainly Josephus' story is presented as such. For other notices of Ebionites see Iren. I.26.2; Eus. H. E. III.27.1-2; Jer. Ep. 112.13.1-2; In Isa. 1:12; In Matt. 12:2; Orig. C. Cels. V.61; in Matt. XVI.12.

[2] "Ebion" is presented as the founder of the Ebionites at Hippol. Haer. VII.35.1; Ps.-

shapes, who practically formed the snake-like shape of the mythical many-headed hydra in himself. He was of the Nazoraeans' school, but preached and taught differently from them.

1,2   For it was as though a person were to collect a set of jewelry from various precious stones, and a garment from clothing of many colors, and dress up to be conspicuous. Ebion, in reverse, took any item of preaching from every sect if it was dreadful, lethal and disgusting, if it was ugly and unconvincing, if it was full of †contention, and patterned himself after them all. (3) For he has the Samaritans' repulsiveness but the Jews' name, the viewpoint of the Ossaeans, Nazoraeans and Nasaraeans, the nature of the Cerinthians, and the badness of the Carpocratians. And he has the Christians' name alone—most certainly not their behaviour, viewpoint and knowledge, and the Gospels' and apostles' agreement as to faith!

1,4   But since he is practically midway between all the sects, he is nothing. The words of scripture, "I was almost in all evil, in the midst of the church and synagogue,"[3] are fulfilled in him. (5) For he is Samaritan, but rejects the name with disgust. And while professing to be a Jew, he is the opposite of Jews—though he does agree with them in part. I shall prove this later with God's help, through the proofs of it in my rebuttal of them.

2,1   For Ebion was contemporary with the Nazoraeans and, <since he was> their ally, was derived from them. (2) In the first place, he said that Christ was generated by sexual intercourse and the seed of a man, Joseph[4]—I have already said that he agreed with the others in everything, with this one difference, his attachment to Judaism's Law of the Sabbath, circumcision, and all other Jewish and Samaritan observances. (3) But like the Samaritans he goes still further than the Jews. He added the rule about care in touching a gentile,[5] (4) and that a man must immerse himself in water every day he has been with a woman,[6] after he leaves her—any water he can find, the sea or other. (5) Moreover, if he meets anyone while returning from his plunge and immersion in the water, he runs back again for another immersion, often with his clothes on too![7]

Tert. 3; Jer. Adv. Lucif. 23; Doctr. Pat. 41; Tert. De Carn. Chr. 14; 18; 24; De Virg. Vel. 6; Praescr. 10; 33.

[3] Prov. 5:14.

[4] Cf. Eus. H. E. III.27.2; Orig. in Matt. 16:12.

[5] At Jos. Bel. II.119 Essenes are said to wash after touching foreigners. Cf. the Essene rules against contact with gentiles at IQ S 5,11-20; CD 12,6-11; 13,14-15. At Clem. Hom. XIII.4 it is said that Christians do not eat at a gentile table.

[6] Cf. Lev. 15:18; GR 16,21-22; Book of John 92,18-19 et al. The rule is given as a Christian one at Clem. Hom. VII.8.2.

[7] Cf. Hippol. Haer. IX.15.4;5.

2,6   At present this sect repudiates celibacy and continence altogether,[8] like the others of its kind. For they once took pride in virginity because of James the Lord's brother, if you please, < and so > address their treatises to "elders and virgins."

2,7   They got their start after the fall of Jerusalem. For since practically all who had come to faith in Christ had settled in Peraea then, in Pella, a town in the "Decapolis"[9] the Gospel mentions, which is near Batanaea and Bashanitis—as they had moved there then and were living there, this provided an occasion for Ebion. (8) And as far as I know, he first lived in a village called Cocabe in the district of Qarnaim—also called Ashtaroth—in Bashanitis. There he began his bad teaching—the same place, if you please, as the Nazoraeans whom I have mentioned already. (9) For since Ebion was connected with them and they with him, each party shared its own wickedness with the other. Each also differed from the other to some extent, but they copied each other in malice. But I have already spoken at length, both in other works and the other Sects, about the locations of Cocabe and Arabia.

3,1   And originally, as I said, Ebion declared that Christ is begotten of the seed of a man, Joseph. Beginning later, however, various of his followers gave conflicting accounts of Christ, as though they were bent on the untenable and impossible. (2) But I think the reason may be that because Elxai—the false prophet < I mentioned earlier > in the tracts called "Sampsaeans," "Ossenes" and "Elkasaites"—was connected with them, they give some imaginary description of Christ and the Holy Spirit as he did.

3,3[10]   For some of them even say that Adam is Christ—the man who was formed first and infused with God's breath.[11] (4) But others among them say that Christ is from above; that he was created before all things; that he is a spirit, higher than the angels and ruler of all; that he is called Christ, and the world there is his portion.[12] (5) But he comes here when he chooses,[13] as he came in Adam and appeared to the patriarchs[14] with Adam's body on. And in the last days the same Christ who had come to Abraham,[15] Isaac and Jacob, came and put on Adam's body, and he appeared to men, was crucified, rose and ascended.

---

[8] Cf. Ep. Clem. Ad Jac. 7.1-2, and see Sect 19, note 4.
[9] Cf. Matt. 4:25.
[10] With. 3.3-5 cf. Hippol. Haer. IX.14.1.
[11] Cf. Victorinus Rhetor in Gal. 1:19; Clem. Hom. III.20-21; Recog. I,45.4.
[12] Cf. Clem. Hom. III.19.2.
[13] Cf. Clem. Hom. III.20.3.
[14] Cf. Clem Hom. III.20.2; Recog. I.33-34; 52.3.
[15] Cf. Clem. Recog. I.33.1-2.

3,6   But again, when they choose to, they say, "No; the Spirit—that is, the Christ—came to him and put on the man called Jesus."[16] And they get all giddy from supposing different things about him at different times.

3,7   They too accept the Gospel according to Matthew. Like the Cerinthians and Merinthians, they too use it alone. They call it, "According to the Hebrews," and it is true to say that only Matthew put the setting forth and the preaching of the Gospel into the New Testament in the Hebrew language and alphabet.[17]

3,8   But by now some will have replied that the Gospel of John besides, translated from Greek to Hebrew, is in the Jewish treasuries, I mean the treasuries at Tiberias. It is stored there secretly, as certain converts from Judaism have described to me in detail. (9) And not only that, but it is said that the book of the Acts of the Apostles, also translated from Greek to Hebrew, is there in the treasuries. So the Jews who have been converted to Christ by reading it have told me.

4,1   One of them was Josephus—not the ancient Josephus, the author and chronicler, but a Josephus of Tiberias, < born > during the old age of the Emperor Constantine of blessed memory. This Josephus was awarded the rank of count by the Emperor himself, and was authorized to build a church for Christ in Tiberias itself, and in Diocaesarea, Capernaum and the other towns. He also suffered a great deal from the Jews themselves before he came to the Emperor's notice.

4,2   For this Josephus was one of their men of rank. There are such persons, called "apostles," < who > stand next after the patriarch.[18] They attend on the patriarch, and often stay with him day and night without intermission, to give him counsel and refer matters of law to him. (3) The patriarch at that time was called Ellel. (I think that was how Josephus pronounced his name, unless I am mistaken because of the time). He was descended from the Gamaliel who had been one of their patriarchs. (4) One may suspect, and others have suggested this as well, that these patriarchs were descended from the first Gamaliel, the Savior's contemporary, who gave the godly counsel of stopping the abuse of the apostles.

4,5   When Ellel was dying he asked the bishop who then lived near Tiberias for holy baptism, and he received it from him *in extremis* for allegedly medical reasons. (6) For he had sent for him, as though for a doctor, by Josephus, and he had the room cleared and begged the bishop, "Give me the seal in Christ!" (7) The bishop summoned the servants

---

[16] Cf. Hippol. Haer. VIII.34.1. For further references see Sect 28, note 3.
[17] Cf. Iren. I.26.2; Eus. H. E. III.27.4; Jer. C. Pelag. III.2.
[18] Cf. Eus. In Isa. 18:1-2; Jer. in Gal. 1:1.

and ordered water prepared, as though intending to give the patriarch, who was very sick, some treatment for his illness with water. They did what they were told, for they did not know. But pleading indulgence for his modesty the patriarch sent them all out, and was allowed the laver and the holy mysteries.

5,1   Josephus told me <this> in conversation. For I heard all this from his own lips and no one else's, in his old age when he was about seventy or even more. (2) For I was entertained at his home in Scythopolis; he had moved from Tiberias, and owned a notable estate there in Scythopolis. Eusebius of blessed memory, the bishop of Vercelli in Italy, was Josephus' guest, since Constantius had banished him for his orthodox faith. I and the other brethren had come there to visit him, and we were entertained too, along with Eusebius.

5,3   Now when I met Josephus at his home, asked him about himself, and found that he had been a prominent Jew, I also inquired his reason, and why it was that he had come over to Christianity. And I heard all this plainly (from him), not at secondhand from anyone else. (4) And since I believe the trouble over the man because of the Hebrew translations in the treasuries is worth recording for the edification of the faithful, I deliberately give Josephus' entire reason.

5,5   Josephus was not only privileged to become a faithful Christian, but a despiser of Arians as well. In that city, Scythopolis, he was the only orthodox Christian—they were all Arian. (6) Had it not been that he was a count, and the rank of count protected him from Arian persecution, he could not even have undertaken to live in the town, especially while Patrophilus was the Arian bishop. Patrophilus was very influential because of his wealth and severity, and his familiar acquaintance with the Emperor Constantius. (7) But there was another, younger man in town too, an orthodox believer of Jewish parentage. He did not even dare <to associate> with me in public, though he used to visit me secretly.

5,8   But Josephus told me something plausible and amusing, though I guess that <here he was joking too>. He claimed that after his wife died, fearing that the Arians might take him by force and make him a cleric—to soften him for conversion to the sect they would often promise him higher preferments if need be, and to make him a bishop. Well, he claimed this was why he had married a second wife, to escape their appointments!

6,1   But I shall resume my description of the reason for the patriarch's conversion, and also make Josephus' own reason plain in every detail to those who care to read it, in the words he used to me. (2) "Just as the patriarch was being granted baptism," he told me, "I peeped in through the cracks in the doors and saw what the bishop was doing to the patriarch—found it out, and kept it to myself. (3) For besides," Josephus said, "the patriarch had a very ample sum of money ready, and he reached out, gave it to the bishop, and said, 'Offer it for me. It is written that things are bound and loosed on earth through the priests of God, and <that> these are what will be loosed and bound in heaven.'[19] (4) When this was over," he said, "and the doors were opened, the patriarch's visitors asked him how he felt after his treatment, and he replied, 'Great!' He knew what he was talking about!"

6,5   Then <after> two or three days, with frequent visits from the bishop in the character of a physician, the patriarch fell asleep with a good hope in store. He had entrusted his own son, who was quite young, to Josephus and another very capable <elder>. (6) All business, then, was transacted through these two, since the patriarch, as a boy, was still childish, and was being brought up under their supervision.

6,7   During this time Josephus was considering what he should do, for because of the mysteries, his mind was often troubled over the subject of baptism. Now there was a "gazophylacium" there which was sealed—"gaza" means "treasure" in Hebrew. (8) As many had different notions about this treasury because of its seal, Josephus plucked up the courage to open it unobserved—and found no money, but books money could not buy. (9) Browsing through them he found the Gospel of John translated from Greek to Hebrew, as I said, and the Acts of the Apostles—as well as Matthew's Gospel, which is actually Hebrew. After reading from them he was once more distressed in mind, for he was somehow troubled over the faith of Christ. But he was prodded for two reasons now, his reading of the books and the patriach's initiation. Still, as often happens, his heart was hardened.

7,1   While all his time was occupied with these things, the boy Ellel had left to be reared as patriarch was growing up. (No one usurps the positions of authority among the Jews; a son succeeds a father.) (2) Just as the lad was reaching full vigor some idle youths of his age, who were used to evil, unfortunately met him. (I guess he was called Judas, but because of the time I am not quite sure.) (3) The youths of his age got him into many bad habits, seductions of women and unholy sexual unions. They undertook to help him in his licentious <deeds> with certain magic devices—made certain love-philtres and compelled free women, by incantation, to be brought against their will for his seduction.

7,4   Josephus and his fellow elder, who were obliged to attend the boy, bore this with difficulty. Often they charged him verbally, and admonished him. But he preferred to listen to the young men, and he hid

---

[19] Cf. Matt. 18:18.

his indecencies and denied them. And Josephus did not dare to voice his accusations of him openly; he admonished him, however, as though from professional duty.

7,5   Well, they went to Gadara for the hot baths. There is an annual gathering there. Persons who wish to bathe for a certain number of days arrive from every quarter, to rid themselves of their ailments, if you please—though it is a trick of the devil. For where God's wonders have been, the adversary has already spread his deadly nets—men and women bathe together there!

7,6   There happened to be an unusually beautiful free woman in the bath. With his accustomed licentiousness the young man brushed against the girl's side as he strolled about in the hot-air room. (7) But being Christian, she naturally made the sign of the cross. (There was no need for her to break the rules and bathe in mixed company. These things happen to simple laypersons, from the laxity of the teachers who do not forewarn them through their instruction.) (8) Still, that God might make his wonders manifest, the youngster, I mean the patriarch, failed in his enterprise. For he sent emissaries to the woman and promised her gifts; but she insulted his messengers and did not yield to the pampered youth's futile efforts.

8,1   Then, when his helpers learned of the passion the boy had betrayed for the girl, they undertook to equip him with more powerful magic—as Josephus himself described to me minutely. (2) After sunset they took the unfortunate lad to the neighboring cemetery. (In my country there are places of assembly of this kind, called "caverns," made by hewing them out of cliffsides.) (3) Taking him there the cheats who were with him recited certain incantations and spells, and did some things, with him and in the woman's name, which were full of impiety.

8,4   By God's will the other elder, Josephus' partner, found this out; and on realizing what was happening, he told Josephus. And he began by bemoaning his lot, and said, "Brother, we are wretched men and vessels of destruction! What sort of person are we attending?" (5) Josephus asked what the matter was, and no sooner were the words out of his mouth than the elder seized his hand and took Josephus to the place where the persons doomed to die, with the youth, were holding their assembly in the cemetery for magic. (6) They stood outside the door and eavesdropped on their proceedings, but withdrew when they came out. (It was not dark yet; it was just about sundown, and visibility was still good.) (7) After the monsters of impiety had left the tomb Josephus went in and saw certain vessels and other †implements of jugglery on the ground. He made water on them and covered them with a heap of dust, he said, and left.

8,8   But he knew the kind of woman on whose account they had plotted these wicked things, and he watched to see whether they would win. (9) When the sorcerers did not win—the woman had the aid of the sign and faith of Christ—he learned that the young man had waited for the girl's arrival on three nights, and later quarrelled with those who had performed the jugglery, because it had not succeeded. (10) This made Josephus' third lesson—where Christ's name was, and the sign of his cross, the power of sorcery did not prevail. But at this point he was by no means convinced that he should become a Christian.

9,1   Then the Lord appeared to him in a dream, and said, "I am Jesus, whom your forefathers crucified; but believe in me." When even this did not convince him, he became very ill and was given up for lost. But the Lord appeared to him again, and told him to believe and he would be healed. And he promised and recovered, but again remained obstinate.

9,2   He became ill a second time in turn, and was given up as before. When his Jewish kin supposed that he was dying, they told him the words they continually repeat among themselves as a secret. (3) An elderly scholar of the law came and told him secretly,[20] and said, "Believe < in > Jesus, crucified under Pontius Pilate the governor, Son of God first yet later born of Mary; the Christ of God and risen from the dead. And believe that he will come to judge and quick and the dead." I can truthfully say that, in outline, that same Josephus distinctly told me this.

9,4   But I have also heard this sort of thing from someone else. He was still a Jew, from fear of the Jews, but he often spent time in Christian company, and he honored Christians and loved them. He travelled with me in the wilderness of Baithel and Ephraim, when I was going up to the mountains from Jericho, and I said something to him about Christ's incarnation, and he did not dispute it. (5) I was amazed—he was learned in the Law and capable of disputation—and I asked why he did not dispute, but agreed with me about Jesus Christ our Lord. I had got no further than this when he too revealed to me that he had been dying himself, and that they had told him secretly, in a whisper, "Jesus Christ, the crucified Son of God, will judge you." (6) But let this be my record here, based on true report concerning these persons and with regard to this formula.

10,1   Josephus was still sick. And though, as I said, like the others he had heard "Jesus Christ will judge you" from the old man, he was still hardened. But the Lord in his lovingkindness again said to him in a

---

[20] Mysteries are said over the heads, and into both ears of the dying for their salvation at PS 239-41.

dream, "Lo, I heal you; but rise up and believe!" But though he recovered again, he did not believe. (2) When he was well the Lord appeared to him in a dream once more, and demanded to know why he did not believe. But the Lord promised him, "If, as an assurance of faith, you choose to work any miracle in my name, call upon me and I will do it."

10,3   There was a madman in the city who roamed the town, I mean Tiberias, naked. If he was dressed he would often tear his clothing apart, as such people will. (4) Josephus wished to test the vision, and though he still doubted it, was awed. So he brought the man inside, shut the door, took water, made the sign of the cross over it, and sprinkled it on the madman with the words, "In the name of Jesus of Nazareth the crucified begone from him, demon, and let him be made whole!"

10,5   Falling down with a loud cry, the man lay motionless for a long time foaming profusely and retching, and Josephus supposed he had died. (6) But after a while he rubbed his forehead and arose. And on standing up and seeing his nakedness he hid himself and covered his privy parts with his hands, for he could no longer bear to see his own nakedness. (7) In proof of his comprehension and sanity, after Josephus had dressed him in one of his own himatia, he came and offered many thanks to him and to God, for he realized that he had been cured through Josephus. He spread word of him in town, and this miracle became known to the Jews there. (8) Much talk ensued in the city, with people saying that Josephus had opened the treasuries, found the Name of God in writing, read it, and was working great miracles. And what they were saying was true, though not in the way they thought.

10,9   Josephus, however, still remained hardened in heart. But the merciful God, who continually arranges occasions of good for those who love him, supplies them to those to whom he allows salvation. (11,1) As things turned out for Josephus himself, after Judas, the patriarch we spoke of, grew up—I guess he was called that—to repay him, he awarded him the revenue of the apostolate. (2) He was sent to Cilicia with a commission, and on arriving there collected the tithes and firstfruits from the Jews of the province, from every city in Cilicia. (3) At this time he lodged next to the church, I do not know in what city. But he made friends with the bishop there, <went to him> unobserved, borrowed the Gospels and read them.

11,4   <He was> very solemn, if you please, and immaculate, as apostles are—as I said, this is what they call the rank. And he was always intent on what would make for the establishment of good order, and he purged and demoted many of the appointed synagogue-heads, priests, elders and "azanites" (meaning their kind of deacons or assistants). He was thus hated by many. As though in an attempt to defend themselves against him, they showed no little zeal in prying into his affairs and finding out what he was doing. (5) For this reason a crowd of meddlers burst in upon him at home in his residence, and caught him perusing the Gospels. They took the book and seized the man, dragged him along on the ground with outcries, bore him off to the synagogue with no light mistreatment, and whipped him as the Law prescribes. (6) This made his first trial; however, the bishop of the town arrived and got him out. They caught him on a journey another time, as he described to me, and threw him into the river Cydnus. <When they saw> the current take him they presumed he had gone under and drowned, and were glad of it.

11,7 But he was given holy baptism a little later—for he was rescued (from the river). He went to court, made friends with the Emperor Constantine, and told him his whole story—how he was a Jew of highest rank and how the divine visions kept appearing to him, since the Lord was summoning him to his holy calling, and the salvation of his faith and knowledge. (8) But the good emperor—a true servant of Christ, and, after David, Hezekiah and Josiah, the king with the most godly zeal—rewarded him with a rank in his realm, as I have said already. (9) He made him a count and told him to ask what he wanted in his turn.

Josephus asked only this very great favor from the emperor—permission by imperial rescript to build Christ's churches in the Jewish towns and villages where no one had ever been able to found churches, since there are no Greeks, Samaritans or Christians among the population. (10) This <rule> of having no gentiles among them is observed especially at Tiberias, Diocaesarea, Sepphoris, Nazareth and Capernaum.

12,1 After receiving the letter and the authorization along with his title, Josephus came to Tiberias. He also had a draft on the imperial treasury, and the honor of a salary from the emperor as well.

12,2 So he made his first foundation in Tiberias. There was a very large temple in the town already, I think they may have called it the Adrianeum. The citizens may have been trying to restore this Adrianeum, which was standing unfinished, for a public bath. (3) When Josephus found this out, he took the opportunity; and as he found that there were already four walls raised to some height, made of stones four feet long, he began the erection of the church from that point.

12,4 But lime was needed, and the other building material. He therefore had a number of ovens, perhaps seven altogether, set up outside the city. (In the language of the country they call these "furnaces.") But the ingenious Jews, who are ready for anything, did not spare their continual sorcery. Those natural-born Jews wasted their time on magic and jugglery to put a spell on the fire, but did not entirely succeed.

12,5 Well, the fire was smouldering and doing no good; in a manner of speaking it had deviated from its own nature. When those whose task it was to feed the fire with fuel—I mean brushwood or scrub—told Josephus what had been done, he rushed from the city, stung to the quick and moved with zeal for the Lord. (6) He ordered water fetched in a vessel, (I mean a flask, but the local inhabitants call this a "cacubium,") < and > took this vessel of water in the sight of all—a crowd of Jews had gathered to watch, eager to see how it would turn out and what Josephus would try to do. Tracing the sign of the cross on the vessel with his own finger, and invoking the name of Jesus, he cried out, (7) "In the name of Jesus of Nazareth, whom my fathers and those of all here present crucified, may there be power in this water to set at naught all sorcery and enchantment these men have wrought, and to work a miracle on the fire that the Lord's house may be finished." (8) With that he wet his hand and sprinkled the water on each furnace; and the spells were broken, and in the presence of all, the fire blazed up. And the crowds of spectators cried, "There is (only) one God, the help of the Christians," and withdrew.

12,9 Though they harmed the man on many occasions, he eventually restored part of the temple at Tiberias and finished a small church. He then left, but came to Scythopolis and made his home. However, he completed buildings in Diocaesarea and certain other towns. (10) So much for my account and description of these events, which I recalled here because of the translation of the books, the rendering from Greek to Hebrew of the Gospel of John and the Acts of the Apostles.

13,1 But I resume the sequence of my argument against Ebion— because of the Gospel according to Matthew the progress of the discussion obliged me to give the sequel of the knowledge which had come my way. (2) Now in what they call a Gospel according to Matthew,[21] though it is not entirely complete, but is corrupt and mutilated—and they call this thing "Hebrew"!—the following passage occurs. "There was a certain man named Jesus, and he was about thirty years of age,[22] who chose us. And coming to Capernaum he entered into the house of Simon surnamed Peter, and opened his mouth and said, (3) Passing beside the Sea of Tiberias I chose John and James, the sons of Zebedee,[23] and Simon and Andrew and < Philip and Bartholomew, James the son of Alphaeus and Thomas >, Thaddaeus, Simon the Zealot, and Judas Iscariot.[24]

---

[21] Cf. Jer. C. Pelag. III.2.
[22] Cf. Luke 3:23.
[23] Cf. Matt. 4:18. What precedes is a combination of Gospel passages: Mark 1:21;29; Matt. 5:2; Matt. 4:18.
[24] Cf. Matt. 10:2-4 and Luke 6:14-16. But the list given here is not identical with either.

Thee likewise, Matthew, seated at the receipt of custom, did I call, and
thou didst follow me.[25] I will, then, that ye be twelve apostles[26] for a
testimony to Israel." (4) And, "John came baptizing, and there went out
unto him Pharisees and were baptized, and all Jerusalem. And John had
a garment of camel's hair, and a girdle of skin about his loins. And his
meat," it says, "was wild honey, whose taste was the taste of manna, as
a cake in oil."[27] (5) This, if you please, to turn the speech of the truth
into falsehood, and substitute "a cake in honey" for "locusts"!

13,6   But their Gospel begins, "It came to pass in the days of Herod,
king of Judaea, <in the high-priesthood of Caiaphas>, that <a
certain> man, John <by name>, came baptizing with the baptism of
repentance in the river Jordan, and he was said to be of the lineage of
Aaron the priest, the son of Zacharias and Elizabeth, and all went out
unto him."[28] (7) And after saying a number of things it adds, "When
the people had been baptized Jesus came also and was baptized of John.
And as he came up out of the water the heavens were opened, and he
saw the Holy Spirit in the form of a dove which descended and entered
into him. And (there came) a voice from heaven saying, Thou art my
beloved Son, in thee I am well pleased,[29] and again, This day have I
begotten thee.[30] And straightway a great light shone round about the
place.[31] Seeing this," it says, "John said unto him, Who art thou,
Lord?[32] And again (there came) a voice to him from heaven, This is my
beloved Son, in whom I am well pleased.[33] (8) And then," it says, "John
fell down before him and said, I pray thee, Lord, do thou baptize me.
But he forbade him saying, Suffer (me), for thus it is meet that all be
fulfilled."[34]

14,1   See how their utterly false teaching is all lame, slanted, and
nowhere straight! (2) Cerinthus and Carpocrates use the same <so-
called> Gospel <of Matthew> in their own circles, if you please, and
prove Christ's origin from Joseph's seed and Mary from the beginning
of Matthew, by the genealogy. (3) But these people have something else
in mind. They falsify the genealogical tables in Matthew, and start its
opening, as I said, with the words, "It came to pass in the days of Herod,

---

[25] Cf. Matt. 9:9.
[26] Cf. Clem. Recog. I.40.4; Clem. Alex. Strom. VI.48.2.
[27] Cf. Matt. 3:4-5; Numb. 11:8.
[28] Cf. Luke 1:5; Mark 1:4-5.
[29] This is closest to Luke 3:21-22.
[30] Heb. 1:5; Ps. 2:7.
[31] Cf. Justin Dial. 7; Ps.-Cypr. De Rebapt. 17.
[32] Acts 9:5.
[33] Cf. Matt. 3:17.
[34] Cf. Matt. 3:14-15.

king of Judaea, in the high-priesthood of Caiaphas, that a certain man, John by name, came baptizing with the baptism of repentance in the river Jordan'' and so on. (4) This is because they mean that Jesus is really a man, as I said, but that Christ, who descended in the form of a dove, has entered him—as we have found already in other sects—< and > been united with him. Christ himself < is from God on high, but Jesus > is the product of a man's seed and a woman.

14,5   But again they deny his humanity, on the basis of the Savior's words, if you please, when he was told, ''Behold thy mother and thy brethren stand without''—''Who are my mother and my brethren? And he stretched forth his hand toward his disciples and said, These are my brethren and mother and sisters, these that do the will of my Father.''[35] (6) This means that Ebion is full of all sorts of trickery, as I said, and shows himself in many forms. And that makes him a monstrosity, as I indicated above.

15,1   But they use certain other books as well—Clement's so-called Peregrinations of Peter, if you please, though they corrupt the contents while leaving a few genuine items. (2) Clement himself fully convicts them of this in his general epistles which are read in the holy churches, because his faith and speech are of a different character than their spurious productions in his name in the Peregrinations. He himself teaches celibacy, and they will not have it. He extols Elijah, David, Samson and all the prophets, whom they abhor.[36]

15,3   They have made everything in the Peregrinations their own and lied about Peter in many ways, saying that he was baptized daily[37] for purification as they are. And they say he abstained from living flesh and dressed meat as they do, and any other meat-dish—since both Ebion himself, and Ebionites, abstain from these[38] entirely. (4) When you ask one of them why they do not eat meat they have nothig to say, and foolishly answer, ''Since it is produced by the congress and intercourse of bodies, we do not eat it.'' Thus, according to their own foolish regurgitations, they are wholly abominable themselves, since they are results of the intercourse of a man and a woman.

16,1   They also receive baptism, apart from their baptisms daily. And they celebrate mysteries year after year, if you please, in imitation of the

---

[35] Matt. 12:47-50.

[36] David is (perhaps) repudiated at Clem. Hom. III.25.5. The prophets are repudiated at Clem. Hom. III.53.2; GT 52; Acts of Paul VII.1.10. Mandaean literature contains violent attacks on the Jewish prophets, e.g. at GR 25,22-26,28; 43,29-44,28.

[37] Cf. Clem. Hom. X.1.1-2; XI.1.1-2; Recog. IV.3.1; VIII.1.1.

[38] Clem. Hom. VIII.15.3-4; XII.6.1-4; Recog. VIII.6.4.

sacred mysteries of the church, using unleavened bread—and the other part of the mystery with water only.[39]

16,2   But as I said, they set two divine appointees side by side, one being Christ, but one the devil.[40] And they say that Christ has been allotted the world to come, but that this world has been entrusted to the devil[41]—by the Almighty's decree, if you please, at the request of both. (3) And they say that this is why Jesus was begotten of the seed of a man and chosen, and thus named Son of God by election, after the Christ who had come to him from on high in the form of a dove. (4) But they say he is not begotten of God the Father, but was created as one of the archangels,[42] and that he is ruler both of angels and of all creatures of < the > Almighty; and he came and instructed us < to abolish the sacrifices >. (5) As their so-called Gospel says, "I came to abolish the sacrifices, and if ye cease not from sacrifice, wrath will not cease from you."[43] These and certain similar things are their crafty devices.

16,6   They say that there are other Acts of apostles; and these contain much utterly impious material, with which they deliberately arm themselves against the truth. (7) They prescribe certain degrees and directions in the "Degrees of James," if you please, as though he discoursed against the temple and sacrifices, and the fire on the altar— and much else that is full of nonsense.

16,8   Nor are they ashamed to accuse Paul[44] here with certain †false inventions of their false apostles' villainy and imposture. They say that he was a Tarsean—which he admits himself and does not deny. But they suppose that he was of Greek parentage, taking the occasion for this from the (same) passage because he frankly said, "I am a man of Tarsus, a citizen of no mean city."[45] (9) They then claim that he was Greek and the son of a Greek mother and father, but that he had gone up to Jerusalem, stayed a while, and desired to marry a daughter of the †high priest. He therefore became a proselyte and was circumcised. But since

---

[39] Bread and water eucharists are mentioned at Acts of Paul, Hamburg Codex; James, *The Apocryphal New Testament*, p. 573; Vercelli Acts of Peter and James p. 304; Acts of Thomas, James, p. 418. Water is a Mandaean sacramental drink at Book of John p. 5 note 1; Mandaean Prayer Book p. 58, note 1.

[40] Cf. Clem. Hom. III.19.2; VIII.21; XV.7.4; XX.2.1; Recog. I.24.5; IX.3-4.

[41] Cf. Man. Hom. 41,18-20.

[42] Perhaps cf. Clem. Recog. I.45. Another "Ebionite" Christology is given at Hippol. Haer. VII.34.3-4.

[43] Cf. Clem. Hom. III.26.3; 56.4; Recog. I.37.3; 39.1; IV.36.4; GR 9,83; 33,2; 43,8-10.

[44] Cf. Clem. Recog. I.70-71; Iren. I.26.2; Orig. C. Cels. V.65; Hom. 19 In Jerem. 18:12.

[45] Cf. Acts 21:39.

he still could not get that sort of girl he became angry, and wrote against circumcision, and the Sabbath and Legislation.

17,1   But he is making a completely false accusation—this dreadful serpent with his poverty of understanding. For "Ebion," translated from Hebrew to Greek, means "poor". For he is indeed poor, in understanding, hope, and actual fact, since he takes Christ for a mere man, and thus hopes in him with poverty of faith. (2) But their boastful claim, if you please, is that they are poor because they sold their possessions in the apostles' time and laid them at the apostles' feet, and have gone over to poverty and renunciation;[46] and thus, they say, they are called "poor" by everyone. (3) But there is no truth to this claim of theirs either; he was really named Ebion. I suppose the poor, wretched person got the name from his father and mother by prophecy.

17,4   And how many other shocking, false, utterly wicked observances they have! When one of them falls ill or is bitten by a snake, he gets into water and invokes the names in Elxai—heaven and earth, salt and water, winds and "angels of righteousness" <as> they say, bread and oil[47]—and begins to say, "Help me, and rid me of my pain!"

17,5   But I have already indicated just above, that Ebion knew nothing of this. His followers who later became associated with Elxai have the circumcision, the Sabbath and the customs of Ebion, but Elxai's imagination. (6) They thus believe that Christ is a figure in the form of a man, invisible to human eyes, ninety-six-miles—plus twenty-four schoena, if you please!—tall; twenty-four miles, six schoena wide; and some other measurement through. Opposite him the Holy Ghost stands invisibly as well, in the form of a female, with the same dimensions. (7) "And how did I find the dimensions?" he says. "I saw from the mountains that the heads were level with them, and by observing the height of the mountain, I learned the dimensions of Christ and the Holy Spirit." (8) I have already spoken of this in the Sect, "Against Ossaeans." I allude to it now, however, or it might be thought that I fail from forgetfulness to mention characteristics of any nation and sect which are also found in others.

18,1   Ebion too preached in Asia and Rome, but the roots of these thorny weeds come mostly from Nabataea and Banias, Moabitis, and Cocabe in Bashanitis beyond Adrai—in Cyprus as well. (2) They marry their children by compulsion even when they are too young—with the permission of their teachers, if you please! (Ebionites have elders and heads of synagogues, and they call their church a synagogue, not a

---

[46] Cf. Acts 4:34-35.
[47] Cf. Hippol. Haer. IX.15.4-6.

church; they take pride only in Christ's name.) (3) And they do not just allow people to contract one marriage; even if somebody wants a release from his first marriage and to contract another, they permit it—they allow everything without hesitation—down to a second, and a third, and a seventh marriage.

18,4 They acknowledge Abraham, Isaac and Jacob, Moses and Aaron—and Joshua the son of Nun[48] simply as Moses' successor, not as of any importance. But after these they acknowledge no more of the prophets, but even anathematize David and Solomon and make fun of them. Similarly they disregard Isaiah and Jeremiah, Daniel and Ezekiel, Elijah and Elisha; for they pay them no heed and blaspheme their prophecies,[49] but accept the Gospel only. (5) They say, however, that Christ is prophet of truth[50] and Christ; < but > that he is Son of God by promotion, and by his connection with the elevation given to him from above. The prophets, they say, are prophets of < their own > understanding,[51] not of truth. (6) He alone, they would have it, is prophet, man, Son of God, and Christ—and yet a mere man,[52] as I said, though owing to virtue of life[53] he has come to be called Son of God.

18,7 Nor do they accept Moses' Pentateuch in its entirety; certain sayings they reject.[54] When you say to them, of eating meat, "Why did Abraham serve the angels the calf and the milk? Why did Noah eat meat, and why was he told to by God, who said, 'Slay and eat?' Why did Isaac and Jacob sacrifice to God—Moses too, in the wilderness?" he will not believe that and will say, "Why do I need to read what is in the Law, when the Gospel has come?"

18,8 "Well, where did you hear about Moses and Abraham? I know you admit their existence, and put them down as righteous, and your own ancestors."

18,9 Then he will answer, "Christ has revealed this to me,"[55] and will blaspheme most of the legislation, and Samson, David, Elijah, Samuel, Elisha and the rest.

19,1 But the scum is altogether refuted by the Savior, who refutes the whole of his deceitful teaching, expressly and by a sort of shortcut, with

---

[48] The Book of Joshua is appended to the Samaritan Pentateuch, perhaps for similar reasons.

[49] The Ebionites are also said to reject the canonical prophets at Method. Conviv. VIII.10.

[50] This idea is common in Clem. Hom. and Recog.

[51] Cf. "prophecies among those who are born of woman" Clem. Hom. II.52.1.

[52] The divinity of Christ is denied at Clem. Hom. XVI.15.2.

[53] Cf. Hippol. Haer. VII.34.1-2.

[54] Cf. Clem. Hom. II.45; 51; XVIII.19-20.

[55] Cf. the discussion of the nature of revelation at Clem. Hom. XVII.18.

one utterance, "John came in the way of righteousness, neither eating nor drinking, and they say, He hath a devil. The Son of Man came eating and drinking, <and they say, Behold a man gluttonous and a wine-bibber.>"[56] (2) And he certainly does not mean that John never by any chance ate, or that the Savior ate anything and everything—with the suspicion of forbidden foods as well. (3) The passage makes the meaning of the truth plain, since "He is a glutton and a wine-bibber" can mean only the eating of meat and the drinking of wine; and "neither eating nor drinking" means that John did not take meat and wine, but only locusts and honey—water too, obviously.

19,4   But who does not know that the Savior arose from the dead and ate (flesh)? As the holy Gospels of the truth say, "There was given unto him bread, and a piece of broiled fish. And he took it, and did eat, and gave to his disciples."[57] And he did the same at the Sea of Tiberias, both by eating fish and by giving it to his disciples to eat. (5) And a great deal can be said on this subject. But I must now come to the detailed refutation of their belated, unsound preaching, and compose their rebuttal.

20,1   And first, it must be said that Christ is not a mere man. If someone is conceived <like> a man in every way, it cannot be that he will be given to the world as a "sign"; as the Holy Ghost foretold of him in saying to Ahaz, "Ask thee a sign." And since Ahaz did not ask, the prophet then said, "The Lord himself shall give you a sign. Behold the Virgin shall conceive."[58]

20,2   Now if a woman has been joined to a husband and married, she cannot be called a virgin. But she who has truly conceived the Word of God without a husband may properly be called a virgin— (3) as Isaiah, again, says in another passage, "A voice of a cry from the city, a voice from the temple, a voice of the Lord of recompense, that rendereth recompense to his enemies. Before she that travailled hath brought forth, before the pain of her travail came, she escaped and was delivered of a man child. Who hath heard of such a thing? Or who hath seen such things? Or hath the earth travailled in one day and brought forth a nation at once? For Zion hath travailled and brought forth her children. And it was I who gave this expectation, and they did not remember, saith the Lord."[59] (4) But what is the "expectation," and what are the "children"? This can mean only that a virgin gave birth without labor, a thing that had never happened. And that even though John, the child

---

[56] Matt. 11:18-19.
[57] Luke 24:42-43; John 21:13.
[58] Isa. 7:11;14.
[59] Isa. 66:6-9.

Elizabeth bore by promise for his sake, <was born with labor, he leaped in the womb (from expectation) before his birth>.

20,5 So how can they declare the Savior a mere man, conceived of a man's seed? How will he "not be known," as Jeremiah says of him, "He is a man, and yet who will know him?"[60] (6) For the prophet, describing him, said, "Who will know him?" But if he meant a mere man, surely his father would know him, and his mother, his relatives and neighbors, those who lived with him and his fellow townsmen. (7) But that which came to birth is born of Mary, while the divine Word came from above. He was truly begotten not in time and without a beginning, not of a man's seed but of the Father on high. But in the last days he consented to enter a virgin's womb and fashion his flesh from her, patterned after himself. This is why Jeremiah says, "And he is a man, but who will know him?"[61] For he came from above as God, the only-begotten divine Word.

20,8 But the misguided Ebionites are very unfortunate to have abandoned the testimonies of prophets and angels and contented themselves with the misguided Ebion—who wants to do what he likes, and practice Judaism even though he is estranged from Jews. (9) <For> when Gabriel made his announcement to Mary, as soon as she said, "How shall this be, seeing I know not a man?" he pledged his word and said, "The Spirit of the Lord shall come upon thee, and the power of the highest shall overshadow thee. Therefore also that which is born of thee shall be called holy, Son of God."[62] (10) By saying, "that which is born," he showed that the flesh and the rest of the humanity <are> from her, but that the power of the highest and the Holy Spirit overshadowed the holy Virgin from above, from heaven, and the only-begotten Son, the divine Word, has descended from on high. <He thus indicates> both that Christ became man, and that he was born of her in truth. (11) And how much more of this sort there is! But as I promised I do not cover a wide range, or I might make my treatise very large.

21,1 But next I shall discuss their other slanders, of Peter and the other apostles. They claim that every day, before eating so much as bread,[63] Peter had undergone immersions. (2) Observe their quibble, and the falsity of the scummy teaching! To deceive themselves, if you please, since they are defiled themselves and often have much to do with sex, they use the water lavishly for their own reassurance, and think that they have purification through baptisms. (3) And they venture to say

---

    [60] Jerem. 17:9.
    [61] Jerem. 17:9.
    [62] Luke 1:34-35.
    [63] Cf. IQ S 3,4-5;8-9; 4,21; 5,13-14, and see the references at Note 37.

these offensive things about the apostles, even though the Lord exposes
their badness, since, when he came to wash Peter's feet, Peter said,
"Thou shalt never wash my feet," and the Savior's answer was, "If I
wash not thy feet thou hast no part with me." (4) And when Peter
replied, "Not the feet only, but also the head," the Lord returned, "He
that is washed once needeth not < to wash > his head, but his feet only;
for he is clean every whit."[64]

21,5   He showed then, that we must not employ immersions, customs
of no value, and commandments and teachings of men, as he says in the
Gospel with the prophet, "This people honoreth me with their lips, but
their heart is far from me. But in vain do they worship me, teaching for
doctrines the commandments of men."[65] (6) Why did he fault the
Pharisees and Scribes, with their diligent immersions of themselves, and
of their platters, cups and the rest? And why does he declare absolutely,
"To eat with unwashen hands defileth not a man?"[66] Thus not only did
he put a stop to the immersion of these things. He even indicated that
there is no need to wash one's hands, and if one would rather < not >,
it does him no harm.

22,1   But how can their stupidity about eating meat not be exposed
out of hand? In the first place, the Lord ate the Jewish Passover. Now
the Jewish Passover was a sheep and unleavened bread—the flesh of a
sheep roasted with fire and eaten, (2) as his disciples say to him, "Where
wilt thou that we prepare for thee that thou mayest eat the Passover?"
And the Lord himself says, "Go ye into the city, and ye shall find a man
bearing a pitcher of water and ye shall follow whithersoever he goeth, and
say ye to the goodman of the house, Where is the guest-chamber, where
I shall keep the Passover with my disciples? And he shall show you an
upper room furnished; there make ready."[67]

22,3   But the Lord himself says in turn, "With desire I have desired
to eat this Passover with you."[68] And he said, "this Passover," not
simply "Passover," so that no one would practice it in accordance with
his own notion. Passover, as I said, was roast meat and the rest. (4) But
of their own will these people have lost sight of the consequence of the
truth, and have altered the wording—which is evident to everyone from
the sayings associated with it—and made the disciples say, "Where wilt
thou that we prepare for thee to eat the Passover?" And the Lord, if you

---

[64] John 13:8-10.
[65] Matt. 15:8-9.
[66] Matt. 15:20.
[67] Mark 14:12-15.
[68] Luke 22:15.

please, says, "Have I desired meat with desire, to eat this Passover with you?"

22,5   But how can their tampering go undetected, when the consequence cries out that the "mu" and "eta" are additions? Instead of saying ἐπιθυμίᾳ ἐπεθύμησα they added the μή as an afterthought. Christ actually said, "With desire I have desired to eat this Passover with you."[69] But they misled themselves by writing in meat and making a false entry, and saying, "Have I desired meat with desire to eat this Passover with you?" But it is plainly demonstrated that he both kept the Passover, and, as I said, ate meat.

22,6   But they will also be refuted with the vision shown St. Peter, in the form of the sheet which contained all sorts of wild beasts, domestic animals, reptiles and birds, and the Lord's voice saying, "Arise, slay and eat!" And when Peter said, "Not so, Lord; nothing common or unclean hath entered into my mouth," the Lord replied, "What God hath cleansed, that call not thou common."[70]

22,7   There are two ways of demonstrating the truth. If they say that St. Peter's words, "Nothing common or unclean < hath > at any time < entered into my mouth >," covered all foods—so that he would have called cattle, goats, sheep and birds unclean—they will be refuted at once by his previous mode of life. (8) He was of Jewish extraction, and met the Savior (only) after marrying, fathering children,[71] and having a mother-in-law. But Jews eat flesh, and the eating of meat is not an abomination to them, or forbidden. (9) Since he had always eaten meat, then—even if we say (this was only) until he met the Savior—this will prove that he considered nothing unclean which was not said to be. For he never, in fact, attributed commonness or uncleanness to meat of all sorts, but (only) to the kinds the Law called common or unclean.

22,10   But again—once it is established that he was not saying that all sorts of meat were common, but that he said this of the kinds called common and unclean in the Law—to teach him what Christ's holy church is like, God told him to consider nothing common. "For all things are pure, when they are received with thanks and praise to God."[72] (11) At all events, though the riddle referred to the call of the gentiles, (and was meant) to keep Peter from considering the uncircumcised profane or unclean, the vision that appeared to Peter had no bearing on people, as anyone can see, but meant the foods prohibited in the Law. And their silly argument is a total failure.

---

[69] Luke 22:15.
[70] Acts 11:7-9.
[71] The legend of Peter's daughter is given at The Act of Peter BG 8502,4.
[72] Cf. Rom. 14:20 and 1 Tim. 4:3.

23,1   To convince their dupes they pretendedly take the names of the apostles, and have forged books and inscribed them with their names, in impersonation, if you please, of James, Matthew, and other disciples. (2) Among these names they include the apostle John's, making their stupidity altogether apparent. For not only does he refute them entirely by saying, "In the beginning was the Word, and the Word was with God, and the Word was God."[73] (3) <It is clear from the same Gospel>, moreover, that he <accepts> the testimonies of the holy prophets. By the Holy Spirit's inspiration, and his fine precision in giving the Savior's words about the purposes that were fulfilled, as I said, in Christ, John in his Gospel gave the testimonies of the prophets from whom the Ebionites have estranged themselves.

23,4   He showed at once how John the Baptist answered the messengers the Pharisees had sent him with, "I am the voice of one crying in the wilderness, Make straight the way of the Lord, as said the prophet Isaiah."[74] (5) And again, when the Lord overturned the tables of the money-changers and said, "Make not my Father's house an house of merchandise," John himself said, "They remembered that it was written, The zeal of thine house hath eaten me up,"[75] and took the testimony from the prophets, I mean from David. And again, John himself said, "Isaiah saw, being in the Spirit."[76]

24,1   Again, while St. John was preaching in Asia, it is reported that he did an extraordinary thing as an example of the truth. Though his way of life was most admirable and appropriate to his apostolic rank, and he never bathed, he was compelled by the Holy Spirit to go to the bath, and said, "Look what is at the bath!" (2) To his companions' surprise he actually went to the bathing-room, approached the attendant who took the bathers' clothes, and asked who was in the bathing-room inside. (3) And the attendant stationed there to watch the clothes—some people do this for a living in the gymnasia—told St. John that Ebion was inside. (4) But John understood at once why the Holy Spirit's guidance had impelled him, as I said, to come to the bath for the record, to bequeathe to us the essence of the truth—who Christ's servants and apostles are, and the sons of that same truth; but what the evil one's vessels are, and the gates of hell. Though these cannot prevail against the rock, and God's holy church which is founded on it. (5) John immediately became disturbed and cried out in anguish; and as a testimony in proof of uncontaminated teaching he said, in an aside audible to all, "Brothers, let us get away

---

[73] John 1:1.
[74] John 1:23.
[75] John 2:16-17.
[76] John 12:41.

from here quickly! Or the bath may fall and bury us with Ebion, in the bathing-room inside, because of his impiety.''[77]

24,6   And no one need be surprised to hear that Ebion met John. The blessed John had a very long life, and survived till the reign of Trajan.[78] (7) But anyone can see that all the apostles distinguished Ebion's faith (from their own), and considered it foreign to their kind of preaching.

25,1   And how much can I say about the blasphemous things they call St. Paul! First, they say that he was Greek and of gentile parentage, but that he had later become a proselyte. (2) Why does he say ''an Hebrew of Hebrews'' of himself, then, ''of the seed of Abraham,'' of the tribe of Benjamin, concerning the Law, a Pharisee, being more exceeding zealous of the traditions of my fathers?''[79] (3) And he says elsewhere, ''Are they Israelites? So am I. Are they the seed of Abraham? So am I,''[80] and, ''Circumcised the eighth day, brought up at the feet of Gamaliel, and an Hebrew of Hebrews.''[81]

25,4   What frightful shrieks and snake-like hisses from the horrid serpents! How poisonous their nonsense is! Whose word shall I take? Ebion's and his kind, or St. Peter's, who says, ''As my brother, Paul, hath written unto you, which things are deep and hard to be understood, which they who are unlearned and unstable pervert by their own ignorance?''[82] (5) But St. Paul himself testifies for Peter in turn, and says, ''James, John and Cephas, who seemed to be pillars, gave to me and Barnabas the right hand of fellowship.''[83] Even if he said that he was from Tarsus, this is no excuse for the attitude of those who hunt for words < of their own invention >—to their own ruin and < their > converts'. (6) For that matter, scripture also says that Barnabas—once he was called Joseph, but his name was changed to Barnabas, or ''son of consolation''—was a Cypriote Levite. And it is by no means true that, because he was a Cypriote, he was not descended from Levi. Just so, even though St. Paul came from Tarsus, he was not foreign to Israel.

25,7   For many were dispersed because of the wars in the reign of Antiochus Epiphanes and at other times, both by being taken prisoner, and by †fleeing because of a seige. The captives stayed on in certain places, while everyone who had chosen to leave for this reason settled where he could. (8) Thus, because of the frequency with which Israel had to flee from its enemies, the holy Jeremiah said of it, ''And if thou passest over

---

[77] This story is told of John and Cerinthus at Iren. III.3.4.
[78] Cf. Iren. III.3.4.
[79] Phil. 3:5; Gal. 1:14.
[80] 2 Cor. 11:22.
[81] Phil. 3:5; Acts 22:3.
[82] 2 Pet. 3:15-16.
[83] Gal. 2:9.

to the Citians, there also shalt thou have no rest."[84] (9) Now anyone can see that Citium means the island of Cyprus, for Citians are Cypriotes and Rhodians. Moreover, the Cypriote and Rhodian stock had settled in Macedonia; thus Alexander of Macedon was Citian. And this is why the Book of Maccabees says, "He came out of the land of the Citians;"[85] Alexander of Macedon was of Citian descent.

25,10 But to find my place again, after giving these facts because of the chance remark. I say that many of the emigrants who had settled in the other countries were descended from Israel. (11) For they were also called natives of each country. Thus Jethro's daughters told their father how Moses had helped them when he drove the shepherds away and watered their sheep. And they went and told their father about it, and when he said, "How is it that ye are come so soon today?" (12) they answered, "An Egyptian delivered us from the shepherds, and also drew water for us and watered our flock." And Jethro answered at once, "Why brought ye him not hither, that he may eat bread?"[86]

25,13 But who does not know that Moses was the son of Amram and Jochabed, Amram was the son of Kohath, Kohath of Levi, Levi of Jacob, Jacob of Isaac, and Isaac of Abraham? And their line of noble stock and descendants had surely not died out because Moses is called "Egyptian!" (14) But these people whom Ebion led astray have left the road, and have their minds set on many crooked ways, and a path that goes uphill.

26,1 Again, they are proud of their circumcision,[87] and boast, if you please, that this is the sign and mark of the patriarchs and the righteous men who have lived by the Law; and they think that it makes them their equals. Moreover they argue for this from Christ himself, like Cerinthus. (2) Echoing his silly argument they too say, "It is enough for the disciple that he be as his master. Christ was circumcised; you be circumcised too!"[88]

26,3[89] ...and that the seeds of the imposture may be altogether discredited. As the sea has a bridle, bars, and gates determined by God; as sand is the sea's boundary and its commandment is, "Hitherto shalt thou come, but no further; in thyself shall thy waves be shattered,"[90] as < it says >—so will they be exhausted within themselves. (4) But there the words about the boundary are uttered by God, to discipline the sea by divine decree. Here, however, wickedness on its own initiative, and

---

[84] Isa. 23:12.
[85] 1 Mac. 1:1.
[86] Exod. 2:18-20.
[87] Cf. Iren. I.26.2.
[88] Cf. Ps.-Tert. 3.3. The scriptural verse is Matt. 10:25.
[89] There is a lacuna here.
[90] Job 38:11.

the imposture that blinds the mind and perverts pious reason, has raised waves of a sort against itself beforehand. It wears out the shocking notions it states first with other waves of itself, and is always being shattered within itself < and > destroying itself.

26,5   Or, it is like a dreadful serpent savaging itself, and becoming its own consumer by bending round from the tail and eating itself. (6) They say this was once done by asps sealed up in jars, when they had all consumed each other, and at length the most vigorous and cruelest remained. But when it was left alone and got hungry, certain Egyptian naturalists report that it would eat itself up, beginning with its own tail. Hence they named it appropriately and from the Gorgon's head called it an "aspidogorgon." (7) So the lame-brained Ebion and his supporters have cut themselves up beforehand, and destroyed from the outset the very things that made them proud.

26,8   For Christ was born a child, and did not circumcise himself. But glory to the merciful God! To avoid admitting the facts Ebion has anticipated himself, so that this even becomes a refutation for him. (9) If he said that Christ had come down from heaven as God and been circumcised on the eighth day by Mary, then—since he was God and would be allowing this of his own consent—this would provide the scum with the argument for circumcision. But since he introduces the idea that Christ was generated as a mere man by men, the child is no longer responsible, even though he was circumcised the eighth day. (10) He did not circumcise himself, but was circumcised by men. Children do not circumcise themselves, and are not responsible for their own circumcisions; their parents are. Children know nothing, are ignorant infants, and have no idea what their parents do to them.

27,1   But we say that he has both come from heaven as God and stayed in the Virgin Mary's womb as long as any baby, to take his incarnate humanity in its fullness from the virgin womb, and provide a dispensation in which he was also circumcised—truly, and not in appearance—on the eighth day. (2) "For he came to fulfil the Law and prophets, not to destroy them."[91] He did not come to declare that the Law was foreign to him but that it was given by him, though it had remained typical until his coming. Thus the lacks in the Law would be fulfilled in their turn, in him and by him, so that the types, come to spiritual fulfilment, might be preached in truth, by him and his apostles—types no more, but truth.

27,3   For in this the saying of the Law was fulfilled, one that had stood until his time, and was abolished and yet brought to fulfilment in

---

[91] Cf. Matt. 5:17.

him—the words of Zipporah, "The blood of the circumcision of my child hath ceased to flow."[92] (4) And she did not say, "I circumcised my child"—the angel who was sent to her was not providing for circumcision, and did not leave for fear of the blood of circumcision. But in token that the blood of the circumcision of the Child to come must cease to flow, < he made sure that she would say, "The blood of my child hath ceased to flow" >. And on hearing this, and having arranged for it, he left.

27,5   And which child's blood, mark you, but the child's of whom the prophet said, "They shall wish that they were burned with fire. For unto us a child is born, unto us a son is likewise given?"[93] (6) In indication of the true humanity, he showed that what was born was truly a child; but he said, "Unto us a son is given," to show that God's Word from above and God's Son himself had been given, and by entering the womb had become man, both human and divine—himself God, himself man; himself a Son given from above, himself a child (humanly) born.

27,7   At this point the blood of circumcision finally ceased to flow, as he says in the Gospel—when Greeks arrived to see him, approached Philip, and told him, "Show us Jesus," and Philip told John and John told Jesus, "Certain Greeks desire to see thee."[94] (8) And the Lord replied at once, "Now hath come the glory of God," to show that the circumcision of the body, which had served for a while as a type, was passing away, but that the uncircumcision of the body, since it sees Christ and has comprehended him in truth, possesses a greater circumcision in spirit.

28,1   But if they choose to say, "Then why was Christ circumcised?"—you misguided souls, I have already told you why! He was circumcised for many reasons. (2) First, to prove that < he had > actually < taken > flesh, because of Manichaeus and those who say he has (only) appeared in semblance. (3) Then, to show that the body was not of the same nature as the Godhead, as Apollinarius says, and that he had not brought it down from above, as Valentinus says. (4) And to confirm the fact that the circumcision he had given anciently had served a legitimate purpose until his arrival and to deprive the Jews of an excuse. For if he had not been circumcised they could have said, "We could not accept an uncircumcised Christ."

28,5   And besides, after commanding Abraham to be circumcised—as a visible mark, but in token of the true and invisible mark that had been given him—Christ needed to confirm this by being circumcised

---

[92] Cf. Exod. 4:25.
[93] Cf. Isa. 9:5-6.
[94] Cf. John 12:20-22.

(himself). (6) For the visible circumcision was instituted because of Abraham's doubt, when the holy and righteous man asked, in apparent uncertainty, "Shall a son be born unto him that is an hundred years old?" and, "Shall Sarah in her old age bear a son?"[95] And the Lord at once said, "Take me a ram three years old, and a goat, and an heifer,"[96] and so on. And about sundown, when Abraham had seen burning torches, an oven and the rest, (7) God reprovingly told him, "Thy seed shall be a stranger in a land that is not theirs, and they shall enslave them for four hundred years."[97] And for a safeguard, because of the doubt that had led Abraham to say, "Shall a son be born to him that is an hundred years old?"[98] he laid physical circumcision on him and his, to keep them from forgetting the God of their fathers when enslaved by idolatrous, unbelieving Egyptians. They would see their circumcision, be reminded and feel abashed, and not deny him.

28,8   And until Christ this remained the case, and because of it he too consented to be circumcised, and became true man; though he had come from above from the Father as divine Word, and did not doff the Godhead but truly wore flesh. (9) He was circumcised with full humanity and making all his dispensations in truth—to deprive the Jews of their excuse, as I said, for the refutation of Manichaeans and others, and so that, being circumcised himself, he could with reason abolish circumcision and suggest that another kind was greater. It was not as though he contrived a circumcision for himself because he had none. He had, but showed that there is no further need of this, but of the greater.

29,1   And that he was God at birth straightway, and not a mere man, the magi will plainly show. For after two years—as they told Herod the time the star had risen, "two years ago at the most"[99]—they came to Jerusalem. And on learning by inquiry that Christ must be born in Bethlehem, these magi left again with the star as their guide, and came from Jerusalem to Bethlehem. (2) And they entered and found him with Mary his mother, and fell down and worshipped him and offered their gifts. (3) Now if he is worshipped at once, he is not a mere man at birth, but God. And he does not become Christ thirty years later, and not after the baptism. He was born of a virgin as Christ straightway, God and man. (4) And thus the angels hymn him at once with, "Glory to God in the highest, and on earth peace, good-will among men."[100] And they an-

---

[95] Gen. 17:17.
[96] Gen. 15:9.
[97] Gen. 15:13.
[98] Gen. 17:17.
[99] Matt. 2:16.
[100] Luke 2:14.

nounce to the shepherds, "Unto you is born this day, in the city of David, Christ the Lord."[101]

29,5 And this is not the only proof, deluded Ebion! At the age of twelve moreover, he is found "sitting in the midst of the priests and elders, both questioning them and disputing with them,"[102] and "They were amazed at the gracious discourse which proceeded out of his mouth."[103] (6) And he was not doing this after his thirteeth year, permitting you to say that he became Christ when the Spirit came to him. He did it, as I said, directly on turning twelve, as is written in the Gospel according to Luke.

29,7 But even earlier too, when Joseph and Mary went up to Jerusalem during his childhood to worship at the feast and started back, Jesus stayed behind. And they looked for him on the road and among their relatives—Mary had relatives—and could not find him. (8) But she went back and found him, and said, "Son, what hast thou done to us? Behold, thy father and I have sought thee sorrowing." (Joseph was in the position of father to him, for he was not his actual father.) (9) Then the Lord answered her, "Why is it that ye sought me? Wist ye not that I must be in my Father's house?"[104] indicating that the Temple had been built in the name of God, that is, of his own Father. (10) Now if he knew both the Temple and his Father from childhood, Jesus was not a mere man at birth. And he was not called Christ and Son (only) after thirty, once the (thing in the) form of the dove had come to him. He taught at once, and with full assurance, that he belonged in his Father's house.

29,11 And for proof that Joseph was not his father but <was> in the position of a father, hear what the same evangelist says, the one who wrote in the person of Mary, "Thy father and I have sought thee sorrowing."[105] He writes in turn, "And Jesus began to be about thirty years of age, being, as was supposed, the son of Joseph."[106] By saying, "as was supposed," he proved that Jesus was not his son, but was supposed to be.

30,1 But I lack time for a full discussion in proof of the truth, and in refutation of Ebion's weak-mindedness and the weak-mindedness of his false school. (2) How can it not be plain that Joseph was not father to Jesus, but was held to be in the position of father? "Behold," scripture says, "the Virgin shall conceive and bear a son;"[107] it did not say, "Behold, the wife!" (3) And again, it says elsewhere, "And the heifer

---

[101] Luke 2:11.
[102] Luke 2:46.
[103] Luke 4:22.
[104] Luke 2:48-49.
[105] Luke 2:48.
[106] Luke 3:23.
[107] Isa. 7:14.

shall bear, and they shall say, It hath not borne.''[108] Some Manichaeans
and Marcionites say that Jesus was not born—hence, ''She shall bear,
and they shall say, She hath not borne.'' For Mary has not given birth
from impregnation by a man's seed, yet they tell the mad lie that she has.
Thus the heifer has in truth borne God, in truth borne man.

30,4   And to show that ''heifer'' means the Virgin, and that what she
left behind her was a purification for the defiled, hear the Law saying,
''*Take* unto thee a fiery-red heifer,''[109] and indicating the chosen vessel
of Mary < with its words, ''*Take* unto thee an heifer.'' But it said, ''fiery-
red,'' > because of the fiery red of the Savior's Godhead that was contained in the Virgin; for ''God,'' says scripture, ''is a consuming
fire.''[110] (5) And the Law says, ''a fiery-red heifer, upon whose neck hath
never come yoke,''[111] to show that the Virgin, not knowing the yoke of
marriage to a husband, is a ''heifer.''

30,6   But why should I give the full discussion? As Isaiah, again, said
in the person of the Lord, ''Take unto thee a sheet cut from a great, new
papyrus-roll''[112]—''cut'' because, although she is the product of a man's
seed, the Virgin has been cut off from union with men and is cut off from
the intercourse natural to man. (7) For all human beings are generated
by the seed of a man. But while Christ's generation was given its
humanity naturally by a woman, the Virgin Mary, it was cut off un-
naturally from the line of human descent. Thus Jacob says of him,
''Thou didst come up, my son, from a shoot''[113]—not, ''Thou didst
come up from a seed.'' (8) And thus the holy Isaiah the prophet says,
or rather the Lord says to him, ''Take to thee a sheet (cut from) a
papyrus-roll''[114]—meaning the form of intercourse, since men write their
entire record in that form. As it says in the hundred and thirty-eighth
psalm, ''In thy book shall all be written; they shall be fashioned in a day,
and no one is in them.''[115] For it compared the womb with a book.

30,9   This is why David says, ''Thine eyes did see my unbaked
substance.''[116] That is, ''You knew me after conception, before my formation; and even earlier, before my conception.'' (31,1) But the Hebrew
author makes the word marvellously plain. He called the ''unbaked
substance'' a ''golem,'' which means a grain or granule of flour—

---

[108] This is from the Apocryphon of Ezekiel. See Resch, *Agrapha* II,pp. 305-306.
[109] Numb. 19:2.
[110] Deut. 4:24.
[111] Numb. 19:2.
[112] Isa. 8:1.
[113] Cf. Gen. 49:9.
[114] Isa. 8:1.
[115] Cf. Ps. 138:16.
[116] Ps. 139:16.

something which has not yet come together to form a loaf, and is not yet kneaded. Instead, it is like a particle or fleck detached from a grain of wheat, or the tiny speck that is left by fine flour. (2) He thus represented what is detached from a man for insemination as a thing of exactly the same shape and said—to give it in Greek translation—"the unbaked substance." In other words, he said, "'Thine eyes did see' the unformed substance yet in the womb, or before the womb"—"God knoweth all things before they be,"[117] as scripture says. But what is meant by "book" and "sheet" is "womb."

31,3 And he did not say, "Take to thyself a roll," or, "Take to thyself a papyrus," but "Take a piece"—contrary to men's proper custom—because of the womb's suitability for writing. He said, "new," because the Virgin is new and immaculate. (4) And < "great" >; for great indeed before God and man is Mary, the holy Virgin! How can we not call her "great," when she contained the Uncontainable, whom heaven and earth cannot contain? Yet he, though uncontainable, was contained by his own choice and consent, willingly, not of necessity. Great, then, is the "sheet," and new! Great, because of the marvel; new, because virgin.

31,5 "And write on it," he says, "with a man's pen."[118] Not, "Someone will write on it with a man's pen," or—to allow Ebion an excuse—"A man will write on it." If he had said, "A man will write on it," Ebion could say that a man, Joseph, sowed, and that Christ was generated from the seed of a man. (6) But he told Isaiah, "Write!" about 753 years before the event, so that, from the length of the interval, the truth might be apparent to everyone—since no one could have sired the child who would be born, 753 years ahead of time. (7) Then did he tell the prophet, "Write!" for no reason? No, but to show that the Holy Spirit, who was in the prophet, would himself become the true agent of the incarnate Christ's conception. For, "The Holy Ghost shall come upon thee,"[119] and so on, said the angel Gabriel to Mary. (8) But "with a man's pen" means, "in the image of a man." "For Christ Jesus is man, but he is mediator between God and men,"[120] since he came from on high as divine Word, but came from Mary as man, though not begotten of man's seed.

31,9 And this is why the prophet says immediately, "And he went in unto the prophetess,"[121] to show that Mary is a prophetess. Not

---

[117] Susannah 42.
[118] Isa. 8:1.
[119] Luke 1:35.
[120] Cf. 1 Tim. 2:5.
[121] Isa. 8:3.

Ahaz's wife—some make this mistake, and claim that the words refer to Hezekiah. (10) Hezekiah was eleven years old by this time. For the prophecy, "Behold, the Virgin shall conceive,"[122] was made in the third year of his father's reign. And after the death of Ahaz, who reigned for fourteen years and (then) died, the scripture says at once, "And Hezekiah began to reign; twenty < and five > years old was he when he began to reign."[123] (11) So how can Hezekiah, (who reigned for twenty years after his father), be born during his father's reign because of the prophecy that Emmanuel would be born of a virgin, when his father reigned for fourteen years? Instead, will it not be evident to the wise that Hezekiah had already been born when the prophet made the prophecy during the reign of Ahaz, Hezekiah's father? (12) Especially since Ahaz's wife is no prophetess, as anyone can see. Mary, who said prophetically, "For from henceforth all generations of the earth shall call me blessed,"[124] is the prophetess. To her came Gabriel, with the tidings that the Spirit who had spoken in Isaiah would come upon her and she would bear a son, our Lord Jesus Christ, through the Holy Ghost—not by the seed of a man, the blasphemy of the foolish, mistaken Ebionites.

32,1   But both the lame-brain's Sabbath observance and circumcision, and his baptisms every day, stand discredited; Jesus did his best to heal mostly on the Sabbath. And not just because he heals, but also because of his two ways of healing. (2) He directs the patients he has healed on the Sabbath to pick their mattresses up and walk. Moreover, he made clay on the Sabbath and anointed the blind man's eyes—but making clay is work. (3) Hence, since they had learned from his association with them, and from his teaching, that the Sabbath was abolished, the apostles plucked ears of grain on the Sabbath, rubbed them in their hands, and ate them. But it was a "second Sabbath after the first," as the Gospel indicates.

32,4   The Law designated various Sabbaths. The Sabbath proper, which recurs week by week. And the one that is a Sabbath because of the occurrences of the true new moons and the feasts that follow, such as the days of Tabernacles, and of Passover when they sacrifice the lamb and eat unleavened bread afterwards. Further, when they keep the single, annual fast which is called the "Greater Fast," and the other, which they call the "Lesser." (5) For when these days occur, on the second day of the week or the third or the fourth, this too is designated a Sabbath for them.

---

[122] Isa. 7:14.
[123] 2 Kings 18:1-2.
[124] Luke 1:48.

32,6   Hence, after the Day of Unleavened Bread had come and been designated a Sabbath day, on the Sabbath proper following the Day of Unleavened Bread which was treated as a Sabbath, it was found that the disciples went through the standing grain, plucked the ears, and rubbed and ate them. (7) They were proving that the prohibition which is fixed on the Sabbath has been relaxed at the coming of the Great Sabbath— Christ, who gave us rest from our sins, and of whom Noah was a type. On seeing him at birth his father named him Noah by prophecy, and said, "He will give us rest from our sins, or deeds of cruelty."[125]

32,8   But Noah gave no rest from sins. Lamech made the prophecy of Christ, whose meaning is truly Noah—"Noah" means "rest"—and "Sebeth," which means "rest and Sabbath." (9) In other words, "Christ," in whom the Father and his Holy Spirit have rested. And all holy men have found rest in him by desisting from sins. He is the greater, eternal Sabbath, of which the lesser, temporary Sabbath was a type. This served until his coming, it had been prescribed by him in the Law, and it was abrogated and fulfilled in him in the Gospel. For this is what he meant when he said, "The Son of Man is Lord even of the Sabbath day."[126]

32,10   Hence the disciples broke the Sabbath with confidence. Even the priests before them broke it in the Temple by sacrificing and offering sacrifices to God, to keep the constant, daily sacrifice from coming to an end. And not only did the priests themselves prophesy the Sabbath's abrogation by not remaining idle; circumcision broke the Sabbath too.

32,11   When a child was born on the Sabbath, as one often was, there was an abrogation of the Sabbath and circumcision. Dissolution was thus predicted for both. Obviously, if those who were to circumcise the child born on the Sabbath chose to be exact about the eighth day, and they found that it fell on Sabbath and still circumcised the child, they performed a work and broke the Sabbath. (12) But if they put it off to keep from breaking the Sabbath, they then performed the circumcision on the ninth day, and violated circumcision itself, and its mandatory term of eight days.

33,1   Nor was the original circumcision final. It was given for a sign, as a reminder of things to come, and because of the holy Abraham's doubts when, as I said, he was reproved for them—and as a type of the Greater Circumcision, which fulfils all things equally in those to whom it is allowed. (2) If the former circumcision had been for sanctification and the inheritance of the kingdom of heaven, Sarah would have been

---

[125] Cf. Gen. 5:29.
[126] Matt. 12:8.

deprived of the kingdom—and Rebecca, Leah, Rachel, Jochabed, Miriam the sister of Moses, and all the holy women. They could not have inherited the kingdom of heaven, since they could not have the circumcision of Abraham, which the Ebionites say God had given him. But if these are not deprived of the kingdom of heaven though they have no circumcision, the physical circumcision of our day is of no use.

33,3   But why does Ebion boast of circumcision, when both idolaters and Egyptian priests have it? So do the Saracens, also called Ishmaelites, and the Samaritans, Idumaeans and Homerites. Most of these do this, not because of the Law, but from some senseless custom.

33,4   And it will simply take a lot of my time to spend it on Ebion's nonsense—his vain reliance on the literal wording of the Savior's, "It is enough for the disciple that he be as his master,"[127] for his boast that his own circumcision derives from Christ's. Yet this was cut off altogether in him, and was abolished through him! (5) However, since the oaf takes this saying of the imitation of Christ, I do not mind showing that this is not why it was said.

33,6   The Lord explains immediately that he did not say it on this account, but because of persecutions, and because of the Jewish violence towards him. He says, "If they have persecuted me, they will also persecute you; if they have hated me, they will hate you also."[128] "Call ye not me teacher and Lord? And ye say well, for so I am.[129] If they have called the master of the house Beelzebul, how much more shall they call them of his household?"[130] (7) And, "The servant cannot be above his lord, nor the disciple above his teacher. But let the servant be perfect in all things, as his teacher"[131]—in other words, ready for persecution, defamation, and whatever may be inflicted on him. (8) Hence St. Paul also said, "Be ye imitators of me, as I also am of Christ."[132] And this was not because he imitated his Master inappropriately; he did not say, "I am God," or, "I am the Son of God," or, "I am the divine Word." For he says, "I am the least of the apostles," and, "He was seen of me also, as of one born out of due time."[133]

34,1   But if you take this wording to mean the imitation of Christ, Ebion, and if you would like to be as your teacher—or rather, as your Lord—in the circumcision you have silly notions < about >, stop

---

127 Matt. 10:25.
128 John 15:20.
129 John 13:13.
130 Matt. 10:25.
131 Matt. 10:24; Luke 6:40.
132 1 Cor. 11:1.
133 1 Cor. 15:8-9.

mimicking him in circumcision! This will not help you. The Lord has made it obsolete, as I have shown plainly through many items of evidence. (2) For he came and fulfilled it, and gave us the perfect circumcision of his mysteries—not of one member only, but by sealing the entire body and cutting it off from sin. And not by saving one portion of the people, males alone, but by truly sealing the entire Christian people, men and women both, and <advancing> them ungrudgingly to the inheritance of the kingdom of heaven. And not by an inadequate provision of the seal, in a feeble manner, to only one class, males alone; but by revealing the kingdom of heaven to an entire people through his seal, his commandments, and his good teaching.

34,3   But if you want to be like the Lord, Ebion—that is, if you want to be like the teacher—you are very wrong. Stop mimicking him in circumcision. Call Lazarus from the grave, or raise another dead man; cleanse lepers, grant sight to the blind, or heal a paralytic from birth, if you can! But you cannot; you do the opposite because you are a prisoner of unbelief, chains of flesh, and insatiable demands of law. (4) Now if you could not do even these things—and you cannot, because of your wrong belief—I deny <that you are> like Christ. You cannot become like God, for you are a mortal man, and under a delusion. Nor can you call on Christ's name for miracles—and even if you do, you cannot work them. (5) But if you had any success in making a paralytic rise to his feet, since he stood by the name of Jesus he could get understanding from him too, and would not tolerate your Sabbath observance. From the name of his Healer he <could> learn, "Take up thy bed and go unto thine house on the Sabbath day."[134]

34,6   But I have already said how each of them makes a different suggestion about Christ. Ebion himself did at one time, by saying that he originated as a mere man from sexual intercourse. But at other times the Ebionites who derive from him say that Christ has a heavenly power from God, "the Son," and that the Son dons Adam and doffs him when convenient. By the power of God I have refuted their various opinions.

34,7   But why should I spend any further time on tidal beaches by the sea, which are flooded here and dry there, and fish are often stranded on some of them and injure people's feet when they cross their high parts? (For some of the fish are poisonous, I mean sting-rays, sea-snakes, sharks and sea-eels, as I have just now said.) (8) I shall leave this spot in its turn, thanking God that I have also put this sect to flight, not half-heartedly but even with a painstaking refutation. (9) But let us address ourselves to others next, beloved, and pray for God's help, that he himself may bring our promises to fulfilment through us.

---

[134] Mark 2:11; John 5:8;16.

31.

Against Valentinians,[1] also called Gnostics. Number eleven, but thirty-one of the series

1,1 After these so-called Ebionites I shall pass to the sect of the Valentinians. For I have made my way through †the Ebionites' wickedness, and have promised < to refute > the others that follow by the power of God—though they look like other wild beasts; though they have the poisons, bites and venom of serpents, visible in their teachings as in a gaping maw; and though they † < act like > a fire-breathing dragon, or a dreadful serpent and basilisk. I shall give the best refutation I can of the Valentinians, who also call themselves Gnostics. (2) There are ten varieties of Gnostic, each as much smitten as the other with one plague of dreams about their syzygies, ogdoads, and male and female aeons. I shall no longer arrange the treatise by the times of the (sects') succession, but (simply) pass from one to the other.

1,3 For all of these sprouted from the ground at once like toadstools. And like stunted, smelly shoots, thistly grass, and a den full of scorpions, they all came to life at one time, and like the ugliness of toadstools—as I said—appeared in an instant. This has been said of them already, by the most holy Irenaeus. (4) For they all arose simultaneously. And though each borrowed its poor excuse for existing from the other, each, in its desire < to invent > still more than the other, had already thought of its own kind of wicked invention to show off with. (5) And they all called themselves Gnostics, I mean Valentinus and the Gnostics before him, as well as Basilides, Satornilus and Colorbasus, Ptolemy and Secundus, Carpocrates, and many more.

1,6 But though I have named them all here because they all emerged at once and had the rank growth of < their teaching > at the same time, I shall still discuss the badness of each one's sowing separately. For the present I shall go to the heresiarch and tragic poet before us, I mean to Valentinus and his teaching, part of this larger subject of "knowledgeability"—though < this is full > of contemptible silliness, and the wise find it contemptible and ridiculous.

2,1 Valentinus comes next in time after the persons I placed ahead of him—Basilides and Satornilus, and Ebion, Cerinthus, Merinthus and their schools. For all these had their rank growth in the world at the same

---

[1] Sect. 31 is drawn from an untitled and otherwise unknown Valentinian work, which is quoted verbatim; from Iren. Praef.-I.11.5, also quoted verbatim; and, to a slight degree, from oral sources. For other discussions of Valentinianism see Hippol. Haer. VI.3.21-23; Ps.-Tert. 4.1-6; Eus. H. E. IV.22.5; Justin Dial. 35; Tert. Adv. Val.; Praescr. 33; Test. Tr. 56,1-5.

time; or rather, Cerinthus, Merinthus and Ebion had theirs a little earlier. They grew up with the ones I had mentioned already, before mentioning them.

2,2   Most people do not know Valentinus' nationality or birthplace; indicating his birthplace has not been an easy business for any writer. I have heard a rumor, however, as though by word of mouth. So I shall not overlook it, and though I cannot give his birthplace—to be honest, it is a disputed point—I shall still not ignore the rumor that has come to me. (3) Some have said he was born a Phrebonite, a native of Paralia in Egypt, but was given the Greek education in Alexandria.

2,4   Hence, in imitation of Hesiod's Theogony < and > the thirty so-called gods in Hesiod's own work, Valentinus learned to produce heathen mythology himself, got the notion from those who had lost the truth in his time and before, and wanted to fool the world with the same things as Hesiod's, though changing their names. (5) For he too introduces thirty gods, aeons, and heavens. Depth is the first of these, as he said in his own weak-mindedness—just as the originator of his notion, Hesiod, surely said, "Chaos is the eldest of the gods."[2] But who can fail to see that "chaos" and "depth" are the same sort of thing?

2,6   But mark the scum's overblown invention, and his wicked teaching! As I said, he sets thirty aeons, whom he also calls gods, side by side, and says that there are fifteen males and as many females. (7) He and his school say that each aeon is male and female, and a pair; but they say there are fifteen pairs, which they call "syzygies." Altogether there are thirty aeons, and each female brings forth the next aeons with the male as sire. They are as below, with each male's name beside the female's for contrast: (8) Ampsiou Auraan, Boukoua Thardouou, Ouboukoua Thardeddein, Merexa Atar, Barba Oudouak, Esten Ouananin, Lamertarde Athames, Soumin Allora, Koubiatha Danadaria, Dammo Oren, Lanaphek Oudinphek, Emphiboche Barra, Assiou Ache, Belim Dexiarche, Masemon.[3]

2,9   That is how they go together in male and female pairs. But in consecutive order they go, Ampsiou, Auraan, Boukoua, Thardouou, Ouboukoua, Thardeddein, Merexa, Atar, Barba, Oudouak, Esten, Ouananin, Lamertarde, Athames, Soumin, Allora, Koubiatha, Danadaria, Dammo, Oren, Lanaphek, Oudinphek, Emphiboche, Assiou, Ache, Belim, Dexiarche, Masemon.

---

[2] Hesiod Theogony 116.
[3] There are only 29 "names"; either a word has fallen out, or Epiphanius miscounted. The text of Epiphanius actually gives 33 words, of which Holl eliminated four as duplications. The sense is irrecoverable; Holl suggests that the whole may have been a Hebrew prayer or the like, which has been corrupted into unintelligibility.

2,10   The translations of these names are,[4] Depth < and > Silence.
Mind and Truth. Word and Life. Man and Church. Advocate and
Faith. Paternal and Hope. Maternal and Love. Ever-Mindful and
Understanding. Desired—also called Light—and Blessedness. Ec-
clesiasticus and Wisdom. Profound and Mingling. Ageless and Union.
Self-Engendered and Blending. Only-Begotten and Unity. Immoveable
and Pleasure. (11) Counted in consecutive order from the highest, un-
nameable being whom they call Father and Depth, to our heaven, the tal-
ly of the thirty aeons is, Depth, Silence, Mind, Truth, Word, Life, Man,
Church, Advocate, Faith, Paternal, Hope, Maternal, Love, Ever-
Mindful, Understanding, Desired—also called Light—Blessedness, Ecclesiasticus, Wisdom, Profound, Mingling, Ageless, Union, Self-
Engendered, Blending, Only-Begotten, Unity, Immoveable, Pleasure.

3,1   And this is their fictitious romance of the thirty aeons, and their
nonsense of a "spiritual Pleroma,"[5] if you please, in pairs! (2) If, for purposes of comparison, one were to set it beside the one in Hesiod,
Stesichorus, and the other Greek poets, he would find that, put parallel,
they are just the same. And from this he will learn that the leaders of the
school of these opinions profess to speak in mysteries about nothing that
is remarkable. (3) They have simply copied the Greeks' affected habit of
composing the imposture and teaching of heathen mythology, making no
changes except for their altered foreign coinage. (4) For Hesiod says this
sort of thing too: First of all comes "Chaos"—their way of saying
"Depth." Then Night, Erebus, Earth, Aether, Day, Passion, Skill,
Destiny,[6] Woe, Lot, Retribution, Reproach, Friendship, Death,
Lawlessness, Prize, Bane, Desire, Oblivion, Sleep, Combat, Bestower of
Rest, Hauteur, Kindly, Radiance, Allayer of Care, Deceit, Sweet-
Singing, Strife.

3,5   And this consecutive tally of males and females makes thirty.
However, if one should wish to see how they falsely unite one to one, he
would find the ones the poets thought appropriate united and coupled as
follows. (6) For example, by joining Depth to Night and Silence, they
brought about the generation of Earth. But others say that Heaven, the
one they have also called Hyperion—he was united with Earth and has
sired males and females, and so with the rest in succession throughout
their entire composition, as the myth's interminable, silly nonsense has
it.

---

[4] For this list see Iren. I.1.1-3, Hippol. Haer. VI.30.3-5; Tert. Adv. Val. 8.1-2.

[5] Cf. Iren. I.1.3.

[6] Up until this point, the names given correspond with those at Hesiod Theogony
116-125.

3,7   He would find that they are joined and coupled like this and can be put in the following order: Chaos, Night. Erebus, Earth. Aether, Day. Passion, Skill. Destiny, Woe. Lot, Retribution. Reproach, Friendship. Death, Lawlessness. Prize, Bane. Desire, Oblivion. Sleep, Combat. Bestower of Rest, Hauteur. Kindly, Radiance. Allayer of Care, Deceit. Sweet-Singing, Strife. (8) But if one studied their fabrication, and wanted to find how (since they were vainly inspired < to > evil by the sources of the madness of the poets of the world and of Greece) < they changed the same error > into a piece of useless labor and trouble for nothing, he would find that they were so much the more in error.

4,1   Thus they searched still higher, if you please, and thought they could find a Defect too, with their own deranged fancy. This Defect they call Almighty and Demiurge, and maker of creatures.[7] (2) They say that it in turn has created a latter Ogdoad with seven heavens, patterned after the former Ogdoad—and it is in the Ogdoad itself,[8] and has made seven heavens after it.[9]

4,3   To Defect they join an unattached aeon with no female, which has come here from the Pleroma in search of the soul. The soul came from above, from its mother, Wisdom, whose name they choose to represent and forge as Achamoth.[10] The unattached aeon they < choose > to call Savior, Limit,[11] Cross, Limit-Setter, Conductor, and Jesus—who passed through Mary like water through a conduit.[12] (4)[13]He is a light from the Christ on high, and is therefore named Light for his father, after the Light on high; Christ, after the Christ on high; Word, after the Word on high; and likewise Mind and Savior. (5) He continually ascends above his father, the Demiurge, and brings with him, to the supernal syzygies of the Pleroma,[14] any who put their trust in him.

4,6   What frivolity on their part, and silly talk in proportion! But as I said, I shall also present < what Hesiod said for comparison, to refute them and > the way in which they have coupled their foolishness with the

---

[7] Iren. I.5.2 has been combined with I.16.3. Cf. Hippol. Haer. VI.32.8-9; 36.1; Exc. Theod. 33.3; Tert. Adv. Val. 18. "Defect" is a common term in Nag Hammadi.

[8] The Ogdoad (or heaven above the seven heavens) appears, e.g., at Apoc. Paul 23,30-24,1; Test. Tr. 55,1;3, and very frequently in Nag Hammadi and other Gnostic literatures.

[9] Iren. I.5.2. Cf. Hippol. Haer. VI.32.8-9; Tert. Adv. Val. 20.2.

[10] "With this Defect ... Achamoth" is based on the combination of Iren. I.2.4. and I.8.4. Cf. Hippol. VI.32.4.-5; Tert. Adv. Val. 10.3.

[11] Iren. I.2.4, I.3.1. Cf. Hippol. Haer. VI.30.5-6; Tert. Adv. Val. 10.3; Exc. Theod. 35.1; 42.1-3.

[12] Iren. I.7.2. Cf. Ps.-Tert. 4.5; Test. Tr. 45,14-15.

[13] With 31,4,4 cf. Iren. I.2.6; I.7.2; Exc. Theod. 35.1; 40.2; Hippol. Haer. VI.36.3; 47.3; 59.2; Tert. Adv. Val. 12.4.

[14] Cf. Gr. Seth 57,7-11.

fabrication of the poets and heathen myth. (7) For after the thirty, <Hesiod too introduces> the one in the middle with no female; and after it again, the Ogdoad in pairs, whose source is the Demiurge. It too can be listed in this way, and the names are as follows. Exepaphus is the first. Porphyrion, Clotho, Rhyacus, Lachesis, Epiphaon, Atropus, Hyperion, Asterope.

4,8   And this is the stage-piece of these poets. It also contains many other names of what they call gods, male and female, variously named by various of them. There can even be 365[15] of them, and they are still dreamed of to give occasion to the other sects, which have mounted this tragic piece in their turn. (9) For after the ones already mentioned, Hesiod, Orpheus and Stesichorus say that Uranus and Tartarus have come into being and Cronus and Rhea; Zeus, Hera and Apollo; Poseidon and Pluto—and, for the rest, any number of what they call <gods>. For the deceitful error to which their notion gave rise was considerable; and by craving nonsense and inventing it, it fabricated many myths. (10) And this is the error which appears to be deceiving the minds of these deluded (Valentinians). But people with godly enlightenment of mind find these things ridiculous straightaway.

4,11   But here, passing this by and once more <following> the lists from their own books, I shall give the citation of their reading, I mean their book, word for word and phrase for phrase. It follows:

5,1   "Greeting from <unsearchable> Mind Unfailing to the unfailing among the discerning, the soulish, the fleshly, the inhabitants of the world, and in the presence of the Majesty![16]

5,2   "I make mention before you of mysteries unnameable, ineffable, and higher than the heavens, not to be comprehended by principalities, authorities, subordinates or all commingled, but manifest to the Ennoia of the Changeless alone.

5,3   "When, <in> the beginning, the Self-Progenitor[17] encompassed all things within himself, though they were within him in ignorance[18]—he whom some call ageless Aeon, ever new, both male and female,[19] who encompasses all and is yet unencompassed[20]—(4) the Ennoia within him (desired to break the eternal bonds). Her some have

---

[15] See Sect 24, note 4.

[16] μέγεθος is a common Gnostic term for the Supreme Being; see Apocry. Jas. 15,25 et al.

[17] For Self-Progenitor (Autogenes) see Index NHL.

[18] Cf. Gos. Tr. 22,25-33; Tri. Trac. 60,1-37; 72, 22-25.

[19] Cf. Iren. I.11.5; Ascl. 21. The masculo-feminine aeon is a common motif in Gnostic literature.

[20] Cf. Eug. 73,7-9; SJC 96,1-3; Val. Exp. 22,26-28 and other Gnostic passages.

called Ennoia, others, Grace,[21] but properly—since she has furnished treasures of the Majesty to those who are of the Majesty—those who have spoken the truth have termed her Silence.[22] For the Majesty has accomplished all things by reflection without speech.[23] (5) Wishing to break the eternal bonds,[24] the imperishable <Ennoia>, as I said, softened the Majesty from longing for his repose. And by coupling with him she showed forth the Father of Truth. Him the perfect have properly termed Man,[25] since he was the antitype of the Unbegotten who was before him.

5,6   "Hereafter Silence, to exhibit the union by nature of Light[26] with Man—though their coming together was the will for it—showed forth Truth. She was properly named Truth by the perfect, for she was truly like her own mother, Silence. For this was Silence's desire, an equal apportionment of the lights of male and female, that the <oneness> in them might also be made manifest, by themselves, to those to be separated[27] from them as perceptible lights.

5,7   "Hereafter Truth, in an exhibition of her mother's wantonness, softened her own Father toward her. They came together in immortal intercourse and ageless union, and showed forth a spiritual tetrad, male and female, the antitype of the already existig tetrad, (which was Depth, Silence, Father and Truth).[28] Now this is the tetrad stemming from the Father and Truth: Man, Church, Word, and Life.[29]

5,8   "Then, by the will of the all-encompassing Depth, Man and Church, remembering their father's words, came together and showed forth a dodecad[30] of wanton †males-and-females. The males are Advocate, Paternal, Maternal, Ever-Mindful, Desired, that is, Light, Ecclesiasticus; the females, Faith, Hope, Love, Understanding, Blessed One, Wisdom.

5,9   "Next, in their own version of the gift of union, Word and Life had congress—though their congress was the will for it—and by coming together showed forth a decad[31] of wantons, also male and female. The

---

[21] For Grace as an Aeon see Index NHL, and Iren. I.1.1; I.13.2.

[22] For Silence as an Aeon see Index NHL.

[23] Almost the same statement is made at Eug. 88,7-11; SJC 112,5-10. For "reflection" (ἐνθύμησις) see Eug. 73,10; SJC 96,6 et al; Exc. Theod. 7.1-3; also Keph. 116,13 and elsewhere in Manichaean literature.

[24] "Yet (the Son) wanted (his fruit) to become known," Tri. Trac., 57,26-27.

[25] For Father and Truth as a pair see Iren. I.11.1; for Man, see Iren. I.12.4; I.14.3.

[26] "Man of Light" is a common Gnostic expression; so, e.g., at GT 24, and passim in PS.

[27] Cf. Exc. Theod. 36.2.

[28] Iren., I.1.9.

[29] Iren. I.1.1. Cf. Val. Exp. 29,25-28; 35-37. For Depth see Tri. Trac. 60,16-22 et al.

[30] Cf. Val. Exp. 30,18-19; 33-36.

[31] Cf. Val. Exp. 30,16-17; 30-32.

males are Profound, Ageless, Self-Engendered, Only-Begotten, Immoveable. These acquired their names <to> the glory of the All-Encompassing. The females are Copulation, Uniting, Intercourse, Union, and Pleasure. They acquired their names to the glory of Silence.

6,1 "On completion[32] of the triacad headed by the Father of Truth—earthlings count it without comprehension and go back and count again whenever they encounter it, having yet to reach a tally;[33] but it is Depth, Silence, Father, Truth, Man, Church, Word, Life, Advocate, Paternal, Maternal, Ever-Mindful, Desired, Ecclesiasticus, Faith, Hope, Love, Understanding, Blessed One, Wisdom, Profound, Ageless, Self-Engendered, Only-Begotten, Immoveable, Copulation, Uniting, Intercourse, Union, and Pleasure—(2) then, by his knowledge unsurpassable, the All-encompassing decreed that another Ogdoad be named, to correspond to the principal Ogdoad which already existed, so that this would remain in the Thirty. (It was not the Majesty's purpose to be counted.) With the males (of the first Ogdoad) he matched the males Sole, Third, Fifth and Seventh—and the females Dyad, Tetrad, Hexad and Ogdoad.[34] (3) This Ogdoad, named in correspondence with the prior Ogdoad—Depth, Father, Man, Word, and Silence, Truth, Church and Life—was united with the lights and became a full Triacad.

6,4[35] "And the prior Ogdoad <was> at rest. But Depth departed from Majesty to be united with the multitude of the Triacad. For he consorted with Truth, and the Father of Truth came together with Church, and Maternal had Life to wife, and Advocate had Henad, and Henad was joined with the Father of Truth, and the Father of Truth was with Silence. But the spiritual Word consorted with ... by spiritual intercourse and immortal commingling, for the Self-Progenitor was at last rendering his rest indivisible.

6,5 "On the completion of its profound mysteries the Triacad showed forth imperishable lights[36] by consummating marriage among immortals. These were termed children of the Intermediate Region[37] and—since they lacked intelligence—were undifferentiated, reposing unconscious without Ennoia. Unless one understand this in its entirety, he achieves nothing by treating of it.

---

[32] For the completion of the thirty see also Val. Exp. 30,16-30.

[33] Cf. 1 Apoc. Jas. 27,1-5, "If you want to give (the seventy-two heavens) a number now, you will not be able to do so until you cast away from yourself blind thought, this bond of flesh which encircles you."

[34] Perhaps cf. the numbering of the Aeons at Iren. I.11.5; Hippol. Haer. I.5.2.

[35] With what follows, cf. Tri. Trac. 68,26-28.

[36] Cf. Hippol. Haer. VI.34.2-3.

[37] μεσότης is common in Nag Hammadi and other Gnostic literature. See, e.g., Gos. Phil. 66,8-16; 76,33-36; Para. Shem 6,13; 13,14-16; PS 188; 197.

6,6 "Then, when the lights had been made—there is no need to enumerate their great number but to consider it is needful, since, for the knowledge of ineffable mysteries, each has been allotted its own name—(7) Silence, desirous of bringing all things safely to the choice of knowledge, consorted by immortal intercourse but intellectual desire with the second Ogdoad which answers to the first. Her intellectual desire, however, was the Holy Spirit[38] which is among the holy churches. Sending this to the second Ogdoad, she persuaded it also to be united with her. (8) Marriage was thus consummated in the regions of the Ogdoad, with Holy Spirit united with Sole, Dyad with Third, Third with Hexad, Ogdoad with Seventh, Seventh with Dyad, and Hexad with Fifth. (9) The whole Ogdoad came together with ageless pleasure and immortal intercourse—for there was no parting from one another; their commingling was with blameless pleasure—and showed forth a Pentad of wantons with no females. Their names are, Emancipator, Limit-Setter, Thankworthy, Free-Roaming, Conductor. These were termed sons of the Intermediate Region.

6,10 "I would have you know (this). Ampsiou, Auraan, Boukoua, Thardouou, Ouboukoua, Thardeddein, Merexa, Atar, Barba, Oudouak, Esten, Ouananin, Lamertarde, Athames, Soumin, Allora, Koubiatha, Danadaria, Dammo, Oren, Lanaphek, Oudinphek, Emphiboche, Barra, Assiou, Ache, Belim, Dexiarche, Masemon." This ends my partial citation < from > their literature.

7,1 Valentinus also preached in Egypt. Thus his seed is still in Egypt, like the remains of a viper's bones, in Athribitis, Prosopitis, Arsinoitis, Thebais, and Paralia and Alexandria in Lower Egypt. Moreover, he went and preached in Rome.[39] (2) But on reaching Cyprus—† < and > really having an actual shipwreck—he departed from the faith and became perverted in mind. Before this, in those other places, he was thought to have a bit of piety and right faith. But on Cyprus he finally reached the last degree of impiety, and sank himself in this wickedness which he proclaims.

7,3 As I said, both he and his school call our Lord Jesus Christ Savior, Christ, Word, Cross, Conductor, Limit-Setter and Limit. (4) But they say he has brought his body down from above and passed through the Virgin Mary like water through a pipe. He has taken nothing from the virgin womb, but has his body from above, as I said. (5) He is not the original Word; nor is he the Christ after the Word, who

---

[38] For Holy Spirit as a Valentinian Aeon see Iren. I.2.5; I.11.1; Hippol. Haer. VI.31.4.

[39] Iren. III.4.3; Tert. Praescr. 30; Adv. Val. 4.

is above among the aeons on high. But they claim that he has been emitted only[40] to come and rescue the spiritual race from above.

7,6   They deny the resurrection of the dead, and make some fictitious, silly claim that it is not this body which rises, but another which comes from it, a body they call "spiritual."[41] <There is salvation> only of those "spiritual" persons in their community and of the others—<the> so-called "soulish" ones—provided that the soulish practice righteousness. But the ones they call "material," "fleshly," and "earthly" perish altogether and cannot be saved at all.[42] (7) Each essence returns to its own origins[43]—the material is abandoned to matter, and the fleshly and earthly to the earth.

7,8   For they believe in three classes[44] of persons, spiritual, soulish and material. They say that they are the spiritual class—as well as "Gnostics"—and have no need of work, simply of knowledge and the afterthoughts of their mysteries. Each of them may do anything with impunity and think nothing of it; they say they will be saved in any case, since their class is spiritual. (9) But the other class of humanity, which they call soulish, cannot be saved of itself unless it saves itself by work and righteousness. They say, however, that the material class of people can neither hold knowledge, nor receive it even if a member of this class wants to, but must perish body and soul.

7,10   Since their own class is spiritual it is saved with another body, something deep inside them,[45] an imaginary thing they call a "spiritual body." (11) But when the soulish have worked hard and risen above the Demiurge, they will be given, on high, to the angels[46] who are with Christ. They recover no part of their bodies; just their souls are given as brides to the angels with Christ, once it appears that they have full knowledge and have risen above the Demiurge.

8,1   Such is their overblown story, and there is more than this. I merely enumerated the things I thought naturally needed to come out, as far as I †knew them—(2) where he came from, when he lived, from whom he took his cue, what his teaching was, with what others he propagated evil in the world. And as I said, I recalled his teaching in part. (3) But I do not want to write the rest of his quibbles myself, since I have found the treatise against him in the works of the ancient author, the most holy Irenaeus. Thus far I have related these few things, but for the

---

[40] Cf. Hippol. Haer. VI.36.3; Iren. I.3.1.
[41] Cf. Ps.-Tert. 4.5; On Res. 47,38-48,3 and, less clearly, Gos. Phil. 57,5-19.
[42] This contrast is made at Iren. I.6.1; I.7.5. Cf. Tri. Trac. 106,6-18.
[43] Cf. Gos. Phil. 53,20-21.
[44] Manichaean variations on this theme occur at Keph. 120,31-33; 269,17-25.
[45] Cf. Hippol. Haer. VI.36.3.
[46] This is a slip on Epiphanius' part, since at Iren. I.7.5 this is said of the spiritual.

rest I shall make the whole presentation from him, a servant of God—I mean Irenaeus.

From the Writings of St. Irenaeus[47]

9,1   Certain persons reject the truth and introduce novel falsehoods, and "endless genealogies which," as the apostle says, "minister questions rather than godly edifying which is in faith."[48] With the specious argument they have villainously hammered together, they mislead the minds of the simple and take them captive, (2) by tampering with the oracles of the Lord and becoming bad expositors of things that have been said well. And they destroy many by leading them away, with pretended knowledge, from him who framed and ordered this whole creation, as though they had something higher and greater to display than the God who has made heaven, earth, and everything in them. (3) In a plausible fashion they win the innocent, with rhetoric, to the habit of inquiry. But they destroy them without plausibility by making their attitude blasphemous and impious towards the Creator,[49] when they have no ability to distinguish truth from falsehood.

9,4   For error is not shown as it is, lest it become detectible stripped. Villainously decked in a cloak of plausibility, it presents itself as truer than the truth itself— < an absurd thing even to say! > —to give the simple that impression by its outward show. (5) It has been said of such persons by a greater man than I, that if a piece of glass is artificially made to resemble a stone, the real precious pearl and of very great value, it will fool some people, if no one there is competent to test it and expose the villainous craft. And when bronze is mixed with silver, what guileless person can readily assay it?

9,6   Now I have read the treatises of the "disciples of Valentinus," as they say themselves, and have met some and understood what they think. To see that—even through no fault of mine—none (of us) are snatched away like sheep by wolves since, under the outer layer of lambskin, they may not know the persons the Lord has warned us of, whose speech is <like ours> but whose thought is different, (7) I feel, beloved, that I must disclose to you the monstrous, abstruse mysteries which "all cannot receive,"[50] since all have not spat their brains out! When you under-

---

[47] 9,1 through 32,9 are quoted directly from Iren. Praef.-I.11.1. Cf. Tert. Adv. Val.; Hippol. Haer. VI.29-31 and, less directly, 32-37.

[48] 1 Tim. 1:4.

[49] That is, the Demiurge. See Index NHL.

[50] Matt. 19:11.

stand them too you can make them known to all who are with you, and urge them to beware of the abyss of folly and blasphemy of God.

9.8 And I shall also give a brief, clear explanation, as far as I can, of the opinion of those who are now repeating the same teaching; I mean Ptolemy and his followers. This is a culling from the school of Valentinus. And as well as my modest ability allows, I shall give <others> the resources for its refutation, by showing that what they say is uncouth, untenable, and incompatible with the truth, (9) though I am neither accustomed to composition nor trained in rhetoric. Love, however, impels me to disclose, to you and to all who are with you, the teachings that have been concealed till now, but by God's grace have now come to light. "For there is nothing covered that shall not be revealed, and hid, that shall not be known."[51]

10,1 As I live among Celts and am mostly occupied with a barbarian language, you will not look for rhetoric, which I have not learned, from me—or ability at composition, in which I have no practice, or elegance of style, or persuasiveness, of which I know nothing. (2) Instead you will receive with love what I have written you with love, simply, truly, and in everyday speech, and make it grow yourself—as you can, being abler than I—as though you had gotten seeds and shoots from me. (3) In the breadth of your intellect you will make what I have said in brief bear fruit in great measure—and will powerfully present, to those who are with you, the information I have given you feebly. (4) And as I have done my best not only to let you know their views—which you have been wanting to learn for a long time—but also to provide the means of proving their falsity you, by the grace the Lord has given you, will you do your best to convey them to the rest, so that people may no longer be carried away with their specious argument, which goes like this:

10,5 They say there is a perfect Aeon, pre-existent in invisible, nameless heights. Him they call Prior Principle, First Progenitor,[52] and Depth. He is uncontainable and invisible, eternal and unbegotten, and has existed in calm and deep tranquility for boundless ages of time. And with him also is Ennoia, whom they term both Grace and Silence.[53]

10,6[54] At some time Depth conceived of emitting a first principle of all from himself, and like a seed[55] he deposited the emanation he had conceived of emitting <in> his co-existent Silence, as in a womb. (7) Receiving this seed and becoming pregnant, Silence brought forth

---

[51] Matt. 10:26.
[52] Cf. "The Lord of the Universe is not called Father, but προπάτωρ" Eug. 74,21-24.
[53] See Notes 18 and 21.
[54] With 10,6-11 cf. Tert. Praescr. 33.
[55] For the thought cf. Tri. Trac. 60,29-37; 61,7-9.

Mind,[56] the like and equal of the One who had emitted him and alone capable of holding the Father's majesty. This Mind they also call Only-Begotten, and Father and first principle of all. (8) But with him Truth has been emitted, and this is the first, original Pythagorean tetrad,[57] which they also call the root of all. For it is Depth and Silence, and then Mind and Truth.

10,9   Realizing why he had been emitted, Only-Begotten himself emitted Word and Life:[58] the father of all who were to come after him, and the principle and form of the entire Pleroma. But from Word and Life, Man and Church have been emitted in a pair.[59] (10) And this is the original Ogdoad, the root and ground of all things, which they call by four names, Depth, Mind, Word, and Man. (For each is male and female as follows: First Progenitor, to begin with, is united in a pair with his own Ennoia. Only-Begotten, or Mind, is united with Truth, Word with Life, and Man with Church.)

10,11   After these Aeons had been emitted to the glory of the Father, they themselves desired to glorify him with something of their own,[60] and put forth emanations in pairs. Word and Life emitted ten other Aeons after the emission of Man and Church, and they say their names are Profound and Copulation, Ageless and Union, Self-Engendered and Pleasure, Immoveable and Intercourse, Only-Begotten and Blessed One. These are < the > ten Aeons they claim have been emitted by Word and Life.[61]

10,12   But Man too, with Church, emitted twelve Aeons.[62] They favor these with the names of Advocate and Truth, Paternal and Hope, Maternal and Love, Ever-Mindful and Understanding, Ecclesiasticus and Blessedness, Desired and Wisdom.

10,13   These are the thirty Aeons[63] of their imposture, which have been kept secret and are not known. This is their invisible, spiritual Pleroma, with its triple division into ogdoad, decad and dodecad. (14) And hence, they say, the Savior—they will not call him "Lord" either—did nothing openly for thirty years, to indicate the mystery of these Aeons. (15) Moreover, they say, these thirty Aeons are made very

---

[56] Mind appears in this role at Val. Exp. 22,30-38; 23,36-37; 24,19-20. For other references to Mind see index NHL.

[57] The Tetrad also appears at Val. Exp. 29,35-38.

[58] For life in a comparable role see Val. Exp. 24,21-22; for Word and Life, Val. Exp. 29,26-37; 31,36-37.

[59] Cf. Val. Exp. 29,28.

[60] With this idea cf. Tri. Trac. 68,3-5.

[61] Cf. Val. Exp. 30,16-17.

[62] Cf. Val. Exp. 30,18-19.

[53] Cf. Val. Exp. 30,16-20.

plainly known in the parable of the laborers sent into the vineyard.[64] For some are sent about the first hour, some about the third, some about the sixth, some about the ninth, and others about the eleventh. If you add these hours they make thirty—one, three, six, nine and eleven are thirty—and they hold that the Aeons are made known by the hours. (16) And these are the great, marvelous, ineffable mysteries which they produce—and, of the things the scriptures say in great quantity, these are all that it is possible to compare and match with their fabrication.

11,1   They say their First Progenitor is known only to Only-Begotten, that is to Mind, who originated from him.[65] To all the rest he is invisible and incomprehensible.[66] Only Mind, they believe, enjoyed the contemplation of the Father and rejoiced in the perception of his immeasurable greatness. (2) And he meant to tell the remaining Aeons[67] how old and vast the Father's greatness was, and how it was without beginning, uncontainable, and impossible to see. But by the Father's will Silence restrained him, since it was her desire to elevate them all to a conception (ἔννοια) of their First Progenitor, and a yearning to seek him.[68]

11,3   Similarly the other Aeons had a sort of silent yearning to see the originator of their seed, and examine their beginningless root.[69] (4)[70] But Wisdom, by far the last and the youngest Aeon of the twelve emitted by Man and Church, sprang forward, and without union with her consort, Desired, experienced a passion of †presumption masked as love, because she lacked Mind's fellowship with the perfect Father. (The passion had begun in Mind and Truth, but fell suddenly on this errant Aeon.) But the passion was a search for the Father; for as they say, she wished to comprehend his greatness.

11,5   Then, since she could not because she had set herself an impossible task, and since she had fallen into deep distress[71] at the vastness of the depth, the Father's unsearchability, and her love for him, she stretched farther and farther forward. And she would finally have been engulfed and utterly dissolved by his sweetness[72] if she had not encountered the

---

[64] Matt. 20:1-16. Gnostics are said to know the true sense of this parable at Apocry. Jas. 8,8-9.

[65] Cf. Apocry. Jn. 4,15-22.

[66] Cf. Tri. Trac. 60,16-29.

[67] A comparable role is played by the Father himself at Tri. Trac. 61,1-18.

[68] The Father himself does this at Tri. Trac. 65,11-17; 71,35-72,8.

[69] The Aeons' search for their origin is mentioned, e.g., at Gos. Tr. 17,5-6; Tri. Trac. 61,24-28; 71,7-11; U 229-30.

[70] Versions of the myth that follows appear at On Res. 46,35-37; Tri. Trac. 76,13-30; 77,25-27; Nat. Arc. 94,4-8; Orig. Wld. 108,14-19; I Apoc Jas. 34,12-15; Gr. Seth 50,25-34; PS 45-46; GL 564,18-19 et al.

[71] Cf. Gos. Tr. 17,10-11; Tri. Trac. 77,11-36.

[72] For the Father's "sweetness" cf. Tri. Trac. 72,11-19.

power which makes all things firm, and keeps watch over them outside of the ineffable majesty. (6) This power they call Limit.[73] Restrained and made fast by Limit, coming to herself with difficulty, and convinced of the Father's incomprehensibility, she abandoned her former resolution, with the passion that had followed from that terror-stricken wonder.

12,1 But some give their mythical account of Wisdom's passion and conversion like this: From attempting an impossible and unattainable feat, she gave birth to a formless essence,[74] the kind a female could.[75] (2) On observing it she was first unhappy over its incomplete formation.[76] Then she became afraid that its very existence might come to an end as well—then distraught and at her wits' end, from trying to see why this had happened, and how to hide it. (3) But after this submersion in the passions she received a conversion, and tried to return to the Father; and after some time in this enterprise was exhausted, and became the Father's suppliant.[77] (4) The other Aeons, but Mind especially, joined in her supplication.[78] This, they say, was the origin of the essence of matter, the ignorance, grief, fear and distraction (of Wisdom).

12,5 It was for this reason that the Father emitted Limit in his own image, unpartnered and with no female, through Only-Begotten. (They sometimes conceive of the Father as paired with Silence, but sometimes, also, as above both male and female.) (6) They also call Limit Cross, Redeemer, Emancipator, Limit-Setter, and Conductor.[79] They say that Wisdom was purified and supported by Limit, and restored to her syzygy.[80] (7) For now that her Resolution, with the passion[81] which had arisen later, was separated from her, she remained within the Pleroma. But her Resolution, with the passion, was separated and walled off by Limit,[82] and once outside him was a spiritual essence <like> a sort of natural germ of an Aeon, but shapeless and without form because it

---

[73] For Limit or comparable ideas see Tri. Trac. 75,13-17; 76,30-34, and the entries listed in Index NHL; Mand. PB 256 pg. 213.

[74] Versions of this myth occur at Gos. Tr. 17,10-20; Tri. Trac. 78,8-17; Apocry. Jn. 9,25-10,19; Orig. Wld. 99,23-34; Zost. 9,16-17; GR 78,25-28; 241,21-23; Keph. 93,1-2;29-30 et al.

[75] An allusion to the common belief that the male parent contributes the form of the offspring, the female, the matter.

[76] In Mandaean literature, Rucha d' Qudsha often laments the imperfection of her offspring, GR 99,23-28; 100,37-101,5; 175,19-27 et al.

[77] Versions of this occur at Tri. Trac. 81,30-35; Apocry. Jn. 13,13-26; Ex. Soul 128,26-129,2; Zost. 10,8-9; Val. Exp. 34,23-34. And note the psalms of repentance in Pistis Sophia.

[78] Cf. Tri. Trac. 82,1-9; 86,29-32; Apocry. Jn. 14,1-6.

[79] Cf. the list of names for the "Cross of Light," which are given at Acts of John 98.

[80] Cf. PS 166; GR 311,37-312,9; Book of John 36,10-37,4 et al; Keph. 72,3-6.

[81] For "passion" cf. Tri. Trac. 95,2-3.

[82] The cross plays a comparable role at Test. Tr. 40,25-29.

understood nothing. And for this reason they call it a sterile fruit and a female.

13,1   But after its banishment outside the Pleroma of Aeons and its mother's restoration to her syzygy, to see that no Aeon would suffer as she had, Only-Begotten emitted yet another pair by the Father's foresight, Christ and Holy Spirit, to fix and support the Pleroma. <They say> that the Aeons were restored to their senses by these.[83] (2) For Christ taught them the nature of union, that <only those> who comprehend the unbegotten <are fit for union> with it;[84] and to proclaim mutually their realization that the Father is uncontainable and incomprehensible and cannot be seen or heard, or is known through Only-Begotten alone. (3) Also that the Father's incomprehensibility is the cause of the others' eternity, while his comprehensibility, or Son, is the cause of their birth and formation. And this is what the just emitted Christ did among them.

13,4   But once they were all made equal, Holy Spirit taught them to give thanks and †explained the true repose.[85] And thus, they say, the Aeons were made alike in form and sentiment, and all became Minds, all Words, all Men, and all Christs. And the females similarly all became Truths, Lives, Spirits and Churches. (5) But when all things were confirmed in this state, they say, and had come to repose at last, with their great good cheer they hymned First Progenitor very joyfully.

13,6   And to make a return for this beneficence each one of the whole Pleroma of Aeons, with Christ's and Holy Spirit's consent and their Father's endorsement, pooled and contributed what was best and brightest in it with one design and purpose. They brought these things fitly together, united them becomingly, (7) and produced an emanation to the honor and glory of Depth,[86] a kind of consummate beauty and star of the Pleroma, its perfect Fruit, Jesus. He is also called Savior; Christ; Word after his father; and All,[87] because he is of all. And angels[88] of like nature were emitted with him in †this honor, to be his bodyguard.

14,1   This, then, is the trouble they say was within the Pleroma, and the misfortune of the Aeon who suffered and all but perished from <her experience> of deep †grief in search of the Father, and her congealing by the efforts of Limit, Cross, Redeemer, Emancipator, Limit-Setter and

---

[83] Cf. Gos. Tr. 24,9-20; Tri. Trac. 73,1-8.

[84] Something like this is done by Spirit at Tri. Trac. 71,35-72,19; 73,1-8.

[85] Cf. the "rest" at Tri. Trac. 70,18.

[86] The same idea appears at Tri. Trac. 86,23-87,11, and a comparable one at Corp. Herm. XIII.2.

[87] Cf. Tri. Trac. 65,23-25; Silv. 101,22-26; 102,5; GT 77; Vercelli Acts of Peter 39; Corp. Herm. XIII.2.

[88] The thought appears in more sophisticated form at Tri. Trac. 87,17-31.

Conductor. And the production, later than the Aeons, of the first Christ and Holy Spirit by their Father in his repentance. And the composite constitution, by loan, of the second Christ, whom they also term Savior.

14,2   Since not everyone can accommodate the knowledge of these things, they have not been said openly. They have been made known mystically by the Savior, to those who can understand, in the following parables. (3) The thirty Aeons are made known—as I said—by the thirty years in which they claim the Savior did nothing openly; and by the parable of the laborers in the vineyard. (4) And they say that Paul obviously names these Aeons many times, and further that he has even preserved their order in the words, "unto all the generations of the aeons of the aeon."[89] (5) We too indicate those Aeons by saying, "unto the aeons of the aeons,"[90] at the eucharist. And wherever "aeon" or "aeons" are mentioned, they hold that the reference is to those.

14,6   The emission of the dodecad of Aeons is made known through the Lord's disputation with the doctors of the Law at the age of twelve and the choosing of the apostles; there are twelve apostles. (7) And the remaining eighteen Aeons are made manifest by what they say about the Lord spending eighteen months with the disciples after the resurrection. Moreover, the eighteen Aeons are clearly made known by the first two letters of his name, "iota" and "eta." (8) And they say that the ten Aeons are similarly indicated by the "iota" which begins his name. And this is why the Savior has said, "One iota or one tittle shall not pass away till all things come to pass."

14,9   The passion the twelfth Aeon experienced is suggested, they say, by the defection of Judas, the twelfth apostle, and because (the Savior) suffered in the twelfth month—they hold that he preached for one year after the baptism. (10) Further, this is indicated very clearly by the woman with the issue of blood. For after suffering for twelve years she was healed by the Savior's arrival, through touching the hem of his garment. And the Savior said, "Who touched me?"[91] to teach his disciples of the mystery which was enacted among the Aeons, and the healing of the suffering Aeon. (11) For the woman who suffered for twelve years is that power, <which> would have been <totally> dissolved when—as they say—she was extended and her essence ran endlessly, if she had not touched the Son's garment—the Truth of the first Tetrad, made known by the hem of the garment. But she came to a halt and ceased from the passion. For the power of the Son which issued forth—they hold that this is Limit—healed her, and separated the passion from her.

---

[89] Eph. 3:21.
[90] Cf. Tri. Trac. 67,38-39.
[91] Mark 5:30.

14,12   And that Savior, the product of all, is the All, is shown, they say, by the words, "every male that openeth the womb."[92] For since he is the All, he opened the womb of the suffering Aeon's Resolution, †the one who was banished outside the Pleroma. They also call her a second Ogdoad; I shall speak of her a little later. (13) And they say that, "And he is all,"[93] was obviously said on this account by Paul, and again, "All are for him, and of him are all,"[94] and, "In him dwelleth all the Pleroma of the Godhead."[95] And they interpret, "to gather all in one in Christ, through God,"[96] <in this sense>, and anything else of the kind.

15,1   Then they declare of their Limit, the one they have more names for, that he has two operations, stabilizing and divisive.[97] Insofar as he stabilizes and supports, he is Cross; but insofar as he divides and separates, he is Limit. (2) They say the Savior has made his operations known in the following ways. First the stabilizing, with the words, "He who doth not bear his cross and follow me, cannot be my disciple,"[98] and <again>, "Take up thy cross and follow me."[99] (3) But his divisive operation with the words, "I came not to send peace, but a sword."[100] John too, they say, has made the same thing known by saying, "The fan is in his hand. He will throughly purge his floor, and will gather the wheat into his garner; but the chaff he will burn with fire unquenchable."[101] (4) And with this he has shown Limit's operation. For they interpret the fan as that Cross, which consumes everything material as fire consumes chaff, and yet winnows the saved as a fan winnows wheat. (5) But they say the apostle Paul has also mentioned this Cross with, "For the preaching of Cross is to them that perish foolishness, but unto them that are saved he is a power of God,"[102] and again, "God forbid that I should glory in anything save in the Cross of Christ, through whom the world is crucified unto me, and I unto the world."[103]

15,6   They say this sort of thing of their Pleroma, and their fictional account of everything, and make every effort to harmonize things which have been said well with things which they have invented badly. And not only do they try to produce their proofs from the Gospels and apostolic

---

[92] Luke 2:23.
[93] Cf. Col. 3:11.
[94] Cf. Rom. 11:36.
[95] Col. 2:9.
[96] Eph. 1:10.
[97] Cf. Val. Exp. 25,22-24; 26,26-34; 27,30-37.
[98] Luke 14:27.
[99] Cf. Mark 8:34 parr.
[100] Matt. 10:34.
[101] Luke 3:17.
[102] 1 Cor. 1:18.
[103] Gal. 6:14.

writings, by twisting the meanings and tampering with the interpretations. (Even) more skillfully, and in a dishonest fashion, they square <what they like> from the Law and prophets with their fabrication— (7) these have numerous parables and allegories which can be carped at in many respects, †owing to the doubtfulness of their interpretation. They thus capture from the truth those who do not keep firm their faith in one God, the Father almighty, and one Lord Jesus Christ, the Son of God.

16,1   But what they say is outside the Pleroma is something like this. When the Resolution of the Wisdom on high, whom they also call Achamoth,[104] was separated, with the passion,[105] from the Pleroma <on high>, they say that of necessity she was stranded in a shadowy, empty region.[106] For she found herself outside of light and Pleroma, without shape and form like an untimely birth,[107] because she had understood nothing. (2) But in pity for her the Christ <on high> reached out to her through Cross, and gave her form by his own power—only the form[108] pertaining to essence, not the form pertaining to knowledge. Having done so he withdrew by contracting his power and left <her>, so that she would realize the passion she had because of leaving the Peroma, and yearn for something better.[109] For she had a certain savor of immortality, left <her> by Christ and Holy Spirit. (3) Hence she is given both names: Wisdom, after her father—for Wisdom is said to be her "father"—and Holy Spirit, after the Spirit who is with Christ.

16,4   Formed and become conscious, but immediately emptied of Word, or Christ, who had been with her invisibly, she started up to seek the light that had left her—and could not overtake it, because prevented by Limit.[110] And here, to prevent her from starting forward, Limit said, "Iao!"[111] This, they claim, is the origin of the name, Iao.

16,5   Unable to pass Limit because of her entanglement with the passion, and left alone outside, she was subject to every portion of the pas-

---

[104] "Echamoth" is distinguished from "Echmoth" at Gos. Phil. 60,10-15; Achamoth appears at 1 Apoc. Jas. 34,3; 35,5-12; 36,5. A "hylic Sophia' is mentioned at Gos. Egypt. 57,1.

[105] With this "passion" cf. Tri. Trac. 95,2-3.

[106] This is something like the description of Chaos given at Orig. Wld. 98,23-99,22.

[107] There is a different version of this at Tri. Trac. 78,29-79,4, and yet another at Orig. Wld. 99,2-22. Some of these traits are wrongly applied to Christ at Jer. in Amos 3:9-10.

[108] Cf. the repairing of Sophia at Apocry. Jn. 13,33-14,13. See also Val. Exp. 26,22-26; 27,32-33.

[109] The Logos stimulates the best desires of his defective offspring at Tri. Trac. 83,11-32.

[110] Cf. Val. Exp. 33,25-32.

[111] Jesus cries "Iao" three times at PS 353.

sion in its multiplicity and variety. She suffered grief because she had not overtaken the light; fear of being without life as she was without light; and desperation besides. She was altogether in ignorance. (6) And unlike her mother, the first Wisdom Aeon, she did not have an alternation of the passions but a conflict between them. But another disposition had visited her as well—conversion[112] to him who had brought her to life.

16,7   She, they say, has become the system and substance of the matter of which this world is composed.[113] The whole soul of the world and the Demiurge originates from the conversion, while the rest arises from the fear and the grief. Everything wet comes from her tears, everything bright from her laughter; and the world's physical components from her grief and terror. (8) For at times, as they say, she would weep and grieve at being left alone in the dark and void. But at other times she would think[114] of the light that had forsaken her, interrupt her weeping, and laugh.[115] Again, she was sometimes afraid, at other times at her wits' end and distraught.

17,1   And why bother? It would be left for us to discuss a lot of dramatics and imagining here; each of them proudly explains in a different way from which element of what sort of passion a substance had its origin. (2) Indeed, it makes sense to me that they do not care to teach everyone openly—just those who can afford even high prices for mysteries of such sublimity![116] (3) For these are no longer like the ones of which our Lord has said, "Freely ye have received, freely give."[117] They are recondite, monstrous, deep mysteries, obtainable with great effort by those who love lies. (4) For who would not spend all he has to learn that seas, springs, rivers, and everything wet has originated from the tears of the suffering Aeon's Resolution, but the light from her laughter, and the world's physical components from her terror and perplexity?

17,5   But I would like to make a contribution of my own to their produce. As I see that some water—springs, rivers, rain and the like—is fresh, while sea-water is salt, I have an idea that not all water emanates from her tears. Tears are salty. (6) Obviously, then, it is this salt water that comes from the tears. But it is likely that, since she fell into great

---

[112] Cf. the conversion of the Logos at Tri. Trac. 81,8-82,14—also Val. Exp. 34,10-34—and the repentance and prayers of Pistis Sophia at PS 46-52 and many other places.

[113] Matter is given a comparable origin at Tri. Trac. 85,7-12.

[114] Cf. Tri. Trac. 82,4-6.

[115] Cf. Sophia's laughter at Val. Exp. 34,35-38.

[116] The imparting of teaching or mysteries for payment is forbidden at Apocry. Jn. 31,34-37; Jeu 100.

[117] Matt. 10:8.

anguish and perplexity, she perspired as well. Therefore, on their premise, one must suspect that springs and rivers, and any other fresh water, originates from her < sweat >. (7) For since tears are of one quality, it is not credible that fresh water on the one hand, and salt on the other, issues from them. This is more credible, that the one is from the tears and the other from the sweat. (8) < However >, since certain kinds of water are both hot and bitter, you should realize what she did to emit those, and from which part of her. These are the sorts of conclusion that fit with their premise!

17,9   When their Mother had passed through all the passions and barely surmounted them, they say she addressed herself to supplication[118] of the light, or Christ, who had left her. As he had returned to the Pleroma he likely did not care to come down again. But he sent Advocate < to > her[119]—that is, Savior—(10) once the Father had put all power in him and put all under his authority, and the Aeons had done the same, so that "all things might be created in him, visible and invisible, thrones, godheads, dominions."[120]

17,11   He was sent to her, with his angelic companions.[121] They say that at first, out of respect for him, Achamoth veiled herself in modesty. But then, seeing him with all his bounty, she ran to him, and drew strength from his appearing.

17,12   He gave her the form which pertains to knowledge[122] and effected the cure of her passions by separating them from her. He did not ignore them—they could not be destroyed like the former Wisdom's passions, because they were already habitual and strong.[123] But he set them apart by the act of separating them from her, and he mixed and solidified them, and from incorporeal passions changed them into incorporeal matter. (13) Then he put serviceability and an outward form in them in the same way, so that they became compounds and bodies for the generation of two essences, the inferior one < made from > the passion, and the passionate one made from the conversion.[124] And they therefore say that Savior has wrought with power.[125]

17,14   When Achamoth got out of the passion,[126] joyfully caught sight of the lights with him[127]—that is, of the angels who were with

---

[118] See notes 77 and 78.
[119] Cf. Ex. Soul 132,6-16; PS 98-99.
[120] Col. 1:16.
[121] A comparable thought appears at Tri. Trac. 87,26-31; 89,15-20; PS 99 et al.
[122] Cf. Tri. Trac. 62,1-3.
[123] From this point through 17,13 cf. Val. Exp. 35,30-37.
[124] At Ascl. 22 gods and men are said to be made from different parts of nature.
[125] Something similar is said of the Logos at Tri. Trac. 96,35-97,5.
[126] For "passion" cf. Tri. Trac. 95,2-3.
[127] "The Savior and those who are with him" appear at Tri. Trac. 95,35-36.

him—and yearned for them, they teach that she conceived fruit in
<their> image, a spiritual embryo conceived in the likeness of Savior's
bodyguards.

18,1   As they tell it, there were now these three things: that which
came from the passion, which was matter; that which came from the conversion, which was the soulish; and that which she had conceived, the
spiritual. Thus her next concern was their formation. (2) But she could
not form the spiritual, since it was the same as herself. Instead she addressed herself to forming the soulish essence which stemmed from her
conversion, and emitted the things she had learned from Savior. (3) And
first, they say, from the soulish essence she formed the Father and King
of all things[128]—the things of his own kind, the soulish things they call
"right"—and those which stem from the passion and matter, the things
they call "left." (4) For they say that <he> formed everything after
him, instigated by the Mother without knowing it. Thus they call him
Male-and-Female Progenitor, Without Progenitor, Demiurge, and
Father, and say he is father of those on the right, the soulish; demiurge
of those on the left, the material; but king of them all.[129] (5) For they say
that, in her desire to create all things in honor of the Aeons, Resolution
has made their images—or rather, Savior has made them through her.[130]
She herself has retained †the image of the invisible Father, since she is
unknown to the Demiurge. He, however, has retained the image of the
Only-begotten Son; and the archangels and angels he has made, that of
the remaining Aeons.

18,6   Thus, as maker of everything soulish and material, they say he
has become Father and God of the things outside the Pleroma. For by
separating the two commingled essences and making corporeal things
from incorporeal, he has created everything heavenly and earthly, and
become Demiurge of material and soulish, right and left, heavy and
light, rising and sinking. (7) For they say he has made seven heavens and
is their Demiurge above them. And thus they call him Hebdomad; but
the Mother, Achamoth, they call Ogdoad,[131] since she retains the
number of the original, first Ogdoad of the Pleroma. (8) But they say the
seven heavens are intelligible heavens, and suppose that they are angels.
The Demiurge is an angel too, but like a god. And thus they also say that

---

[128] Cf. Tri. Trac. 100,19-30.

[129] Something comparable is said of the sun at Corp. Herm.XVI.12-13.

[130] The Logos works through the Demiurge at Tri. Trac. 100,31-35; the Spirit works
through the Demiurge at Tri. Trac. 101,9-19.

[131] "A great aeon whose name is Ogdoad" is found at SJC 102,3-4; "the Eighth of
darkness" is found at the Book of John 25,8; 41,17; 95,3-4 et al.

since Paradise is above a third heaven[132] it has the significance of a fourth archangel, and that Adam had something of it while he lived in it.

18,9 They claim that the Demiurge thinks he makes these things <entirely> by himself,[133] but that he has made them because Achamoth emits them. <For> he has made heaven without knowing heaven; formed man though ignorant of man; and †produced earth with no knowledge of earth. (10) And in every case they similarly say that he did not know of the forms of the things he was making, or the Mother herself, but believed that he alone was all. (11) But they claim that, from her wish to give him this sort of preferment, the cause of this creating of his has been the Mother, the source and origin of her own being, but the "lord" of the entire transaction. (12) They call her Mother and Ogdoad, and Wisdom, Earth, Jerusalem, Holy Spirit, and in the masculine, Lord. She inhabits the Intermediate Region[134] and is above the Demiurge, but is below, or outside, the Pleroma till the consummation.

19,1 Since they say that the material essence is composed of three passions—fear, grief and perplexity—what is soulish has its origin from the fear and the conversion.[135] (2) They hold that the Demiurge originated from the conversion, but everything else that is soulish, such as the souls of brute beasts, wild creatures and men, originated from the fear. (3) <And> thus, because he is too weak to know the spiritual, the Demiurge has believed that he alone is God, and has said, through the prophets, "I am God, there is none besides me."[136]

19,4 But they teach that wicked spiritual beings[137] come from the grief. This is the origin of the Devil, whom they also call Ruler of the World, and of demons, angels, and anything spiritual that is wicked. (5) But they say the Demiurge is a soulish son of their Mother, while the Ruler of the World is a creature of the Demiurge. And the Ruler of the World knows what is above him, for he is a wicked spirit; but as the Demiurge is soulish, he does not.[138] (6) Their Mother dwells in the place above the heavens, the Intermediate Region, the Demiurge in the heavenly place, the Hebdomad, <but> the Ruler of the World, in our world.

---

[132] Paradise may be comparably located at Orig. Wld. 110,2-6.
[133] Comparable ignorance is mentioned at Tri. Trac. 79,12-16; 84,3-7; 100,36-101,5; 101,20-25; 105,29-35; Orig. Wld. 100,19-21; GR 266,18-24.
[134] Pistis Sophia is conducted to a comparable place at PS 165-166.
[135] "Powers" result from the "prayer and remembering" of the Logos at Tri. Trac. 82,10-24.
[136] See Sect 25, Note 8.
[137] Cf. Eph. 6:12.
[138] Cf. the ignorance of the similar beings mentioned at Tri. Trac. 79,12-19; 80,24-30.

19,7   As I said, the world's physical components are derived from the consternation and bewilderment, the more †distracting (part of the passion)—earth answering to the motionlessness of consternation, water to the movement of fear, air to the fixity of pain. But they teach that fire is inherent in them all as death and decay, just as ignorance lies concealed within the three passions.

19,8   After creating the world the Demiurge also made the man of dust—not by taking him from this dry earth but from the invisible essence, the overflow and runoff of matter. Into him, they declare, he breathed soulishness. (9) And this is the man created "in an image and a likeness;"[139] and in image he is the material man, very like God but not of the same nature. But "in likeness" he is the man with a (living) soul;[140] hence his essence is also said to be a "spirit of life," stemming from a spiritual effluent. (10) Later, they say, the garment of skin was put on him; this they hold to be the perceptible flesh.

19,11   But they say the Demiurge is also unknowing of their Mother Achamoth's spiritual embryo which she brought forth, spiritual in nature like the Mother, at the sight of the angels about Savior. Nor does he know that it was implanted in him unawares, without his knowledge, so as to be sown through him in the soul which stems from him and in this material body, to be incubated < and > grown in these, and to get ready for the reception of full < Reason >.[141] (12) Thus, they say, the Demiurge was unaware of the spiritual man whom Wisdom also sowed, with ineffable < power and > providence, through his breath.[142] For as he knew nothing of the Mother, so he knew nothing of her seed[143]—which they also call Church,[144] a replica of Church on high.[145] (13) They regard this as the man within them,[146] so that they have their soul from the Demiurge, their body from earth and its fleshliness from matter, but their spiritual man from the Mother, Achamoth.[147]

---

[139] Gen. 1:26.

[140] With what follows cf. the creation of the "psychic and material body" at Apocry. Jn. 19,3-6; also Keph. 120,31-33; 269,17-25.

[141] Cf. Tri. Trac. 123,3-15; GL 455,31; 463,34-35; 483,15-20; Book of John 120,5-7 et al.

[142] Comparable are the powers breathed into the mixture that becomes the soul, at PS 14; 336-337. Note also the "hidden Adam" which is mentioned at GL 486,17-19; 577,1-25.

[143] "Seed" in this sense is common in Nag Hammadi; cf. e.g., Tri. Trac. 95,31-36; Gos. Phil. 85,21-23; Nat. Arc. 96,27; 97,9; Val. Exp. 37,23;38; 39,12;15;20; 40,19.

[144] "Church" appears in similar sense at Tri. Trac. 94,17-23.

[145] The Church on high seems to mean the totality of the aeons at Tri. Trac. 57,23-59,26.

[146] For "inner man" cf. Let. Pet. 137,20-22; PS 338-339 and many other passages in this document.

[147] Comparable accounts of man's composition are found at the non-Gnostic Silv.

20,1 Thus there are three principles.[148] They say the material principle, which they also call "left," must perish, since it can receive no
breath of immortality.[149] But the soulish, which they also term "right,"
is midway[150] between spiritual and material and goes wherever it is in-
clined.[151] (2) The spiritual, however, has been sent out to be formed here
in conjunction with the soulish,[152] and educated with it in life.[153] And
they say that this is the salt,[154] and the light of the world.[155] For the
soulish needed even sensible means of instruction; this is why a world has
been made, they say. (3) And the Savior has also come for this soulish
principle, to save it, since it too has power of self-determination.

20,4 They claim that the Savior has received the first-fruits[156] of the
principles he was to rescue. He has received spirituality from Achamoth,
has donned the soulish Christ from the Demiurge, and from the dispensation has been clothed with a body whose essence is soulish, but which,
by an ineffable art, has been made to become visible, tangible and passible. But they say he has received nothing material at all, since matter is
not susceptible of salvation.

20,5 The consummation will come when everything spiritual has
been given form and perfected in knowledge.[157] This means the spiritual
men, who have perfect knowledge of God and are initiates of <the>
mysteries[158] of Achamoth; they suppose that <they themselves> are
these persons. (6) But soulish people, who are established by works and
mere faith and lack perfect knowledge,[159] were taught soulish things. We
of the church, they say, are these people.[160] (7) And so they declare that
doing good is essential for us—we cannot be saved otherwise.[161] But they
hold that they will surely be saved in any case, not by doing but because
they are spiritual by nature.[162] (8) For as the earthy cannot have

---

92,11-93,33, and at Acts of Thomas 165, Keph. 69,17-25, cf. 120,31-33. Perhaps cf. also
Corp. Herm. IX.9.
[148] There is a very full account of these at Tri. Trac. 103,13-104,3; 106,3-18;
118,14-124,25.
[149] Cf. Tri. Trac. 119,8-20.
[150] The vital are said to be in the "middle area" at Tri. Trac. 103,19-21.
[151] Cf. Tri. Trac. 119,20-24.
[152] Cf. Tri. Trac. 123,3-22.
[153] The spirit and the soul are said to be saved together at Apocry. Jas. 11,39-12,5;
GL 566,18-567,23; 583,2; 587,22 et al.
[154] Sophia is called salt at Gos. Phil. 59,30-34. Cf. Matt. 5:13.
[155] Cf. Matt. 5:14.
[156] Cf. Test. Tr. 32,22-24.
[157] Cf. the account of the restoration given at Tri. Trac. 123,12-124,3.
[158] The learning of "mysteries" is the core of the teaching of Pistis Sophia and Jeu.
[159] Cf. Tri. Trac. 118,37-119,7; 129,34-131,13.
[160] Cf. Tri. Trac. 122,13-123,3.
[161] Perhaps cf. Tri. Trac. 130,11-30.
[162] Cf. Tri. Trac. 119,16-18; 2 Apoc. Jas. 59,1-10. In Pistis Sophia souls which have

salvation—they say it is not susceptible of it—so the spiritual, in turn, which they claim to be, does not admit of corruption, whatever deeds they engage in by the way. (9) For as gold buried in mud does not lose its beauty but retains its own nature, since the mud has no power to harm the gold, they too, they say, in whatever material acts they engage, cannot be harmed or lose their spirituality.[163]

21,1   Hence, the most perfect ones may do with impunity all the forbidden things of which the scriptures assert that those who do them will not inherit the kingdom of God.[164] (2) In fact they eat foods sacrificed to idols without distinction, and believe they are in no sense defiled by them. They are the first to gather for any holiday celebration the heathen hold in honor of the idols—and some do not even avoid the murderous spectacle, hateful to God and man, of battles with beasts and gladiatorial combat. (3) Some even serve the pleasures of the flesh to excess and say they render carnal things to the carnal and spiritual to the spiritual. (4) And some secretly seduce the women to whom they teach this, as women have often confessed with the rest of the imposture, after being deceived by some of them and then returning to God's church. (5) Some, even open in their shamelessness, have enticed any women they want away from their husbands, and regarded them as their own wives. (6) Others again, pretending at first to live modestly with them as sisters, have been exposed in time when the sister became pregnant by the brother.

21,7   But though they do many other detestable, ungodly things, they cast off on us as ignorant boors with no understanding, because from fear of God we guard against sin even in thought and speech. But they exalt themselves above us and call themselves "perfect"[165] and "seed of election." (8) For they say that we receive grace on loan,[166] and so will be deprived of it. But as their rightful possession they have the grace descended from above, from the ineffable, unutterable syzygy; and therefore it will be added to them. And for this reason it is absolutely essential that they continually study the mystery of the syzygy.

21,9   Of this too they convince the stupid, and say in so many words, "Whoever has come into the world and not loved a woman so as to

---

received the higher mysteries are certain of salvation, 286-291. They are assured in advance of forgiveness for subsequent sin, 302-303, though this is limited to twelve sins, and repentance is required after each, 303. But they are lost if they die impenitent, 305-306; 308, cf. also 309 et al. Mandaeism, on the other hand, rejects this type of teaching, cf. Book of John 226,2-3.

[163] This is said of a pearl at Gos. Phil. 62,17-26.

[164] Gal. 5:21.

[165] Cf. PS 77; 126 et al; Man. Hom. 53,8 et al. The term "perfect" is of frequent occurrence in Nag Hammadi, and is also a common term for the Mandaean initiate.

[166] Cf. "the names which they received on loan," Tri. Trac. 134,20.

possess her, is not of the truth, and will not depart to the truth. But he who is of the world and has possessed a woman, will not depart to the truth, for he has possessed a woman in lust."

21,10   And so we, whom they call "soulish" and say are "of the world," need continence and good deeds as our means of entering the Intermediate Region.[167] But not they, the ones called "spiritual" and "perfect." No deed enters the Pleroma, but the seed which is sent from there in its infancy, <though> it matures here.

21,11[168]   But they say that when all the seed matures, their Mother, Achamoth, leaves the Intermediate Region, enters the Pleroma, and receives the product of all the Aeons, Savior, for her bridegroom, forming a syzygy of Savior and the Wisdom of Achamoth. This is the meaning of "bridegroom and bride"; "marriage chamber"[169] is the entire Pleroma. (12) The spiritual will doff their souls, become intellectual spirits, enter the Pleroma[170] untouched and unseen,[171] and be given as brides to Savior's angels.[172] (13) The Demiurge too will move to Mother Wisdom's place,[173] that is, in the Intermediate Region. And the souls of the righteous will also rest in the Intermediate Region—for nothing soulish can enter the Pleroma.[174] (14) But they teach that after that, the fire latent in the world will flash forth, catch, consume all matter,[175] be consumed with it,[176] and pass into nothingness. They declare that the Demiurge knew none of this before the Savior's advent.

22,1   But there are those who say that he too emitted a Christ[177]—a son of his own, and soulish <himself>—<and> has spoken of him through the prophets. This is the one who passed through Mary like water through a pipe. On him, at the baptism,[178] that Savior from the Pleroma, the product of all, descended in the form of a dove. The spiritual seed from Achamoth came into him as well. (2) They maintain, then, that our Lord was a compound of these four, reflecting the original, first tetrad: the spiritual, which was from Achamoth; the soulish, from

---

[167] "The soul" seeks the "place of righteousness" which is "mixed," at PS 282.

[168] With 21,11-12 cf. Val. Exp. 39,28-35.

[169] Cf. Gr. Seth 57,13-18.

[170] Restoration to the Pleroma is mentioned at Treat. On Res. 44,31-32.

[171] Cf. Acts of Thomas 148.

[172] Cf. the account of the ascent at Corp. Herm. I.26.

[173] A kind of rehabilitation of Ialdabaoth may be intended at SJC 121,6-13. Cf. Para. Shem 22,25-23,2.

[174] Cf. "that curtain between the immortals and those that come after them" SJC 117,21-24.

[175] Cf. Gr. Pow. 40,9-23; 46,29-33; Man. Hom. 39,23-24; 41,5.

[176] Cf. Gr. Pow. 40,21-23; 46,29-32.

[177] Sabaoth creates a Christ at Orig. Wld. 105,24-29.

[178] See Sect 28, Note 3.

the Demiurge; the dispensation, which was prepared with an ineffable art; and Savior, which was <the> dove that came down to him. (3) And Savior remained impassible; he could not suffer, since he could not be touched or seen. Hence when Jesus was brought before Pilate, the spirit of Christ that had been implanted in him was taken away.

But the seed from the Mother has not suffered either, they say; it too is impassible, †since it was spiritual and invisible even to the Demiurge. (4) To conclude, their "soulish Christ" and the one mysteriously prepared by the dispensation suffered, so that the Mother could exhibit the type of Christ on high <through> him—the Christ who was stretched out by Cross and gave Achamoth the form pertaining to essence. For they say that all these things are types of the others.

22,5 They say that the souls with Achamoth's seed are better than the rest. Thus they are more loved than the others by the Demiurge, though he does not know why, and thinks that he is responsible for their quality. (6) And so, they say, he appointed them prophets, priests and kings. And they interpret many passages as utterances of this seed through the prophets, since it is of a higher nature. They say that the Mother too has said a great deal about the higher things; however, they <claim> that <much has been said> through †the Demiurge and the souls which he created. (7) And to conclude, they cut the prophecies up by holding that one part is uttered by the Mother, one by the seed, one by the Demiurge. (8) But Jesus has similarly said one thing by Savior's inspiration, one by the Mother's, one by the Demiurge's, as I shall show in due course.

22,9 But the Demiurge, who did not know what was above him, was angry at those sayings. He despised them and had various explanations of their cause: the spirit prophesying, with some anger of its own; man; the admixture of inferior things. (10) And he remained in this ignorance till the Savior's coming. But when the Savior came, they say, he learned everything from him, and gladly joined him with his entire host. (11) And he is the centurion of the Gospel, who tells the Savior, "For I also have under my authority soldiers and servants, and whatsoever I command, they do."[179] (12) He will fulfil his function in the world as long as necessary, especially to care for the church and because he knows the reward in store for him—that he will go to the Mother's place.

23,1 They suppose that there are three kinds of men, the spiritual, the earthy, and the soulish, just as there were Cain, Abel and Seth— <to

---

[179] Matt. 8:9; Luke 7:8. With the enlightenment of the Demiurge cf. Nat. Arc. 95,13-17; 31-34; Orig. Wld. 104,26-31; Para. Shem 22,17-23,8; GR 88,21-34; 355,23-357,33; 360,21-370,19; Book of John 30,8-11 et al; PS 197.

prove > the three natures even from these, not as individuals here but as types. (2) The earthy kind departs to corruption. If the soulish chooses what is better, it rests in the Intermediate Region; if it chooses what is worse, it too will depart to that sort of place.[180] (3) But they hold that when the spiritual (seeds) which Achamoth sows among them have been trained and nurtured here in righteous souls from then till now—since they are sent as infants—they will later be awarded to Savior's angels as brides, when they are deemed mature.[181] But of necessity their souls will have gone to eternal rest in the Intermediate Region with the Demiurge. (4) And again they subdivide the souls themselves, and say that some are good by nature, others evil by nature. And it is the good souls that become fit to receive the seed; the souls which are evil by nature would never welcome that seed.[182]

24,1   Since such is their subject—which no prophets proclaimed, which the Lord did not teach or the apostles transmit, (yet) which they take extreme pride in knowing better than the others—they read from uncanonical writings, busily plait what is said there into ropes of sand, and rather than let their forgery appear unevidenced, (2) try to match parables of the Lord, oracles of the prophets, or words of the apostles convincingly with what they have said. They violate the arrangement and sequence of the scriptures, and as much as they can manage, dismember the truth. (3) They change things and refashion them, and, by making one thing out of another, completely fool many with their poorly assembled show of the accommodated oracles of the Lord.

24,4   It is as though a beautiful portrait of a king had been carefully made of fine gems by a wise craftsman, and someone destroyed the image of the man he saw, moved those gems and recombined them, and produced a likeness of a dog or fox, and poorly made at that. (5) And then he stated categorically that this was the beautiful portrait of the king which the wise craftsman had made, and he displayed the gems the former craftsman had fitted together well into the king's portrait, but the latter had changed badly into a likeness of a dog—and defrauded the less experienced, who have no conception of what a king looks like, with the show of the gems, and convinced them that this latter poor effigy of the fox was the former lovely portrait of the king. (6) They have cobbled old wives' tales together in exactly the same way, and then they extract words, sayings and parables from here and there, and want to match the oracles of God with their stories.

---

[180] Cf. in a sense Corp. Herm. I.19.
[181] Cf. Dia. Sav. 138,16-20.
[182] Different sorts of souls are distinghuished at Tri. Trac. 105,29-106,5.

25,1   We have spoken of all the things they match with what is inside the Pleroma. Here are the sorts of things they try to adapt from scripture to the things outside the Pleroma. (2) They say the Lord has come for the passion near the end of the world to exhibit the passion that overtook the last of the Aeons; and with this "end" to indicate the end of the Aeons' trouble. (3) They explain the twelve-year-old girl, the ruler of the synagogue's daughter, whom the Lord came and raised from the dead, as a type of Achamoth, to whom their Christ gave form when he was extended, and whom he brought to an awareness of the light that had left her.

25,4   They say it was because of Savior's manifesting <himself> to Achamoth when she was outside the Pleroma like an untimely birth,[183] that Paul, in the First Epistle to the Corinthians, has said, "Last of all he was seen of me also, as of one born out of due time."[184] (5) In the same epistle he has similary revealed the coming of Savior to Achamoth with his companions by saying, "The woman ought to have a veil on her head because of the angels."[185] And that Achamoth veiled <her face> in shame when Savior came to her, Moses has made evident by covering his face with a veil.

25,6   And they claim the Lord has indicated the passions she suffered <when abandoned by the light>. With his words on the cross, "My God, why hast thou forsaken me?"[186] he has shown that Wisdom was abandoned by the light and prevented from starting forward by Limit. With, "My soul is exceeding sorrowful,"[187] he has shown her grief; with, "Father, if it be possible, let this cup pass from me,"[188] her fear. Similarly her bewilderment, with, "and what I should say, I know not."[189]

25,7   They teach that he has shown three kinds of men in the following ways. The material, by replying, "The Son of Man hath not where to lay his head," to the man who said, "I will follow thee."[190] The soulish, by answering the man who said, "Lord, I will follow thee, but let me first bid farewell to them which are at home in my house," with, "No man having put his hand to the plow and looking back is suitable in the kingdom of heaven."[191] (8) (They say this man was one of the intermediate kind.) They claim that the man who professed to have per-

---

[183] Cf. Nat. Arc. 94,13-15; Orig. Wld. 99,9-11;23-26.
[184] 1 Cor. 15:8.
[185] 1 Cor. 11:10.
[186] Matt. 27:46; Mark 15:34.
[187] Matt. 26:38.
[188] Matt. 26:39.
[189] John 12:27.
[190] Matt. 8:19-20; Luke 9:57-58.
[191] Luke 9:61-62.

formed most righteousness and then would not follow, but was kept from maturing by wealth,[192] was similarly soulish. (9) But the spiritual kind, by saying, ''Let the dead bury their own dead; but go thou and preach the kingdom of God;''[193] and by saying of Zacchaeus the publican, ''Make haste and come down, for today I must abide at thy house.''[194] For they declare that these were of the spiritual kind.

25,10   And they say that the parable of the leaven the woman is said to have hidden in three measures of meal[195] shows the three kinds. For they teach that Wisdom is called a woman, but that ''three measures of meal'' are the three sorts of men, spiritual, soulish, earthy. And they teach that ''leaven'' means the Savior himself.

25,11   <And> Paul has spoken expressly of earthy, soulish, and spiritual men—where he says, ''As is the earthy, such are they also that are earthy;''[196] where he says, ''The soulish man receiveth not the things of the spirit;''[197] and where he says, ''A spiritual man examineth all things.''[198] And they say that ''The soulish man receiveth not the things of the Spirit,''[199] refers to the Demiurge, who is soulish and does not know the Mother, who is spiritual; or her seed; or the Aeons in the Pleroma.

25,12   Because the Savior took the firstfruits of those he was to save, Paul has said, ''If the firstfruits be holy, the lump is also holy.''[200] They teach that ''firstfruits'' means the spiritual but ''lump'' means ourselves, the soulish church, whose lump they say he received and raised in himself, since he himself was leaven.

26,1   And they say that by his statement that he has come for the <sheep> that was lost,[201] he showed that Achamoth strayed outside the Pleroma, and was formed by Christ and sought out by Savior. (2) For they explain that ''lost sheep'' means their Mother, by whom they hold that the church here has been sown. But ''straying'' means the time she spent outside the Pleroma, on <all> the passions from which they think matter originated.

26,3   They explain that the woman who swept the house and found the drachma[202] means the Wisdom on high, who lost her Resolution but

---

192 Cf. Matt. 19:16-22.
193 Matt. 8:22; Luke 9:60.
194 Luke 19:5.
195 Cf. Matt. 13:33.
196 1 Cor. 15:48.
197 1 Cor. 2:14.
198 1 Cor. 2:15.
199 1 Cor. 2:14.
200 Rom. 11:16.
201 Cf. Matt. 18:12; Luke 15:4.
202 Luke 15:8. Cf. Apocry. Jas. 8,9.

found her later, when all had been purified by Savior's arrival. This, they think, is why she was restored to her place within the Pleroma.

26,4   They say that Simeon, who took Christ up in his arms, gave thanks to God, and said, "Lord, now lettest thou thy servant depart in peace according to thy word,"[203] is a type of the Demiurge. He learned of his translation when Savior came, and gave thanks to Depth.

26,5   And they declare that Achamoth is very obviously shown by Anna, whom the Gospel proclaims a prophetess, and who had lived seven years with a husband and always remained a widow after that, till she saw and recognized the Savior and spoke of him to everyone.[204] Achamoth saw Savior briefly < then > with his companions, and always remained in the Intermediate Region afterwards, waiting for him[205] to return and restore her to her syzygy. (6) And her name has been disclosed—by the Savior with, "And Wisdom is justified by her children;"[206] but by Paul with, "Howbeit we say, 'Wisdom' among them that are perfect."[207]

26,7   And they claim that Paul has mentioned the syzygies within the Pleroma, and in one instance specified them. For of the syzygy in the world he wrote, "This is a great mystery, but I speak concerning Christ and Church."[208]

27,1   They teach further that John, the disciple of the Lord, has revealed the former Ogdoad. Their exact words are, (2) "John, the disciple of the Lord, desiring to speak of the generation of all by which the Father emitted all, posits as God's first production a 'Beginning,' which he has called both 'Son' and 'Only-Begotten God.' In this, in germ, the Father emitted all. (3) He says that 'Word' has been emitted by him, and in Word the entire essence of the Aeons, to which Word himself later imparted form. Since John is speaking of a first act of generation, he rightly begins his teaching at the 'Beginning,' that is, the Son and the Word.

27,4   "But this is what he says. 'In Beginning was Word, and Word was with God, and Word was God. The same was in Beginning with God.'[209] (5) After distinguishing the three at first—God, Beginning and Word—he puts them together again, to show the emission of the two, Son and Word, and their union with each other and the Father as well. (6) For Beginning was in the Father and of the Father, and Word was in Beginning and of Beginning. So he was right in saying, 'In Beginning

---

203   Luke 2:29.
204   Cf. Luke 2:36-38.
205   Cf. Ex. Soul 132,16-21.
206   Luke 7:35.
207   1 Cor. 2:6.
208   Eph. 5:32.
209   John 1:1-2.

was Word,' for Word was in Son. 'And Word was with God' is right, for Beginning <was> indeed <with the Father>. 'And Word was God' is apt, for what is begotten of God is God. <And by>, 'The same was in Beginning with God,' he indicated the order of the emissions.

27,7 "He said, 'All things were made by him, and without him was not anything made,'[210] for Word was the cause of the form and generation of all the Aeons after him. But, says John, 'That which was made in him is Life.'[211] Here he even disclosed a syzygy. He said that all things have their origin through Word, but that Life has her origin in Word.

27,8 "Hence, she whose origin was in him is closer to him than those whose origin was through him; for she is his companion, and bears fruit by him. (9) For John adds, 'And Life was the light of men.'[212] In saying 'Man' at this point, he has disclosed Church under the same name, to show the syzygy's partnership through the one name; for Man and Church come from Word and Life. (10) And he termed Life the 'light of men', since men are enlightened—that is, formed and made manifest—by her. But Paul says this too, 'Whatsoever is made manifest is light.'[213] Therefore, since Life made Man and Church manifest and brought them forth, she is called their light.

27,11 "With these words, then, John has clearly indicated both the rest, and the second tetrad: Word and Life, Man and Church. (12) But indeed, he has disclosed the first tetrad as well. For in describing the Savior and stating that everything outside the Pleroma has been formed by him, he calls him the fruit of the entire Pleroma. (13) For he has called him a 'light' that shines in darkness and is not comprehended by it, since, though Savior set all the products of the passion in order, he was not known by them. (14) But John calls him 'Son,' 'Truth,' 'Light,' and 'Word made flesh, whose glory,' he says, 'we beheld; and his glory was as that of an Only-Begotten, given him of the Father, full of Grace and Truth.'[214] (15) He says it as follows: 'And Word was made flesh and dwelt among us, and we beheld his glory, the glory as of an Only-Begotten of a Father, full of Grace and Truth.'[215] Thus he also disclosed the first tetrad exactly as it is, by saying Father, Grace, Only-Begotten, and Truth. (16) In this way John has spoken of the first Ogdoad, mother of all the Aeons. For he has said Father, Grace, Only-Begotten, Truth, Word, Life, Man, and Church.''

---

[210] John 1:3.
[211] John 1:4.
[212] John 1:4.
[213] Eph. 5:13.
[214] John 1:14.
[215] John 1:14.

28,1 You can see the way they deceive themselves, beloved, their abuse of the scriptures to try to prove their fabrication from them. This is the reason I cite their actual words, to show you the villainy of the method from them, and the wickedness of the imposture. (2) In the first place, if John intended to reveal the higher Ogdoad, he would have kept to the order of the emanation, and placed the first Tetrad, which they say is the most venerable, among the names that come first. He would then have added the second, showing the order of the Ogdoad by the order of the names. He would not have mentioned the first Tetrad after such a long interval, as though he had forgotten it completely and then recalled it at the last minute.

28,3 And next, if he meant to indicate the sygyzies, he would not have left Church's name out. He might have been equally content to name the males in the case of the other syzygies—they too can be understood to go with (their females)—to maintain uniformity throughout. <Or>, if he were listing the consorts of the rest, he would have revealed Man's too, and not left us to get her name by divination.

28,4 <Their> falsification of the exegesis is obvious. John proclaims one God almighty, and one Only-begotten, Christ Jesus, through whom he says all things were made. <He says> that he is Son of God, that he is only-begotten, that he is maker of all, true light that enlightens every man, creator of the world, he who came unto his own, and that he himself became flesh and dwelt among us. (5) But these people pervert the exegesis as much as they plausibly can, and hold that Only-Begotten, whom they also call Beginning, is one of the series of emanations. But they hold that Savior was a different one, that Word, Only-Begotten's Son, was a different one, and that Christ, who was emitted to rectify the Pleroma, was another. (6) They have taken each thing they say from the truth <and> changed it for their own purpose by misusing the names, so that, to hear them tell it, among so many names John makes no mention of the Lord, Christ Jesus. (7) For although he has said Father, Grace, Only-begotten, Truth, Word, Life, Man, and Church, on their premise he has said it of the first Ogdoad, in which there is no Jesus yet and no Christ—John's teacher!

28,8 But the apostle himself has made it plain that he has not spoken of their syzygies, but of our Lord Jesus Christ, whom he also knows as the Word of God. (9) For in summing up about the Word, which he has already mentioned at the beginning, he adds the explanation, "And the Word was made flesh, and dwelt among us." But on their premise Word did not become flesh; he never even left the Pleroma. That was Savior, who was the product of all the Aeons, and of later origin than Word.

29,1 Fools, learn that Jesus himself, who suffered for us, who dwelt among us, is the Word of God! If some other Aeon had become flesh for our salvation, the apostle would presumably have spoken of another. But if the Word of the Father, who descended, is †also the one who ascended—the only-begotten Son of the only God, made flesh for man at the Father's good pleasure—then <John> has not written "word" of any other, or of an Ogdoad, but of the Lord Jesus Christ.

29,2 Nor, in their view, has the Word predominately become flesh. They say that Savior put on a soulish body which, by ineffable providence, had been prepared by the dispensation to become visible and tangible. (3) But flesh is the ancient thing God formed from the dust, like Adam; and John has revealed that this is what God's Word has truly become.

29,4 And this destroys their first, original Ogdoad. Once it is established that Word, Only-Begotten, Life, Light, Savior and Christ are one and the same and God's Son, and that he himself was made flesh for us, the stage-platform for <their> Ogdoad is destroyed. And with this wrecked their whole pantomine—which they falsely dream to disparage the scriptures and fabricate their own dramatic piece—fails of its purpose.

29,5 Then they collect words and names which lie scattered throughout scripture, move them from their natural setting, as I said, to an unnatural one, and do the same sort of thing as the persons who set themselves subjects at random and then try to declaim them in lines from Homer. (6) It thus seems to the simple that Homer has composed the words on that subject which has been declaimed extemporaneously. And by the artificial sequence of the words, many are rushed into believing that Homer must have written these words in this order. (7) So with the one who wrote as follows, in lines from Homer, about Heracles' being sent for the dog in Hades by Eurystheus. (There is nothing to prevent me from mentioning even these by way of illustration, since <the> enterprise of both parties is one and the same.)

(8) So spake Eurystheus, son of Sthenelus,
Who came from Perseus' house, and sent away
Much-laboring Heracles, to fetch from Hell
The loathed Hades' dog. With heavy sighs
He hastened through the town, like to a lion
Bred in the mountains, trusting in its strength.
All they that loved him bare him company,
Young maids, and elders who had much endured,
Mourning for him as on his way to death.

But lo, gray-eyed Athena, in her heart—
For hers was kin to his—knowing his toil,
Sent Hermes to his aid.

29,9   What innocent person could fail to be swept off his feet by these words, and think that Homer had written them in that way, on this subject? But anyone familiar with the subject of Homer will recognize < the words but not their subject > , (10) since he knows that some are spoken of Odysseus, some actually of Heracles, but some of Priam, and Menelaus and Agamemnon. He will take them and put each one back it its own < book > , and remove < this > subject from consideration. (11) Thus he who holds the rule of the truth upright within him, the rule he has received by baptism, will recognize the names, expressions and parables from scripture, but not this blasphemous subject. (12) For though he will commend the gems, he will not allow the fox as a substitute for the king's portrait. He will restore each thing that is said to its own position, fit it to the truth's naked body, and prove that their forgery is without foundation.

30,1   < But > to allow us to go over their mime and give the refutation—this piece is beyond redemption—I suppose it might be well first to show how the very authors of this story differ among themselves, as though they stemmed from different spirits of error. (2) In this way too we may understand perfectly—even before it is demonstrated—that the truth the church proclaims is sure, and the one they have counterfeited is falsehood.

30,3   For though it is dispersed the whole world over, to the ends of the earth, the church, from the apostles and their disciples, has received the faith in one God, the Father Almighty, maker of heaven, earth, the seas, and everything in them. (4) And in one Christ Jesus, the Son of God, made flesh for our salvation. (5) And in the Holy Spirit, who through the prophets has proclaimed the dispensations, the coming, the birth of the Virgin, the passion, the resurrection, and the bodily assumption into heaven of the beloved < Son > , Christ Jesus our Lord, and his coming from heaven in his Father's glory to gather all things in one and raise the flesh of all mankind; (6) that, by the invisible Father's good pleasure, every knee in heaven, on earth, and under the earth may bow to Christ Jesus, our Lord, God, Savior and King, and every tongue confess him. And that he may pronounce a righteous judgment on all, (7) and consign the spirits of wickedness, the angels who have transgressed and rebelled, and wicked, unrighteous, lawless and blasphemous men, to the eternal fire; (8) but grant life, bestow immortality, and secure eternal glory for the righteous and holy, who have kept his commandments and abode in his love, some from the first, others after repentance.

31,1   The church, as I said, has received this message and this faith. Though it is dispersed all over the world it guards them as carefully as if it lived in one house. It believes in accordance with them, as though it had one soul and the same heart. It preaches, teaches and transmits them in unison, as though with one mouth. (2) Even if the languages of the world are different, the meaning of the tradition is one and the same. The Churches founded in Germany have not believed differently or transmitted the tradition differently—or the ones founded among the Iberians, the Celts, in the east, in Libya, or in the center of the earth. (3) As the sun, a creature of God, is one and the same the world over, so the light < of the mind >, the proclamation of the truth, shines everywhere and illumines all who are willing to come to a knowledge of truth. (4) The ablest speaker of the church's leaders will say nothing different from these things, for no man is above his master.[216] Nor will the feeblest speaker diminish the tradition. For as faith is one and the same, someone with much to say of it does not enlarge it, and someone with little to say does not diminish it.

31,5   No one can know more or less with understanding by changing the actual subject (of our knowledge) and inventing a new God different from the creator, maker and sustainer of all—as though he were not enough for him—or a different Christ or Only-Begotten. (6) He can, however, by giving a further explanation of what has been said in parables, and suiting it to the subject of the faith. He can by expounding God's dealings with mankind and his provision for them, and making it plain that God bore with the rebellion of the angels who transgressed, and the disobedience of men. (7) By proclaiming the reason why one and the same God has made things temporal and eternal, heavenly and earthly, and why, though invisible, God appeared to the prophets, not in one form but so as to be perceived differently by different ones. By disclosing the reason why men have been given a number of covenants, and teaching the nature of each. (8) By inquiring why God confined all in disobedience so as to have mercy upon all, and giving thanks for the reason why God's Word became flesh and suffered—and by telling why the advent of God's Son came in the last times, which is to say that the beginning appeared in the end.

31,9   He can by unfolding what scripture says of the end and the things to come; not hiding God's reason for making the gentiles, who once were reprobate, fellow-heirs and of the same body, and partakers with the saints; (10) by making it known that this mortal flesh will put on immortality, this corruptible, incorruption; by proclaiming that God

---

[216] Cf. Matt. 10:24.

will say, "That which was not my people is my people, and she who was not beloved, is beloved,"[217] and, "More are the children of the desolate than the children of the married wife."[218]

31,11   For it was at these things and others like them that the apostle cried, "O the depth of the riches both of the wisdom and knowledge of God! How unsearchable are his judgments, and his ways past finding out!"[219] It was not because had gotten so blasphemous that he went on to discover the Creator and Demiurge's Mother above him, and their erring Aeon's Resolution! (12) And not <at> lying still more about the Pleroma above her in turn—a Pleroma of thirty Aeons then, †of a countless tribe of them now—as these teachers say, who are truly barren of divine understanding. Meanwhile all the true church, as I said, holds one and the same faith the world over.

32,1   Now let us also see their unstable views—how it is that, when there are perhaps two or three of them, they cannot agree on the same things, but make pronouncements contrary in facts and names. (2) For Valentinus, the first of the so-called Gnostic sect to change its principles into a form characteristic of a school, blurted them out as follows. He declared that there is <an> unnameable pair, one of which is called Ineffable, and the other Silence. (3) Then a second pair has been emitted from this, and he calls one Father, and the other Truth. Word and Life, and Man and Church, are the fruit of this Tetrad; and this is the first Ogdoad. (4) And he says that ten powers have been emitted from Word and Life, as we mentioned, and from Man and Church, twelve—one of whom, by rebelling and coming to grief, has caused the rest of the trouble.

32,5   And he supposed that there were two Limits. One is between Depth and the rest of the Pleroma, and separates the begotten Aeons from the unbegotten Father;[220] the other one separates their Mother from the Pleroma. (6) And Christ was not emitted from the Aeons in the Pleroma. Along with a certain shadow he was brought forth by the Mother when she got outside, in memory of better things. (7) Since he was male and could, he cut the shadow off and returned to the Pleroma. But after the Mother was abandoned with the shadow and emptied of spirit, she bore another son; and this is the Demiurge, whom he also terms autocrat of all beneath him. But like the persons falsely termed Gnostics, of whom we shall speak, Valentinus held that a left-hand archon was also emitted with the Demiurge.

---

[217] Hos. 2:25; Rom. 9:25.
[218] Isa. 54:1.
[219] Rom. 11:33.
[220] Cf. Val. Exp. 27,34-38.

32,8   And he sometimes says that Jesus was emitted by the one whom their Mother inhaled, <and> exhaled into all things—that is <by> Desired. Or sometimes by the one who returned to the Pleroma, that is, by Christ—or sometimes, by Man and Church. (9) And he says that the Holy Spirit was emitted by Truth to examine the Aeons and make them fruitful, by entering them invisibly. Through him the Aeons bring forth the fruits of the truth.

This concludes Irenaeus against the Valentinans

33,1   The elder I mentioned, Irenaeus, <gave> these facts and others like them; he was fully equipped by the Holy Spirit. Sent into the ring by <the> Lord as a champion athlete, and anointed with the heavenly favors of the true faith and knowledge, he wrestled their whole silly subject down and beat it, and went over every bit of their nonsense. (2) But he gave a fine further refutation of them in his next book, the second, and the others. He seemed to want to drag his opponent after he had already been thrown and beaten, to make a public spectacle of him, and to find the shameless though feeble challenge of weak-mindedness in him even when he was down.

33,3   I, however, am content with the few things I have said, and the things these compilers of the truth have said and written. And I can see that others have done the work—I mean Clement, Irenaeus, Hippolytus, and many more, who have given the Valentinians' refutation even remarkably well. I have no wish to add to the work as I said, since these men satisfy me, and my intent is precisely the same. Even from the wording of the Valentinians' teachings their refutation will be †perfectly apparent to any person of understanding.

34,1   In the first place their ideas are at variance, and each professes to demolish the other's. Secondly, there is no proof of their mythological constructions. No scripture said these things—not the Law of Moses or any prophet after Moses, not the Savior or his evangelists, certainly not the apostles. (2) If these things were true, the Lord who came to enlighten the world, and the prophets before him, would have told us something of the kind in plain language. And then the apostles too. They confuted idolatry and all sorts of wrongdoing, and were not afraid to write against any unlawful teaching, and opposition. (3) Especially when the Savior himself says, ''Unto them that are without, in parables; but to you must †the parables' interpretation be told, for knowledge of the kingdom of heaven.''[221] (4) It is plain that he explained any parables he told in the Gospels immediately. He surely says who the mustard seed is, who the

---

[221] Cf. Mark 4:11.

leaven is, the woman who put the leaven in the three measures, the vineyard, the fig tree, the sower, the best soil.

34,5   And these people are falsely inspired, because haunted by devils. The most holy apostle Paul says of them, "In the latter times some shall depart from the teaching, giving heed to fables and doctrines of devils."[222]

34,6   And again, St. James says of this sort of teaching, "This wisdom descendeth not from above, but is earthly, sensual, devilish. But the wisdom that is from above is first of all pure, then peaceable, easy to be intreated, without partiality, full of mercy and good fruits,"[223] and so on. But not one fruit of this wisdom is visible in these people. (7) With them there is "confusion and every unlawful work,"[224] spawn of devils and serpents' hisses, with each one saying something different, in a different way, at a different time. In them no mercy or pity is apparent, just hair-splitting and disagreement; no purity, no peace, no fairness.

35,1   But again, since the argument demands it, I do want to mention a few of their statements and refute them, even though I promised to finish. I do not care about the correct technique of speaking, but about benefiting the reader. (2) Now then, they say that the twelfth Aeon, the one which became defective, dropped out of the twelve entirely, and the number twelve was gone. (3) But they say that this is what happened †when Judas, the twelfth apostle, defected, and this eliminated the number twelve. And so of the woman with the issue, and the one who lost the one drachma out of her ten. (4) However, it is established that the twelfth Aeon cannot be represented by Judas, as the most holy Irenaeus has said already. Judas has perished utterly, but the so-called twelfth Aeon of their fabrication was not emptied. They say themselves that Conductor, or Limit-Setter, stood in front of her and told her, "Iao!" and this made her firm.

35,5   Nor can the woman who bled for twelve years be compared with their dramatic piece; she was healed after the twelve years in which she was afflicted with bleeding. She did not stay healthy for eleven years and bleed in the twelfth; she bled in the eleven, but was healed in the twelfth. (6) Nor did the woman with the ten drachmas lose the one for good, allowing for their story of the lost Aeon of matter; she lit the lamp and found the drachma.

36,1   Since all their stories are refuted at once by these two or three arguments, the sons of prudence and children of God's holy catholic church will understand them as melodrama, ineffective, and come too

---

[222] 1 Tim. 4:1.
[223] Jas. 3:15;17.
[224] Jas. 3:16.

late. (2) For not to make the treatise endlessly long by attacking the same people, I shall make my last mention of them with this sketch, set a bound to their wickedness though it is so great, and go on to the next. (3) I call on God as the guide and help of my weakness, to preserve me from this sect and the ones I have mentioned before it—and the ones I plan to exhibit to studious people, who want a precise knowledge of all the foolish talk in the world, and the chains which cannot hold.

36,4   For in a way, by planting his dreams in many people after him and calling himself a Gnostic, Valentinus fastened a number of scorpions together in one chain, as in the old and well-known parable. It says that scorpions, one after another, will form a sort of chain to a length of ten or more, let themselves down from a roof or housetop, and so inflict their damage on men by guile. (5) Thus both he, and the so-called Gnostics who derive from him, have become authors of imposture. Each has taken his cue from him, been instructed by another, added to the imposture after his teacher, and introduced another sect clinging to the one before it. (6) And thus the so-called Gnostics have been divided successively into different sects themselves; but, as I said, they have taken their cue from Valentinus and his predecessors. (7) Still, since we have trampled on them, and on the sect of this Valentinus, with the teaching of the truth, let us pass them by. Let us, however, examine the rest by the power of God.

32.

Against Secundians[1] with whom Epiphanes and Isidore are associated. Number twelve, but thirty-two of the series

1,1   I have now passed Valentinus' sect by, after getting very tired in his crop of thistles and < going through it >, if I may say this, with considerable trouble and hard field labor. I shall go to what is left of his thistly crop, and his snake's carcass. (2) I pray the Lord for the Holy Spirit, that through him I may be able to shield souls from harm by my teaching in God, and my grave speech, and may suck the poisons out of those who have this infection already. (3) But I shall begin to say, of each of the following in turn, which of those who stemmed from Valentinus yet taught a different crop of teachings than his, succeeded which.

1,4   Now Secundus, who was one of them yet more conceited, explained everything like Valentinus; but he made a louder noise in the

---

[1] Sect 32 is based on Iren. I.11.2-5 and Clem. Alex. Strom. III.5.1-3. Cf. Hippol. Haer. VI.38.1-2; Tert. Adv. Val. 37-38.

idiots' ears. (5)² Being Valentinian as I said, but more conceited than Valentinus, he said that the first Ogdoad is a right-hand tetrad and a left-hand tetrad, and so taught that the one is called "light," and the other, "darkness." (6) However, the power that fell away and got into difficulty was not one of the thirty aeons, but came after the thirty aeons. It was thus one of <their fruits, which> originated lower down, after the other Ogdoad. (7) But on Christ and the other doctrines he held precisely the same position as Valentinus, the furnisher of his own venom and the supplier of his poison.

1,8   Since few of his ideas are enlisted from anywhere else, I feel I should be content with the ones I have mentioned, which are refutable even of themselves. But I shall still say a little about him too, or it may appear that I pass the subject by because I cannot deal with it.

1,9   If their tetrads are ranged on the right and left, it will be found that something is required between the right and left. (10) Anything with a right hand and a left stands between its right and left hands, and there can be no right or left except as distinguished from a body in between. (11) Now then, Secundus you fool—and anyone fooled by yourself—the center, by which both right and left are determined, (12) must be some one thing. And the right and left it determines cannot be alien to this one thing. And the whole must inevitably be traced back to the thing that is one; and nothing whatever can be above it, or inferior to or below it, except the things it has created. (13) And to those who see the truth it will be obvious that God is one, Father, Son and Holy Spirit. But if God, the source of all, is one, there is no "left" in him or other defect, and nothing inferior except for the things he has made. However, anything after the Father, Son and Holy Spirit has been made well, and has been brought into being, with unstinting generosity, by himself.

2,1   But even supposing a different snake of this sort goes on to answer me that the right and left are outside of the One, while he himself is the middle, and he takes the right-hand things to himself and rejoices in them, and names them "right" and "light"; but he abhors the left-hand things as strange to him and lying on his left. He will have to tell me where he gets this geometry that allows him a good definition of an unalterable right and left. (2) Right or left in us is aptly named from the limbs, which are fixed in the body and never interchangeable. (3) But anything outside us can be "right" one minute and "left" the next. The south, or meridial region, will be called "right" by anyone facing east, and the northerly, or arctural region, "left." (4) But conversely, if one turns west he will find the regions named differently. The southerly and

---

² Cf. Iren. I.11.2; Hippol. Haer. VI.38.1; Tert. Adv. Val. 38.

meridial, which was "right" a minute ago, changes in turn into "left." And the arctural, or northerly, which has been on one's left, changes into his right. (5) Very well, where did the fraud find his divinely ordained geometry? And how much silly talk there is like this, confusing everything!

2,6 But he claims that Deficiency came after the thirty Aeons. All right, Mister, tell me where you got hold of the nature of Deficiency, or the rebellious power! (7) If you found it < growing > from a shoot of the things on high, not a result of creation but a product of generation—both you and your master determine that created things are not results of creation; < you suppose > that everything which is generated in its turn grows up by generation and participation, with each nature receiving from each. (If so), on your terms you are surely attacking yourself. (8) For if both the later power and its rebellion are the products of the things on high, and if, in a manner of speaking, it sprouted and grew from them, it therefore partakes of the benefits on high. For the later power is in touch with the Pleroma and the Pleroma with the later power, and there can be no difference between them either way, since they are both in contact at their ends. (9) And in a word, you unhappiest of the unhappy, you will be convicted of getting the fodder for your imposture from a demon's second sowing.

3,1 But so as not to omit any group's customs or teachings—even if each has many innovators, who proudly go beyond their teachers by inventing story after story—I shall continue to describe those who are in this sect itself, but say something different from the ones above. (2) I am speaking of Epiphanes[3] the pupil of Isidore, who degraded himself to a further depth of misery under the cover of hortatory speeches. In fact, he took his cue from his own father, Carpocrates; but he was connected with Secundus' sect, and a Secundian himself. (3) For there was considerable difference between all these misguided persons, and a sort of miscellaneous tangle of nonsensical talking.

3,4 This Epiphanes as I said, who was a son of Carpocrates and whose mother's name was Alexandria, is connected with the Secundians. On his father's side he was a Cephallenian. < But > he died early at the age of seventeen,[4] as though the Lord had something better in mind for the world, and was removing its worthless thorns. (5) After his death though, those who had strayed on his account did not get over the plague they had caught from him. (6) At Same he is still honored as a god; the

---

[3] Epiphanes is probably connected with Secundus because of the clause, "qui et clarus (= ἐπιφανής) est magister eorum," said of an anonymous Gnostic teacher at Iren. I.11.2. See also Hippol. Haer. VI.38.2; Clem. Alex. Strom. III.5.1-3; Tert. Adv. Val. 37.

[4] Clem. Alex. Strom. III.5.2.

natives have dedicated a temple to him, and have sacrifices and mysteries every new moon. They have erected altars to him and founded a well-known library in his name, the one called the Library of Epiphanes. (7) The Cephallenians are so far gone in error that they sacrifice and pour libations to him, and have banquets and sing hymns to him in his temple which they have dedicated.[5] (8) But it was because of his over-education both in the arts and Plato,[6] that they got the entire deception from him—about the heresy and the other imposture, the one that made the Samians into crazy idolaters.

3,9   Epiphanes, then, was associated with Secundus and his following. For he copied Secundus' ejection of poison, that is, his wordy babble of harmful, snake-like corruption. (4,1) They claim, however, that Isidore[7] in his exhortations is the author of their wickedness. But I cannot tell for certain whether he agreed with them himself and was originally one of them, or whether he was another preacher with philosophical training. In any case these people are all in the same line.

4,2   In the first place Epiphanes himself, with his father and the leader of his sect, Carpocrates, and those about him, ruled that men's wives are to be held in common. He took his cue for this from Plato's Republic[8] and got what he himself wanted. (3) But he begins by saying that on the Savior's authority there are three kinds of eunuch in the Gospel—the eunuch made by men, the eunuch from birth, and the eunuch who becomes one willingly for the kingdom of heaven's sake.[9] (4)[10] "Therefore," he says, "those who are so of necessity do not become eunuchs deliberately. But those who make themselves eunuchs for the kingdom of heaven's sake <make this> calculation, they say, because of the consequences of matrimony, for fear of preoccupation <with earning> a living. (5) <And by> 'It is better to marry than to burn, set not thy soul on fire,'[11] he says that the apostle means, 'Stand firm and fear night and day, do not fall from continence. For a soul that stands firm is awarded its hope.'

4,6   "'Stand firm against a contentious woman then,'[12] says Isidore in the Ethics in these very words"—as I said, he is quoting the exhortation—"'lest you be enticed away from God's grace. Once you

---

[5] Clem. Alex. Strom. III.5.2.
[6] Clem. Alex. Strom. III.5.2.
[7] Isidore is mentioned at Clem. Alex. Strom. II.113.3-6; III.1.1-3; VI.53.2-4; Test. Tr. 57,6-8.
[8] Cf. Clem. Alex. Strom. III.8.1-2.
[9] Matt. 19:12. Cf. Clem. Alex. Strom. III.1.1-2.
[10] 4,4-5,3 is quoted from Clem. Alex. Strom. III.1.1-3.2.
[11] Cf. 1 Cor. 7:9.
[12] Cf. Prov. 21:19.

have ejaculated the fire,[13] pray with a good conscience. But when your
state of grace succumbs at demand and you are unsuccessful at last and
cease from it, fall! Marry!'"[14]

4,7 Then, again, he says, "'But one who is a youth, or poor, or on
the decline'"—that is, ill—"'and prefers not to choose marriage should
not leave his brother,'"[15] The unhappy man plays the knave and invites
certain evil suspicions besides, <for> he says, (8) "'let him say, Since
I have entered the holies I cannot be affected. But if he feels a presenti-
ment let him say, Lay your hand on me, brother, lest I sin; and he will
receive aid in intellect and sense.[16] Let him but will to achieve the good,
and he will attain it.'"

4,9 Then again, he says, "'At times we say, We will not sin, with
our lips, but our minds are devoted to sin. From fear a man like this does
not do as he desires, lest he be assessed the penalty. Mankind has certain
members which are essential and natural, <but some which are
natural> only. Its garment (of flesh) is natural and essential, but while
the organ of desire is likewise natural, it is <not> essential.'"

5,1 "I have quoted these remarks," the author who wrote against
them <says>, "to expose those who do not live uprightly," and Basilideans, Carpocratians, and those who are named for Valentinus and
Epiphanes, whose associate was the Secundus I mentioned before him.
(2) For whether the first transmitted them to the second or the second to
the first, each traded with each other for his horrors. And though they
differ to a degree they put themselves in one sect, (3) "and so held that,
because of their maturity, they had license even to sin. Even if they sinned now they would be saved by nature in any case—due to their natural
election, (I suppose), since not even the original authors of these doctrines permit them to do that."

5,4[17] "As though aspiring to something loftier and on a higher plane
of knowledge, these also speak of the first tetrad, as follows: 'Before all
else there is a certain prior principle of which there can be no preconception, and which is unutterable and cannot be named; I call it Soleness.
With this Soleness there co-exists a power which in turn I term
Singleness. (5) Without being emitted themselves this Singleness and
Soleness, which I call the One, emitted a principle intelligible in all
respects, unbegotten and invisible, a principle which speech terms In-

---

[13] Cf. Keph. 26,15-17.
[14] Holl suggests reading μή with κατορθώσας rather than with σφαλῆναι, giving this
rendering.
[15] Cf. GT 25.
[16] Cf. Keph. 128,18-23.
[17] 5,4-7,5 are in part quoted, in part summarized from Iren. I.11.2-5. Cf. Hippol.
Haer. VI.38.2-4; Tert. Adv. Val. 37.

dividual. (6) With this Individual there co-exists a power of the same
nature, and I term it the One. These powers, Soleness and Singleness,
Individual and the One, emitted the remaining emanations of the
Aeons.'''

6,1   Next those who had compiled the truth <about> them well
refuted <them> in their own treatises. Clement did, whom some call
Clement of Alexandria, and others, Clement of Athens. (2) Moreover St.
Irenaeus has come forward to ridicule those dramatics of theirs by saying, (3) "Alas and alack!" of the words we have just quoted. "'Tragic'
is a really good word for a misfortune like that of the authors of these
ridiculous specimens of such coinage—and for impudence so great that
he gave names to his lie without a blush. (4) For in saying, 'Before all
else there is a certain prior principle of which there can be no preconception; I call it Soleness'—and again, 'With this Soleness there co-exists a
power which in turn I term Singleness'—he has made the plainest sort
of admission that the words are a fabrication of his, and that he himself
has given names to the fabrication which have never been given by
anyone else. (5) And he has plainly ventured to coin them himself; and
if he had not lived the truth would not have had a name. (6) Hence there
is nothing to prevent someone else from assigning names of this sort for
the same purpose."

6,7   Then in conclusion the blessed Irenaeus—as I said—proposes
ridiculous terms himself and says jokingly that different names of his own
are worth just as much as their silliness. He makes up family trees of
melons, cucumbers and gourds as though they were right there, and from
what they have read the studious can see †their <aptness>.

7,1   "But others in turn have given the following names to the first,
original Ogdoad: First, Prior Principle; next, Inconceivable; but third,
Ineffable, and fourth, Invisible. (2) And from the first, Prior Principle,
Beginning has been emitted in the first and fifth <place>.[18] From Inconceivable, Incomprehensible has been emitted in the second and sixth
place; from Ineffable, in the third and seventh place, Unnameable; from
Invisible, Unbegotten. (This is) the Pleroma of the first Ogdoad. (3) To
seem more perfect than the perfect and more gnostic than the Gnostics,
they hold that these powers are before Depth and Silence—but to these
people one could rightly say, 'Drivelling sophists!'

7,4   "Indeed, their opinions about Depth himself differ. Some say he
is unattached, not male, not female, not a thing at all. Others give him

---

[18] "(I) stood upon the first aeon which is the fourth aeon" Zost. 6,19-20; "I stood
upon the second aeon which is the third" 7,6-8; "...the fourth aeon which is the first,"
7,20-21.

the nature of a hermaphrodite and say he is male and female. (5) Others again attach Silence to him as bedfellow to form a first syzygy,'' and thus dramatically produce the rest from him and her. (6) And the amount of foolish dreaming in them, which lulls their minds into deep slumber, is considerable.

7,7   But why waste my time at length? From what has been said the subject of the Secundians, and their refutation and rebuttal, can be glimpsed by all who care to cling to their life and not be fooled by empty myths. (8) I shall say no more about them. Passing this sect by I shall < go > to the rest to look for a safe way and level path by which to traverse and refute their evils—to lead myself and my hearers to safety by God's power, through the teaching and true contemplation of our Lord. (9) Treading this viper underfoot with the sandal of the Gospel— like the mousing viper, which resembles many vipers—let us examine the rest.

33.

Against Ptolemaeans.[1] *Number thirteen, but thirty-three of the series*

1,1   Ptolemy follows Secundus and the man named Epiphanes, who took the cue for his own opinion by barter from Isidore. He belongs to the same sect of the so-called Gnostics, and with certain others < is one of > the Valentinians, but has suppositions which are different from his teachers'. His adherents take pride in his very name, and are called Ptolemaeans.

1,2[2]   This "Ptolemy, with his supporters, presents himself to us as still more adept" than his own teachers, and has invented still more additions to their outline. (3) "He invented two consorts for the God they call Depth, and bestowed them on him. But he also called these 'dispositions,'[3] Conception (ἔννοια) and Will." (4) Conception had always co-existed with him, continually conceiving of emission; but Will arose in him later. "For he first conceived of emitting < something >," says Ptolemy, "and then willed to. (5) Thus when Conception and Will, these two dispositions or faculties"—again, he calls them faculties—"had been blended as it were, the emission of Only-Begotten and Truth as a pair

---

[1] Sect 33 is drawn from Iren. I.12.1-3, and from the Epistle of Ptolemy to Flora, which is quoted in its entirety. Cf. Hippol. Haer. VI.38.5-7.

[2] 1,2-3,5 is partially quoted, and partially paraphrased from Iren. I.12.1-3. Cf. Hippol. Haer. VI.38.5-7.

[3] For "dispositions" cf. Tri. Trac. 63,34-36. With Depth's "two consorts" cf., in a sense, Val. Exp. 24,19-22, "He is [one] who appears [in Silence] and [he is] Mind of the All. [He was] dwelling secondarily with [Life].''

took place. (6) These came forth as representations and visible images of the Father's two invisible dispositions; Mind of Will, and Truth of Conception. And thus the male became an image of <the later> Will, <but> the female, of the unbegotten Conception. (7) Will, then, was a faculty of Conception. For Conception had always conceived of the emission, but by herself could not emit what she had conceived of. But when the faculty of Will supervened, she then emitted that of which she had conceived.''

2,1   What nonsense of the lame-brain! This cannot even be detected in a man if he is sane, let alone in God. (2) Homer strikes me as more sensible with his portrayal of Zeus' becoming worried, fretting and angry, and lying awake all night to plot against the Achaeans, because Thetis had demanded that the Greek leaders, and the Greeks themselves, be punished for their insult to Achilles. (3) Ptolemy has thought of nothing more suitable in glorification of what he calls Father of all and Depth, than what Homer has said of Zeus. (4) Or rather, he has understood him to be ''Zeus, since he got the notion from Homer. For'' <one> can fairly say that, to disgorge so much impudence on his part, <he must have had>''Homer's apprehension'' of Zeus and the Achaeans ''rather than <the apprehension> of the Lord of all, who at the moment of conceiving it has likewise accomplished what he willed. And he also conceives of what he has willed at the moment of willing, for he conceives when he wills, and wills when he conceives. (5) He is all conception, all will, all mind, all light, all eye, all ear, all fount of all that is good,'' and is subject to no vicissitudes. He is God, and is not worried or at a loss like Depth, or Zeus. For in speaking of Depth, Ptolemy mimicked Homer speaking of Zeus.

2,6   But next, for the fraud's further refutation, I subjoin the tempting yet dangerous words he actually wrote himself to a woman named Flora. Otherwise it might be thought that I confute the cheat from hearsay only, without reading his false teaching first. For besides the things I have mentioned, he even ventures to insult God's Law which was given through Moses. Here are his words:

Ptolemy's Letter to Flora

3,1   After noting the discrepant opinions about it, my good sister Flora, I think you too can see at once that not many before us have understood the Law given through Moses, or had accurate knowledge of the giver himself, or his commandments. (2) Some say it was given by our God and Father. But others, who go in the reverse direction, maintain that it was given by our adversary the devil, author of corruption—as, indeed, they ascribe the creation of the world to him, and call him father and maker of this universe.

3,3 <But surely> these parties did nothing but stutter while they sang their rival songs and, each in its own way, they completely missed the truth of the matter. (4) It is evident, since logical, that this Law has not been made by the perfect God and Father; it is imperfect and needs to be fulfilled by someone else, and its ordinances do not suit the nature and intent of such a God. (5) Again, <as> the Savior has said, †it is not †appropriate to attribute a Law which †does away with †iniquity to the iniquity of the adversary— <as fools would>, and persons incapable of drawing inferences. For our Savior has declared that "A house or city divided against itself cannot stand."[4]

3,6 And further, to deprive the liars beforehand of their unfounded wisdom, the apostle says that the creation of the world is <the Savior's> prerogative, that all things were made by him and without him nothing is made, and that creation is the work of a righteous God who hates iniquity, not a god of corruption.[5] <This latter> is the view of improvident persons, who take no account of the Creator's providence, and are not merely blind in the eye of the soul, but in the eye of the body as well.

3,7 From the foregoing it will be plain to you that they have completely missed the truth. Each party has got into this predicament in its own way—the one through its ignorance of the God of justice; the other through not knowing the Father of all, whom none but the only one who knows him has come to make known. (8) But as the <knowledge> of both has been vouchsafed to me, it is left to me to tell you, and give you an accurate description, both of the nature of the Law itself and of its author, the lawgiver. I shall prove <my> assertions from the words of our Savior, which are the only sure guide to the perception of the truth.

4,1 First, it must be understood that not all of that Law in the five books of Moses has been made by one legislator. That is, it is not made by God alone; some of its provisions are made by men. And the words of the Savior teach us that there are three divisions in it. (2) One division is God himself and his legislation, but another is Moses—not as God legislates through him, but as Moses too made certain provisions on his own notion. And another division is the elders of the people, for it is plain that <they> too have inserted certain commandments of their own.

4,3 You may now learn how the truth of this can be proved from the words of the Savior. (4) In his discussion with those who argued about the bill of divorce with him—the bill of divorce which the Law had sanctioned—the Savior told them, "Moses for the hardness of your hearts permitted a man to divorce his wife. For from the beginning it was

---

[4] Matt. 12:25.
[5] Cf. John 1:1;3.

not so. For God," he said, "hath joined this pair together, and what the Lord hath joined," he said, "let not man put asunder."[6] (5) Here he proves that <the> Law of God, which forbids a wife's divorce from her husband, is one law; but the law of Moses, which permits this couple's separation because of the hardness of their hearts, is another.

4,6   Indeed, Moses' legislation runs contrary to God's in this, for separation is the contrary of not <separating>. If, however, we examine Moses' purpose in making this law, we shall find that he made it of necessity, not of his own choice, owing to the frailty of those for whom it was made. (7) When forbidden to divorce their wives, they could not honor God's intention. Some were living with their wives unwillingly, and so risked being turned further to wickedness, and destroyed in consequence. (8) On his own initiative then, to end this discontent by which they risked destruction as well, Moses gave them a second law, the law of the bill of divorce, as though to take a lesser evil, in a pinch, in place of a greater. (9) If they could not keep the former law, they would at least keep this, and not be turned to iniquities and evils which would result in their utter destruction. (10) When we find Moses legislating in opposition to God, it is with this intent. But it is undeniable that Moses' law is shown here to be other than God's, even if for the present we have proved it with (only) one example.

4,11   The Savior also makes it plain that certain traditions of the elders are intermixed with the Law. "For God said, Honor thy father and thy mother that it may be well with thee," he says. (12) "But ye," he says to the elders, "have said, That wherewith thou mightest be profited by me is a gift to God; and ye have nullified the Law of God by the tradition of your elders. (13) Isaiah cried this out, saying, 'This people honoreth me with their lips, but their heart is far from me. But in vain they do worship me, teaching for doctrines the commandments of men.'"[7] (14) From these passages it is plainly evident that that Law as a whole is divided into three. In it we have found Moses' own legislation, the legislation of the elders, and the legislation of God himself. And this division of that Law as a whole which I have made here has shown which part of it is true.

5,1   But the one portion, the Law of God himself, is again divided into some three parts. One is the pure legislation unmixed with evil, and this is properly termed the "law" which the Savior came not to destroy, but to fulfil. (If he fulfilled it, it was not foreign to him, <but it needed fulfillment>; it was not perfect.) Another part is mixed with inferior

---

[6] Matt. 19:8;6.
[7] Matt. 15:4-9.

matter and injustice, and the Savior abolished this as incongruous with
his nature. (2) And another division is the typical and allegorical laws in
the image of things which are spiritual and excel them. This the Savior
transformed from a perceptible, phenomenal thing to something spiritual
and invisible.

5,3   And the pure Law of God, unmixed with inferior matter, is the
Decalogue itself—those ten commandments engraved on the two tablets
to prohibit what must not be done and enjoin what must. These required
fulfilment by the Savior, for though they had the legislation in its pure
form they lacked perfection.

5,4   The law intermixed with injustice is the law of the requital and
repayment of those who committed the first injustice, and it orders an eye
knocked out for an eye and a tooth for a tooth, and murder in requital
for a murder.[8] For the second party does no less of an injustice, and
commits the same act, changing it merely in its order. (5) In any case
this commandment was and is just, though owing to the frailty of its recipients it was given in violation of the pure law. But it does not fit with
the nature and goodness of the Father at all. (6) It is perhaps appropriate,
but is rather a matter of necessity. For in requiring the murderer to be
murdered in retaliation, making a second law, and presiding over two
murders after forbidding the one, he who opposed even the one murder
by saying, "Thou shalt not kill,"[9] was an unwitting victim of necessity.
(7) Thus the Son who came from him has abolished this portion of the
Law, while acknowledging that it too was a law of God—<as> he has
†conformed to the old school in other matters, and in his words, "It is
God who said, He that curseth father or mother, let him die the death."[10]

5,8   But this is the Law's typical part, the part in the image of things
which are spiritual and excel it. I mean the laws of sacrifices, circumcision, the Sabbath, fasting, the passover, unleavened bread and the like.
(9) Since all these were images and allegories, they were transformed
when the truth appeared. Outwardly and in bodily observance they were
abrogated; spiritually they were adopted, with the names remaining the
same but the actions altered. (10) The Savior did command us to offer
sacrifices, not of dumb animals or their odors but of spiritual hymns,
praises, and thanksgiving, and charity and beneficence to our neighbors.
(11) He also wants us to have a circumcision, not of the bodily foreskin
but of the spiritual heart—(12) <and> to keep the Sabbath, for it is his
will that we desist from evil works. (13) And to fast—but it is his will that

[8] Cf. Lev. 24:20.
[9] Exod. 20:15.
[10] Matt. 15:4.

we keep not the bodily fast but the spiritual, which includes abstinence from all evil.

We do observe outward fasting, however. This can make some contribution even to the soul as well if it is done with reason—not to mimic anyone, or by custom, or for the sake of the day, as though there were a day designated <for> it. (14) At the same time it serves as a reminder of the true fast, so that those as yet unable to keep that may have a reminder of it through the outward one.

5,15   That the Passover and Feast of Unleavened Bread were likewise images, Paul the apostle makes plain by saying, "Christ, our Passover, is sacrificed," and, "that ye may be unleavened, having no part of leaven"—by "leaven" now he means evil—"but that ye may be a new lump."[11]

6,1   Thus even the Law which is admittedly God's has three divisions—the one fulfilled by the Savior, (for "Thou shalt not kill," "Thou shalt not commit adultery," and "Thou shalt not bear false witness" are included in his prohibition of anger, lust and oaths). (2) There is also the division that is altogether annulled. "An eye for an eye and a tooth for a tooth,"[12] which is mixed with injustice and contains an act of injustice itself, was annulled by the Savior through its opposites. (3) But opposites cancel each other: "For I say unto you that ye resist not evil by any means, but if a man smite thee, turn to him the other cheek also."[13] (4) There is also the division which has been altered and transformed from physical to spiritual—this allegorical legislation in the image of the things that excel it. (5) For since the images and allegories were indications of other things, it was right to perform them as long as the truth was not here. But since the truth is here we must do what befits the truth, not the image.

6,6   The Savior's disciples have proved these divisions, and so has the apostle Paul. For our sakes he proved the part which consists of images with the Passover and Feast of Unleavened Bread, as I have said already. And the part consisting of the law which is mixed with injustice by saying, "The law of commandments contained in ordinances is abolished."[14] And the part consisting of the law with no admixture of inferior matter through his words, "The Law is holy, and the commandment holy and just and good."[15]

---

[11] 1 Cor. 5:7.
[12] Matt. 5:38.
[13] Matt. 5:39.
[14] Cf. Eph. 2:15.
[15] Rom. 7:12.

7,1   I think you have been given sufficient proof, so far as this can be done concisely, of the human legislation which has invaded the Law, and of God's Law itself with its triple division. (2) It remains for me to identify this God who gave the Law. But I feel this has been shown you too in my earlier remarks, if you have listened carefully. (3) If, as I have explained, the Law was not given by the perfect God himself, and certainly not by the devil—it is wrong even to say that—then this lawgiver is someone other than these. (4) But this is the demiurge and maker of this entire world and everything in it. As he differs in essence from the other two <and> stands between them, he may rightly be awarded the title of "Intermediate." (5) And if, in his own nature, the perfect God is good—he is indeed, for our Savior has declared that his Father, whom he made manifest, is the one and only good God.[16] And if a god of the adversary's nature is evil, and characterized as wicked by his injustice—then a God who stands between them, and is neither good[17] nor, certainly, evil or unjust, may properly be called "just," and is the arbiter of his sort of justice.

7,6   As he is begotten, not unbegotten, this God will be inferior to the perfect God and subject to his justice. (There is one Unbegotten, the Father, of whom are all things; all, each in its own way, have been framed by him.) But he will be greater and possess more authority than the adversary, and be of an essence and nature different from the essence of both. (7) For the essence of the adversary is corruption and darkness, since he is material and composite. The essence of the unbegotten Father of all is incorruption and self-existent light, simple and uniform. This God's essence displays a sort of dual capacity, but in himself he is image of the better.

7,8   Do not let this trouble you for now, despite your desire to learn how these natures, that of corruption and <that of> the intermediate, also arose from one first principle of all, though they differ in kind. And yet this first principle is <simple>, and we confess and believe it to be, and it is, unbegotten, imperishable and good—and it is the nature of the good to beget and bring forth its like and its own kind. (9) God willing, you shall learn their origin and begetting next, since you are adjudged worthy of the apostolic tradition which I have received in my turn, together with the assessment of all its statements by the standard of our Savior's teaching.

7,10   I have not been slow to send you these few words, my sister Flora, and had written the brief statement already, making the matter

---

[16] Cf. Matt. 19:17.
[17] This is said of the ὑλικὸς θεός, the καλὸς κόσμος, at Corp. Herm. X.10.

sufficiently plain. They will be of the utmost value to you in what follows as well, if, like good, productive soil which has received fertile seeds, you bear the fruit which they engender.

The end of the Letter to Flora

8,1 Who can be content with these words, and the lunacy of this charlatan and his allies—I mean Ptolemy and his associates, who have concocted fabrications at such length and basted them together? (2) None of the ancient tragic poets, or the imitative ones after them—Philistion I mean, and that writer of the incredible, Diogenes—or all the others who wrote the myths down and recited them, (3) could fabricate falsehood to the extent that these have manufactured horrors for themselves; impudently attacking their own life, and smothering their followers' minds with foolish questions and endless genealogies! (4) They themselves did not understand what was under their noses. And yet they professed to survey the heavens with measurements of some sort, and adopted the profession of midwives for mothers who were supposed to be in heaven, non-existent ones who were supposed to exist. (5) If a man who is an utter fool hears it from them he will be easily captivated by their lie, believing that they have taught him something sublime. (Scripture says, "Every bird flocketh with its kind, and a man will cleave to his like.")[18] (6) But if a person of understanding and good sense happens on them he will laugh at the extent of their silliness, and from the very subject of what they say, will know its refutation. For they are altogether guilty of arming their unproductive labor's lies against themselves.

8,7 Where did you learn Depth's dimensions, you gentleman and lady Ptolemaeans? And the pregnant (Aeons') deliveries, and what got them pregnant? (8) You profess to give us the knowledge, as though you had been there and seen the origins of the beings in heaven, and were older even than Depth, as you call him. (9) But no prophet has ever said this. Not Moses himself, not the prophets before him, not the prophets after him, not the evangelists, not the apostles—unless you mean the works of heathen mythology by Orpheus, Hesiod, Hicesius and Stesichorus! In their writings the generations of men were turned into names for gods, and human events were dramatized by poetic fabrication. (10) For they too held beliefs of this kind; < and > by making gods of Zeus, Rhea, Hera, Athena, Apollo, and Aphrodite, and honoring the children of their wickedness, they got the world to imagine polytheism and idolatry.

---

[18] Sir. 13:16.

8,11 But refuting and exposing you and your kind will not be of much further use to me, Ptolemy. Your forebears have already gotten the refutation in sufficient measure. Since I have engineered your own disgrace by the remarks I made earlier, I shall go over the others' imposture. I call on God to aid my modest ability, that I may detect each people's clumsily invented subject, and make a spectacle of it; and I ask God's grace for my promise of zeal.

9,1 But to keep the three cheap expressions you boastfully sent to your girl, Flora, from passing unchallenged, Ptolemy—the snake-like teachings always deceive "silly women laden with sins,"[19] as the apostle said. I quoted the words themselves here at the proper time, and will accordingly give their refutation next—a necessary one, for I might leave the root of your tare-like crop (in the soil).

9,2 You claim that the Law has three divisions, Mister, and that one owes something to God, but one comes from Moses and one from the elders. (3) You cannot show < the part > you think was written by the elders; this much is plain. The traditions of the elders are nowhere in the Law. In your ignorance both of the books and the truth you are imagining them, by quibbling at each accurate form of knowledge and †altering its consequences. (4) The Jews call the traditions of the elders "repetitions," and there are four of them. One is handed down in the name of Moses, a second in the name of Rabbi Aqiba as they call him, a third in the name of Adda or Judah, and a fourth in the name of the sons of Hasmonaeus. (5) You trouble-maker with your fickle disposition, where can you show that the words the Savior mentions, "He who shall say to his father Korban, that is, a gift, he shall profit nothing from him,"[20] were spoken in the five books of the Pentateuch and God's legislation? (6) You cannot show that. Your argument fails then, since the saying is nowhere in the Pentateuch. And you have deceived Flora, your dupe, for nothing.

9,7 Neither were Moses' < laws > made without God's consent. They were made by God through Moses, as is shown by the Savior's own verification. The very evidence you introduced, you have assembled against yourself. (8) In the Gospel the Lord says, "Moses wrote for the hardness of your hearts."[21] But Moses did not write what he wrote without God's permission; his legislation was inspired by the Holy Ghost.

9,9 For the Lord in the Gospel said, "What God hath joined together, let not man put asunder."[22] And to teach us how God joined

---

[19] 2 Tim. 3:6.
[20] Mark 7:11.
[21] Matt. 19:8.
[22] Matt. 19:6.

them, he <joined> the (explanatory) saying to this, "For this cause shall a man leave his father and his mother and shall cleave to his wife, and they twain shall be one flesh." (10) (Only) at this point does he add, "That which God hath joined together, let not man put asunder."[23]

And yet the Lord said no such thing when he formed Adam and Eve; he said only, "Let us make him an helpmeet like himself."[24] (11) It was said by Adam—when he awoke and said, "This is now bone of my bone and flesh of my flesh. She shall be called wife, for she was taken out of her husband."[25] He then said, "Therefore shall a man leave his father and his mother, and shall cleave unto his wife, and they twain shall be one flesh."[26]

9,12   Now God did not say this, Adam was the speaker; yet in the Gospel the Lord bears witness that the words spoken by Adam are the words of God. He thus proved, by the very subject (of the words), that in the former case Adam spoke, but uttered his words by the will of God; while here Moses made laws because God had given him the legislation. And these two expressions of yours have fallen already; and not after a long chain of reasoning but by actual use.

9,13   And making laws is God's prerogative; this much is plain. And God makes laws everywhere, some temporary, some typical, some to reveal the good things to come, whose fulfillment our Lord Jesus Christ made known in the Gospel when he came.

10,1   But I shall take up your other distinction—a triple one again—between gods, and show that this is another of your quibbles, and simply the work of a charlatan. (2) What sort of third God do we have here—made up of two likenesses, nothing else but two, with no wickedness or injustice, as you said, and no goodness or luminous essence either? "Just" because he is in the middle? (3) As you in fact have nothing to do with any justice, you naturally do not know what justice is, and think it is something other than goodness. You will be exposed completely, you tamperer, you stranger to the truth! Justice comes from nowhere else than from goodness, and no one can become good without being just.

10,4   And so, in praise of the legislation and its just men, the Lord said, "Ye garnish the tombs of the prophets, and build the sepulchres of the just, and your fathers killed them."[27] But where have prophets and just men come from, if not from the Father's goodness? (5) And, to prove that the just man belongs in the category of goodness, he said, "Be ye

---

[23] Matt. 19:5-6.
[24] Gen. 2:18.
[25] Gen. 2:23.
[26] Gen. 2:24.
[27] Matt. 23:29; Luke 11:47.

like unto your Father which is in heaven, for he maketh his sun to rise on good and evil, and sendeth rain on just and unjust."[28] This was to make it plain that just is good and good is just, and that evil is unjust, and unjust, evil.

10,6   Nor can you prove the intermixture of the Law (with evil) that you spoke of. You are guilty of a vexatious prosecution of the Law, and of ascribing some intermixture to it because it has said, "eye for eye and tooth for tooth,"[29] and because it murders the murderer. (7) But it will be shown, from our Lord Jesus Christ's own treatment of the matter, that there was no intermixture; the legislation was the same, and it had the same effect as the Savior's commandment, "If a man smite thee on the right cheek, turn to him the other also."[30] (8) The Law had always secured this <too> by saying "an eye for an eye," or in other words, "Turn your cheek to him." To avoid what would happen if he struck a blow, a man would present his cheek to the person striking him— knowing that if he put an eye out, he would get the same because of the Law.

11,1   A father disciplines his children, and progresses with the discipline by suiting it to each age. He rightly does not discipline a little baby like a boy, a boy like a youth, or a youth like a grown man. (2) An infant is disciplined with a finger, an older child with a slap of a hand, a boy with a strap, and a youth with a stick. But by law a man is punished with a sword for the more serious offenses. And thus the Lord fitly gave each generation the laws that were suitable to it. (3) He chastened the earlier generations with fear, as though he were talking to little children who did not know the power of the Holy Spirit; but he considered full grown adults worthy of full mysteries.

11,4   Even in the Gospel he often <tells> the disciples something like, "Ye know not what I do, but ye shall know hereafter"[31]—that is, "when you grow up." And again, "They knew not until he was risen from the dead."[32] (5) And Paul says, "Ye were not able, neither yet are ye able,"[33] to show that commandments become more advanced as time goes on. They are the same, but changed to another state. For the young, they are given in one form; for the more mature, in another.

11,6   For in requiring "eye for eye,"[34] the Law did not tell them to put one eye out after another, but, "If someone puts an eye out, the eye

---

[28] Matt. 5:45.
[29] Lev. 24:17;20.
[30] Matt. 5:39.
[31] John 13:7.
[32] John 2:22.
[33] 1 Cor. 3:2.
[34] Lev. 24:20.

of the person who put it out will be put out.'' And to spare his own body, everyone would offer his cheek for the blow, rather than strike one. (7) And what is now stated clearly in the Gospel was observed from that time on—compulsorily then, as by children under correction, but now by choice, as by adults from conviction.

11,8   But if you claim that this is involvement with evil—to say "an eye for an eye" and have a murderer put to death—then observe! Even of the day of judgment we see the Savior saying, "His Lord shall come''—but he said this of himself, since he is Lord of all—and he says, "and cut the servant himself asunder and appoint his portion with the unbelievers.''[35] (9) In other words, by quibbling about words again you arm yourself even against the Savior; and you could say that he is not good but just, and is different from the Father—though he is begotten of a good Father, and is good himself. (10) You can even separate him from the Father's essence, Mister—you who appear to us once more as a dissector and surveyor of the laws, and divide everything into threes!

11,11   And you touch on a little bit of the truth by saying that parts of the Law are written allegorically to serve as types, and then you can fool people about the rest by your little bit of truth. (12) "These things" indeed "happened unto them typically, and were written for our admonition on whom the ends of the ages have come,''[36] <as> the most holy apostle said of circumcision, the Sabbath and so on. (13) But I wish you would tell the truth about everything, and stop inflicting your nonexistent third, intermediate God on us—or rather, stop inflicting him on yourself and your dupes!

12,1   But now, scum, I feel that enough has also been said about your expressions. I have finished refuting them and shall go to the sects remaining, with my usual invocation of the same God that he aid my modest ability to discover the rebuttal of each spurious heresy. (2) For it has been shown above that with his own piping—as though he were rising out of the sea and summoning sharks and a viper with it—Ptolemy deceived Flora and others with her by means of a letter. (3) But by entangling him in the net of the truth—in the Gospel the Lord declared that this stands for the kingdom of heaven—and by exposing him as one of the bad fish by bringing his unsound words to light, I have overcome him with the teaching of the true faith. (4) Having thrashed him by the power of God let us give thanks to God ourselves, and set ourselves, as I said, to go on to the rest as well.

---

[35] Matt. 24:50-51.
[36] 1 Cor. 10:11.

ANACEPHALAEOSIS III

Here, also, are the contents of the third Section of the first Volume, which contains thirteen Sects.

34,1   34.   Marcosians. A Marcus was a fellow-student of Colorbasus, and he also introduces two first principles. He denies the resurrection of the dead, and initiates his female dupes <by creating> certain illusions with chalices †which are turned dark blue, and purple, by incantation. (2) Like Valentinus, he too holds that everyting †is made of the twenty-four sounds of the alphabet.

35,1   35.   Colorbasus. Colorbasus described the same things himself. But he was somewhat different from the other sects, I mean from Marcus and Valentinus, and taught the emanations and ogdoads in another way.

36,1   36.   Heracleonites too are carried away with the stories about the ogdoads, but differently from Marcus, Ptolemy, Valentinus and the others. (2) Moreover, like Marcus they "redeem" their dying members at the end with oil, balsam and wine, and pronounce certain Hebrew invocations over the head of the person being pretendedly redeemed.

37,1   37.   Ophites, who extol the serpent and think he is Christ, and have an actual snake, the familiar reptile, in a sort of basket.

38,1   38.   Cainites, who repudiate the Law and the Speaker in it, with the ones before them; and they deny bodily resurrection, and extol Cain by saying he belongs to the stronger power. (2) But with him they also deify Judas, together with Korah, Dathan and Abiram, and the men of Sodom besides.

39,1   39.   Sethians. These in turn glorify Seth, and claim he is the child of the Mother on high, who regretted her emission of Cain and then, after Cain's banishment and the killing of Abel, had congress with the Father on high and produced the pure seed of Seth—from whom all humanity was then derived. (2) They too had the doctrines of first principles and authorities, and all the ones the others have.

40,1   40.   Archontics. These in turn trace the universe to many archons, and say that all phenomena derive from them. But they are also guilty of a certain type of vice. (2) They reject bodily resurrection and slander the Old Testament. But they have both the Old and the New Testaments, though they deal with every word to suit themselves.

41,1   41.   Cerdonians, named for Cerdo, <who> received his share of the imposture in succession from Heracleon, but who added to the deceit. He migrated from Syria to Rome, and did his preaching during the episcopate of Hyginus. (2) He preaches that two first principles are the opposites of each other, and that Christ is not begotten. He repudiates resurrection and Old Testament alike.

42,1   42. Marcionites. Marcion of Pontus was the son of a bishop, but he seduced a virgin and, after his excommunication by his own father, went into exile. (2) He arrived at Rome, and asked for a remission of punishment from the <elders> of the time. Because he could not get it, he grew angry and taught doctrines contrary to the faith by his introduction of three first principles, a good, a just, and an evil one; and by saying that the New Testament is foreign to the Old Testament and the Speaker in it.

42,3   He rejects bodily resurrection and administers not just one baptism, but even two and three after lapses into sin. When catechumens die other Marcionites are baptized for them. He unhesitatingly allows even women to baptize, if you please!

43,1   43.   Lucianists. An ancient Lucian—not the modern one born in Constantine's time—taught doctrines in all respects like Marcion's. But he too, if you please, has further ones different from Marcion's.

44,1   44.   Apelleans. This man too, Apelles, abuses the whole process of creation and the creator like Marcion and Lucian. (2) But unlike them he did not introduce three first principles, but one first principle and one God, who is the very highest and cannot be named. But the one God has himself made another. And this God who was made <by him>turned out bad, and made the world in his inferiority.

45,1   45.   Severians. A Severus in turn, after Apelles, rejects wine and the vine and tells the story that it was born of the dragon-like Satan and earth, who had had relations. (2) He repudiated his wife, claiming she belonged to the left-hand power. (3) He further introduces certain names for archons and certain uncanonical books. Like the other sects he rejects bodily resurrection and the Old Testament.

46,1   46.   Tatianists. Tatian flourished in company with the holy martyr, Justin, who was also a philospher. But after Justin, the martyr and philosopher, died, Tatian unfortunately became acquainted with Marcion's doctrines. He was instructed by him, and both taught doctrines like his and added different ones. He was said to have come from Mesopotamia.

This will summarize the three Sections of Volume One, which deals with forty-six sects.

34.

Against Marcosians.[1] *Number fourteen, but thirty-four of the series*

1,1[2]   A Marcus, who founded the so-called Marcosians, was one of these (Gnostics) originally, but dared to vomit different evils out on the world. He suceeded Secundus, Epiphanes, Ptolemy and Valentinus, but was moved to gather a larger crowd of scum. (2) For he attracted female and male dupes of his own; the wretch knew the most about magical trickery, and so was taken for a corrector of the other cheats. (3) But since he deceived all these men and women into regarding him as the most knowing of all, and possessed of the greatest power from the unseen, unnameable realms, this is proof positive that he is the forerunner of the Antichrist. (4) For he combined Anaxilaus' comic performances with the villainy of the so-called magicians, and by this means deceived and bewitched those who saw and trusted him, and drove them to consternation. His successors still achieve this, even today.

1,5   Those who see the <results> of his jugglery believe that miracles of some sort are wrought by the hands of Marcus, and such Marcosians as do these things. (6) For they have lost their own minds, and—not knowing how to estimate them—do not see that what we might call his comic piece is made to come into being by magic. For they have been carried away with an evil opinion, and have gone entirely mad themselves.

1,7   It is said that they prepare three chalices of white vinegar mixed with white wine, and just as Marcus finishes the incantation, which is supposed to be a eucharistic prayer, these are transformed, with one <turning> blood-red, another purple, and another dark blue. (8) But rather than commit myself to a second hard task I had better be content with the work against Marcus himself, and his successors, by the most holy and blessed Irenaeus. I hasten to publish it here word for word, and it runs as follows. For St. Irenaeus says this himself, in giving his glimpse of the things they did:

From the Writings of St. Irenaeus[3]

2,1   While pretending to consecrate liquids mixed with wine, and spinning his invocation out at length, he makes them turn purple and

---

[1] Sect 34 is entirely dependent upon Iren. I.13.1-21.5, which it quotes verbatim. Cf. Hippol. Haer. VI.39.1 etc.
[2] 1,1-3 is paraphrased from Iren. I.13.1.
[3] 2,1-20,12 is quoted from Iren. I.13.2-21.3.

scarlet. This makes it appear that Grace, one of the powers above the universe, is shedding drops of her blood into his cup at his invocation. And those who witness this are extremely anxious for a taste of that drink, so that the Grace this magician summons may shower on them as well.

2,2   Again, he would give women chalices which were mixed already, and tell them to consecrate them while he looked on. And when they had, he would bring another chalice out, much larger than the one his dupe had consecrated, and pour the contents of the smaller one the woman had consecrated into the one he had brought in.

<He would say a eucharistic prayer> with the added words, (3) "May she that is before all, the inconceivable and ineffable Grace, fill thine inner man and increase in thee her knowledge, by sowing the grain of the mustard seed in the good ground." (4) And by making the poor woman mad with some such words he would appear to be a wonder-worker, for the big chalice would be filled from the little one and even overflow from it. And he has fooled many completely with other performances quite similar, and won them to his following.

2,5   He probably has a familiar spirit too, through which he both appears to prophesy himself, and causes the women he considers worthy to share his grace to prophesy. (6) (He spends most of his time on women, and on the best-dressed, the highest-ranking, and the wealthiest.) In his effort to subject them to himself he often softens them by saying, "I desire to share my grace with you, for the Father of all continually beholds your angel before his face. But the Majesty's place is in us; we must be restored to the One. (7)[4] First receive Grace from me and through me. Prepare yourself as a bride awaiting her bridegroom, that you may be what I am, and I what you are. Place the seed of the light in your bridal chamber. Receive the bridegroom from me; contain him and be contained in him. Lo, Grace has descended upon you; open your mouth and prophesy!"

2,8   But if the woman answers, "I have never prophesied and do not know how," he gives another set of invocations to his dupe's consternation, and tells her, "Open your mouth <and> say any old thing, and you will be prophesying!"

2,9   And made conceited and feather-brained by that, fevered in soul with the expectation of prophesying, her heart beating too hard, she (10) will pluck up the courage to babble silly things at random—all vain and impudent, since she has been made feverish by a vain spirit. (Of such

---

[4] With 2,7 cf. the discussions of the marriage chamber at Gos. Phil. 67,23-30; 69,1-70,4; 74,12-24; 82,23-30. See also Ex. Soul 132,12-26.

<prophets> a greater man than I has said, "An impudent and shameless thing is a soul made feverish by empty air.") (11) And from then on she takes herself for a prophetess and is grateful to Marcus for bestowing his own grace on her, and not only attempts to repay him with the gift of her money—he has made a great deal that way—but with physical union too. For she is eager to be united with him entirely, to be restored to the One with him.

2,12   Already—though he took care to cajole them like the rest by telling them to prophesy—some of the more faithful women, who fear God and were not fooled, have spat, cursed, and left a † juggler like that, <with his pretense of breathing a divine thing>. (13) They know perfectly well that prophecy is not put into men by the sorcerer Marcus. Those to whom God sends his grace from above have prophecy as a divine gift, and they speak where and when God wills, not when Marcus says so. (14) Something that gives an order is greater, and has more authority, than something that is given an order; the one takes precedence while the other is subject. Hence if Marcus, or anyone else, orders prophecy—and at their dinners they make a regular game of having each other prophesy <by> lot, and divine for them as their passions dictate—then, though he is only a man, the one who orders it is greater than the prophetic spirit, and has more authority.

But that is not possible. (15) Such spirits as are at their bidding and speak when they choose, are earthy and feeble, though presumptuous and impudent. They are sent by Satan for the deception and ruin of those who fail to maintain the vigor of the faith they originally received through the church.

3,1   But that Marcus administers philtres and love-potions to some of the women if not all, to outrage their bodies as well, they have often confessed on returning to God's church—and to having been corrupted in body by him, and having loved him with great passion. (2) Even one of our deacons in Asia had this misfortune because he welcomed Marcus into his home. His wife was a handsome woman, and she was seduced both in mind and body by this sorcerer, and followed him for a long time. (3) Then, when the brethren had brought her to repentance with great difficulty, she spent the rest of her life in confession, mourning and lamenting her seduction by the magician.

3,4   Certain of his disciples too, who wander about in the same area, have deceived and seduced many women by proclaiming themselves so perfect that no one can rival the greatness of their knowledge—not even Paul or Peter or any other apostle. (5) (They) claim that <they> know more than all, they alone have drunk in the greatness of the knowledge of the ineffable power, and they are higher than any power. (6) Hence

they are free to do everything,[5] and fear nothing under any cir-
cumstances. Because of their redemption they have become untouchable
by the judge, and invisible to him. But even if he were to apprehend them
they would stand before him with their redemption and say this:[6]

3,7 "O Counsellor of God and the primordial mystic Silence, †
<thou through whom> the Majesties, who ever behold the Father's
face, draw their forms heavenward with thy leading and guidance—the
forms that greatly-daring one imagined because of First Progenitor's
goodness and emitted us † <in their image>[7]—† and who had then a
dreamlike notion of the things on high: (8) Lo, the judge is nigh and the
herald bids me make my defense. But do thou, understanding the affairs
of us both, render an account to the judge for <us> both, as one!" (9)
And the Mother hears them without delay and puts Homer's helmet of
invisibility on them, so that they may escape the judge unseen.[8] Drawing
them up instantly she conducts them to the marriage chamber, and gives
them to their own bridegrooms.

3,10 By saying and doing such things they have completely fooled
many women in our own region too, the Rhone valley. These women are
branded in conscience and some even confess it openly. Others, who are
ashamed to do this but have quietly <withdrawn> somehow, despair of
God's life and in some cases have become entirely apostate; while others
vacillate, in the proverbial predicament of being neither in nor out. This
is their fruit from the seed of the children of knowledge!

4,1 This Marcus <then>, who says that only he, in his uniqueness,
has become the womb and receptacle of Colorbasus' Silence, has brought
forth the actual <seed> of Defect, which was somehow sown in him
here. (2) The all-sublime Tetrad has descended to him herself, from the
invisible, ineffable realms, in feminine form[9]—the world could not bear
her masculine one, he says. To him she disclosed herself; and to him and
him alone she told the origin of all things, which she had never revealed
to any god or man. Her words were as follows:

4,3 "At the first, when the Father <who has> no <father>, who is
inconceivable and without essence, who is neither male nor female, will-

---

[5] A comparable idea is stated at Corp. Herm. IX.4.

[6] The challenge of the soul by hostile powers and its apologia to them is common in
Mandaean literature, e.g. at GR 184,10-185,7; GL 444,14-27; Book of John 82,23-25;
Mand. PB 175, p. 178. Comparable material from other literature is cited at Sect 26 Note
65.

[7] Cf. "those who had come forth from him in an imaginary way" Tri. Trac. 78,6-7.

[8] Cf. Gos. Phil. 70,5-8; 76,22-25.

[9] "Now I have come the second time in the likeness of a female" Tri. Prot. 42,17-18.
See also Tri. Trac. 64,32-37, "if he had formerly revealed himself suddenly to all the
exalted ones among the aeons who had come forth from him, they would have perished."

[10] With 4,3-9 cf. Hippol. Haer. VI.42.2-45.1.

ed that his unutterability become utterable and his invisibility be given form,[11] he opened his mouth and pronounced a word[12] like himself. It stood by him and showed him what he was, manifest itself as a form of the invisible.[13] (4) But the pronouncing of the name took the following form. He spoke the first word of his name, which was a beginning, and its syllable was made up of four sounds. <And> he subjoined the second syllable, and it too was made up of four sounds. Next he pronounced the third, and it was a syllable with ten sounds. And he pronounced the final one, and it had twelve sounds. The pronouncing of the entire name, then, took thirty sounds, but four syllables.

4,5[14]   "Each of the sounds has its own letters, its own impression, its own pronunciation and forms and representations. There is not one of them that sees the form of that of which it is a sound. No syllable knows † it,[15] and certainly not the pronunciation of its neighbor. As though it pronounced the All it thinks that what † it pronounces names the whole. (6) For though each is (only) part of the whole, it makes its own noise as though it named the All; and it does not stop until, with its one utterance, it reaches the last letter of the last sound."

4,7   She said that the restoration of all will come when all have arrived at the one letter, and utter one and the same exclamation. She supposed that "Amen," when we pronounce it together, is an image of this exclamation. But it is the sounds which give form to the Aeon which is without essence and unbegotten. And they are forms—the Lord has termed them "angels"—continually beholding the Father's face.[16] (8) She called the common, spoken names of the sounds Aeons, words, roots, seeds, fullnesses and fruits; but said that the individual names peculiar to each one are observably included in the church's name.

4,9   The last letter of the <last> of these sounds has made its noise. <The> echo of it came forth in the image of the sounds, and produced sounds of its own. From these, she says, the things here (now) have been reconstituted,[17] and the things before them brought into being. (10) But

---

[11] Cf. Tri. Trac. 57,24-31; 66,13-16; 67,18-19.

[12] The Son is "the word of [the] unutterable" at Tri. Trac. 66,15-16. Perhaps cf. Thunder 14,9-15.

[13] The First Father beholds himself within himself at Eug. 74,21-75,12 = SJC 98,24-99,13.

[14] With what follows, perhaps cf. Thunder 20,32-35, "I am the name of the sound, and the sound of the name. I am the sign of the letter and the designation of the division."

[15] Cf. the ignorance of the Aeons at Tri. Trac. 60,16-26; 72,22-29. But unlike the sounds here, the Aeons are said not to speak 72,25.

[16] Cf. Matt. 18:10.

[17] διακεχοσμῆσθαι, the Stoic term for the periodic reconstitution of the universe, was read by Hippolytus and is presupposed by Holl. The variant, γεγεννῆσθαι, does not carry this connotation; but it does not seem to suit the context as well.

the letter itself, she said, whose echo was simultaneous with the echo below, was taken up by its own syllable to make the whole complete.[18] The echo has remained below, as though discarded.

4,11   But she says that the sound itself, from which the letter descended in company with its own pronunciation, has thirty letters. Each of the thirty letters contains other letters, the ones by which the letter's name is said. (12) And the other letters are named with other letters in turn, and the others with others, so that the throng of the letters issues without end. But you can understand this better from the following example:

5,1   The sound, delta, contains five letters: delta itself, epsilon, lamda, tau and alpha. These letters, in turn, are written with other letters, and the others with others. (2) Now if the delta's whole essence keeps coming out endlessly, with letters continually generating other letters and succeeding each other, how much greater than that sound is the sea of the letters! (3) And if the one letter is endless in this way, see the depth of the letters of the whole name of which Marcus' Silence held that First Progenitor is made! (4) And hence the Father, who knows the name's uncontainability, has permitted each of the sounds—which he also calls Aeons—to cry its own pronunciation aloud, since one cannot pronounce the whole.

5,5   After explaining this to him Tetrad said, "Now I wish to show you the Truth herself. I have brought her down from the habitations above so that you may see her naked and observe her beauty—hear her speak, moreover, and admire her wisdom. (6) See her head, alpha and omega, at the top. Her neck, beta and psi. Her shoulders and arms, gamma and chi. Her breasts, delta and phi. Her diaphragm, epsilon and ypsilon. Her belly, zeta and tau. Her privy parts, eta and sigma. Her thighs, theta and rho. Her knees, iota and pi. Her shins, kappa and omicron. Her ankles, lamda and xi. Her feet, mu and nu." This is the body of the sorcerer's "Truth," this is the form of the sound, this is the impression of the letter. (7) And he calls this sound "Man," and says it is the source of all speech, the origin of every sound, the utterance of everything unutterable, and the mouth of the Silence who cannot be spoken of.

5,8   "And this is her body. But raise <the> thought of your mind aloft, and hear the self-begetting utterance, the dispenser of fatherly bounty, from the Truth's own mouth."

6,1   When Tetrad had said this, Truth looked at him, opened her mouth, and spoke a word. But the word was a name, and the name was

---

[18] Cf. "the one who ran on high" at Tri. Trac. 86,4-15; "[the] invisible [Spirit] ran up to his place" Mars. 9,28-10,2.

the one we know and say, "Christ Jesus." And after naming it she fell silent at once. (2) But while Marcus was waiting for her to say something further, Tetrad came forward again and said, (3) "How trivial you considered the word you heard from the lips of Truth! The one you know, and think you <have> always <had>, is not a name. You only have a sound; you do not know its meaning.[19] (4) 'Jesous' is a name with six letters, a digamma, and is known by all who are called. But among the Aeons of the Pleroma the name is complex, and it has a different form and impression and is known by those of the brethren whose Majesties are always in its presence.[20]

6,5   "Learn, then, that these twenty-four letters of yours are effluences which copy the three powers comprising the sum total of the powers on high. (6)[21] Regard the mute consonants, of which there are nine, as copies of the Father and Truth, for they are "mute"—that is, ineffable and unutterable. (7) Regard the voiced consonants, of which there are eight, as copies of Word and Life; they are between the mutes and vowels, as it were, and receive the effluence of the ones above them, and the vapor of the ones below.[22] (8) But regard the vowels, of which in turn there are seven, as copies of Man and Church; for it was by Man that <the> voice came forth and gave form to the whole. For the echo of the voice provided a form for them.

6,9   <Thus> there are Word and Life with the eight letters, Man and Church with the seven, and Father and Truth with the nine. (10) But the number which had been evacuated in the Father came down upon the sum that lacked (a number). It was sent to the sum it had left to remedy the situation, so that the addition of the sums would be uniform and make the value of all of them the same in all cases. (11) And thus the sum of seven acquired the value of eight, and the <three> spaces became correspondent with the numbers, since they were ogdoads. Added in three operations they gave the sum of twenty-four."

6,12   But when the three sounds are multiplied by four—on his own account Marcus says that these are coupled with the three values making six, and that the twenty-four sounds emanate from this—when they are multiplied fourfold by the total of the ineffable tetrad, they give the same number as the ones he says are the number of the unnameable. (13) The three sounds are worn by the three values in resemblance to the invisible.

---

[19] Cf. Gos. Phil. 53,23-54,4. There all names for holy things are said to be "deceptive" as they are "heard in the world."

[20] Cf. Matt. 18:10.

[21] A comparable discussion of the letters of the alphabet, including a ranking of their relative importance, is found at Mars. 25,17-34,19. The schema given there, however, is not related to the one given here.

[22] Something similar is said of the sun at Corp. Herm. XVI.17.

Our double letters are images of images of these sounds; and when they
are included with the twenty-four sounds (of the alphabet) they give
<the> sum of the thirty (Aeons), by the value which is proportionate
(to the Aeons' value).

7,1   Marcus says that a fruit of this reckoning and dispensation has
appeared in a likeness of its image, in the person of him who went up
the mountain fourth after the six days and became the sixth, and who
came down and was caught hold of on the seventh. He has appeared as
a digamma,[23] though he is an ogdoad and contains the full total of the
sounds. (2) The descent of the dove made <him> manifest when he
came for baptism, for this is alpha and omega—its sum is 801.

7,3   For the same reason Moses has said that man was created on the
sixth day. The dispensation <of the passion> also <took place> on the
sixth day; for <on the sixth day>, the day of <the> preparation, the
last man appeared for the restoration of the first.[24] The sixth hour, at
which he was nailed to the tree, is also the beginning and end of this
dispensation.[25] (4) For because it understands the number six, the perfect
Mind, with its power to make and make afresh, shows the sons of light
its restoration to itself by itself by the appearance of the digamma. This,
he says, is why there is a total of six double letters. For when combined
with the twenty-four sounds, the number six completed the thirty-letter
name.

7,5   "Six has the quantity of seven as its attendant,"[26] says Marcus'
Silence, "to show the fruit of its own initiative. But for now," she says,
"understand this six that is patterned after the digamma as the six who
was divided or cut in two[27] as it were, and remained outside.[28] By emitting it from himself he gave life, through his own power and wisdom, to
this world of the seven values which represent the value of seven; and he
was appointed to be the soul of the visible universe.

7,6   "For his part he has this task as a work he performs voluntarily;
but since they (i.e., the seven vowel sounds) are imitations of the in-
imitable, they serve the Mother's Purpose. (7)[29] And the first heaven ut-
ters the alpha, the next, the epsilon, the third, <the> eta. The fourth,
and midmost of the seven, pronounces the value of the iota, the fifth, the

---

[23] I.e., the ἐπίσημον. This is used of the First Man at Keph. 76,29-30.

[24] I.e., "last man" (= digamma, six) plus "last" plus "first" = ogdoad, eight.

[25] "Sixth hour" plus "beginning" plus "end" = eight.

[26] This is to account for the seven heavens or planets, which do not fit into Marcus'
scheme of sixes and eights.

[27] "Divided and split in two" is an allusion to the form of the digamma.

[28] I.e., The digamma is a mere "mark," ἐπίσημον, rather than being one of the sounds
of the alphabet.

[29] With 7,7-8 cf. the vowels of the Name of God as given at Herm. Disc. 61,8-15.

omicron, the sixth, the ypsilon. But the seventh, the fourth from the middle, cries out the sound, omega," as Marcus' Silence affirms, who talks all sorts of nonsense but never tells the truth. (8) "These values," she says, "all ring out together in harmony and glorify the one who emitted them; and the glory of the sound is sent to First Progenitor. But the echo of this praise drifts earthward," she says, "to become that which forms and generates the things on earth."

7,9   Her proof of this is the new-born babes, whose soul cries out the echo of each of these sounds as they issue from the womb. As the seven values glorify the Word, so the soul in infants glorifies him by weeping and wailing <like> Marcus. (10) David, also, has said, "Out of the mouths of babes and sucklings hast thou perfected praise,"[30] on this account, and again, "The heavens declare the glory of God."[31] And thus, when a soul has troubles and misfortunes, to purge itself it cries, "Oh!" as a sign of praise, so that the soul on high will recognize its kinship with it and send it aid.

8,1   And this was his foolishness about this whole thirty-letter name, and Depth, who grew from the letters of it. And further, about Truth's body <with> its twelve members, <each> composed of two letters, and her voice with which <she conversed without> conversing; and the explanation of the name that was not spoken—and the soul of the world and man, with their disposition in an image. (2) But next, beloved, I shall tell you how Tetrad produced an equal numerical value for him from the names (of the Aeons)—and then, as you have often asked me, you will not be unfamiliar with any of his teachings which I happen to know.

8,3   Here, then, is what their all-wise Silence has to say about the origin of the twenty-four sounds. Oneness co-exists with Soleness. Two emanations from these, Unit and One as we have said, were two times two and made four; for two times two are four. (4) And again, when the two and the four were added they made six; but multiplied by four, these six brought forth the twenty-four forms.

8,5   And the names of the first tetrad, which are understood to be holiest of the holy and not capable of utterance, can be known by the Son alone—what they are, the Father knows. But the ones pronounced in his presence, augustly and with assurance, are Arretos and Sige, Pater and Aletheia.

8,6   The full total of this tetrad is twenty-four sounds. For the name, Arretos, has seven letters, Seige has five, Pater, five, and Aletheia,

---

[30] Ps. 8:3.
[31] Ps. 18:2.

seven. Added together, the twice five and the twice seven, these made up the full twenty-four. (7) Similarly the second tetrad, Logos and Zoe, Anthropos and Ecclesia, gave the same number of sounds. (8) And the Savior's spoken name, Jesous, has six letters, but his unutterable name has twenty-four. "Uios Chreistos" has twelve letters, but the ineffable name in Christ has thirty. And she calls him alpha and omega to disclose the dove, since this is a dove's numerical value.

9,1   But Jesus has the following ineffable origin, she says. From the Mother of all, the first tetrad, the second tetrad[32] came forth like a daughter. This made an ogdoad, and a decad came out of it. Now there were a decad and an ogdoad. (2) Joining the ogdoad once more and multiplying it by ten,[33] the decad produced the next number, eighty. Multiplying the eighty by ten again it generated the total of 800, so that the sum total of the letters which issue from eight times ten is an eight, an eighty, and an 800, or "Jesus." (3) For by the sum in its letters, the name, "Jesus," is 888. You are now clear as to Jesus' origin beyond the heavens, as they explain it. (4) And this is why the Greek alphabet contains eight units, eight tens, and eight hundreds, giving the figure of 888—in other words, Jesus, who is composed of all the numbers. He is thus called "alpha and omega" to indicate his origin from all.

9,5   And again: When the first tetrad was added to itself cumulatively ten was produced; for when one, two, three and four are added they make ten, or iota, and they hold that this is Jesus. (6) But "Chreistos" too, she says, which has eight letters, means the first ogdoad; in union with the iota this brought forth Jesus. (7) He is also called "Uios Chreistos,' which is the dodecad. The name, Uios, has four letters, while Chreistos has eight; when these were added they gave the amount of twelve.

9,8   Before the six-letter mark of this name—that is, "Jesus," its son—appeared, men were deep in ignorance and error. (9) But at the manifestation of the six-letter name, which was clothed with flesh to be perceptible to man and contained the six itself and the twenty-four, men learned † it, shed their ignorance, and ascended from death to life. For the name was their way to the Father of truth. (10) For the Father of all has willed to dissolve ignorance and abolish death. But dissolution of ignorance was the recognition of him. Thus his choice of the Man who, by his will, was disposed in the image of the value on high.

10,1   For the Aeons issued from < the second > tetrad. In the tetrad there were Man and Church, Word and Life. Powers (= "values")

---

[32] For the second Tetrad, see Val. Exp. 29,25-28; 35-38.
[33] There is a comparable, though not identical, multiplication at Val. Exp. 30,30-38.

which overflowed from these, he says, brought the Jesus who appeared on earth into being. (2) The angel Gabriel took the part of Word, the Holy Spirit, of Life, and the power of the highest, of Man, while the Virgin played the role of Church. (3) And this is how Marcus' "man by dispensation" was brought into being through Mary; and on his issuance from the womb the Father of all chose him, through Word, to come to the knowledge of him. (4) And when he came to the water, the number which had withdrawn to heaven and become the twelfth descended on him as a dove. In it was the seed of these people, who were sown together with it, and have descended and ascended with it.

10,5   He says that the actual value which descended was the Father's seed, and contained both Father and Son, the ineffable value of Silence which is known through them, and all the Aeons. (6) And this is the Spirit which spoke through Jesus' mouth, and which confessed itself Son of Man and made the Father manifest; † but it was < certainly > united with Jesus when it came down upon him. And he says that < Jesus >, the Savior by the dispensation, abolished death; but † Christ made the Father manifest. (7) He says, then, that † "Jesus" was the name of the man framed by the dispensation, but was meant to provide a likeness and form for Man, who would descend upon him. In containing him he possessed Man himself, Word himself, Father, Ineffable and Silence, and Truth, Church and Life.

11,1   These things are already beyond "Alas and alack!" and any outcry and lamentation in tragedy. For who can fail to detest the author of such big lies, badly put together, when he sees the truth made into an idol by Marcus, and with the alphabet scribbled on it? (2) The Greeks admit that, compared with anything primordial, it was recently— yesterday and the day before, as we say—that they first received sixteen letters from Cadmus. Then later, as time went on, they themselves invented the aspirates at one point, and the double consonants at another. Last of all, they say, Palamedes added the long vowels. (3) Before the Greeks did this then, there was no Truth! What you call her body, Marcus, is of later origin than Cadmus and his predecessors, later than those who added the rest of the sounds—later even than yourself! For no one but yourself has brought your so-called Truth down (from heaven) < as > an idol.

11,4   But who can put up with your Silence who talks so much nonsense, and who names the unnameable, explains the ineffable, searches the unsearchable, and says that he whom you call bodiless and without form has opened his mouth and uttered a Word—like a beast, made up of parts! (5) And his Word, which is like the one who emitted it and which has become a form of the invisible, is composed of thirty sounds, but four syllables. In that case the Father of all, as you call him, will be composed of thirty sounds but four syllables, in the Word's likeness!

11,6   Or again, who can bear your confinement of the Word of God, the creator, artificer and maker of all, to shapes and numbers—thirty sometimes, sometimes twenty-four, sometimes just six— <and> your dissection of him into four syllables, but thirty sounds? (7) And your reduction of the Lord of all, who established the heavens, to 888, like the alphabet; your subdivision even of the Father himself, who contains all things and yet is uncontained, into a tetrad, an ogdoad, a decad and a dodecad; and your explanation of what you call the Father's ineffability and inconceivability by multiplications like these? (8) You make the essence and subsistence of the One you call incorporeal and without essence out of many letters, with new letters generated by others, though you yourslf were the false Daedalus and the bad sculptor of the power before the all-highest! (9) And by subdividing the essence you say is indivisible into mutes, vowels and voiced consonants, and falsely attributing their voicelessness to the Father of all and his Ennoia, you have brought all who trust you to the very height of blasphemy, and the greatest impiety.

11,10   Hence it was with justice, and appropriately for insolence like yours, that the divinely-inspired elder and herald of the truth has cried out at you in verse and said,

11,11   Maker of idols, scanner of portents, Mark,
        Skilled in in the arts of astrologue and mage,
        Confirming error's teachings by their use;
        To them thou hast deceived thou showest signs,
        Works of the rebel power's enterprise,
        Given thee to perform time and again,
        Through the angelic power of Azazel,
        By Satan, thy true sire, who deemeth thee
        Harbinger of the craft that mimics God!

(12) So far the elder beloved of God. But I shall try to go briefly over the rest of their mysteries however lengthy, and bring to light what has been concealed for a long time. May this make them easy for everyone to refute!

12,1   By combining the origin of their Aeons with the straying and finding of the sheep, these people who reduce everything to numbers try to give a deeper explanation, and claim that all things are made of a unit and a dyad; (2) and they generate the decad by counting from one to four. For the addition of one, two, three and four gave birth to the sum of the ten Aeons. But then again, by proceeding from itself to six—as in "two, four, six"—the dyad displayed the dodecad. (3) And again, when we count in the same way from two to ten the triacad is displayed, with an ogdoad, a decad and a dodecad in it.

12,4 Since the digamma is concomitant with the dodecad, they say that the digamma is (its) accident (πάθος). Hence, when the slip occurred, the sheep that ran off went wrong over the number twelve—since they claim that the defection was from a dodecad. (5) And they find by divination that one rebellious value was similarly lost from the † decad, and this is the woman who lost the drachma, and lit a lamp and found it. (6) After this the numbers that were left—nine in the drachma's case, eleven in the case of the sheep—were also united and gave birth to the number ninety-nine. For nine times eleven are ninety-nine. They say that this is why "Amen" has this total.

12,7 But as they give other explanations I do not mind telling you those, so you will see just what fruit they bear. They hold that the sound, eta, is an ogdoad if we include the six, since it stands eighth after alpha. Then again, by reckoning up the sounds themselves without the six and adding them cumulatively through eta, they display the triacontad. (8) For if <one> enumerates the sounds from alpha through eta, leaving the six out and adding cumulatively, he will arrive at thirty. (9) The total from alpha through epsilon is fifteen. Then seven added to this makes twenty-two. But when eta, or eight, is added to this, it completes the wondrous triacontad. And from this they prove that the Ogdoad is the mother of the thirty Aeons.

12,10 Now since the number thirty is a combination of three numerical values, it was multiplied by three itself and made ninety, for three times thirty are ninety. But the three was also multiplied by itself and generated a nine. And thus, in their view, the Ogdoad gave birth to the ninety-nine. (11) And since the twelfth Aeon (i.e., the letter mu) left the first eleven when it rebelled, they say that the form of the (two) letters (found in the letter mu) is parallel to the shape of the † lamda—for lamda, or thirty, is the eleventh letter—and that its place in the alphabet reflects the provision (just mentioned). For, omitting the digamma, the sum of the letters themselves from alpha through lamda, added cumulatively with lamda itself included, is ninety-nine.

12,12 But from the very shape of the sound it is plain that lamda, the eleventh letter, came down in search of its like to make up the number of twelve (letters), and that it was made complete when it found it. (13) For as though it had come in search of its like, and had found † it and clasped † it to itself, lamda filled the place of the twelfth letter—the letter mu is composed of two lamdas. (14) By knowledge, then, they escape the ninety-ninth place—this is Deficiency, and it is counted with the left hand—and reach the One. When this was added to ninety-nine, it moved them to the right hand.[34]

13,1   As you go through this, beloved, I am well aware that you will roar with laughter <to hear> the kind of foolishness they think is wise. But people deserve to be mourned when they make this sort of feeble effort to disparage such ancient religion, and the amount of the really inexpressible value, and such great dispensations of God, with alpha and beta and numbers.

13,2   Any who leave the church, however, to put their trust in these old wives' tales, <are> truly self-condemned. Paul tells us to repudiate them after a first and a second admonition. (3) But John, the disciple of the Lord, extended their condemnation further and did not even want us to greet them, "For he that biddeth them godspeed is partaker of their evil deeds."[35] (4) And rightly so, for the Lord says, "It is not lawful to greet the impious."[36] And impious beyond all impiety are these persons who say that the creator of heaven and earth, the only God almighty, beyond whom there is no other God, has been emitted by a Deficiency, which itself is the product of another Deficiency. As they see it, then, he himself is the emission of a third Deficiency!

13,5   It is truly imperative that we despise and curse this opinion, keep <even> far away from them, and realize that the more they rely on their frauds and delight in them, the more they are animated by the ogdoad of the evil spirits—(6) just as people subject to fits are in worse condition † the more they laugh, seem to have recovered, and do everything like persons in good health and some things even better. Similarly, the more these people appear to aim high, and exhaust themselves by shooting with a taut string, the less sound of mind they are.

13,7   When the unclean spirit of folly had gone out, and then found them not busy with God but with worldly philosophical inquiries, he took with him seven other spirits more wicked than himself. Making their minds conceited—as becomes those who are capable of conceiving of something higher than God—and fit to be driven out for good, he stored the evil spirits' eightfold folly in them.

14,1   But I want to tell you besides how they say the creation the Demiurge wrought in the image of things invisible was (actually) the work of the Mother, since he did not know (them). (2) They say that the four elements, fire, water, earth, and air, were emitted first as an image

---

[34] This interpretation of the Lost Sheep is found at Gos. Tr. 31,35-32,16.
[35] 2 John 11.
[36] Isa. 48:22.

of the first tetrad before them. When their operations are reckoned in with them—that is, heat, cold, dryness and wetness—they are just like the ogdoad.

14,3   <And> next they enumerate ten powers as follows. Seven circular † bodies, which they also term heavens; then the circle that encloses them, which they also call an eighth heaven; and the sun and moon besides. As these make ten in all, they say they are images of the invisible decad which issued from Word and Life.

14,4   But the dodecad is disclosed by the so-called circle of the zodiac. For they say that the twelve signs are obviously shadows of the dodecad, the daughter of Man and Church. (5) And since the highest heaven was counterpoised against the very swift motion of all (the others)—it bears down on their vault itself, and compensates for their speed with its slowness, so that it revolves from sign to sign in thirty years—they say it is an image of Limit, who surrounds their Mother for whom there are thirty names. (6) And the moon, in turn, which traverses its own heaven in thirty days, portrays the number of the thirty Aeons with the days. (7)[37] The sun too, which makes its revolution in twelve months and circles back to its starting-point, makes the dodecad apparent through the twelve months. But also the days, which are limited to twelve hours, typify the dodecad which <does not> shine.

14,8   But they say that even the hour in fact, which is a twelfth of a day, is composed of thirty parts in the image of the triacontad. (9) The rim of the zodiacal circle itself is made of 360 parts, for each sign has thirty. And thus they say the image of the union of twelve with thirty is retained even by the circle. (10) And further, they insist that even the earth is an obvious type of the dodecad and its children. They claim it is divided into twelve regions, and in each region, from its position directly below it, it receives <a particular> power from the heavens, and bears offspring in the likeness of the power that sends its influence down upon it.

14,11   They say further that the Demiurge wanted to copy the infinity, eternity, boundlessness, and timelessness of the Ogdoad on high, and could not portray its stability and eternity because he was a fruit of Deficiency <himself>. So he has sown its eternity in times, seasons, numbers, and long periods of years, with the idea of mimicking its endlessness by the large number of the periods of time. (12) And here they say that since Truth deserted him falsehood has followed, and his work will therefore be destroyed when the times are fulfilled.

---

[37] With 14,7-8 cf. the treatment of the divisions of time at Tri. Trac. 73,28-74,2; Eug. 83,20-84,11.

15,1 And by saying such things about creation, each one produces <a> further novelty every day if he can. For none of them is ripe unless he bears big lies. (2) But I must tell you which prophetic passages they transform, and supply the rebuttal to them.

For they say that right at the beginning of his work on the creation, Moses exhibited the Mother of all with the words, "With Beginning God created the heaven and the earth."[38] (3) He thus represented their "tetrad," as they say, by naming these four—God and beginning, heaven and earth. And to state that it is invisible and hidden he said, "And the earth was invisible and unformed."[39]

15,4 <But> they hold that he has spoken of the second tetrad, the offspring of the first, by naming an abyss; the darkness that is in them; water; and the Spirit which was borne above the water. (5) After this, to mention the decad, he said light, day, and night; a firmament, evening, and what is called early morning; dry land and sea, and further, vegetation; and tenth, trees. And thus he has disclosed the ten Aeons through the ten names.

15,6 But he gave the same value as the docecad's in the following way. He spoke of sun and moon; stars and seasons; years and whales; <and further> of fish and creeping things; birds and four-legged creatures; wild beasts—and twelfth, besides all these, man. They teach that in this way the Spirit has spoken of the triacontad through Moses.

15,7 Indeed even the man formed in the image of the above value contains the value in himself, from the same source. The brain-stuff is its seat. Four so-called faculties emanate from it in the image of the tetrad mentioned above: sight; hearing; the sense of smell, third; fourth, taste. (8) And the ogdoad is disclosed by the man in the following way. He has two ears; the same number of eyes; and further, two nostrils; and a dual sense of taste, bitter and sweet. (9) They teach that the whole man contains the whole image of the triacontad in the following way. He bears the decad on his hands because of the fingers, but the dodecad in his entire body, which is divided into twelve members. (They divide it like the body of Truth, of which I have spoken.) And the ogdoad, which is ineffable and invisible, is thought to be concealed in the viscera.

16,1 They claim in turn that the sun, the greater light, was created on the fourth day because of the number of the tetrad. (2) They believe that the courts of the tabernacle Moses constructed, which were made of flax, blue, purple, and scarlet, displayed the same image. (3) They declare that the high-priest's robe, which was decorated with four rows of precious stones, indicates the tetrad. And anything <at all> of this sort in scripture, which can be reduced to four, they say is there because of their tetrad.

16,4   But the ogdoad, in turn, is indicated as follows. They say that
man was formed on the eighth day. (They sometimes place his creation
on the sixth day and sometimes <on> the eighth, unless they mean that
the man of earth was made on the sixth, but the man of flesh on the
eighth—they draw this distinction. (5) But some of them <even> hold
that <there was> one man created male-and-female in God's image
and likeness, and that this is the spiritual man; but the man formed from
the earth is a different one.)

16,6   And they say that the provision of the ark during the flood, in
which eight persons were saved, very plainly discloses the saving ogdoad.
David too, who was the eighth brother in order of birth, has the same
significance. Even circumcision furthermore, which is performed on the
eighth day, shows that the above ogdoad is cut off from us. (7) And in
a word, they say that whatever in scripture can be reduced to eight makes
up the mystery of the ogdoad.

16,8   Moreover, they say the decad is indicated by the ten nations
God promised to give Abraham for his possession. Sarah's provision in
giving him her maid Hagar after ten years to have children by, has the
same meaning. (9) And the servant whom Abraham sent for Rebecca,
and who gave her ten gold bracelets at the well; and her brethren, who
kept her for ten days—and further, Rehoboam, who received rule over
ten tribes; the ten courts of the tabernacle; its pillars, ten cubits high;
Jacob's ten sons, who were sent to Egypt to buy food the first time; and
the ten apostles to whom the Lord appeared after the resurrection in
Thomas' absence. In their view these portrayed the invisible decad.

17,1   They also say that the dodecad—the occasion for the mystery
of the passion of Deficiency, from which they hold that the visible world
was made—is conspicuous and evident everywhere in scripture. (2) For
example, Jacob's twelve sons, who were also the ancestors of <the>
twelve tribes; the intricate breastplate with its twelve stones; the twelve
bells; the twelve stones Moses placed at the foot of the mountain, those
too that Joshua set up in the river, and others on the further bank; the
bearers of the ark of the covenant; the stones Elijah set up at the sacrifice
of the calf; the number of the apostles also. And in a word, they say that
everything retaining the number twelve is an indication of their dodecad.

17,3   They contend that they can show the combination of all these,
which they call a triacontad, by the thirty-cubit height of Noah's ark; and
Samuel, who seated Saul at the head of his thirty guests; and David,
when he hid in the field for thirty days, and the thirty who entered the

---

[38] Gen. 1:1.
[39] Gen. 1:2.

cave with him; and because the length of the holy tabernacle was thirty
cubits. And so with anything else they find has the same number.

18,1   < But > to these I feel I must also add the passages they cull
from scripture in the attempt to argue for their First Progenitor, who was
unknown to all before Christ's coming; and to prove that our Lord proclaimed someone else as Father instead of the maker of our universe. (As
I said, they impiously call him a fruit of Deficiency.) (2) They change the
prophet Isaiah's meaning—he certainly said, "Israel doth not know me,
and the people doth not undersand me"[40]—to ignorance of the invisible
Depth. (3) They make Hosea's saying, "There is no truth nor knowledge
of God in them,"[41] pertain to the same; and they assign the words,
"There is none that understandeth, or seeketh after God: They are all
gone out of the way, they are together become unprofitable,"[42] to ignorance of Depth. (4) They also argue that Moses' saying, "There shall
no man see God and live,"[43] refers to him. For a further lie they say that
the creator has been seen by the prophets; but they hold that the
< text >, "There shall no man see God and live," is said of the invisible
majesty which is unknown to all. (5) (And it is plain to everyone that,
"There shall no man see God," is said of the invisible Father and maker
of the universe. However, in the course of the treatise it will be shown
that this does not refer to their added invention, Depth, but to the
Creator, and < that > he is the invisible God.)

18,6   They also say that Daniel means the same when he asks the
angel for the interpretations of the parables, as though he did not know
them. Moreover the angel concealed the great mystery of Depth from
him and told him, "Go thy way, Daniel, for these words are sealed until
the understanding understand, and the white be whitened."[44] And they
boast that they are the "white," and the "understanding." (7) Besides
these, they bring forward an unutterably large number of apocryphal,
spurious scriptures which they have forged themselves, to the consternation of the fools who do not know the true scriptures.

18,8[45]   For this purpose they also employ the fraudulent story that in
the Lord's childhood when he was learning to read, his teacher, as is
customary, told him, "Say Alpha," he answered, "Alpha." (9) And
then when the teacher told him to say "Beta," the Lord replied, "Tell
thou me first what is Alpha, and then will I tell thee what is Beta." And

---

[40] Isa. 1:3.
[41] Hos. 4:1.
[42] Rom. 3:11-12.
[43] Exod. 33:20.
[44] Dan. 12:9-10.
[45] With 18,8-9 cf. Epist. Apost. 4; (Infancy) Gospel of Thomas A VI.3; B VI.6-VII.2.

they interpret this to mean that the Lord alone understands the unknowable, and revealed it in the form of the Alpha.

18,10   They also change some Gospel passages into this sort of thing. For example, the Lord's reply to his mother when he was twelve, "Wist ye not that I must be in my Father's house?"[46] They say he was proclaiming the Father they did not know to them. And this is why he sent the disciples out to the twelve tribes, preaching the God they did not know. (11) And to the person who addressed him as "Good Master," he confessed the truly good God by saying, "Why callest thou me good? One is good, the Father in the heavens."[47] They say that in this case "heavens" means "Aeons."

18,12   And they explain that he has shown the Father's ineffability by <not> speaking, because he gave no answer to those who asked him, "By what authority doest thou these things?"[48] and they were baffled by his counter-question instead. (13) Moreover, when he said, "Oft have I desired to hear one of these words, and have found none to say it," they say the "word" was that of a person who would indicate the truly one God they had not known, by saying "one." (14) Further, by contemplating Jerusalem, weeping for it, and saying, "If thou hadst known, even thou this day, the things that belong unto peace—but they are hid <from> thee,"[49] he has indicated the hiddenness of Depth with the word "hid." (15) Again, by saying, "Come unto me, all ye that labor and are heavy laden, and learn of me,"[50] he has proclaimed the Father of Truth. For they say he promised to teach them something they did not know.

18,16   <In proof> of the foregoing and as though to close their subject, they cite, "I thank thee, Father, Lord of heaven and earth, that thou hast hidden them from the wise and prudent and hast revealed them unto babes. Vah, my Father, for it was good in thy sight. All things are delivered unto me of my Father; and no man knoweth the Father save the Son, and the Son, save the Father, and he to whomsoever the Son shall reveal him."[51] (17) <For> they say that with this the Lord has expressly shown that before he came no one had ever known their discovery, the Father of truth. And they would like to make it out that, since the maker and creator was always known by everyone, the Lord has said this too of the Father whom no one knows, the one they proclaim.

---

[46] Luke 2:49.
[47] Mark 10:17-18.
[48] Matt. 21:23-27 par.
[49] Luke 19:42.
[50] Matt. 11:28-29.
[51] Matt. 11:25-27.

19,1 Their transmittal of "redemption"[52] is invisible and impossible to get hold of, † for the untouchable, invisible Mother is its source and it is therefore unstable and < thus > —since they each transmit it as they choose—there is no giving a simple or summary account of it. There are as many "redemptions" as there are mystagogues of this persuasion. (2) In refutation of them I shall declare at the proper place that (redemption of) this kind has been fobbed off on them by Satan, in denial of the baptism of regeneration to God, and to do away with all of the faith.

19,3 They say that redemption is a necessity for those who have received the perfect knowledge, for their regeneration to the power above all. < It is > impossible to get into the Pleroma otherwise, for in their view redemption takes them down to the bottom of Depth. (4) They suppose that the baptism of the visible Jesus < is > for the remission of sins, but the redemption of the Christ who came down into him is for perfection; and the one is soulish, while the other is spiritual. Baptism has been proclaimed for repentance by John, but redemption has been obtained by Christ for perfection.[53] (5) And this is what he means when he says, "And I have another baptism to be baptized with, and am in great haste for it."[54] Moreover, they say that the Lord laid this further redemption on the sons of Zebedee when their mother asked that they sit in the kingdom with him on his right and left, by saying, "Can ye be baptized with the baptism that I am to be baptized with?"[55] (6) And they claim that Paul has often disclosed the redemption in Christ Jesus in so many words, and that this is the redemption which they transmit in complex, inconsistent ways.

20,1 For some of them prepare a bridal chamber,[56] initiate their candidates with certain invocations, and claim that their rite is a spiritual marriage in the likeness of the syzygies on high. (2) But some take them to water, and use the following invocation as they baptize them: "In the name of the unknowable Father of all; of Truth, Mother of all; and of him who descended upon Jesus for union, redemption, and participation in the powers." (3) To scare the candidates more, others add some Hebrew names as follows: "Basema chamosse baainaoora mistadia rouada, kousta babophor kalachthei." This means something like "More than every power of the Father I call on < thee, who art > termed light, good spirit, and life, for in a body thou didst reign."

---

[52] Baptism = redemption at Tri. Trac. 127,25-128,24.
[53] A comparable distinction seems to be implied at On Bapt. A 41,10-38.
[54] Cf. Luke 12:50.
[55] Mark 10:38.
[56] Baptism is the bridal chamber at Tri. Trac. 128,33-35.

20,4   But when others < perform > the redemption in their turn they use this invocation: "The name hid from every Godhead, sovereignty and truth, which Jesus of Nazareth put on in the girdles of the light of Christ, for Christ lives by Holy Spirit—for angelic redemption, the name of the restoration: (5) Messia oupharegna mempsai men chal daian mosome daea akhphar nepseu oua Jesou Nazaria." And this means something like, "I do not distinguish the spirit, the heart, and the merciful power above the heavens. May I enjoy the benefit of thy name, O true Savior!" (6) This is the invocation of the officiants themselves. The neophyte responds, "I am stablished and redeemed, and do redeem my soul from this world and all that is of this world in the name of Iao, who redeemed his soul for redemption in the living Christ." (7) Then the congregation add, "Peace be to all on whom this name doth abide!" Then they anoint the candidate with oil[57] of balsam; for they say that this ointment typifies the sweet savor which is above all.

20,8   But some of them claim that it is not necessary to take candidates to the water. They mix oil and water and apply them to the candidates' heads with < certain > invocations like the ones we have given, and hold that this is redemption. But they too anoint with oil of balsam.

20,9   Others deprecate all this and claim that the mystery of the ineffable, invisible power must not be performed with visible, perishable creatures, and the mystery of the inconceivable and incorporeal with the perceptible and bodily. (10) Discernment of the ineffable Majesty is perfect redemption in itself.[58] The whole system of ignorance which was brought about by the ignorance and passion of Deficiency is dissolved by knowledge, and thus knowledge is the redemption of the inner man. (11) And redemption is not of the body—for the body is mortal. Nor is it of the soul, for the soul too < comes > from Deficiency, and is a sort of dwelling-place for the spirit. Hence redemption must be spiritual as well. (12) The inner, spiritual man is redeemed through knowledge, and the discernment of all things is enough for them. And this is true redemption.

This concludes the excerpt from Irenaeus

21,1   The blessed elder Irenaeus composed this whole searching inquiry, and gave every detail of all their false teaching in order. Hence, as I have already indicated, I am content with his diligent work and have presented it all word for word, as it stands in his writings. (2) But they

---

[57] Gnostic chrismation appears at Gos. Phil. 69,4-14; Acts of Thomas 27; 121; 157.
[58] "Hidden knowledge" = holy baptism at Apoc. Ad. 85,19-31; renunciation of the world = baptism at Test. Tr. 69,15-31.

will be refuted by the very things the holy man—in contradistinction to their wickedness—has said. We believe what the truth everywhere discloses and sound reasoning suggests in agreement with the standard of piety, and with the Law and prophets, and the ancient patriarchs in succession, and with the teaching of the Savior himself. (3) For < the Lord > and his apostles plainly teach us to confess one God as Father, the almighty sovereign of all, and our Lord Jesus Christ and his Holy Spirit, one holy Trinity uncreate—while all other things were created out of nothing, subsequent to Father, Son and Holy Spirit. (4) Now since these things are confessed plainly and believed, by these holy prophets, evangelists, and apostles, no shifty invention can withstand the truth's bright beam, as I have said in detail often enough in opposition to every sect. (5) It is thus perfectly plain that, like the other sects, this deadly scum is tailoring these big things and making them up to show off and be a nuisance.

22,1 But let us also pass his wickedness by, beloved, and the wickedness of those who are called Marcosians after him. And let us hurry on to the rest to find their roots in turn, and counteract their fruit's bitterness by showing its refutation, and all the facts about them. (2) This is not to harm the reader but for his protection, so that he will come nowhere near any of the sects before this or after it, but will read what they have written, become acquainted with their cant, recognize each one's imposture for what it is, and flee from its snake-like wickedness without, as I said, coming near it.

22,3 The naturalists speak of a viper called the dipsas, which does the following sort of harm. In certain places where there are depressions in the rocks, or little basins hollowed out of rocks for receptacles, the dipsas finds water and drinks, and after drinking puts its poison into these pools of water. Then any animal that approaches and drinks its fill will feel refreshed because it drank, but it will fall right down and die beside the receptacle contaminated by the dipsas' venom. (4) Moreover, if the dipsas strikes someone, his pain from its particularly hot poison will make him thirsty and want a drink, and will impel him to keep coming up and drinking. (5) Each time the victim < feels > such deadly pain and < has some water > he will think that it does his injury some good, but he will vomit his life out later along with the drink, because the very thing he drinks fills his stomach and it cannot hold < any > more. (6) Thus Marcus too causes the death of his dupes with a drink. But since we have been rescued from this poison by the power of God, let us go on to the rest.

35.

Against Colorbasians.[1] *Number fifteen, but thirty-five of the series*

1,1   Colorbasus comes after these. He drew on Marcus' sorcery, but also grew up like a thorn from Ptolemy's root. <But> again, he invented different irritants for the world, like goads, and thought of a greater "experience," if you please, as though he had come down from heaven. (2) He was originally a partner of Marcus[2] whose ideas were like his, for their sect was like a two-headed snake. But like a head cut off a snake's body and still breathing he destroyed many later and wronged them, with his claim that he had shown them something greater than his contemporaries and predecessors, if you please.

1,3[3]   "For he says that the first ogdoad has not been emitted in a descending series, one Aeon by another. As though he had delivered them himself he is positive that the emanation of the six Aeons has been brought forth, at the same time and once for all, by First Progenitor and his Ennoia. And he and his followers no longer say, as the others do, that Man and Church have been brought forth by Word and Life, but that Word and Life have been brought forth by Man and Church. (4) They also say the following in a different way. When First Progenitor conceived of emission, then he was called Father. But since what he emitted was a truth, this was termed Truth. When he willed to show himself, this was called Man. But the Aeons he had previously thought of when he emitted them—this was termed Church. And Man † emits Word; this is the first-born son. But Life also accompanies Word. And thus a first ogdoad was brought to completion.

1,5[4]   "There is also considerable dispute among them about the Savior. Some say he is the product of all and is therefore called 'Well-Pleased,' since all of the Pleroma was pleased to glorify the Father through him.[5] Some say he is the product only of the ten Aeons emitted by Word and Life <and is called 'Word' and 'Life' accordingly>, preserving the names of his progenitors. (6) Others say he is from the twelve Aeons produced by Man and Church, and that thus, as Man's progeny, he confesses <himself> the 'Son of Man.' Others say he originates from Christ and Holy Spirit, <the ones emitted> to make the

---

[1] Sect 35 is entirely dependent upon Iren. I.12.2-4. Cf. Hippol. Haer. VI.39.1.

[2] Epiphanius probably associates the sect described here with Marcus because Irenaeus' treatment of the Marcosians comes next, at I.12.5, and begins, Alius vero quidam exiis qui sunt apud eos.

[3] 1,3-7 is quoted from Iren. I.12.2-4. Cf. Tert. Adv. Val. 36; 39.

[4] With what follows cf. the various names given to the Son at Tri. Trac. 87,6-13.

[5] Cf. "the son in whom the Totalities are pleased" Tri. Trac. 87,1.

Pleroma firm. He is called 'Christ' for this reason, keeping the name of the Father by whom he was emitted. (7) But others, certain bards of theirs as we might say, say that the First Progenitor of the universe, its Prior Principle and the One of whom there can be no preconception, is called Man.[6] And this is the greatest and most hidden mystery—the power which is above the universe and encompasses all things is called Man. And this is why the Savior says he is Son of Man!''

2,1   There too is Colorbasus' bombastic nonsense—no use to the world, and a figment of his imagination. Whoever examines it closely will see from what lies before him that ambition is <the reason> for each of these people's opinions. (2) They each told any lies that occurred to them from vainglory and their desire to gather a following, but not because they spoke prophetically—the Holy Spirit did not speak in them—or were afforded even one excuse by the truth of the prophets and Gospels.

2,3   But the rebuttal of all of these people's falsely styled "knowledge" is the same speech of the truth which was uttered against the previous ones. For though each interprets his intent differently they all belong to the school of Valentinus and his predecessors, and they will all incur the same embarrassment.

2,4   For Colorbasus has also come to offer us a vast imposture consisting of empty talk. He has fabricated a name for us, "Man," and given the name, "Man," to the incomprehensible, invisible, holy God, the Father of all—to combine with his own imposture the saying in which the Savior calls himself Son of Man, and divert the minds of its users away from Christ's trustworthy and perfectly clear confession about himself to an impossibility, and to the nonsense † of discussions about the non-existent ogdoad, as though there were one in the heavens.

2,5   For suppose we grant that, as this pathetic Colorbasus says, Christ called himself Son of Man because his Father on high somewhere is named "Man"—not because of the flesh he took from a virgin womb, that is from St. Mary, when he was conceived by the Holy Ghost. (6) What would he say of the words of the same Jesus Christ our Lord, when he told the Jews, "But now ye seek to kill me, a man that has told you the truth, which I heard of my Father?"[7] (7) And in this case he did not say, "the man, my Father." As a confession of the Father he indicated

---

[6] Jeu is "the great man" at Jeu 122, and "the first man" frequently in Pistis Sophia. Eug. 85,9-13 reads, "Now the first aeon is that of Immortal Man. The second aeon is that of Son of Man, the one who is also called "First Begetter," 77,13-14 and SJC 103,22-104,1. The First Man is the source of all things at Gos. Egyp. 49,8-19; 59.1-3.

[7] John 8:40.

that he is God of all; but of himself, since he had been truly incarnate, he said that he was man.

2,8 The apostles too—as proof positive of the truth, and to show where the names ascribed to the Lord come from—say, "Jesus, a man approved among you by signs and wonders,"[8] and so on. (9) What can you say to this, you most pathetic of all mortals—since you have come from on high with new names for us, and you take pride in daring to attach the name, "Man," to the Lord and Father of all himself, so that the Lord is called Son of Man because Man is his Father's name! (10) Find us some other name to fit the Father, <corresponding with> "man approved!" But you never will!

Even though man also means "male," and we call a male "man" to distinguish him from a woman, you still can make nothing out of this either. (11) No one can be termed male without certain features and members, hidden and visible. We call a woman "man" too, but not "male"; this is why we say both ὁ ἄνθρωπος and ἡ ἄνθρωπος. (12) But when we distinguish sex we call the feminine specifically "woman," but the masculine "male." For when the condition of the sexes is differentiated the distinction between the masculine and feminine sex is this, the words "male" and "woman." But the male and the woman are called "man" synonymously.

3,1 Since this is the case, join me, all you servants of God and lovers of the truth, in laughing at the scummy fraud, Colorbasus! Or rather, mourn for those who have been deceived, and have destroyed themselves and many others. (2) But let us ourselves thank God that the truth guides its sons in a straight path with short, simple words, and that it scatters, overturns, and does away with what is abominable and loud, though it has been given a good appearance with great ingenuity. The truth goes softly, as is plain to see from the prophet's oracle. (3) In accusation of those who waste their energy on cleverness, and invent long-winded verbiage to their own deception, the prophet said, "Forasmuch as ye refuse the water of Siloam that goeth softly, the Lord bringeth up upon you the water of the river, the king of the Assyrians."[9] (4) For "water of Siloam" means the "teaching of him who has been sent." And who can this be but our Lord Jesus Christ, who has been sent from God, his Father? But <he "goes"> softly" because <he> does not <introduce> any idle talk or fiction, but in truth <keeps> his holy bride, whom he calls "dove" in the Songs of Solomon because of the dove's harmlessness, gentleness and great purity.

---

[8] Acts 2:22.
[9] Isa. 8:6-7.

3,5   And the other women, who are not his but have taken his name, he surprisingly called "concubines" and "queens,"[10] because of the kingly name which each one boasts by having "Christ" inscribed on her. (6) But though there are eighty concubines—meaning the sects—and then any number of young women, he says, "One is my dove, my perfect one;"[11] that is, the holy bride and catholic church herself. "Dove," as I said, because of the dove's gentleness, harmlessness and purity; and "perfect" because she has received perfect grace from God, and perfect knowledge from the Savior himself, through the Holy Ghost.

3,7   The bridegroom himself, whose name means "sent,' or "Siloam," has water that flows softly. That is, he has quiet teaching which makes no commotion, and is not imaginary and not boastful. (8) But his bride too is a peaceable dove, with no poison, or teeth like millstones, or stings—like all these people with their snake-like appearance and spouting of venom, each eager to prepare some poison for the world and harm his converts.

3,9   This man is one of them as well. I have hastened to detect him here with divinely-given speech and aid from above, and to squash him like the four-jawed snake called the malmignatte—or crush him quickly like a head cut off from the two-headed viper, the amphisbaena. (10) But I shall pass him by, and once more investigate the rest. And in going over them I shall ask in prayer that I may describe them truthfully, but not harm anyone or be harmed myself.

36.

Against Heracleonites.[1] *Number sixteen, but thirty-six of the series*

1,1   Colorbasus' successor is one Heracleon, for whom the Heracleonites are named; he is no less versed in the <nonsense> of their silly taik. (2) Whatever they say he makes the exact same declaration, since he was originally one of them, and he copied his poison from them. But he exalts himself above them by patterning himself after something else, if you please, to gather his own body of dupes.

1,3   For by patterning themselves after a body with 100 heads or 100 hands, all these people mimicked the Cottus or Briareus—also called Aegaeon or Gyges*—who was once in the Greek poets' legends, or the

---

10 Cf. Song of Songs 6:8.
11 Cf. Song of Songs 6:9.

1 Heracleon is mentioned at Iren. II.4.1, and said to be in agreement with Valentinus about the Aeons. But the source of Sect 36 is the last part of Irenaeus' account of the Marcosians, Iren. I.21.3-5; we do not know why Epiphanius connected this data specifically with Heracleon. For Heracleon see also Hippol. Haer. VI.4; Ps.-Tert. 4.8; Tert. Adv. Val. 4.2.

so-called "many-eyed Argus." (4) These are the sort of prodigies the poets told of them in their recitations, with the fabrication that one had 100 hands and sometimes fifty or sometimes 100 heads, and the other had 100 eyes. (And they say that this is why Hermes is called "Argeiphontes," as the slayer of the many-eyed Argus). (5) So with these (latter). Since each desired to establish his own supremacy he named himself head, and introduced things different from the wasted effort and mad teaching of his instructors. But not to make the composition of the preface very lengthy, I shall address the matter in hand.

2,1[2] As I said, Heracleon, and the Heracleonites who, as I indicated, derive from him make the same sort of claims as Marcus and certain of his predecessors about the Ogdoads, I mean the upper and lower. And then, he imagines the same about the syzygies of the thirty Aeons. (2) He too claims that the Father of all on high is a man—he also called him "Depth." He too says that the Father is neither male nor female, but that the Mother of all—whom he calls both Silence and Truth—comes from him. (3) And the second Mother, who had the lapse of memory, came from her, and he too calls her Achamoth. Then all things were rendered defective because of her.

2,4[3] But he too says more than his predecessors, as follows. He "redeems" those of their people who are dying and at their last gasp, taking his cue from Marcus, but no longer doing it in his style. He handles the matter differently by redeeming his dupes at the point of death, if you please. (5) "For some of them will at times mix oil with water, and apply it to the head of the dying—others apply the ointment known as balsam, and water." But they have in common the invocation as Marcus before him composed it, with the addition of certain names. And the invocation is this: (6) "Messia oupharegna mempsai men chal daian mosome daea akhphar nepseu oua Jesou Nazaria."[4]

2,7 But their reason for doing this, if you please, is that those who receive these invocations at the point of death, with the water and the oil or ointment mixed with it, will "become untouchable by the principalities and authorities on high and invisible to them, allowing their 'inner man' to pass them unseen. (8) For their bodies are left behind in the created world, while their souls are committed to the Demiurge"[5] on high who originated in Deficiency, and so stay there with him. But as I

---

[2] 2,1-3 might be Epiphanius' conjecture on the basis of Iren. II.4.1.
[3] With 2,4-5 cf. Iren. I.21.5. Note that Mandaean extreme unction also involved the use of water, Mand. PB pp. 64-68.
[4] The invocation is taken from Iren. I.21.3.
[5] This is quoted from Iren. I.21.5.

said, their "inner man",[6] <which is> deeper inside them than soul and body, ascends beyond him. This, they hold, has descended from the Pleroma on high.

3,1   To those whom they defraud in this way they give the direction,[7] "If you come upon the principalities" and authorities, remember to say this "after your † departure. (2) 'I am a son of a Father, a Father before me; yet I am a son now. <And> I have come to see all that is mine[8] and all that belongs to others—yet it does not belong to 'others' at all but to Achamoth, who is female and made these things for herself. I derive from the One before her, and return to my own, whence I came.'[9] (3) And so saying he escapes the authorities but encounters the company of the Demiurge" on high, in the vicinity of the first ogdoad. (They too hold that there is a hebdomad below, after the Demiurge. He is in the seventh <heaven> as an eighth, but is defective and ignorant.)

3,4   "And to the company of the Demiurge" the departed "says, 'I am a vessel more precious[10] than the female who made you. If your Mother is ignorant of her own root, I know myself and realize whence I am.[11] And I call upon the imperishable Wisdom, who is in the Father, but who is the Mother of your Mother who has no father or even male consort. (5) A female born of a female made you,[12] because she did not know even her mother and believed herself to be alone. I, however, call upon her Mother.' (6) On hearing this the company of the Demiurge are most disturbed, and recognize their root and the Mother's stock; but the departed goes to his own casting off his chain[13] and 'angel,' that is, <the> soul," (they think there is something else in a man, after body and soul). "And this is all that I have learned about redemption."

4,1[14]   But when the wise hear the extravagant nonsense of their miming, may they laugh at the way each makes rules different from the other's to suit himself, and the way he is not restrained from his own impudence but invents as much as he can. (2) "<And> it is difficult to examine or state all the <doctrines> of people who" are being spawned

---

[6] For "inner man" see Let. Pet. 137,21-22; PS passim; Man. Ps. 173,19-20.

[7] The quotations in 3,1-6 are taken from Iren. I.21.5. There is a fuller version of this speech at 1 Apoc. Jas. 33,13-36,1. Cf. also Orig. C. Cels. VI.31; Apoc. Paul 23,1-28; Apocry. Jas. 8,35-36; PS 289-290; Jeu 129 et al.

[8] Cf. Gos. Truth 21,11-13; 22,19-20; Gr. Seth 61,7-10; Keph. 79,25-26.

[9] Cf. Apocry. Jas. 2,21-24.

[10] With "precious vessel" cf. GR 332,6, cf. 151,18. There are comparable speeches at Nat. Arc. 92,21-27; GL 471,26-35.

[11] Cf. Corp. Herm. I.19.

[12] "And yet they are outsiders, without power to inherit from the male, but they will inherit from their mother only," Auth. Teach. 23,22-26.

[13] Cf. the "bondage of the body" at Para. Shem 35,16-17, and see Corp. Herm. I.26.

[14] 4,1-2 is paraphrased from Iren. I.21.5.

and sprouting up among them "even to this day, and every day find something new to say" and fool their converts with. So again I shall rest content with what has been said about this sect, for I have given the information I too have gleaned about it.

4,3 Who can fail to see that teaching like theirs is pure myth and nonsense? Where did you get your body, Mister—you, or your predecessors? Where did you get your soul? Your inmost man? (4) Even if it was from above, from the spiritual principle on high—as you dramatically say to ensnare your dupes with a promise of hope, so that they may be moved by some goal and seduced by the bewitchment of your dramatic composition. (Even so), tell me, what does the spiritual principle on high have in common with the material? What does the material have in common with the soulish?

4,5 Why would the Demiurge create things that were not his? Why did the <spiritual God> on high tender his spiritual power to the Demiurge, whose work was not good? And why did the Demiurge prefer to blend his own soulishness with the material and bind his own power fast with matter? (6) And if he wishes to blend his own power with it, matter is not strange to him. And if it is strange, who gave him authority over matter? (7) And first, you fraud, tell me whether he hated the soul, that he bound it with matter, or whether he did not know what would happen. But I know you will say neither.

4,8 For I deny that the body is "matter"—anything but!—or that God's creatures are. However, scripture does know another kind of "matter," in addition to everyday matter, which is unimportant, but a handy resource for every craft and trade. I mean the sordid reflection arising from the reason, and <the> filthy thoughts of sin. (9) For noisome, filthy <thoughts> arise <from an evil heart> like a bad smell and unclean effluent from mud, as the blessed David said when he was persecuted and slandered by wicked men, "I was trapped in matter of an abyss,"[15] and so on.

5,1 But since it is your belief, Heracleon, that human bodies and the entire world here are what is called "matter," to what end did the Demiurge blend his own soul with matter? (2) If it was because he did not know evil—no one who does not know what he wants to make, can make it. Not even we accomplish anything in any craft by making what we do not understand. We reflect beforehand on what we want to achieve, and know what we have chosen to achieve before we do it. (3) And although we are feeble, and far inferior to God's power, we know and understand through the understanding he has granted to men. But

---

[15] Ps. 68:3.

God-given understanding has resulted in harm for you, Heracleon, since you do not employ it for a godly purpose but in an evil pursuit.

5,4 But I shall say once more, what is the reason for the mixture of the spiritual with the soulish and material? For the thing that you call an inner man, which is united with the second and third "outer man," I mean with the soul and the body? (5) And if it exists by the will of the power on high, the Father of all—I mean your "Depth"—then, as I said, the creation around us here is commingled with the things on high, and hence not incompatible with them. For it is with the consent of the Father on high that the spark, your "spiritual" and inmost man, has been sent down from him from above. (6) But if you say that the Demiurge who is inferior and defective, or the Mother whom you call Achamoth, has received power—that is, spirituality—from above, then the Demiurge is no longer defective and ignorant, or your so-called "Mother" either. How can anyone be ignorant of the thing he wants? And one who knows the good, and desires it rather than detesting it, is not strange to the good.

6,1 And not to waste my time by occupying myself with the scum's devices, I shall rest content with this. All his nonsense breaks down, since it is plainly acknowledged by everyone that the Lord of all is good, has foreknowledge, and is able to do everything; and that all nature, the present creation, has been well made by him. (2) For nothing can be without God, with the sole exception of sin, which has no original root and no permanence; it appears in us as an import from outside, and in turn is brought to an end by us. Thus, in composing my heresiology, I have everywhere proved (3) that God, the maker and creator of all, the Father of our Lord Jesus Christ, is one; and that his only-begotten Son, our Lord, Savior and God, is one; and that his Holy Spirit is one (4)—one holy, consubstantial Trinity. By this Trinity all things are created well— none evil, but good, to correspond with the Goodness which consented to call them, in that state of goodness, from non-being into being. (5) < To this God >, the Father in the Son, the Son with the Holy Spirit in the Father, be glory, honor and might, forever and ever. Amen.

6,6 But after once more giving a brief rebuttal of this sect I am going on to the rest, and will give my best refutation of each and so complete the overthrow of their pernicious wickedness. (7) For Heracleon may justly be called a lizard. This is not a snake but a hard-skinned beast as they say, something that crawls on four feet, like a gecko. The harm of its bite is negligible, but if a drop of its spittle strikes a food or drink, it causes the immediate death of those who have any. Heracleon's teaching is like that. (8) But as we have detected his poison too, and by God's power have wiped it off the throat or lips of those who would have been harmed, let us go over the rest, as I said, and give the rebuttal of their mischief.

37.

Against Ophites.[1] Number seventeen, but thirty-seven of the series

1,1 With God's help, as I promised by the power of God, I shall also describe the Ophite sect, which follows next after the last stupidities. In some ways it goes in the same direction but in others, the customs and gestures of its members, it is different—so that from the erratic wandering of the disagreement between them, everyone can see that these sects ae guided by error, not truth. The Ophites will now be detected by speech, and their kind of stupidity will be refuted.

1,2 As I said, the Ophites took their cue from the sects of Nicolaus and the Gnostics, and the ones before them. But they are called Ophites because of the serpent which they magnify. For they disgorge strange things too, as though they were stuffed with the stinking food we mentioned before; and in their deception they glorify the serpent, as I said, as a new divinity.

1,3 And see how far the serpent, the deceiver of the Ophites, has gone in mischief! Just as he deceived Eve and Adam at the beginning so even now, (and he does it) by concealing himself, both now and in the Jewish period until Christ's coming. (4) Then, even in later times, he seduces greedy humanity further with the food they received through him by disobedience; and he provokes them to further treachery, and makes them rebels against the true God. He always makes big promises, as he did also at the beginning. Even then he cheated them by saying, "Ye shall be as gods;"[2] then, in time, he completed the multiform, monstrous illusion for them. (5) For he had spawned the blasphemous nonsense of idolatry and polytheism long before, by detaching them from the one true God. They were not gods (then), just as they are not (now); <only> God is God. But he was spawning polytheism, the madness for idols, and a deceitful notion beforehand.

1,6 But the snake which was visible at that time was not the only cause of this. It was the snake who spoke in the snake—I mean <the> devil—and who troubled the man's hearing through the woman. (7) And the tree was not sin either—God plants nothing evil—but the tree gave them knowledge so that they would know good and evil.

---

[1] Sect 37 has many points of contact with Iren. I.30.1-7 and Ps.-Tert. 2.1-4, but its precise source is not certain. Some, at least, of the material comes from oral sources. Cf. Hippol. Haer. V.16-18.
[2] Gen. 3:5.

1,8   And death did not come because of knowledge, but because of disobedience. Indeed the adversary's whole plot at that time was laid to make them disobedient, not for the sake of food. (9) Hence they disobeyed then, and as a perfectly just punishment were expelled from Paradise—not from God's hatred for them, but from his care. For the Lord tells them, "Earth thou art, and unto earth shalt thou return."[3] (10) Like a potter the true Craftsman has charge of his own handiwork and vessel, and if this is later rendered defective by disobedience he should not leave it like that—it is still clay, so to speak, and it has been rendered unuseable, as though by a crack. (11) He should change the vessel into the original lump, to restore it to its pristine splendor and better still at the resurrection, in the regeneration. (12) In other words, <renew> the bodies of those who have committed the most grievous sins, and yet have repented, renounced their particular errors, and matured in the knowledge of our Lord Jesus Christ, allowing the body's resurrection from the earth, once the lump has been softened by the Craftsman and restored to its original form and even better.

2,1   Such was the serpent's plot against Eve. For humanity is greedy to begin with, and is always led on by the doctrines and empty promises of worthless talk. (2) And for a long time the serpent stayed in hiding, and did not disclose the whole of its poisonous emission. But later, after Christ's incarnation, it coughed the entire poisonous, wicked intent of its malice up and spat it out; for in its dupes' minds it proposed itself for glorification and worship as God.

2,3   But one can recognize the same serpent as the author of the deception, both from this school of its followers and from the visible snake. Indeed, sacred scripture calls the devil a serpent; not because he looks like one, certainly, but because to men he appears extremely crooked, and because of the treacherous fraud which was originally perpetrated through a snake.

2,4   But to those who recognize the truth this doctrine is ridiculous, and so are its adherents who exalt the serpent as God. No longer able to deceive the masculine reason, which has received the power of the truth from the Lord, the devil turns to the feminine—that is, to men's ignorance—and convinces the ignorant, since he cannot fool sound reason. (5) He always makes his approach to feminine whims, pleasures and lusts—in other words, to the effeminate ignorance in men, not to the firm reason which understands everything logically and by the law of nature recognizes God. (6) For their snake says it is Christ. Or rather,

---

[3] Gen. 3:19.

it does not—it cannot talk—but the devil does, who predisposed their thought to take this direction.

2,7   Thus, when he sees the snake, who will not recognize the adversary and get away? This is why the Lord made this very snake an enemy of mankind, since it is nothing but the devil's instrument and prey, and the devil deceived the man in Paradise through it—so that, on seeing its enmity, they would flee from the plot of the visible snake's treachery, and practically hate even the sight of it.

3,1   As a way of introducing what they consider mysteries with a myth—the mysteries are mimes' recitations and full of absurdity and stupidity—these so-called Ophites too ascribe all knowledge to this serpent, and say that it was the beginning of knowledge[4] for men. (2)[5] For the following are myths indeed. They claim that Aeons were emitted from the Aeon on high, and that Ialdabaoth came into being on a lower level. But he was emitted because of the weakness and ignorance[6] of his own mother, the Prunicus on high. (3)[7] For they say this Prunicus had come down into the waters and become mingled with them,[8] but could not ascend because of being mingled with the heaviness of matter. For she has been intermingled with the waters and matter, and can no longer withdraw. (4) But she heaved herself up with an effort and stretched herself out, and this was the origin of < the > upper heaven. And as she was fixed in place, no longer able to go up or come down but fixed and stretched out in the middle, (so) she remained. (5) For she could not sink down because she had no affinity (with what was below); but she could not go up because she was heavy from the matter which she had acquired.

3,6   But when Ialdabaoth[9] was emitted because of her ignorance he went right to the bottom and begot seven sons,[10] who begot seven heavens.[11] But Ialdabaoth closed off the area above him and hid it from view, so that the seven sons he had emitted, who were lower down than he, would not know what was above him,[12] but just him alone. And they

---

[4] The serpent is "the instructor" at Nat. Arc. 89,32; 90,6; Orig. Wld. 119,7; 120,2-3. Cf. Iren. I.30.5; Hippol. Haer. V.16.8; Ps.-Tert. 2.1.
[5] With 3,2-5 cf. Iren. I.30.2-3 and Ps.-Tert. 2.2. But in Ps.-Tert. it is Ialdabaoth rather than Prunicus who becomes involved with matter.
[6] With this characterization of Ialdabaoth's emission cf. Tri. Trac. 105,10-19. For Prunicus see Sect 25 Note 13.
[7] With 3,3-4 cf. Iren. I.30.3.
[8] Cf. Corp. Herm. I.14.
[9] For Yaldabaoth see Index NHL.
[10] Cf. Iren. I.30.3; Nat. Arc. 95,1-5; Corp. Herm. I.9; 4Q Serekh Shiroth 'Olath Ha-Shabbath.
[11] Cf. Apocry. Jn. 11,4-6.
[12] Cf. Tri. Trac. 79,12-19; 80,24-30; 100,36-101,5; Nat. Arc. 95,1-6. With the entire legend cf. Ps.-Tert. 2.3.

say that he, Ialdabaoth, is the God of the Jews. (7) But this is not so, heaven forbid! God the Almighty will judge them, for he is God both of Jews and Christians, and of everyone—not any Ialdabaoth, as their silly mythology has it.

4,1[13]   Then, they say, since the heights had been closed off by Ialdabaoth's design, these seven sons he had begotten—whether they were aeons, or gods, or angels, they use various terms for them— fashioned the man in the image of their father, Ialdabaoth. Not easily or quickly, however, but in the same way in which the former sects contrived it in their drivel. For these people also say, "The man was a thing that crawled, like a worm, able neither to raise his head nor get to his feet."[14] (2) But the Mother on high, whose name was Prunicus, wished to empty Ialdabaoth[15] of his power which he had gotten from her.[16] As a scheme against him she acted through him on the man his sons had formed, to drain his power and send a spark[17] of him upon the man—the soul,[18] if you please! (3) And then, they say, the man got up, rose in mind above the eight heavens, recognized the Father on high who was above Ialdabaoth, and praised him.[19]

4,4   And then Ialdabaoth was distressed because the things far above him were recognized. Bitterly he stared down at the dung of matter,[20] and sired a power that looked like a snake, which they also call his son.[21] (5) And so, they say, this son was sent on his mission and deceived Eve. But she listened to him, gave him credence as a son of God, and because of her belief ate from the tree of knowledge.[22]

5,1   Then, whenever they describe this foolishness and the absurdity of this practice—after they have composed the tragic piece, as we might call it, and this comic drama—they begin to give us certain indications in support of their false "gods," as they call them. They say, "Are not our entrails also, by which we live and are nourished, shaped like a serpent?"[23] (2) And for their dupes' benefit they introduce any number of

---

[13] With 4,1-2 cf. Ps.-Tert. 2.3, and see Sect 23 Notes 9 and 10.

[14] Cf. Ps.-Tert. 2.3; Iren. I.30.6.

[15] Cf. Iren. I.30.5-6.

[16] Cf. Apocry. Jn. 10,20-21; 11,8-9; 13,2-4.

[17] For "spark," cf., e.g., Apocry. Jn. 6,13; Para. Shem 31,23-29; 33,30-34; 46,13-17; GL 467,30-31.

[18] Something comparable is said at Tri. Trac. 105,11-106,5.

[19] Cf. Iren. I.30.5; Ps.-Tert. 2.4; Apocry. Jn. 20,28-33; GR 107,14-15; GL 465,14-17.

[20] Cf. the grief of the First Father at Orig. Wld. 107,18-34, and see GR 243,10-16.

[21] Cf. Iren. I.30.5; Ps.-Tert. 2.4; Acts of Philip 130.

[22] Cf. Iren. Haer. I.30.7; Ps.-Tert. 2.4; Apocry. Jn. 22,3-9. But in this last case it is Christ, not the serpent, who gives the command to eat.

[23] Cf. the shape of Nous at Iren. I.30.5. See Also Hippol. Haer. V.17.11.

further points in support of their imposture and silly opinion. "We magnify the serpent for this reason," they say; "he* has been the cause of knowledge for the many."

5,3 They say that Ialdabaoth did not want the Mother on high, or the Father, remembered by men. But the serpent convinced them and brought them knowledge, and taught the man and woman the whole of the knowledge of the mysteries on high. (4) Hence his father— Ialdabaoth, that is—was angry because of the knowledge he had given men,[24] and threw him down from heaven.[25] (5) And therefore those who possess the serpent's portion and nothing else, call the serpent a king from heaven.[26] And so, they say, they magnify him for such knowledge and offer him bread.

5,6 For they have an actual snake, and keep it in a sort of basket. When it is time for their mysteries they bring it out of the den, spread loaves around on a table, and call the snake to come; and when the den is opened it comes out. And then the snake—which comes up of its own purpose and villainy, already knowing their foolishness—crawls onto the table and coils up on the loaves. And this is what they call a perfect sacrifice.

5,7 And so, someone has told me, not only do they break the loaves the snake has coiled on and distribute them to the recipients, but they each kiss the snake besides. The snake has either been charmed into tameness by some sort of sorcery, or cajoled for their deception by some other work of the devil. (8) But they worship an animal like this, and call what has been consecrated by its coiling around it the eucharistic element.[27] And they offer a hymn to the Father on high—again, as they say, through the snake—and so conclude their mysteries.

6,1 But anyone would call <this> foolishness and full of nonsense. And it will not require refutation by research in sacred scripture; to anyone with godly soundness of mind its absurdity will be self-evident. The silliness of all of their drivel will be seen at once. (2) For if they say, "Prunicus," as I have said already, how can one fail to detect the unsoundness of their notion from the very name? Anything which is called

---

[24] "You are the tree of knowledge, which is in Paradise, (from) which the first man ate and which opened his mind, (so that) he became enamored of his co-likeness, and condemned other alien likenesses, and loathed them," Orig. Wld. 110,31-111,1. Cf. 118,24-119,19; Nat. Arc. 88,24-89,3; 89,31-90,19; PS 247; 349. For a (Jewish Gnostic?) amulet picturing Adam, Eve and the serpent, see Goodenough, *Jewish Symbols*, Vol. 8 p. 170.
[25] Cf. Iren. I.30.7; Nat. Arc. 87,4-7.
[26] Cf. Hippol. Haer. V.16.14.
[27] Cf. Ps.-Tert. 2.1.

"wanton" is unseemly; but if it is unseemly, it deserves no place of honor. And how can the unseemly be worthy of praise?

6,3   And how can it be anything but mythology to say that Prunicus drained Ialdabaoth, and that the spark went down below from the one who had been drained; but that once it had lodged in the man, it recognized the one above the one who had been drained? (4) How very strange that the man, with the tiniest of sparks in him, recognizes more than the angels who have fashioned him! For the angels or sons of Ialdabaoth, did not recognize the things above Ialdabaoth; but the man they had made did, by means of the spark!

6,5   Ophites refute themselves with their own doctrines by glorifying the snake at one moment, but claiming at the next that he came to Eve as a deceiver, with their statement that "He deceived Eve."[28] (6) And they sometimes proclaim him Christ, but sometimes a son of the higher Ialdabaoth, who wronged his sons by shutting off the knowledge of <the> realms on high from them—and who broke faith both with the Mother and with the Father on high, to keep the sons he had sired from honoring the Father above him.

6,7   How can the serpent be a heavenly king if he has rebelled against the Father? If he gives knowledge, why is he denounced as having fooled Eve with a deception? One who instills knowledge through deceit is no longer giving knowledge, but ignorance in place of knowledge; and one can see, in fact, that among them this is an actuality. For they have ignorance and think it is knowledge—though when they call their "knowledge" deceit and ignorance, in this they are telling the truth!

7,1   They cite other texts as well, and say that Moses too lifted the bronze serpent up in the wilderness and exhibited it for the healing of persons whom a snake had bitten.[29] For they say this sort of thing serves as a cure for the bite. (2) But again, they make these declarations against themselves. For if the bites were snake's bites, and these bites are harmful, then the serpent is not good. The thing Moses held up in those times effected healing by the sight of it—not because of the nature of the snake but by the consent of God, who used the snake to make a sort of antidote for those who were bitten then. (3) It is no surprise if a person is cured through the things by which he was injured. And let no one speak ill of God's creation—as other erring persons do in their turn.

7,4   However, this image was made beforehand for the people in the wilderness, for the reason the Lord gives in the Gospel after he comes: "As Moses lifted up the serpent in the wilderness, even so must the Son

---

[28] 2 Cor. 11:3.
[29] Cf. Ps.-Tert. 2.1; Hippol. Haer. V.16.7-8.

of Man be lifted up''[30]—and this has been done. (5) For dishonoring the Savior like serpents they were injured by the plot of the serpent, I mean the devil. And as healing came to the bitten by the lifting up of the serpent, so, because of the crucifixion of Christ, deliverance has come to our souls from the bites of sin that were left in us.

7,6   But the same people use this very text literally as evidence, and say, "Do you not see how the Savior said, 'As Moses lifted up the serpent in the wilderness, even so must the Son of man be lifted up?'[31] And on this account," they say, "he also says, 'Be ye wise as the serpent and harmless as the dove,'[32] in another passage." And what God has rightly ordained for us as clues to a teaching they cite for their own deluded purpose.

8,1   For Jesus Christ our Lord and the divine Word, begotten of the Father before all ages, without beginning and not in time, is no serpent—heaven forbid! He himself came in opposition to the serpent. (2) If he says, "Be ye wise as the serpent and harmless as the dove,"[33] it is our task to inquire and learn why he introduced these two portraits, of the serpent and of the dove, for our instruction. (3) There is nothing wise about a snake except for <the> two following things. When it is being hunted it knows that its whole life is in its head, and it is afraid of the commandment God once gave about it for the man's sake, "Thou shalt watch for its head, and it shall watch for thy heel."[34] So it coils its whole body over its head and hides its skull, but with extreme villainy surrenders the rest of its body. (4) In the same way the only-begotten God, who came forth from the Father, wills that we surrender our whole selves to fire and sword in a time of persecution and a time of temptation, but that we guard our "head"—in other words, that we do not deny Christ, since "The head of every man is Christ, and the head of the woman is the man, and the head of Christ is God,"[35] as the apostle says.

8,5   Again, as the naturalists say of it, the snake has another kind of wisdom. When it is thirsty and goes from its den to water to drink, it does not bring its poison. It leaves this in its den, and then goes and takes its drink of the water. (6) Let us mimic this ourselves, and not bring evil, pleasure, passion, enmity or anything else in our thoughts when we go to God's holy church for prayer or God's mysteries.

8,7   For that matter, how can we imitate the dove either without keeping clear of evil—though certainly, in many ways doves are not ad-

---

[30] John 3:14.
[31] John 3:14.
[32] Matt. 10:16.
[33] Matt. 10:16.
[34] Gen. 3:15.
[35] 1 Cor. 11:3.

mirable. (8) They are incontinent and ceaselessly promiscuous, lecherous and devoted to the pleasure of the moment, and weak and small besides. (9) But because of the harmlessness, patience and forbearance of doves—and even more, because the Holy Ghost has appeared in the form of a dove—the divine Word would have us imitate the will of the Holy Ghost and the harmlessness of the harmless dove, and be wise in good but innocent in evil.

And all of their dramatics are destroyed. (10) Straight off, when he says, "I fear, lest by any means, as the serpent beguiled Eve through his villainy, so your minds should be corrupted from the sincerity and simplicity of Christ, and from righteousness,"[36] the apostle assigns villainy and treachery to no one else than the devil and the serpent. (11) You see how the apostle declared that the serpent's treatment of Eve was seduction, fearful villainy, and deception, and how he showed that it had done nothing admirable.

9,1 Hence their stupidity is a perfectly discernible and obvious matter, to anyone willing to know the teaching of the truth, and the knowledge of the Holy Spirit. (2) And not to waste time, now that I have also sailed through this fierce, hazardous storm, I shall ready my barque for its other ocean voyages, carefully guarding my tongue by God's power and the prayers of saints, (3) so as to espy the tossing of the wild waves as I sail by, and the forms of the poisonous beasts in the seas, but be able to cross and reach the fair haven of the truth by prayer and supplication, untouched by the poison of sea-eel, sting-ray, dragon, shark and scorpaena. (4) In my case too, the letter of, "They that go down to the sea shall tell the virtues of the Lord,"[37] will be fulfilled. So I shall make my way to another sect after this, to give its description.

38.

Against Cainites.[1] Number eighteen, but thirty-eight of the series

1,1 Certain persons are called Cainites because they take the name of their sect from Cain. For they praise Cain and count him as their father, as though, in a manner of speaking, they too were being driven by a different surge of waves, without being outside of the same swell and surf. And as though they were peering out of thorny undergrowth but

---

[36] 2 Cor. 11:3.
[37] Ps. 106:23-24.

[1] Sect 38 is based upon Iren. I.31.1-2, and some other sources whose identity is not certain. Cf. Ps.-Tert. 2.5-6.

were not outside of the whole heap of thorns, even though they differ in name. For there are many kinds of thorn, but the hurt of injury by thorns is in them all.

1,2[2]   Cainites say that Cain is descended from the stronger power and the authority on high; so, moreover, are Esau, Korah and his companions, and the Sodomites. But Abel is descended from the weaker power. (3) <They regard> all these as worthy of their praise and kin to themselves. For they are proud of their relationship to Cain, the Sodomites,[3] Esau and Korah. And these, they say, belong to the perfect knowledge from on high. (4) Therefore, they say, though the maker of this world made it his business to destroy them, he could do them no harm; they were hidden from him and translated to the aeon on high, where the stronger power comes from. For since they were her own, Wisdom allowed them to approach her.

1,5[4]   And therefore, they say, Judas had found out all about them. For they claim him as kin too and consider him particularly knowledgeable, so that they even attribute a short work to him, which they call a Gospel of Judas. (6) And they likewise forge certain other works against "Womb."[5] They call this "Womb" the maker of this entire vault of heaven and earth. And as Carpocrates does, they say that no one will be saved otherwise than by progressing through all acts.

2,1   For as each of them does the unspeakable with this excuse, and performs obscenities and commits every sin in the world, he invokes the name of each angel, if you please—both real angels, and their fictitious ones. And he attributes a godless commission of every sin on earth to each of them, by offering his own action in the name of any angel he wishes. (2) And each time they do these things they say, "This or that angel, I perform thy work. This or that authority, I do thy deed." (3) And they call this perfect "knowledge," since their reason for turning with confidence to the godless acts of obscenity comes, if you please, from the mothers and fathers of sects whom we have mentioned already. I mean the Gnostics and Nicolaus, and their allies, Valentinus and Carpocrates.

2,4   Further, I have learned of a book in which they have forged certain statements full of iniquity, and it contains such remarks as, "This is the angel who blinded Moses. These are the angels who hid the

----

[2] 1,2-2,3 seems to be paraphrased from Iren. I.31.1. Cf. Ps.-Tert. 2.5-6.

[3] The Sodomites are witnesses to the truth at Para. Shem. 29,12-29. Cf. what is said of Sodom and Gomorra at Gos. Egyp. 56,4-13; 60,9-18.

[4] With 1,5-6 cf. Ps.-Tert. 2.5.

[5] "Womb" in some comparable sense occurs in the Nag Hammadi corpus, e.g., at Para. Shem 4,10-24; Apocry. Jn. 5,5; Pr. Thank. 64,25-30.

companions of Korah, Dathan and Abiram, and removed them elsewhere."[6]

2,5   But again, others forge another short work, full of filthy lewdness, in the name of the apostle Paul—the so-called Gnostics use it too. They call it an Ascension of Paul, taking their cue from the apostle's statement that he has ascended to the third heaven and heard unutterable words, which no man may say. And these, they say, are the unutterable words.[7]

2,6   But they teach these things and their like to honor the wicked and repudiate the good. For < they claim >, as I said, that Cain belongs to the stronger power and Abel to the weaker. These powers had intercourse with Eve[8] and sired Cain and Abel; and Cain was the son of the one, Abel of the other.[9] (7) But Adam and Eve were < also > offspring of powers or angels like these. And the children the powers had begotten, I mean Cain and Abel, quarrelled, and the son of the stronger power murdered the son of the lesser and weaker.

3,1   But they too mix the same mythology with their legacy of ignorance about the same deadly poisons, and advise[10] their followers that everyone must choose the stronger power, and separate from the lesser, feeble one—that is, from the one which made heaven, the flesh and the world. And he must rise above it to the highest through the crucifixion of Christ. (2) For this is why he came from above, they say, so that the stronger power might act in him by defeating the weaker and betraying the body. (3)[11] And some of them say this; others, something different. Some say that Christ was betrayed by Judas because Christ was wicked, and wanted to pervert the provisions of the Law. For they commend Cain and Judas, as I said, and say, "This is why he has betrayed him; he intended to abolish things that had been properly taught."

3,4   But others say, "No, he betrayed him despite his goodness because of the heavenly knowledge. For the archons knew," they say, "that the weaker power would be drained if Christ were given over to crucifixion. (5) And when Judas found this out," they say, "he was anx-

---

[6] Orig. Wld. 106,26-107,17 mentions books which might be comparable in character.

[7] Cf. 2 Cor. 12:2-4. In the Latin Apocalypse of Paul (given at James, *Apocrypha of the New Testament*, pp. 526-535) 21, we read, "And I heard there words which it is not lawful for a man to utter; and again he said, Yet again follow me, and I will show thee what thou mayest relate and tell openly." The Nag Hammadi Apocalypse of Paul does not mention the unutterable words.

[8] Cf. Apocry. Jn. 23,35-24,25, or the archons' attempt on Eve at Nat. Arc. 88,17-30.

[9] A comparable story is told at Orig. Wld. 116,33-117,18.

[10] Or, "As a plot against their followers, they too mix the same mythology (i.e., that one must choose between powers) in with their gift ..." But this would strain the construction.

[11] With 3,3-5 cf. Ps.-Tert. 2.5.

ious and did all he could to betray him, and performed a good work for
our salvation. And we must commend him and give him the credit, since
the salvation of the cross was effected for us through him, and the revelation of the things on high which that occasioned.''

3,6   But they are altogether deluded, since they neither honor nor applaud anyone who is good. It is obvious that this crop, I mean crop of
ignorance and deceit, has been sown in them by the devil. (7) The scriptural words, ''Woe unto them that call good evil and evil good, that put
darkness for light and light for darkness; that call sweet bitter and bitter,
sweet,''[12] are fulfilled in them. (8) Old and New Testaments speak out
in every way to denounce Cain's impiety. These on the contrary, lovers
<of> darkness that they are and imitators of evildoers, hate Abel but
love Cain and give their applause to Judas. (9) But they † dress a rotten
''knowledge'' up by setting up two powers, a weaker and stronger, which
quarrel with each other but see to it that no one on earth can change his
mind; of those who are born here, some are naturally derived from evil,
and others from goodness. They say that no one is good or bad by choice,
but by nature.

4,1   And first, let us see how the Old Testament says of Cain, ''Thou
art cursed from the earth, which hath opened her mouth to receive thy
brother's blood from thy hand,'' and again, ''Thou art cursed in thy
works, and shalt go sighing and trembling upon the earth.''[13] (2) And the
Lord in the Gospel said the same thing about him that the Old Testament
did, when Jews said, ''We have God as our father.''[14] The Lord told
them, ''Ye are sons of your father the devil, for he is a liar because his
father was a liar. He was a murderer, and abode not in the truth. When
he speaketh a lie he speaketh of his own, for his father was a liar also.''[15]

4,3   From hearing this statement the other sects allege that the devil
is the father of he Jews, and that he has a different father, and his father
in turn has a father. (4) But they are speaking with impudence and blin-
ding their reason. They are tracing the devil's ancestry to the Lord of all,
the God of the Jews, the Christians, and all men, by saying that he is the
father of the devil's father—the God who gave the Law through Moses
and has done so many wonders!

4,5   This is not true, beloved. To begin with, the Lord himself, who
cares for us in all ways, <meant> Judas when he said that their father
was the devil—to keep us from deserting the natural interpretation by
making one quibble and supposition after another. (6) In telling his

---

[12] Isa. 5:20.
[13] Gen. 4:11-12.
[14] John 8:41.
[15] John 8:44.

disciples, "Have I not chosen you twelve, and one of you is a devil?"[16] he has called Judas both "Satan" and "devil"; but he means devil in intent, not devil by nature. (7) Again, in another passage he says, "Father, Lord of heaven and earth, keep those whom thou hast given me. While I was with them I kept them, and none of them is lost but the son of perdition."[17] (8) Once more, he says elsewhere, "The Son of Man must be betrayed as it is written of him, but woe unto him by whom he shall be betrayed. It were better for him if he had not been born,"[18] and so on.

4,9   Hence we know from every source that he was speaking of Judas to the Jews. "For of whom a man is overcome, of the same he is brought in bondage;"[19] and the person whom one believes is one's father, and the author of one's belief. (10) The Lord says, "Ye are sons of your father, the devil,"[20] because they believed Judas instead of Christ, just as Eve at the beginning turned from God and believed the serpent. (11) Then, he says it because Judas was not merely a liar but a thief as well, as the Gospel says. That was why he gave him the bag—so that he would have no excuse when, from greed, he delivered his master to men.

4,12   Who is Judas' father then, the "liar before him," but Cain, whose mimic Judas was? For Cain lied to his brother in seeming affection, deceived and cajoled him with the lie, and took him out to the plain, raised his hand, and killed him. (13) Thus Judas too says, "What will ye give me, and I will deliver him unto you?"[21] and, "Whomsoever I kiss, that same is he; hold him fast." And the betrayer said, "Hail, Master,"[22] when he came, honoring him with his lips, but with heart far removed from God.

5,1   Hence this Judas, who became their father by denial of God and betrayal, and who was a Satan and devil, not by nature but in intent, has himself become a son by imitation of the murderer and liar, Cain. For Cain's "father" before him was a liar too—not Adam, but the devil—(2) and Cain imitated him in fratricide, hatred and falsehood, as well as in contradiction of God by saying, "Am I my brother's keeper? I know not where he is."[23] (In the same way the devil says, "Doth Job fear God for nought?"[24] to the Lord.) (3) For the devil himself deceived Adam and

---

[16] John 6:70.
[17] John 17:11-12.
[18] Matt. 26:24.
[19] 2 Pet. 2:19.
[20] John 8:44.
[21] Matt. 26:15.
[22] Matt. 26:48-49.
[23] Gen. 4:9.
[24] Job 1:9.

Eve with the lie, "Ye shall be as gods and shall not die,"[25] to misrepresent the truth and show pretended frienship. And Cain, in imitation of him, deceived his brother with a pretense of affection by saying, "Let us go out to the plain."[26]

5,4   This is why St. John said, "He that hateth his brother, the same is not made perfect in love, but is of Cain, who slew his brother. And wherefore slew he him? Because his works were evil and he envied his brother's, for they were good."[27] (5) And how can these people not be convicted as well, when they envy Abel, whose works are good, but honor Cain? Pronouncing a severe sentence on them, the Savior expressly says, "Of this generation all righteous blood shall be required, from the blood of righteous Abel which was shed at the beginning unto Zacharias the prophet, whom ye slew between the temple and the altar,"[28] and so on.

6,1   Hence Judas did not betray the Savior from knowledge, as these people say; nor will the Jews be rewarded for crucifying the Lord, though we certainly have salvation through the cross. (2) Judas did not betray him to make him the saving of us, but from the ignorance, envy and greed of the denial of God. (3) Even if scripture says that Christ will be given over to a cross—or even if sacred scripture predicts the offenses we are committing in the last days—none of us, who commit the transgressions, can find any defense by appealing to the testimony of the scripture that foretells them. (4) We do not do these things because scripture †foretold* them. Because we would do them, scripture foretold them— from God's foreknowledge and to remove the suspicion that God, who is good and yet inflicts his wrath on sinners, can have emotion. (5) For God's anger at every sinner does not stem from emotion. Godhead is impassible, and it does not inflict its wrath on men because it has been seized with irritation, or because it is mastered and overcome by anger. God shows his impassibility by telling us beforehand of the judgment to come and the just penalty he assesses, to indicate the impassibility of Godhead.

6,6   Hence, in its foreknowledge, Scripture forewarned and taught us, to spare us an encounter with God's irremediable wrath—a wrath which is not determined by emotion and is not the result of mastery by emotion, but which has been prepared beforehand, with complete justice, for men who commit sin and do not truly repent.

7,1   And so with the cross. The Jews did not crucify the Savior, and Judas did not betray the Savior, because sacred scripture said they

---

[25] Gen. 3:4;5.
[26] Gen. 4:8.
[27] 1 John 3:15; 4:18; 3:12.
[28] Matt. 23:35.

would. But because Judas would betray him, and the Jews would crucify him, sacred scripture foretold this in the Old Testament, and the Lord foretold it in the Gospel. (2) Hence Judas did not betray the Lord—as the Cainites say he did—because he was aware of the good deed that would be done for the world. He betrayed him knowing that he was his master, but not knowing that salvation would come to the world. (3) How could he be the one who saw to men's salvation, when the Savior himself said "son of perdition"[29] to him, "Better for that man if he had not been born,"[30] "Friend, do that for which thou art come,"[31] "One of you shall betray me,"[32] "He that eateth bread with me hath lifted up his heel against me,"[33] (Here the Gospel quotes an earlier text from the Psalter), and "Woe unto him by whom the Son of Man is betrayed?"[34]

7,4   For Judas gave an indication of the whole truth about himself; and even <of> himself he exposed the stupidity of those who applaud him, though he did not mean to. All the same he still repented later after getting the thirty pieces of silver as his price, and returned the money as though he had done something bad—bad for himself, and bad for the executioners as well. (5) But to do a good thing for us and the world by his own effort, the Lord has surrendered himself to become our salvation.

7,6   Hence we do not thank the betrayer, Judas, but the merciful Savior who laid down his life for us—for his own sheep, as he himself said. (7) If Judas thought he had done something good, why did he later say, "I repent that I have betrayed innocent blood,"[35] and return the money? As it was written of him in the prophets, "And he returned the thirty pieces of silver, the price of him that was valued of the children of Israel." And again, in another prophet, "If ye deem proper, give me my price, or forbear."[36] (8) And again, in another prophet, "And they gave the silver, the price of him that was valued, and he said, Cast it into the refiner's furnace, and see whether it be proved, as I was proved of the children of Israel."[37]

8,1   And how much we can gather from sacred scripture about prophecies fulfilled in our Lord—not prophecies of Judas' work for good, but prophecies of the voluntary, not compulsory surrender for us of our Savior and Lord Jesus Christ, the Son of God; and his provision of the

---

[29] John 17:12.
[30] Matt. 26:24.
[31] Matt. 26:50.
[32] Matt. 26:21.
[33] John 13:18; Ps. 40:10.
[34] Matt. 26:24.
[35] Matt. 27:4.
[36] Cf. Zech. 11:12.
[37] Zech. 11:12-13; Matt. 27:9.

cross for our salvation! (2) But I know I am giving a very bulky list of texts—as one more prophet says, "Let his habitation be desolate, and his bishopric let another take,"[38] <indicating that Judas died badly>. (3) For "he fell down and burst asunder in the midst and all his bowels gushed out."[39] And as he hanged himself at the last † it was evident that he had destroyed his whole salvation, by the forfeiture of his hope through his unruly, reckless plot against his master, and his greedy <turn> to the denial of God. (4) Thus the apostles made Matthias one of them in his stead with the words, "from which Judas by transgression fell, that he might go to his own place."[40] (5) And what sort of "place" but the one the Savior had awarded him by calling him a "son of perdition?" For this "place of perdition" was reserved for him in the realm where he obtained a portion in place of a portion and, instead of apostolic office, the place of destruction.

8,6 But I think enough has been said about this, beloved. Let us go to still another to expose once more the obscure, savage, poisonous teachings of the remaining sectarians who, to the world's harm, have been thunderstruck by a false inspiration of the devil. (7) After exposing the opinion—like exposing poisonous dung-beetles!—of such people, who desire what is bad, and after crushing it by God's power because of its harmfulness, let us call on God for aid, sons of Christ, since we intend to inquire into the others.

39.

Against Sethians.[1] *Number nineteen, but thirty-nine of the series*

1,1 "Sethians" is yet another Sect, and that is their name. It is not to be found everywhere, nor is the one before it, the so-called sect of "Cainites;" most of these too have probably been uprooted by now. What is not of God will not stand; it flourishes for a while, but has no permanence at all.

1,2 I think I may have met with this sect in Egypt too—I do not precisely recall the country I met them in. And I discovered some things about it in an actual encounter, by inquiry, but have learned others from the literature.

---

[38] Acts 1:20; Ps. 68:26; 108:8.
[39] Acts 1:18; Matt. 27:5.
[40] Acts 1:25.

---

[1] The sources for Sect 39 are not certain. Hippolytus may be one, as evidenced by the resemblance between Sect 39 and Ps.-Tert. 2.7-9. But the "Sethians" reported at Hippol. Haer. V.19-22 bear no resemblance to the group described here. Part of Epiphanius' information was obtained at first hand.

1,3   These Sethians proudly trace their ancestry to Seth[2] the son of
Adam, magnify him,[3] and attribute to him whatever <is held> to be
virtuous—the signs of virtue and righteousness, and anything of the
kind. What is more, they even call him Christ and maintain that he is
Jesus. (4) But the form in which they give their teaching makes all things
a product of angels, not of the power on high.

2,1   For in this regard they agree with the last sect, the Cainite: Two
men came into existence right at the beginning, and Cain and Abel are
the sons of the two. The angels quarrelled about them and went to <war
with> each other, and thus caused Abel to be killed by Cain. (2) For the
angels' quarrel was a struggle over the human stocks,[4] since these two
men, the one who sired Cain and the one who sired Abel, <were at
odds>. (3) But the power on high, whom they call Mother[5] and Female,[6]
was the winner. (They think there are mothers on high, and females and
males, and all but "kindreds and patriarchies.")

2,4[7]   Since the power who is called Mother and Female won, they
say, she reflected—finding that they had killed Abel—caused the generation of Seth, and put her power in him. In him she planted a seed of the
power from above, and the spark that was sent from above for the first
planting of the seed, and the origin (of it). (5) And this is the origin of
righteousness, and the election of a seed and a stock, so that the powers
of the angels who made the world and the two primordial men would be
purified through this* origin and by this seed. (6) For this reason the
stock of Seth, which is elect and distinct from the other stock, is derived
separately from this origin.

2,7   For time went on, they say, and the two stocks of Cain and Abel
were together, <and> had come together out of great wickedness and
been mixed. The Mother of all kept watch and wanted to make the seed
of men pure, as I said, since Abel had been killed. And she chose this

---

[2] A "seed" or "race" of Seth appears in Nag Hammadi at Gos. Egyp. 54,9-11; 56,3;
59,12-18; 60,25-61,1; Apoc. Ad. 65,5-9; Gr. Seth 63,8-9; Three Stel. 119,2; 120,8-10;
Zost. 130,16-17.

[3] Seth is often a supernatural figure in Gnostic literature: so, e.g., in Gos. Egyp.
51,20-22 and passim in this document; Three Stel. 118,25-32; Mand. PB 105 p. 106;
Man. Hom. 61,23; Man. Ps. 144,1.

[4] "And Cain [killed] Abel his brother, for [the Demiurge] breathed into [them] his
spirit. And there [took place] the struggle with the apostasy of the angels and mankind,
those of the right with those of the left, and those in heaven with those on earth, the spirits
with the carnal, and the Devil against God," Val. Exp. 38,24-33. A comparable struggle
between powers or groups of powers appears at Tri. Trac. 81,10-16; 83,34-84,36; Orig.
Wld. 104,13-17. At Apocry. Jn. 24,15-25, Cain and Abel are in fact Yave and Eloim.

[5] The "Mother" appears to be associated with the begetting of Seth at Apocry. Jn.
24,32-25,7.

[6] With "Female" perhaps cf. Θηλεία, Hippol. Haer. V.19.4.

[7] With 2,4-7 cf. Ps.-Tert. 2.7.

Seth and showed his purity, and planted the seed of her power and purity in him alone.

3,1[8]   But once more Mother and Female saw a great deal of intermingling and unruly desire on the part of angels and men, since the two breeds had become mixed; and she saw that their unruliness had caused certain combinations of breeds. So she returned and brought the flood, and destroyed all humanity <and> the whole stock of her opponents, so that only the pure stock, if you please—the one that derived from Seth and was righteous—would remain in the world to propagate the stock from above, and the spark of righteousness.

3,2[9]   But the angels in turn slipped Ham into the ark without her knowledge, and he was of their seed. For they say that of the eight persons who were saved in Noah's ark then, seven were of the pure stock. But one was Ham who belonged to the other power, and he got in unknown to the Mother on high. (3) Such a contrivance was put into effect by the angels for the following reason. The angels had learned that all their seed would be wiped out in the flood, they say, so they smuggled Ham in by some villainy to preserve the wicked stock which they had created.

3,4   And because of this forgetfulness and error have overtaken men, and inordinate crops of sins and a conglomeration of evil have arisen in the world. And thus the world reverted to its ancient state of disorder, and was as filled with evils as it had been at the first, before the flood. (5) But from Seth by descent and lineage came Christ, Jesus himself, though not by generation; he has appeared in the world miraculously. He is Seth himself,[10] who visited men then and now because he was sent from above by the Mother.[11]

4,1   This is the way they say this all was. But preachings like these are foolish, weak and full of nonsense, as everyone can see. (2) Two men were not formed (at the beginning). One man was formed, Adam; and Cain, Abel and Seth came from Adam. And <the breeds of men> before the flood cannot derive from two men but must derive from one, since the breeds all have their own origins <from> Adam. (3) And again, the whole human race since the flood derives from Noah, one man. It does not derive from different men but from one, Noah, Seth's lineal descendant; and it is not divided into two, but is one stock. (4)

---

[8] With 3,1 cf. Ps.-Tert. 2.8.
[9] With 3,2-3 cf. Ps.-Tert. 2.9.
[10] Seth is certainly identified with Christ at Gos. Egyp. 62,24-64,9, and may be at Apoc. Ad. 76,9-77,18; Gr. Seth 51,20-52,10.
[11] Seth is a sort of savior or revealer at Apocry. Jn. 24,33-25,5; Gos. Egyp. 64,24-65,9; Apoc. Ad. 76,24-77,1 and what follows.

Therefore Noah's wife, his sons Shem, Ham and Japheth, and the three
wives of his sons, all trace their ancestry to Seth, and not to the two non-
existent men of the Sethians' invention.

5,1   They compose books in the names of great men, and say that
seven books are in Seth's name,[12] but give other, different books the
name "Strangers."[13] They say that another, which is filled with all sorts
of wickedness, is in Abraham's name, and they also call it an apocalypse.
And they say that others are in Moses' name, and others are in the names
of other people.

5,2   Reducing their own minds to great folly they say that Seth has
a wife, Horaia. Look at their stupidity, beloved, so that you will recognize their melodrama, mythological nonsense, and fictitious claptrap for
just what it is. (3) There are certain other sects which say there is a power
whom they call, † specifically, "Horaia." Now these people say that the
one whom others regard as a power and call Horaia, is Seth's wife!

5,4   From that we can prove that Seth was a real man—as you know,
beloved—that he got no unusual endowment from above, and that he
was the real brother of Cain and Abel, from one father and one mother.
(5) For scripture says, "Adam knew Eve his wife, and she conceived and
bare Cain;" and she named him Cain, meaning "acquisition," saying,
"I have gotten a son through the Lord God."[14] (6) Again, <of>Abel
it says, "Adam knew Eve his wife and she conceived and bare a son and
called his name Abel."[15] (7) And much farther on, after the death of
Abel, "And Adam knew Eve, his wife, and she conceived and bare a son,
and called his name Seth," meaning "recompense." "For," she said,
"God hath raised up for me a seed instead of Abel, whom Cain slew."[16]
(8) (The words, "I have gotten through God," and "God hath raised up
for me," show that God, the maker of all and the giver of the children,
is one.) (9) And it is clear that Cain and Seth, at least, took wives. For
Abel was killed as a young man and still unmarried.

---

[12] Hippol. Haer. V.2.1 mentions a Paraphrase of Seth, but this may be a mistake for
Paraphrase of Shem. CG VII,2 is entitled Second Treatise of the Great Seth; VII,5, The
Three Steles of Seth. The words, "and you will leave these books upon a mountain" at
Allog. 68,20-21 seem to be an allusion to the legend of the written testimony left by Seth,
and imply that this work was considered to be Seth's. All this merely shows that there
was such a literature, and does not indicate that the "books in the name of Seth" to
which Epiphanius alludes are identical with the Nag Hammadi tractates mentioned here.

[13] Porphyry mentions an Apocalypse of Allogenes at Vita Plotini 16. CG XI,3 is entitled Allogenes, and appears to presuppose a legend something like the one related at
Epiphanius 40,7,1-3. "Strange" is a common Mandaean term for a being from the light
world, as at GR 5,2 and many other passages.

[14] Gen. 4:1.

[15] Cf. Gen. 4:1-2.

[16] Gen. 4:25.

6,1   But, as is apparent in Jubilees or "The Little Genesis," the book even contains the names of both Cain's and Seth's wives[17]—to the utter shame of these people who have recited their myths to the world. (2) For after Adam had had sons and daughters it became necessary that, for the time being, his sons marry their own sisters. Such a thing was not unlawful; there was no other human stock. (3) In a manner of speaking, in fact, Adam practically married his own daughter himself, since she was fashioned from his body and bones and had been formed in union with him by God. And this was not unlawful. (4) And his sons were married, Cain to the older sister, whose name was Saue; and a third son, Seth, who was born after Abel, to his sister named Azura.[18]

6,5   As the Little Genesis says, Adam had other sons too—nine after these three[19]—so that he had two daughters but twelve sons, one of whom was killed while eleven survived. (6) You also have the suggestion of them in the Genesis of the World, the first Book of Moses, which says, "And Adam lived 930 years, and begat sons and daughters, and died."[20]

7,1   But when humanity broadened out and Adam's line grew longer, the strict rule of lawful wedlock was progressively amplified. (2) And then, since Adam had had children and children's children, and daughters were born to them in direct descent, they no longer took their own sisters in marriage. Even before the Law written by Moses the rule of lawful wedlock was reduced to order, and they took their wives from among their cousins. (3) And now, as humanity broadened in this way, the two stocks were commingled—Cain's with Seth's and Seth's with the other, and so were the other breeds of Adam's sons.

7,4   Then finally, when the flood had destroyed all mankind at once, Noah alone was preserved, since he had been found righteous in that generation and found favor with God. (5) But as I said before, he prepared his ark by God's decree, as the true scriptures tell us. The same book of the truth states that he was preserved in it, and with him the seven souls I have mentioned—I mean his his own wife and three sons, and their wives, of whom there were also three.[21] (6) And again, the truth makes it certain that this is why there was something left of man's origin in the world. And so, as time went on from generation to generation and with son succeeding father, the world had come to span five generations.

8,1   And the foundation of Babylon in Assyria took place at that time, and the tower which they built then. (2) But, as I have already explained

---

[17] Jub. 4.9-11.
[18] Jub. 4.9;11.
[19] Jub. 4.10.
[20] Cf. Gen. 5:3-5.
[21] Cf. Gen. 7:7; 1 Pet. 3:20.

in connection with the generations discussed above, in the foregoing
Sects, all humanity then consisted of seventy-two men, who were princes
and patricians. Thirty-two were of Ham's stock and fifteen were of
Japheth's, but twenty-five were of Shem's. And thus the tower and
Babylon were built.

8,3   After this tribes and languages were dispersed all over the earth.
And since the seventy-two persons <who> were then building the tower
were scattered by the languages—because they had been confused, and
<made strangers to> the single language they had known—each has
been infused with a different one by God's will. (4) This was the beginning of all the ways of talking there are even to this day, so that <anyone
who> cares to, can discover the person who originated each language.
(5) For example, Iovan acquired Greek[22]—the Ionians,[23] who possess the
Greeks' ancient speech, are named for him. Theras[24] acquired Thracian;
Mosoch,[25] Mossynoecian; Thobel,[26] Thessalian; Lud,[27] Lydian;
Gephar,[28] Gasphenian; Mistrem,[29] Egyptian; Psous, Axomitian;[30] and
Armot,[31] Arabian. And not to mention them individually, each of the
rest was infused with a language of his own. And from then on the people
who spoke each language after them have multiplied in the world.

9,1   Why is it, then, that these people have spoken their false words,
and mixed their own invention (with the truth) by imagining and dreaming what is not real as though it were, and banishing what is real from
their minds? But the whole thing is the devil's † idea, which he implanted
in human souls.

9,2   But it is amazing to see how he deceived man with many absurdities, and dragged him down to transgression, to fornication, adultery
and incontinence, to madness for idols, sorcery and bloodshed, to rapine
and insatiate greed, to trickery and gluttony, and any number of such
things—yet never before Christ's coming did he venture to utter a
blasphemy against his own master, or think of open rebellion. (3) For he
was awaiting Christ's coming, as he says, "It is written of thee that he
shall give his angels charge concerning thee, and in their hands they shall
bear thee up."[32] (4) He had always heard the prophets proclaim the com-

---

[22] Hippol. Chron. 60.
[23] Hippol. Haer. X.31.4.
[24] Hippol. Chron. 63.
[25] Hippol. Chron. 169.
[26] Hippol. Chron. 61.
[27] Hippol. Chron. 111.
[28] Hippol. Chron. 168.
[29] Hippol. Chron. 95.
[30] Hippol. Chron. 94.
[31] Hippol. Chron. 178.
[32] Matt. 4:6; Luke 4:11.

ing of Christ < and > that there would be a redemption of those who had sinned and yet repented through Christ, and he expected to find some mercy. (5) But when he unfortunately saw that Christ had not accepted his turnaround regarding salvation, he opened his mouth against his own Master and spewed the blasphemy out, and gave men a notion to deny their actual Master but seek the non-existent one.

9,6   Now Sethians too will be exposed as utter dupes in the following way. Seth has died, and the years of his life are recorded. He died after living for 912 years and fathering sons and daughters, as sacred scripture says. (7) And next his son, his name was Enosh, also lived for 905 years, and departed this life after fathering sons and daughters as the same book of the truth says.

10,1   If Seth died then, and his sons in succession lived and died, how can he be the Lord who was conceived of the ever-virgin Mary and consented to human life—who was begotten at no point in time, who is always with the Father as the divine Word subsistent; (2) but who came in the last days, fashioned flesh in his own image from a virgin womb and received the human soul, and thus became perfect man? (3) How can he be the Lord who proclaimed the mysteries of salvation to us, made his disciples workers of righteousness, and instructed men in his teaching, himself and through them? He never revealed the Sethians' teachings or called himself Seth, as they say in their foolishness and, from some sort of drunkenness, have lost the truth.

10,4   But now, though the < rebuttal of the > sect is short, I do not need to extend its refutation, and am content merely with what is here. Their stupidity is easy to prick and is self-refuting and self-exposing, not only in their kidnapping of Christ and the quibbling teaching of their belief and affirmation that he is Seth, but on the subject of the two men as well. (5) For if the powers have their origin from above, nothing which was done by the two powers took place and was done without the one power—whom they also call Mother of all. For the one power turns out to be the cause of the two powers, and nothing that has been done, has been done without it. (6) And once the origin is shown to be one, they will return to the confession that the Master of all, and the Creator and Maker of the whole, is one.

10,7   But since we have said these things about this sect as well, beloved, and since we have exposed the poison of their snake-like brood which is descended from asps, let us move once more to another, in the same order of the treatise.

40.

Against Archontics.[1] Number twenty, but forty of the series

1,1   A sect of Archontics follows these though this is reported in few places, or only in the province of Palestine. But by now they may also have brought their poison to Greater Armenia. Moreover, (2) this tare has already been sown in Lesser Armenia by a man named Eutactus—though he was "disorderly" rather than "orderly." In Constantius' reign, near the time of his death, Eutactus came from Armenia to live in Palestine, learned this bad teaching, and then went home and taught.

1,3   As I said he got it in Palestine, as though getting poison from an asp, from an elderly man named Peter, though he was unworthy of the name. He lived in the district of Eleutheropolis < and > Jerusalem, three mile-stones beyond Hebron; they call the village Kephar Baricha.

1,4   To begin with, this old man had an extraordinary garment, and it was stuffed with hypocrisy. He actually wore a sheep's fleece on the outside, and it was not realized that he was a ravening wolf within. He appeared to be a hermit because he would sit in a certain cave. He gathered many for the ascetic life, if you please; and he was called "father," of all things, because of his age and his dress. He had distributed his possessions to the poor, and he gave alms daily.

1,5   He had belonged to many sects in his early youth. But during Aetius' episcopate he was accused and convicted of being a Gnostic then, and was deposed from the presbyterate—at some time he had been made a presbyter. He was banished by Aetius after his conviction, and he went to live in Arabia, at Cocabe where the roots of the Ebionites and Nazoraeans came from—as I have indicated of Cocabe in many Sects.

1,6   He returned later, however, as though having come to his senses with the approach of old age. But he was secretly carrying this emission of poison inside him, and went unrecognized by everyone until finally, from things he had whispered to certain persons, I unmasked him and he was anathematized and refuted by my poor self. (7) And after that he sat in the cave, abhorred by all and deserted by the brotherhood, and by most who were attending to their salvation.

1,8   This Eutactus—if, indeed, he was "orderly"—was this old man's guest on his way home from Egypt, and imbibed his bad teaching. Receiving this poison as choice merchandise, he brought it back to his own country. As I said, he came from Lesser Armenia, near Satale. (9) Hence, on his return home, he polluted many there, in Lesser Armenia.

---

[1] Sect 40 is based on Epiphanius' own experience, and on Gnostic sources which no longer survive.

For he had unfortunately become acquainted with certain rich men, with a woman of senatorial rank, and with other persons of distinction, and through these prominent people he ruined many of his countrymen. The Lord quickly eliminated him, only he had sown his tare.

2,1   The Archontics too have forged their own apocrypha, and these are their names. They call one book a "Lesser Harmony," if you please, and another a "Greater Harmony." They pile up certain other books, moreover, < and add these > to any they may light on, to give the appearance of confirming their own error through many. (2) And by now they also have the ones called the "Strangers"—there are books with this title. And they take their cue from the Ascension of Isaiah, and from still other apocrypha.

2,3   All the facts < about their sect can be seen > from the book called the Harmony. In it they say there is an ogdoad of heavens and a hebdomad, and that there are archons for each heaven. And certain belong to the seven heavens, one archon to one heaven, and there are bands (of angels) for each archon, and the shining Mother is at the very top in the eighth heaven—like the other sects.

2,4   Some of them are defiled in body by licentiousness; but others make a show of pretended fasting, if you please, and deceive the simple by affecting an ascetic discipline in the guise of hermits. (5) And as I mentioned, they say there is a principality and authority for every heaven and certain angelic servitors, since each archon has sired and created his own retinue.[2] But there is no resurrection of the flesh, only of the soul.[3]

2,6   They execrate baptism, though there may be some who were taken and baptized earlier.[4] They make light of participation in the mysteries, and the goodness of them, as something that is foreign to them and has been instituted in the name of Sabaoth. (Like certain other sects they hold that he is in the eighth heaven, ruling as an autocrat with power over the others.)[5] (7) But they say the soul is the food of the principalities and authorities, and that they cannot live without it, since it is some of the ichor on high and gives them power.[6] (8) But if it has come into

---

[2] Cf. Eug. 88,17-89,2.

[3] A possible explanation of the term, "resurrection of the soul" is furnished by Treat. Res. 47,1-12, "Therefore, never doubt concerning the resurrection, my son Rheginus. For if you were not existing in flesh, you received flesh when you entered this world. Why will you not receive flesh when you ascend into the Aeon? That which is better than flesh, which is for it the cause of life, that which came into being on your account, is it not yours?" On the other hand, this may be no more than a statement of the Pauline doctrine of resurrection, as it appears at 2 Cor. 5:1-4—or of the immortality of the soul.

[4] Baptism is bitterly condemned at Para. Shem 37,19-38,27. Mandaean sources also dislike Christian baptism; it is called the "sign of Ruha" at GR 255,5-10.

[5] For competition among supernatural powers see Sect 39, Note 4.

[6] Cf. Dia. Sav. 122,19; PS 36-37; 39; 46 et al.

the know, and has avoided the baptism of the church and the name of
Sabaoth, the giver of the Law, it ascends heaven by heaven and offers
its defense to each authority, and thus rises above them to the Mother
and Father of all,[7] who is higher. This is the place from which it descended into this world.

2,9   I have already said that they execrate baptism as "deadly flies,
causing the preparation of the oil of sweetness to stink"[8]—as the parable
is given by the Preacher with reference to them and their kind. For they
are truly flies which are deadly and cause death, and spoil the aromatic
oil of sweetness—God's holy mysteries which are granted us in baptism
for the remission of sins.

3,1   But one whose wisdom is like the bee's, which settles on every
plant and gathers what is useful to it, might be surprised to find some
things of great value even in the naturalists. (2) For the wise man does
not lose from any source; he profits by everything. But the unwise will
lose, as the holy prophet says, "Who is wise, and he shall understand
these things? And who hath the word of the Lord, and he shall know
them. For the ways of the Lord are straight, but the transgressors shall
fail in them."[9]

3,3   For I find even in the so-called naturalists—or rather, I observe
this for myself—that dung-beetles, which some call bylari, have the habit
of rolling in foulness and dung, and this is food and a task for them. But
this same filthy food of theirs <is obviously> offensive and bad-smelling
to other insects. (4) For bees too, this dung and foul odor is death, while
to dung-beetles it is work, nourishment, and an occupation. For bees, in
contrast, fragrance, blossoms and perfumes serve as refreshment, property and food, work and an occupation. But such things are the reverse
for the dung-beetles, or bylari.

3,5   Anyone wishing to test them, as the naturalists say, can cause the
death of dung-beetles by taking a bit of perfume, I mean balsam or nard,
and applying it to them. They die instantly because they cannot stand the
sweet odor. (6) Thus these people with their longing for copulation, fornication and wickedness, set their hope on evil things. But if they come
near the holy font and its sweet fragrance, they die blaspheming God and
despising his sovereignty.

4,1   But I shall demolish them with one or two texts. Even though
there are things called principalities and authorities, they have not been
established apart from God, especially not in the heavens. (2) For scripture does know of "angels and archangels," not as ranged in opposition

---

[7] Cf. Corp. Herm. IV.8.
[8] Eccles. 10:1.
[9] Hos. 14:10.

to us, but as "ministering spirits, sent forth to minister for them who shall be heirs of salvation."[10]

4,3   Even on earth in fact there are many "authorities" in each kingdom but they are under one king. "The powers that be are ordained of God," as the apostle says; "Whosoever, therefore, resisteth the power resisteth the ordinance of God, (4) since the rulers are not against the good, but for the good, and not against the truth, but for the truth. Wilt thou not be afraid of the power?" he says. "Do that which is good, and thou shalt have praise of the same. For he beareth not the sword in vain. For he is a minister ordained of God for this very thing, for him that doeth evil."[11] (5) And you see how this worldly authority has been appointed by God, and how it received the right of the sword—not from any other source, but from God for retribution. And because there are principalities and authorities in the world, we cannot say that their king is not a king. They are the principalities and authorities, but their king, also, is the king.

4,6   On earth we see—it is an obvious fact—that the principalities are not opposed to the king but are set under him, to administer the entire kingdom and keep order on earth, where there are murders and wars, mistakes and instructions, instances of order and disorder. And authorities exist for this reason, the good ordering and disposition of all God's creatures in an orderly system for the governance of the whole world. (7) And so in heaven—but most especially there, where there is no envy, jealousy, disorder, contention, discord, conspiracy, robbery or anything else of this nature—authorities are appointed for another task. (8) Which task do I mean but the repetition of the hymn, the unalloyed praise on high? On its account our bountiful God and king willed to grant each of his creatures its proper glory, that the splendor, incomprehensibility and awesomeness of his kingdom might be ever glorified. Archontics have obviously gone wrong from ignorance of the grace of God.

5,1   As I have mentioned already, they say the devil is the son of the seventh authority, that is, of Sabaoth. But Sabaoth is God of the Jews, while the devil is his wicked son, but is on earth to oppose his own father. (2) And his father is not like him—nor, again, is he the incomprehensible God whom they call "Father." He belongs to the left-hand authority.

5,3   People of their sort tell yet another myth, that the devil came to Eve, lay with her as a man with a women, and sired Cain and Abel by her. (4) That was why the one attacked the other—from their jealousy

---

[10] Heb. 1:14.
[11] Rom. 13:1-14; 2 Cor. 13:8.

of each other and not, as the truth is, because Abel had somehow pleased God. Instead they concoct another story and <say>, "They were both in love with their own sister, and that was why Cain attacked Abel and killed him." For as I mentioned they say that they were actually of the devil's seed.

5,5 When they wish to fool someone they cite texts from the sacred books <which say>—I have mentioned this in another Sect as well—<that> the Savior said, "Ye are of Satan," to the Jews and, "Whensoever he speaketh a lie he speaketh of his own, for his father was a liar also."[12] (6) This allows them to say, if you please, that Cain was the <son> of the devil because the Savior said that the devil was a murderer from the beginning, and that the devil was <a liar because his father was>, (7) to show that Cain's father was the devil, and the devil's was the lying archon. In blasphemy against their own head, the fools say that this is Sabaoth himself, (8) since they hold that Sabaoth is a name for some god.

In the previous Sects I have dealt in detail already with the translation of Sabaoth and other names—Eli and Elohim, El and Shaddai, Elyon, Rabboni, Jah, Adonai and Jahveh—(9) since they all translate as terms of praise, and are not given names, as it were, for the Godhead. Here too I hasten to give them in translation. (10) "El" means "God"; "Elohim," "God forever"; "Eli," "my God"; "Shaddai," "the Sufficient"; "Rabboni," "the Lord"; "Jah," "Lord"; "Adonai," "the existent Lord." "Jahveh" means, "He who was and is, the Ever-existent," as he translates for Moses, "'He who is' hath sent me, shalt thou say unto them."[13] "Elyon" is "highest." And "Sabaoth" means, "of hosts;" hence "Lord Sabaoth," means, "Lord of Hosts." (11) For wherever scripture uses the expression, "Sabaoth," <"Lord"> is attached. <Scripture> does not merely cry, "Sabaoth said to me," or, "Sabaoth spoke," but says immediately, "Lord Sabaoth." For the Hebrew says, "Adonai Sabaoth," which means "Lord of hosts."[14]

6,1 And it is in vain that, in the blindness of their minds, they and people like them quibble at things which have been rightly said. (2) As every follower of the truth will find, there is no reference to the devil in what the Savior said to the Jews; he made the statement to them on Judas' account. (3) They were no children of the Abraham who entertained him beneath the oak of Mamre, before his incarnation. They

---

[12] John 8:44.
[13] Exod. 3:14.
[14] Cf. "Adonaios who is called Sabaoth", Gos. Egyp. 58,14-15.

sentenced themselves to become sons of the treason of Judas, who is called Satan and devil by the Lord, as he says, "Have I not chosen you twelve, and one of you is a devil?"[15] (4) And thus, to give an interpretation of his evil ways, the Lord said, "Whensoever he speaketh a lie he speaketh of his own."[16] And the Gospel also says, in another passage, "He was a thief, and himself bare the bag."[17] (5) As his father, then, Judas, who was called "devil," got Cain, who deceived his brother Abel with a lie and killed him—and falsely said, "I know not,"[18] when he was asked, "Where is Abel thy brother?" by the Lord. (6) For his mimicry of the actual devil's behavior he too, as he deserved, has fittingly been termed his son by the Savior. For "Of whom a man is overcome, of the same is he also brought in bondage."[19] And whatever each of us does, he will have those who have done it before him as fathers, because of his imitation of them. (7) It has been clearly explained, then, that the Savior's saying, "Ye are children of the devil"—and again, "Whensoever he speaketh a lie he speaketh of his own, for his father was a liar"[20]—was a reference to Judas and Cain. (8) Accordingly, "For his father was a liar," referred to the devil himself, since each of these has done his sort of work. For in breathing into the serpent's mouth the devil has spoken all lies, and this is how he deceived Eve then.

6,9   And their erroneous stories stand discredited even though scripture says, "As Cain slew his brother, for he was of the devil."[21] It has been fully demonstrated <that> Cain was called the devil's son because his behavior was similar and he mimicked his wickedness—not, as they think, because Eve conceived of the devil's seed, as in conjugal union and sexual intercourse, and bore Cain and Abel.

7,1   But again, the same people say that Adam had intercourse with his own wife, Eve, and as his own actual son, sired Seth. And then, they say, the power on high came down with the ministering angels of the good God (2) and snatched Seth himself—they also call him "Stranger"—and bore him aloft somewhere, and nurtured him for some time to prevent his being killed.[22] And long afterwards it brought him back down to this world and made him spiritual, and yet physical <in

---

[15] John 6:70.
[16] John 8:44.
[17] John 12:6.
[18] Gen. 4:9.
[19] 2 Pet. 2:19.
[20] John 8:44.
[21] 1 John 3:12.
[22] This is said of Shitil at GL 443,8-11, and of John the Baptist at Book of John 116,10-19. Something comparable is said of Sabaoth at Nat. Arc. 95,19-22; Orig. Wld. 104,17-22.

appearance >, so that the < Demiurge >, and the other authorities and principalities of the god who made the world, would not prevail against him. (3) And they say he no longer worshipped the creator and demiurge, but recognized the power that cannot be named and the good God on high,[23] < and > that he worshipped him, and revealed many things about the maker of the world and its principalities and authorities.

7,4   And † hence they have forged certain books in the name of Seth himself, and say they are given by him—others in the name of him[24] and his seven sons. (5) (For they say he had seven < sons >, called "Strangers,"[25] as I also mentioned in other Sects—I mean The Gnostics and The Sethians.)

7,6   They also say that there are other prophets, a Martiades and a Marsianus, and that they were snatched up into the heavens and came down three days later.[26] (7) And they produce many forgeries in telling their stories and fabricating blasphemies against the true God Almighty, the Father of our Lord Jesus Christ, as though he were an archon and an originator of evil. Of this they are convicted by their very words.

7,8   For if an originator of evils is also an evildoer—as I have said in the other Sects—how can God not be found good at once, since he legislated against fornication, adultery, rapine and covetousness? For they too say he is God of the Jews—but he gave the Jews the Law, in which he forbade all these things of which they call him the originator! And how can he be called Satan's father, when he has given so many warnings against Satan?

7,9   And suppose he is foreign to the God they call high, and is not God the Almighty himself—our King and Lord, < proclaimed > in Law, Prophets, Gospels and Apostles, himself God the Lord, and Father of our Lord Jesus Christ. Why does the Lord himself plainly teach (that he is) in the Gospel, and say, "I thank thee, Father, Lord of heaven and earth,"[27] to show that his Father is God of all?

8,1   And again, to indicate that there will be a resurrection of the dead, the Son of this God says, "Destroy this temple, and in three days

---

[23] Sabaoth recognizes Pistis in this way and worships her at Orig. Wld. 103,32-104,3. Adam recognizes "the likeness of his own foreknowledge" and hence begets Seth at Apocry. Jn. 23,35-25,2.

[24] See Sect 39, note 12.

[25] Cf. "they are from other races, for they are not similar" at Three Stel. 120,11-13. And see Sect 39, Note 13.

[26] "The powers of all the great aeons have given homage to the power which is in Marsanes. They said: 'Who is this who has been these things before his face, that he has thus revealed concerning him?'" U 235. Marsanes is also mentioned at Eus. H. E. VI.12. CG X,1 is titled "Marsanes."

[27] Matt. 11:25.

I will raise it up."[28] But by "temple" he meant his own body, which would be "destroyed" by the hands of men—that is, killed. (2) But something which was not a body but an apparition—this is something else they say[29]—could not have fallen into men's hands and been raised the third day, as he promised. (3) By such a provision it is proved that the resurrection of the dead is undeniable, and <that> the soul does not need a speech of defense to give before each authority—this too is a fabrication of theirs, as we have said—but needs the Lord's deed of kindness, recommended by works and faith. (4) So says the most holy Paul, writing the following words to Timothy: "That thou mayest know how thou oughtest to behave thyself in the house of the Lord, which is the church of the living God, the pillar and ground of the truth,[30] which the many having deserted have turned unto fables and words of folly,[31] understanding neither what they say nor whereof they affirm,[32] of whom are Phygelus and Hermogenes."[33] (5) In his second epistle, moreover, he says that Hymenaeus and Philetus are in error as to the truth.[34] They too were followers of this sect. They proclaimed another God and endless genealogies, (6) and implanted fresh error in men by saying that the world was not made by God but by principalities and authorities, and that the resurrection has already come in the children who are begotten by every parent, but that there will be no resurrection of the dead. And see the character of the truth, brothers, as well as the refutation of their disorder.

8,7 But I suspect that enough has been said about these too. I shall pass this sect by and make my way to the rest, remarking only that, with the great variety of its names for archons, this sect seems very like the tangled malignity of serpents. (8) For in a way the poisonous emission of their imposture has been taken at random from many snakes. It has the dragon's arrogance, for example, the treachery of the toad that inflates itself, the pull in the opposite direction of the gudgeon's breath, the pride of the quick-darting serpent, and calamine's characteristic of being thrown aside. (9) But now that we have crushed all their heads with the essence of the truth, beloved, let us go on to the rest, and by God's inspiration try to disclose the error of each.

---

[28] John 2:19.
[29] For Gnostic examples of docetism or comparable ideas, see 2 Apoc. Jas. 57,10-19; Gr. Seth 53,23-26; 55,17-57,6; Apoc. Pet. 80,27-30; 81,3-83,15; Man. Ps. 191,4-8; 196,22-26; Acts of John 87-99; 101-102; Acts of Paul VII.1.14. Melch. 5,2-11, though a Gnostic source, polemicizes against docetism.
[30] 1 Tim. 3:15.
[31] 2 Tim. 4:4.
[32] 1 Tim. 1:7.
[33] 2 Tim. 1:15.
[34] Cf. 2 Tim. 2:17.

41.

Against Cerdonians.[1] *Number twenty-one, but forty-one of the series*

1,1   After these, and Heracleon, comes one Cerdo. He is of the same school, and took his cue from Simon and Satornilus. He was an immigrant from Syria who had come to Rome and appeared there, utterly wretched as he was, to his own destruction and his followers'. (2) For the human race is wretched when it leaves God's way and strays, and it has perished by separating itself from God's calling. (3) The proverb of the dog with its mind on the reflection <of the food> which it had in its mouth, is appropriate for people like these. Looking into a pond, and thinking that the reflection in the water was larger than the food in its mouth, it opened its mouth and lost the food it had. (4) So with these, since they had found the way, and yet wanted to get hold of the reflection which had formed in their imaginations—not only did they lose the nourishment which God had graciously put in their mouths, as it were, but they also brought destruction on themselves.

1,5   Cerdo, then, lived in the time of Hyginus, ninth in succession from the apostles James, Peter and Paul. Since his preaching has some of the other heresiarchs' foolishness it appears to be the same. But he has a variation of it, and this is what his is like:

1,6   He too has preached two first principles to the world, and two gods, if you please! One is good, and unknown to all, and him Cerdo has called the Father of Jesus. And one is the demiurge, who is evil and can be known, and has spoken in the Law, appeared to the prophets, and often become visible.

1,7   Christ is not born of Mary and has not appeared in flesh. As he exists in appearance he has also been manifest in appearance, and done all that he has done in appearance. And Cerdo too rejects the resurrection of the flesh, and repudiates the Old Testament, which was given by Moses and the prophets, as something foreign to God. (8) But Christ has come from on high, from the unknown Father, to put an end to the rule and tyranny of the world-creator and demiurge here—the very story that many of the sects have told. (9) After a short time in Rome he imparted his venom to Marcion, and Marcion thus succeeded him.

2,1   Since this sect is just as detectible (as the last), my remarks about it will be brief. And once again, I shall begin the refutation of Cerdo from the very things he says. (2) For that there cannot be two first principles at once is obvious. Either the two principles are derived from some one;

---

[1] Sect 41 appears indebted to Iren. I.27.1. Cf. also Hippol. Haer. VII.37.1; Ps.-Tert. 6.

or the one is a second principle, while the other is the cause and principle of the second. So we shall either need to find a cause for the two or find which of them is the principle of the other and therefore <its cause>, as I said. (3) And thus our reasoning leads inevitably to the one, the actual first principle, the source either of the second or of both, as I have shown.

2,4   But the two first principles cannot exist at once, nor can the one be different from the other. For if they are different, there are two of them; but by being two, they have become more than one. But since the one, first number is required, "two" is implied by the number which is "one", and comes before it, and is the cause of "two." (5) For "two," which comes after the number "one"—or, after the single, first principle—cannot be its own cause. The unit, which comes first of all, is always required.

2,6   For if the two turn out to be of one accord and to have a mutual complaisance and agreement, in that the one remains in existence with the consent of the other while the other enjoys its partnership with the first, what conflict is there between them? (7) But if they are in conflict, and each is just as strong as the other, then, although Christ came to do away with the one, he will no longer be capable of destroying its tyranny. It will stand its ground and have the ability to struggle with the invisible, unnameable power on high and hold out, and can never be destroyed.

3,1   The fool says that both the Law and the prophets belong to the inferior and contrary principle, whereas Christ belongs to the good one. (2) Then why did the prophets predict the things that were patterned after Christ—unless the power that spoke in the Law, the prophets, and the Gospels was one and the same? As he says, "Lo, here am I that speak in the prophets," and so on. (3) And why did the Lord in the Gospel also † cry out, "Had ye believed Moses, ye would have believed me also, for he wrote of me?"[2]

3,4   And I could say a great deal about proof-texts, just as Cerdo did to gather his own school, when he emerged in the world at an evil juncture and led his misguided following astray. (5) But I shall pass it by as well. Like a bembix or wasp—flying insects with stings, that suddenly take wing and dart at us—I have finished it with God's utterly clear faith; (6) with the saving teaching of our Lord Jesus Christ, who said, "See ye be not deceived, for many false prophets shall come in my name;"[3] and with the teaching of the apostle, who spoke of these false Christs, false teachers and false brethren, and warned us against them. <And> I shall proceed to the rest in our series, and give the description of the others.

---

² John 5:46.
³ Luke 21:8.

42.

Against Marcionites.[1] *Number twenty-two, but forty-two of the series*

1,1 Marcion, the founder of the Marcionites, took his cue from Cerdo and appeared before the world as a great serpent himself. And because he deceived a large number of people in many ways, even to this day, he became head of a school. (2) The sect is still to be found even now, in Rome and Italy, Egypt and Palestine, Arabia and Syria, Cyprus and the Thebaid—in Persia too, moreover, and other places. For the evil one in him has lent great strength to the deceit.

1,3 It is very commonly said that he was a native of Pontus[2]—I mean Helenopontus and the city of Sinope. (4) In early life he was an ascetic, if you please, for he was a hermit, and the son of a bishop of our holy catholic church. But in time he unfortunately became acquainted with a virgin, cheated the virgin of her hope and degraded both her and himself.[3] For her seduction he was excommunicated by his own father.[4] (5) (From deep respect for the distinguished persons who took good care of the church, his father was exemplary in the performance of his episcopal duties.) (6) Though Marcion pleaded at length, if you please, and asked for a remission of sentence, he could not obtain it from his own father. For the distinguished old bishop was not only distressed because Marcion had fallen, but because he was bringing the disgrace on him as well.

1,7 As Marcion could not wheedle what he required out of him he felt unable to bear the people's ridicule and fled from his city, and he arrived at Rome itself after the death of Hyginus, the bishop of Rome. (Hyginus was ninth in succession from the apostles Peter and Paul.)[5] Meeting the elders who were still alive and had been taught by the pupils of the apostles, he asked for admission to the church; and no one allowed it to him. (8) Finally, inflamed with jealousy at not getting the headship of the church as well as entry into it, he thought of an expedient, and took refuge in the sect of the fraud, Cerdo.

---

[1] Sect 42 utilizes Marcion's canon, and a treatise on it written at an earlier date by Epiphanius himself. The other documentary sources of this section are unclear. Epiphanius is certainly influenced to some extent by Iren. I.27.2-3, but by no means limited to this. Other discussions of Marcion appear at Hippol. Haer. X.19; Ps.-Tert. 6.2; Eus. H. E. V.13.4; Tert. Adv. Marc.; Praescr. 30.

[2] Cf. Iren. I.27.2; Hippol. Haer. VII.29.1; X.19.1; Ps.-Tert. 6.2; Justin Apol. 26.5; 58.1; Tert. Adv. Marc. I.1.4; III.6.3.

[3] A similar story is told of Apelles at Tert. Praescr. 30.

[4] Cf. Ps.-Tert. 6.2.

[5] Cf. Ps.-Tert. 6.2.

2,1[6] And first, at the very beginning as it were, and at the starting-point of the matters in question, he put this question to the elders of the time: "Tell me, what is the meaning of, 'Men do not put new wine into old bottles, or a patch of new cloth unto an old garment; else it both taketh away the fullness, and agreeth not with the old. For a greater rent will be made?'"[7]

2,2 On hearing this the good and most sacred elders and teachers of God's holy church gave him the appropriate and fitting answer, and equably explained, (3) "Child, 'old bottles' means the hearts of the scribes and Pharisees, which had grown old in sins and had not received the proclamation of the Gospel. (4) And 'the old garment' received a 'worse rent,' just as Judas received a further rent through no one's fault but his own, because, though he had been associated with the eleven apostles and called by the Lord himself, he had grown old in greed, and not received the new, holy, heavenly mystery's message of hope. (5) For his mind was not in tune with the hope above, and the heavenly calling of the good things to come rather than worldly wealth and vanity, and the love of passing hope and pleasure."

2,6 "No," Marcion retorted, "there are other explanations." <But> since they were unwilling to receive him, he asked them openly, "Why will you not receive me?"

2,7 Their answer was, "We cannot do so without your worthy father's permission. Faith is one and concord is one, and we cannot oppose our excellent colleague, and your father."

2,8 Then Marcion became jealous and was roused to great anger and pride, and since he was that sort of person he made the rent. He became head of his own sect and said, "I shall rend your church, and make a permanent rent in it." He did indeed make a rent of no small proportions, but by rending himself and his converts, not the church.

3,1 But he took his cue from Cerdo, the charlatan and swindler. For he too proclaims two first principles. But to add to him in turn, I mean to Cerdo, he exhibits something different and says there are three principles.[8] One is the unnameable, invisible one on high which he also calls a "good God," but which has made none of the things in the world. (2) Another is a visible God, creator and demiurge.[9] But the devil is a kind of third god and in between these too, the visible and the invisible. The

---

[6] With 2,1 cf. Tert. Adv. Marc. III.15.1; IV.11.10, and the somewhat different version at Ps.-Tert. 6.2.

[7] Matt. 9:16-17; Luke 5:36.

[8] Cf. Eus. H. E. V.13.4; Hippol. Haer. VII.31.1-2; X.19.1; Ath. De Decret. Nic. Syn. 464A; Adam. Rect. Fid. I.2; Cyr. Jerus. Cat. XVI.4; 7.

[9] Cf. Corp. Herm. X.10; XIV.8; Ascl. 16.

creator, demiurge and visible God is the God of the Jews, and he is a judge.[10]

3,3   Celibacy[11] is also preached by Marcion himself, and he preaches fasting on the Sabbath. Marcionite mysteries are celebrated in front of the catechumens,[12] if you please. He uses water in the mysteries.

3,4   For fasting on the Sabbath he gives this reason: "Since it is the rest of the God of the Jews who made the world and rested the seventh day, let us fast on this day, to do nothing appropriate to the God of the Jews." (5) Like many sects, he denies the resurrection of the flesh; he says that resurrection, life and salvation are of the soul only.[13]

3,6   Marcionite baptism is not simply given once. They allow it to be given even as many as three times[14] and more to anyone who wishes, as many have told me. (7) But he got into this way of allowing three baptisms and even more, because of his ridicule by his disciples who had known him, for his transgression and the seduction of the virgin. (8) Since the scum was in grievous sin after he had seduced the virgin in his own town and fled, he invented his own second baptism. He said it is all right to give as many as three baths, that is, baptisms, for the remission of sins, so that if one falls away the first time he may repent and receive a second baptism—and a third similarly, if he transgresses after the second.[15]

3,9   But to start his ridicule anew, to show that he was cleansed again after his transgression and from then on ranks among the guiltless, he cites a text which he falsely claims will prove the point—a potentially deceptive one, but it does not mean what he says. (10) He says that after the Lord's baptism by John he told the disciples, "I have a baptism to be baptized with, and why do I wish to if I have already accomplished it?"[16] And again, "I have a cup to drink, and why do I wish to if I have already fulfilled it?" And because of this he decreed the giving of more baptisms (than one).

4,1   But this is not all. He rejects both the law and all the prophets, and says that prophets like these have prophesied by the inspiration of the archon who made the world.[17] (2) And he says that Christ has

---

[10] Cf. Book of John 183,2.

[11] Cf. Hippol. Haer. VII.30.3; X.19.4; Clem. Alex. Strom. III.12.1-2; 25.2; Tert. Adv. Marc. I.14.5; 29.1.

[12] Cf. Jer. In Gal. 6:6; Tert. Praescr. 41.

[13] Cf. Iren. I.27.3; Hippol. Haer. X.19.3; Adm. Rect. Fid. 7. Gos. Phil. 56, 26-57,22 appears to deny resurrection of the flesh, while at the same time attempting to justify the scriptural language which states the idea.

[14] Three baptisms of this kind are spoken of at PS 310.

[15] Cf. Tert. Adv. Marc. IV.15.1.

[16] Luke 12:50; Mark 10:38.

[17] Cf. Ps.-Tert. 6.2; Tert. Adv. Marc. I.19.4; IV.34.15. For a Gnostic indictment of the God of the Law see Test. Tr. 45,14-48,26.

descended from on high, from the invisible Father who cannot be named, for the salvation of souls, and to confound the God of the Jews, the Law, the prophets, and anything of the kind.[18] (3) The Lord has even gone down to Hades to save Cain, Korah, Dathan, Abiram, Esau, and all the gentiles who had not known the God of the Jews. (4) But he has left Abel, Enoch, Noah, Abraham, Isaac, Jacob, Moses, David, and Solomon there. For they recognized the God of the Jews as maker and creator, he says, and have done what is appropriate to him, and did not dedicate themselves to the invisible God.

4,5   They even permit women to give baptism! For, seeing that they even venture to celebrate the mysteries in front of catechumens, everything they do is simply ridiculous.[19] (6) As I indicated, Marcion says resurrection is not of bodies but of souls, and he assigns salvation to these and not to bodies. And he similarly claims that there are reincarnations of souls, and transmigrations from body to body.[20]

5,1   But his futile nonsense is altogether a failure, as I have already argued in other Sects. How can the soul, which has not fallen, rise? How can we speak of its rising, when the soul did not fall? Whatever falls needs to rise; (2) but a body falls, not a soul. Hence common usage is correct in calling the body a "fallen carcass," and so is the Lord himself, who said, "Wheresoever the fallen carcass is, there will the eagles be gathered together."[21]

5,3   We do not shut souls up in tombs. We deposit bodies in the ground and cover them up, and for hope their resurrection can be preached, like the grain of wheat. (4) The holy apostle testified to the grain of wheat and other seeds and so did the Lord in the Gospel, "Except a corn of wheat fall and die, it abideth alone."[22] (5) But the holy apostle says, "Thou fool!" He calls the unbeliever who is entirely in doubt, and who asks, "How can the resurrection be, with what body do they come?" a fool. And to such he says immediately, "Thou fool, that which thou sowest is not quickened except it die."[23] (6) And the scripture gave full proof that there is a resurrection of the grain which has fallen, that is of the body which is buried—not of the soul.

5,7   And how can the soul come by itself? How can it reign alone, when it did good or evil in company with a body? The judgment will not be just, but the reverse!

---

[18] Cf. Iren. I.27.2-3.
[19] Cf. Tert. Praescr. 41.
[20] Cf. Hippol. Haer. VII.30.4.
[21] Matt. 24:28.
[22] John 12:24.
[23] I Cor. 15:35-36.

6,1   And how can Marcion's own count of three principles be substantiated? How can <the God who> does work—either a work of salvation, or the other kinds—in the bad god's territory be considered ''good?'' (2) For suppose the world is not his, and yet he sent his Only-begotten into the world to remove things which he neither begot nor made from another god's world. It will follow, either that he is invading someone else's domain, or that he is poor and has nothing of his own, and is advancing against someone else's territory to get things which he does not already have.

6,3   And how can the demiurge act as judge between both parties? Whom can he judge, then? If he presides over things taken from the God on high, he is more powerful than the God on high—seeing that he hales the possessions of the God on high into his court, or so Marcion thought.

6,4   And if he is really a judge, he is just. But from the word, ''just,'' I shall show that goodness and justice are the same thing. Anything that is just is also good. (5) It is because of his goodness that, with impartial justice, the demiurge grants what is good to someone who has done good. And he cannot be the opposite of the good God in point of goodness, since he provides the good with good on the principle of justice, and the bad with the penalty of retribution.

6,6   Nor, again, can he be good if he gives the good reward to the unrepentantly evil at the end, even though for the present—since both evil and good men have freedom of choice now—he makes his sun rise on good and evil, and provides them with his rain. (7) No one's nature can be good and just if he provides the evil with the reward of salvation in the world to come, instead of hating what is wicked and vile.

6,8   But as to Marcion's third, evil god. If he has the power to do evil and overwhelm the persons in the world—either the good ones from above, or those who belong to the intermediate, just God—it will follow that he is stronger than the two whom Marcion calls Gods. He has the power to seize what belongs to others. (9) And the two will then be adjudged weaker than the one, evil god, for they are unable to resist and protect themselves from the god who seizes what is theirs and turns it to evil.

7,1   And to see the folly of the scum's nonsense, let us observe it again in another light. If the evil god is really evil, and yet he seizes the good men from the good God and the just men from the just God and does not seize only his own, then the evil god cannot be evil after all. For he wants the good, and he claims them at law, because they are superior. (2) But if, besides, he judges his own and exacts a penalty from wrongdoers, this judge of evil men cannot be evil after all. And Marcion's thesis will turn out to be altogether self-refuting.

7,3   But again, tell me, from what source do the three principles have their being? And who settled a boundary for them? If each is circumscribed in its own area, then these three which are bounded in certain places that contain them cannot be perfect after all. The thing that contains each one must be greater than the thing that is contained. And what is contained can no longer be called "God;" the boundary which contains it must be called God instead.

7,4   But even if they met, and each got its own place by the others' leave, and no principle pummels or attacks another once it is on its own ground, the principles cannot be opposed to each other, and none of them can be bad. They mind their own business in a just, peaceable and tranquil fashion, and do not try to overstep.

7,5   But suppose the evil god is overpowered, coerced and oppressed by the God on high, although he has received his allotment and is on his own ground—though no part of this ground appertains to the God on high, and nothing here, I mean in the evil god's territory, is his creation. Rather than "good," the God on high will turn out to be more the tyrant, since he sent his own Son, or Christ, to take what was someone else's.

7,6   And where is the boundary separating the three principles in the scum's account of his thesis? This will require a fourth of some kind— more equitable and wiser than the three, and an expert surveyor. He assigned each its limits and made peace between the three, so that they would not quarrel, or send emissaries into each other's realms. (7) And since he convinced the three principles, this makes him a fourth—both wiser and fairer than the others. And again, he too must be sought in his own place, from which he came to intervene between the three, wisely assigning each its portion to keep them from wronging each other.

7,8   But if the two principles have civic rights in the territory of the one, that is, of the demiurge, with the evil one † always at work in his domain and the good God's Christ a visitor to it—then the judge must not be a mere judge and demiurge, but good as well. He permits the two to do what they please on his property. Or he must be feeble, and unable to prevent the seizure of his property by others.

7,9   But if he is even inferior to the others in power, then his creation cannot be, but would have ceased to be long ago—carried off every day to his own realm by the evil god, and to the realms on high by the good one. And how can the creation still stand? (10) But if you say that it will come to an end eventually, and that it is possible for it to come to a complete end through the good God's assiduity, then will the good God not be responsible for the damage? Yet he never created that which he later saw fit to make good, and he was certainly not its original maker, before most men were wronged, found themselves detained by the judge, and (so) have remained below.

8,1   But again, he cites sacred scripture without understanding it properly, and deceives the innocent by perverting the letter of the apostle's, "Christ hath redeemed us from the curse of the Law, being made a curse for us."[24] He says, "If we were his, he would not 'buy' what was his own. (2) He entered someone else's world as a 'buyer' to redeem us, since we were not his. For we were someone else's creation, and he thus 'bought' us at the price of his own life."

8,3   The fool is wholly unaware that Christ has not become a curse either, heaven forbid! He lifted the curse occasioned by our sin, by crucifying himself and himself becoming the death of death, and a curse on the curse. Thus Christ is no curse but a lifting of the curse, and a blessing to all who truly believe in him.

8,4   And "redeemed" <must> also <be understood> in this sense. Paul did not say "bought;" Christ did not enter another's domain to plunder or buy. If he had bought he would have bought because he did not own, and acquired what he did not have like a poor man. (5) And if our owner had sold us, he would have sold in desperation, and so been under pressure from some moneylender. But this is not the case; Paul did not say "bought," but "redeemed."

8,6   The same holy apostle says a similar thing, "redeeming the time, because the days are evil."[25] And we do not buy days, or pay for days; he said this with reference to † patient <endurance>, and longsuffering's willingness to wait. (7) Thus "redeemed" hinted at the purpose of Christ's acceptance of an incarnation for our sakes <where>by the impassible God undertook to suffer for us, maintaining the impassibility proper to his Godhead and yet <counting> what he undertook to suffer for us <as his own>. He did not buy us from others but adopted the purpose of being crucified for us, by choice and not of necessity. (8) Hence Marcion's reckoning stands refuted at every point. And there are many arguments in rebuttal of his stage-machinery and melodrama, which, contrary to him, are based on careful reasoning and sensible exposition.

9,1   But to come to his writings—or rather, his tamperings. For his only Gospel is Luke, mutilated from the beginning because of the Savior's conception and his coming in the flesh.[26] (2) But he did not simply cut the beginning off, to his own harm <rather> than the Gospel's. He also pruned many words of the truth away, both at the end

---

[24] Gal 3:13.
[25] Eph. 5:16.
[26] Cf. Iren. I.27.2; Ps.-Tert. 6.2; Adam. Rect. Fid. 15; Tert. Adv. Marc. IV.

and in the middle, and has added other things besides what had been written. And he has only this (Gospel) canon, the Gospel according to Luke.

9,3   He also has ten Epistles of the holy apostle, and only these—but not all that is written in them.[27] He deletes some parts of them, and has altered certain sections. He has these two volumes (of the Bible); but he composed other treatises himself for the people he led astray.

9,4   Here are what he calls Epistles: 1. Galatians. 2. Corinthians. 3. Second Corinthians. 4. Romans. 5. Thessalonians. 6. Second Thessalonians. 7. Ephesians. 8. Colossians. 9. Philemon. 10. Philippians. He also has parts of the so-called Epistle to the Laodiceans.

9,5   From the very canon that he retains, of the Gospel and the Pauline Epistles, I can show with God's help that Marcion is a fraud and in error, and can refute him very effectively. (6) For he will be refuted from the very works which he acknowledges without dispute. Precisely from those relics of the Gospel and Epistles which he still has, it will be demonstrated to the wise that Christ is not foreign to the Old Testament, and hence that the prophets are not foreign to the Lord's advent—(7) < and > that the apostle proclaims the resurrection of the body, and calls the prophets righteous, and Abraham, Isaac and Jacob saved—and that all that God's holy church teaches is saving, holy, and firmly founded by God on faith, knowledge, hope and doctrine.

10,1   I shall also give the treatise which I had written against him before—at your instance, brothers—busying myself with the compositon of this. (2) Some years ago, to find what lies this Marcion had invented and what his silly teaching was, I took up his very books which he had † mutilated, his so-called Gospel and Apostolic Canon. From these two books I made a series of < extracts > and selections of the material which was capable of refuting him, and I wrote a sort of outline for a treatise, arranging the points in order, and numbering each saying one, two, three (and so on). (3) And in this way I went through all of the passages in which it is apparent that, like a fool, he still retains these leftover sayings of the Savior and the apostle to his own disadvantage.

10,4   For some of the sayings had been falsely entered by himself, in an altered form and different from the authentic copy of the Gospel and the meaning of the apostolic canon. (5) But others were exactly like both the Gospel and Apostle—unchanged by Marcion, and yet capable of disproving his whole case. By these it is shown that < the > Old Testament is in agreement with the New, and the New with the Old. (6) In turn, other sayings from the same books give intimation that Christ has

---

[27] Cf. Iren. I.27.2; Ps.-Tert. 6.2; Adam. Rect. Fid. II.3; 19.

come in the flesh and been made perfect man among us. (7) Moreover, others in turn confess the resurrection of the dead, and that God is one almighty Lord of all, himself the maker of heaven and earth, and of everything on earth. They do not counterfeit the call of the Gospel, and certainly do not deny the maker and creator of all. Instead they indicate the One who is plainly confessed by the Apostolic Canon and the Proclamation of the Gospel. (8) And here, in what follows, is my treatise, which runs like this.

Preface to the Subject of Marcion's Bible and to Its Refutation

11,1   Whoever cares to make a precise investigation of the deceiver Marcion's spurious inventions, and see the false devices of this victim (of error), should not be slow to read this compilation. (2) I hasten to present the material from his own Gospel which is contradictory to his villainous tampering, so that those who are willing to read the work may have this as a training-ground in acuity, for the refutation of the strange doctrines which he has invented.

11,3   For the canon of the Gospel according to Luke is indicative of † (their) type—its mutilation and its lack of a beginning, middle or end, presents the appearance of a cloak full of mothholes.

11,4[28]   At the very beginning he excised all of Luke's original discussion—his "inasmuch as many have taken in hand,"[29] and so forth, and the material about Elizabeth and the angel's annunciation to the Virgin Mary; John and Zacharias and the birth[30] at Bethlehem; the genealogy and the subject of the baptism. (5) All this he took out and turned his back on, and made this the beginning of the Gospel, "In the fifteenth year of Tiberius Caesar," and so on.[31]

11,6   This, then, was his beginning; and yet, again, he does not continue in order. He falsifies some things, as I said, he adds others helter-skelter, and he does not go straight on but roams freely all over the material. Thus:

1.   "Go shew thyself unto the priest, and offer for thy cleansing, according as Moses commanded—that this may be a testimony unto you,"[32] instead of the Savior's "for a testimony unto them."

2.   "But that ye may know that the Son of Man hath power to forgive sins upon earth."[33]

---

[28] With 11,4-5 cf. Iren. I.27.2; Hippol. Haer. VII.31.5.
[29] Luke 1:1.
[30] Cf. Hippol. Haer. VII.31.5.
[31] Luke 3:1. Cf. Tert. Adv. Marc. I.19.2; IV.7.1.
[32] Luke 5:14. Cf. Tert. Adv. Marc. I.9.9-10.
[33] Luke 5:24.

3. "The Son of Man is lord also of the Sabbath."[34]

4. "Judas Iscariot, which was a betrayer." Instead of, "He came down with them," he has, "He came down among them."[35]

5. "And the whole multitude sought to touch him. And he lifted up his eyes,"[36] and so forth.

6. "In the like manner did your fathers unto the prophets."[37]

7. "I say unto you, I have not found so great faith, no, not in Israel."[38]

8. "Blessed is he who shall not be offended in me,"[39] is altered. For he had it as though with reference to John.

9. "He it is of whom it is written, Behold, I send my messenger before thy face."[40]

10. "And entering into the Pharisee's house he reclined at table. And the woman which was a sinner, standing at his feet behind him, washed his feet with her tears, and wiped and kissed them."[41]

11. And again, "She hath washed my feet with her tears, and wiped and kissed them."[42]

12. He did not have, "His mother and his brethren," but simply, "Thy mother and thy brethren."[43]

13. "As they sailed he fell asleep. Then he arose and rebuked the wind and the sea."[44]

14. "And it came to pass as they went the people thronged him, and a woman touched him, and was healed of her blood. And the Lord said, Who touched me?" And again, "Somebody hath touched me; for I perceive that virtue hath gone out of me."[45]

15. "Looking up to heaven he pronounced a blessing upon them."[46]

16. "Saying, The Son of Man must suffer many things, and be slain, and be raised after three days."[47]

17. "And, behold, there talked with him two men, Elijah and Moses in glory."[48]

[34] Luke 6:5.
[35] Luke 6:16-17.
[36] Luke 6:19-20.
[37] Luke 6:23.
[38] Luke 7:9. Cf. Tert. Adv. Marc. IV.18.1.
[39] Luke 7:23.
[40] Luke 7:27. Cf. Adam. Rect. Fid. II.18; Tert. Adv. Marc. IV.18.7.
[41] Luke 7:36-38.
[42] Luke 7:44-45.
[43] Luke 8:19-20.
[44] Luke 8:23-24.
[45] Luke 8:42-46. Cf. Tert. Adv. Marc. IV.20.7-8.
[46] Luke 9:16.
[47] Luke 9:22. Cf. Tert. Adv. Marc. IV.21.7.
[48] Luke 9:30-31. Cf. Tert. Adv. Marc. IV.22.1; 16.

18.   "Out of the cloud, a voice, This is my beloved Son."[49]

19.   "I besought thy disciples." But in addition to, "And they could not cast it out," he had, "And he said to them, O faithless generation, how long shall I suffer you?"[50]

20.   "For the Son of Man shall be delivered into the hands of men."[51]

21.   "Have ye not read so much as this, what David did: he went into the house of God."[52]

22.   "I thank thee, Lord of heaven."[53] But he did not have, "and earth," or "Father." He is exposed, however; for further on he had, "Even so, Father."

23.   He said to the lawyer, "What is written in the Law?" And after the lawyer's answer he replied, "Thou hast answered right; this do, and thou shalt live."[54]

24.   And he said, "Which of you shall have a friend, and shall go unto him at midnight, asking three loaves?" And then, "Ask, and it shall be given. If a son shall ask a fish any of you that is a father, will he for a fish give him a serpent, or a scorpion for an egg? If, then, ye evil men know of good gifts, how much more the Father?"[55]

25.   The saying about Jonah the prophet has been falsified; Marcion had, "This generation, no sign shall be given it." But he did not have the passages about Nineveh, the queen of the south, and Solomon.[56]

26.   Instead of, "Ye pass over the judgment of God,"[57] he had, "Ye pass over the calling of God."

27.   "Woe unto you, for ye build the sepulchres of the prophets, and your fathers killed them.'[58]

28.   He did not have, "Therefore said the wisdom of God, I send unto them prophets," and the statement that the blood of Zacharias, Abel and the prophets will be required of this generation.[59]

29.   "I say unto my friends, Be not afraid of them that kill the body. Fear him which, after he hath killed, hath authority to cast into hell." But he did not have, "Are not five sparrows sold for two farthings, and not one of them is forgotten before God?"[60]

---

[49] Luke 9:35. Cf. Tert. Adv. Marc. IV.22.1.
[50] Luke 9:40-41. Cf. Tert. Adv. Marc. IV.23.1.
[51] Luke 9:44.
[52] Luke 6:3-4. Cf. Tert. Adv. Marc. IV.12.5.
[53] Luke 10:21. Cf. Tert. Adv. Marc. IV.25.1.
[54] Luke 10:26-28. Cf. Tert. Adv. Marc. IV.26.8.
[55] Luke 11:5;9-13. Cf. Tert. Adv. Marc. IV.20.
[56] Luke 11:29-32.
[57] Luke 11:42. Cf. Tert. Adv. Marc. IV.27.4.
[58] Luke 11:47. Cf. Tert. Adv. Marc. IV.27.8.
[59] Luke 11:49-51.
[60] Luke 12:4-6. Cf. Tert. Adv. Marc. IV.28.3.

30. Instead of, "He shall confess before the angels of God,"[61] Marcion says, "before God."

31. He does not have, "God doth clothe the grass."[62]

32. "And your Father knoweth ye have need of these things,"[63] meaning physical things.

33. "But seek ye the kingdom of God, and all these things shall be added unto you."[64]

34. Instead of, "Your Father," Marcion had, "Father."[65]

35. Instead of, "In the second or third watch," he had, "in the evening watch."[66]

36. "The Lord of that servant will come and will cut him in sunder, and will appoint his portion with the unbelievers."[67]

37. "Lest he hale thee to the judge and the judge deliver thee to the officer."[68]

38. There was a falsification of "There came some that told him of the Galilaeans whose blood Pilate had mingled with their sacrifices" till the mention of the eighteen who died in the tower at Siloam; and of "Except ye repent," and < so forth >, till the parable of the fig tree of which the cultivator said, "I am digging about it and dunging it, and if it bear no fruit, cut it down."[69]

39. "This woman, being a daughter of Abraham, whom Satan hath bound."[70]

40. Again, he falsified, "Then ye shall see Abraham, and Isaac, and Jacob, and all the prophets, in the kingdom of God." In place of this he put, "When ye see all the righteous in the kingdom of God and yourselves thrust"—but he put, "kept"—"out". "There shall be weeping and gnashing of teeth."[71]

41. Again, he falsified, "They shall come from the east and from the west, and shall sit down in the kingdom," "The last shall be first," and, "The Pharisees came saying, Get thee out and depart, for Herod will kill thee;" also, "He said, Go ye, and tell that fox," till the words, "It cannot be that a prophet perish out of Jerusalem," and, "Jerusalem, Jerusalem, which killest the prophets and stonest them that are sent,"

---

[61] Luke 12:8. Cf. Tert. Adv. Marc. IV.28.4.
[62] Luke 12:28. Cf. Tert. Adv. Marc. IV.29.2.
[63] Luke 12:30. Cf. Tert. Adv. Marc. IV.29.3.
[64] Luke 12:31. Cf. Tert. Adv. Marc. IV.29.5.
[65] Luke 12:32.
[66] Luke 12:38.
[67] Luke 12:46. Cf. Tert. Adv. Marc. IV.29.9.
[68] Luke 12:58. Cf. Tert. Adv. Marc. IV.29.16.
[69] Luke 13:1-9.
[70] Luke 13:16.
[71] Luke 13:28. Cf. Tert. Adv. Marc. IV.30.5.

"Often would I have gathered, as a hen, thy children," "Your house is left unto you desolate," and, "Ye shall not see me until ye shall say, Blessed."[72]

42.   Again, he falsified the entire parable of the two sons, the one who took his share of the property and spent it on dissipation, and the other.[73]

43.   "The Law and the prophets were until John, and every man presseth into it."[74]

44.   The material about the rich man, and Lazarus the beggar's being carried by the angels into Abraham's bosom.[75]

45.   "But now he is comforted,"[76] again meaning Lazarus.

46.   Abraham said, "They have Moses and the prophets; let them hear them, since neither will they hear him that is risen from the dead."[77]

47.   He falsified, "Say, We are unprofitable servants: we have done that which was our duty to do."[78]

48.   When the ten lepers met him. Marcion excised a great deal and wrote, "He sent them away, saying, Show yourselves unto the priests;" and yet he made a substitution and said, "Many lepers were in the days of Elisha the prophet, and none was cleansed, saving Naaman the Syrian."[79]

49.   "The days will come when ye shall desire to see one of the days of the Son of Man."[80]

50.   "One said unto him, Good master, what shall I do to inherit eternal life? He replied, Call not thou me good. One is good, God." Marcion added, "the Father," and instead of, "Thou knowest the commandments," says, "I know the commandments."[81]

51.   "And it came to pass that as he was come nigh unto Jericho, a blind man cried, Jesus, thou Son of David, have mercy on me. And when he was healed, he said, Thy faith hath saved thee."[82]

52.   Marcion falsified, "He took unto him the twelve, and said, Behold, we go up to Jerusalem, and all things that are written in the prophets concerning the Son of Man shall be accomplished. For he shall

---

[72] Luke 13:29-35.
[73] Luke 15:11-32.
[74] Luke 16:16. Cf. Tert. Adv. Marc. IV.33.7.
[75] Luke 16:22. Cf. Adam. Rect. Fid. II.10; Tert. Adv. Marc. IV.34.10.
[76] Luke 16:25. Cf. Adam Rect. Fid. II.10.
[77] Luke 16:29;31. Cf. Adam. Rect. Fid. II.10; Tert. Adv. Marc. IV.34.10.
[78] Luke 17:10.
[79] Luke 17:12; 14; 4:27. Cf. Tert. Adv. Marc. IV.35.4;6.
[80] Luke 17:22.
[81] Luke 18:18-20. Cf. Hippol. Haer. VII.31.6; Adam. Rect. Fid. II.17; Orig. De Princ. II.5.1; 5.4; Tert. Adv. Marc. IV.36.4.
[82] Luke 18:35;38;42. Cf. Adam Rect. Fid. IV.14; Tert. Adv. Marc. IV.36.9-10.

be delivered and killed, and the third day he shall rise again."[83] He falsified this in its entirety.

53.   He falsified the section about the ass and Bethphage—and the one about the city and temple, because of the scripture, "My house shall be called an house of prayer, but ye make it a den of thieves."[84]

54.   "And they sought to lay hands on him and they were afraid."[85]

55.   Again, he excised the material about the vineyard which was let out to husbandmen, and the verse, "What is this, then, The stone which the builders rejected?"[86]

56.   He excised, "Now that the dead are raised, even Moses showed at the bush, in calling the Lord the God of Abraham and Isaac and Jacob. But he is a God of the living, not of the dead."[87]

57.   He did not have the following: "Now that the dead are raised, even Moses showed, saying that the God of Abraham, the God of Isaac, and the God of Jacob is God of the living."[88]

58.   Again he falsified, "There shall not an hair of your head perish."[89]

59.   Again, he falsified the following: "Then let them which are in Judaea flee to the mountains," and so on, because of the words subjoined in the text, "until all things that are written be fulfilled."[90]

60.   "He communed with the captains how he might deliver him unto them."[91]

61.   "And he said unto Peter and the rest, Go and prepare that we may eat the passover."[92]

62.   "And he sat down, and the twelve apostles with him, and he said, With desire I have desired to eat this passover with you before I suffer."[93]

63.   He falsified, "I say unto you, I will not any more eat thereof until it be fulfilled in the kingdom of God."[94]

64.   He falsified "When I sent you, lacked ye anything," and so on, because of the words, "This also that is written must be accomplished, And he was numbered among the transgressors."[95]

---

[83] Luke 18:31-33.
[84] Luke 19:29-46.
[85] Luke 20:19.
[86] Luke 20:9-17.
[87] Luke 20:37-38.
[88] Luke 20:37-38.
[89] Luke 21:18.
[90] Luke 21:21-22.
[91] Luke 22:4.
[92] Luke 22:8.
[93] Luke 22:14-15. Cf. Tert. Adv. Marc. IV.40.1.
[94] Luke 22:16.
[95] Luke 22:35;37.

65. "He was withdrawn from them about a stone's cast, and kneeled down, and prayed."[96]

66. "And Judas drew near to kiss him, but he said ..."[97]

67. He falsified what Peter did when he struck the servant of the high priest and cut off his ear.[98]

68. "They that held him mocked him, smiting and striking him and saying, Prophesy, who is it that smote thee?"[99]

69. After, "We found this fellow perverting the nation," Marcion added, "and destroying the Law and the prophets."[100]

70. An addition after, "forbidding to give tribute," is, "and turning away the wives and children."[101]

71. "And when they were come unto a place called Place of a Skull they crucified him and parted his raiment, and the sun was darkened."[102]

72. Marcion falsified the words, "Today shalt thou be with me in paradise."[103]

73. "And when he had cried with a loud voice he gave up the ghost."[104]

74. "And, lo, a man named Joseph took the body down, wrapped it in linen and laid it in a sepulchre that was hewn in stone."[105]

75. "And the women returned and rested the sabbath day according to the Law."[106]

76. "The men in shining garments said, Why seek ye the living among the dead? He is risen; remember all that he spake when he was yet with you, that the Son of Man must suffer and be delivered."[107]

77. He falsified what Christ said to Cleopas and the other when he met them, "O fools, and slow to believe all that the prophets have spoken: Ought not he to have suffered these things?" And instead of, "what the prophets have spoken," he put, "what I said unto you." But he is exposed since, "When he broke the bread their eyes were opened and they knew him."[108]

---

[96] Luke 22:41.
[97] Luke 22:47-48.
[98] Luke 22:50.
[99] Luke 22:63-64.
[100] Luke 23:2.
[101] Luke 23:2.
[102] Luke 23:33;34;44. Cf. Matt. 24:29; Mark 13:24; Tert. Adv. Marc. IV.42.4-5.
[103] Luke 23:43.
[104] Luke 23:46. Cf. Tert. Adv. Marc. IV.42.6.
[105] Luke 23:50;53. Cf. Tert. Adv. Marc. IV.42.7.
[106] Luke 23:56.
[107] Luke 24:5-7. Cf. Tert. Adv. Marc. IV.43.5.
[108] Luke 24:25-26;30-31. Cf. Adam. Rect. Fid. IV.12; Tert. Adv. Marc. IV.43.4.

78. "Why are ye troubled? Behold my hands and my feet, for a spirit hath not bones, as ye see me have."[109]

11,7   But also, I further attach the following citations against the heresiarch to this stock which I have laboriously accumulated against him. Again, I discovered these in his works, in a sort of would-be semblance of the apostle Paul's epistles—not all the epistles, some of them, (8) and these mutilated as usual by Marcion's rascality. (At the end of the complete work I have inserted their names in the order of his Apostolic Canon.) (These citations are) <relics of the truth, which are still preserved in the Epistles>—as, to be honest, <there are> relics of the real Gospel in the Gospel in name which I have given above. All the same, he contrived the whole in a cunning manner and corrupted it.

From the Epistle to the Romans, number four in Marcion but number one in the Apostolic Canon.

1(28).   "As many as have sinned without law shall also perish without law,[110] and as many as have sinned in the Law shall be judged by the Law. For not the hearers of the Law are just before God, but the doers of the Law shall be justified."[111]

2(29).   "Circumcision verily profiteth if thou keep the Law; but if thou be a breaker of the Law, thy circumcision is made uncircumcision."[112]

3(30).   "Which hast the form of knowledge and of the truth in the Law."[113]

4(31).   "For when we were yet without strength, in due time Christ died for the ungodly."[114]

5(32).   "Wherefore the Law is holy, and the commandment holy and just and good."[115]

6(33).   "That the requirement of the Law might be fulfilled in us."[116]

7(34).   "For Christ is the end of the Law for righteousness to everyone that believeth."[117]

8(35).   "He that loveth his neighbor hath fulfilled the Law."[118]

The First Epistle to the Thessalonians, <number five in Marcion's canon>, but number eight in ours.

---

[109] Luke 24:38-39. Cf. Adam. Rect. Fid. V.12; Tert. Adv. Marc. IV.43.6.
[110] Rom. 2:12.
[111] Rom. 2:13.
[112] Rom. 2:25.
[113] Rom. 2:20.
[114] Rom. 5:6.
[115] Rom. 7:12. Cf. Adam. Rect. Fid. II.20; Tert. Adv. Marc. V.13.14.
[116] Rom. 8:4.
[117] Rom. 10:4. Cf. Tert. Adv. Marc. V.14.6.
[118] Rom. 13:8. Cf. Tert. Adv. Marc. V.14.3.

The Second Epistle to the Thessalonians, <number six in Marcion's canon>, but number nine in ours.

From the Epistle to Ephesians, number seven <in Marcion's canon>, but number five in ours.

1(36) "Remember that ye, being in time past gentiles, who are called uncircumcision by that which is called the circumcision in the flesh made by hands; that at that time ye were without Christ, being aliens from the commonwealth of Israel, and strangers from the covenants of promise, having no hope, and without God in the world. But now in Christ Jesus ye who sometimes were far off are made nigh by his blood. For he is our peace, who hath made both one,"[119] and so on.

2(37). "Wherefore he saith, Awake thou that sleepest, and arise from the dead, <and> Christ shall give thee light."[120]

3(38). "For this cause shall a man leave his father and mother, <and> shall be joined unto his wife, and they two shall be one flesh,"[121] minus the phrase, "unto his wife."

<From the Epistle> to the Colossians, number eight <in Marcion's canon>, but number seven in ours.

1(39). "Let no man therefore judge you in meat, or in drink, or in respect of an holyday, or of the new moon and sabbath days, which are a shadow of things to come."[122]

The Epistle to Philemon, number nine <in Marcion's canon>, but number thirteen, or also fourteen, in ours.

The Epistle to the Philippians, number ten <in Marcion's canon>, but number six in ours.

<From the Epistle> to the Laodiceans, number eleven <in Marcion's canon>.

1(<40>). "(There is) one Lord, one faith, one baptism, one God and Father of all, who is above all, and through all, and in all."[123]

From the Epistle to the Galatians, number one <in Marcion's canon>, but number four in ours.

1. "Learn that the just shall live by faith. For as many as are under the Law are under a curse; but, The man that doeth them shall live by them."[124]

2. "Cursed is everyone that hangeth upon a tree; but he that is of promise is by the freewoman."[125]

---

[119] Eph. 2:11-14. Cf. Adam. Rect. Fid. II.18; Tert. Adv. Marc. I.17.12; 14.
[120] Eph. 5:14.
[121] Eph. 5:31. Cf. Tert. Adv. Marc. V.18.9.
[122] Col. 2:16-17. Cf. Tert. Adv. Marc. V.19.9.
[123] Cf. Eph. 4:5-6; Adam. Rect. Fid. II.19.
[124] Gal. 3:11b;10a;12b. Cf. Tert. Adv. Marc. V.3.10;9.
[125] Gal. 3:13; 4:23. Cf. Tert. Adv. Marc. V.3.10; 4.8.

3. "I testify again that a man that is circumcised is a debtor to do the whole Law."[126]

<4.> In place of, "A little leaven leaveneth the whole lump," he put, "corrupteth the whole lump."[127]

<5.> "For all the Law is fulfilled by you; thou shalt love thy neighbor as thyself."[128]

6. "Now the works of the flesh are manifest which are these: Adultery, fornication, uncleanness, lasciviousness, idolatry, witchcraft, hatred, variance, emulations, wrath, strife, seditions, factions, envyings, drunkenness, revellings—of the which I tell you before, as I have also told you in time past, that they which do such things shall not inherit the kingdom of God."[129]

7. "They that are Christ's have crucified the flesh with the affections and lusts."[130]

8. "For neither do they themselves who are circumcised (now) keep the Law."[131]

<From the> First <Epistle> to the Corinthians, number two in Marcion's own canon and in ours.

1(9). "For it is written, I will destroy the wisdom of the wise, and will bring to naught the understanding of the prudent."[132]

2(10). "That, according as it is written, He that glorieth, let him glory in the Lord."[133]

3(11). "Of the first beings of this world that come to naught."[134]

4(12). "For it is written, He taketh the wise in their own craftiness." And again, The Lord knoweth the thoughts of men, that they are vain."[135]

5(13). "For even Christ our passover is sacrificed."[136]

6(14). "Know ye not that he which is joined to an harlot is one body? For two, saith he, shall be one flesh."[137]

7(15). Given in an altered form. In place of, "in the Law," he says "in the Law of Moses." But before this he says, "Or saith not the Law the same also?"[138]

---

[126] Gal. 5:3.
[127] Gal. 5:9.
[128] Gal. 5:14. Cf. Tert. Adv. Marc. V.4.12.
[129] Gal. 5:19-21.
[130] Gal. 5:24.
[131] Gal. 6:13.
[132] 1 Cor. 1:19. Cf. Tert. Adv. Marc. V.5.5.
[133] 1 Cor. 1:31. Cf. Tert. Adv. Marc. V.5.10.
[134] 1 Cor. 2:6.
[135] 1 Cor. 3:19-20. Cf. Tert. Adv. Marc. V.6.12.
[136] 1 Cor. 5:7. Cf. Adam. Rect. Fid. II.18; Tert. Adv. Marc. V.7.3.
[137] 1 Cor. 6:16.
[138] 1 Cor. 9:9;8. "Of Moses" is also in the ecclesiastical text. Adam. Rect. Fid. I.22 also witnesses to its presence in Marcion's canon.

8(16).   "Doth God take care for oxen?"[139]

9(17).   "Moreover, brethren, I would not that ye should be ignorant how that our fathers were under the cloud, and all passed through the sea, and did all eat the same spiritual meat, and did all drink the same spiritual drink. For they drank of a spiritual rock that followed them, and that rock was Christ. But with many of them God was not well pleased. Now these things were our examples, to the intent we should not lust after evil things, as they also lusted. Neither be ye idolaters as were some of them; as it is written, The people sat down to eat and drink, and rose up to play. Neither let us tempt Christ," until the words, "These things happened unto them for examples, and they were written for us,"[140] and so on.

10(18).   "What say I then? That sacrificial meat is anything, or that that which is offered in sacrifice to idols is anything? But the things which they sacrifice, they sacrifice to devils and not to God."[141] But Marcion added, "Sacrificial meat."

11(19).   "A man ought not to have long hair, forasmuch as he is the image and glory of God."[142]

12(20).   "But God hath composed the body."[143]

13(21).   Marcion has erroneously added the words, "on the Law's account," <after>, "Yet in the church I had rather speak five words with my understanding."[144]

14(22).   "In the Law it is written, With men of other tongues and other lips will I speak unto this people."[145]

15(23).   "Let your women keep silence in the church; For it is not permitted unto them to speak; but they are commanded to be under obedience, as also saith the Law."[146]

16(24).   On resurrection of the dead: "Brethren, I make known unto you the gospel which I preached unto you."[147] Also, "If Christ be not raised, it is in vain,"[148] and so on. "So we preach, and so ye believed...[149] that Christ died, and was buried, and rose again the third day...[150] When this mortal shall have put on immortality, then shall be

---

[139] 1 Cor. 9:9. Cf. Tert. Adv. Marc. V.7.10.
[140] 1 Cor. 10:1-9; 11. Cf. Adam. Rect. Fid. II.18; Tert. Adv. Marc. V.7.12-14.
[141] 1 Cor. 10:19.
[142] 1 Cor. 11:7. Cf. Adam. Rect. Fid. V.23; Tert. Adv. Marc. V.8.1.
[143] 1 Cor. 12.24.
[144] 1 Cor. 14:19.
[145] 1 Cor. 14:21. Cf. Tert. Adv. Marc. V.8.10.
[146] 1 Cor. 14:34. Cf. Adam. Rect. Fid. II.18; Tert. Adv. Marc. V.8.11.
[147] 1 Cor. 15:1.
[148] 1 Cor. 15:17.
[149] 1 Cor. 15:11.
[150] 1 Cor. 15:3-4.

brought to pass the saying that is written, Death is swallowed up in victory.''[151]

From the Second Epistle to the Corinthians, number three in Marcion's canon and ours

1(25). ''For all the promises of God have their Yea in him; therefore through him we utter Amen to God.''[152]

2(26). ''For we preach not ourselves, but Christ Jesus the Lord; and ourselves your servants through Jesus. For God who commanded the light to shine out of darkness...''[153]

3(27). ''We having the same Spirit of faith also believe and therefore speak.'' But he excised, ''according as it is written.''[154]

11,9   This is Marcion's corrupt compilation, containing a type and form of the Gospel according to Luke, and an incomplete one of the apostle Paul—not of all his epistles (10) but simply of Romans, Ephesians, Colossians, Laodiceans, Galatians, First and Second Corinthians, First and Second Thessalonians, Philemon and Philippians. (11) < There is no form > of First and Second Timothy, Titus, and Hebrews < in his scripture at all, and > even the epistles that are there < have been mutilated >, since they are not all there but are counterfeits. (12) And < I found > that this compilation had been tampered with throughout, and had supplemental material added in certain passages—not of any value, but in the form of second-rate, harmful heresies against the sound faith, < fictitious > † creatures of Marcion's insane mind.

11,13   I have made this laborious, searching compilation from what he proclaims as scripture, Paul and the Gospel according to Luke, < so that > everyone attempting to oppose his imposture can understand that the altered sayings have been inserted disingenuously, (14) and that any not in their proper places have been stolen from them by his enterprise. For the oaf thought that only these run counter to his false notion.

11,15   But a third < work > of my scholarship is the compilation of whatever material he and we have in common, and whose meaning is the Savior's incarnation and his testimony to the agreement of the New Testament with the Old—and the acknowledgment in the Gospel by the Son of God, that God is the maker of heaven and earth and the same God who spoke in the Law and the prophets, and that this God is his own Father. (16) And this collection of brief memoranda on my subject, taken from authentic copies of Marcion in the form of notes, was written by myself, word for word, as an outline. (17) But lest the difficult parts of

---

[151] 1 Cor. 15:54.
[152] 2 Cor. 1:20. Cf. Adam. Rect. Fid. II.18.
[153] 2 Cor. 4:5-6. Cf. Adam. Rect. Fid. II.19; Tert. Adv. Marc. V.11.11.
[154] 2 Cor. 4:13.

its contents be obscure to some and not understood, once again I shall explain each of the several entries in order, I mean the first entry, the second, the third (and so on), for the same reason that each saying was selected and transferred here. I begin as follows.

Scholion <One>, from Marcion's Own Version of the Gospel

"Go, show thyself unto the priest, and offer for thy cleansing, according as Moses commanded—that this may be a testimony unto you," instead of the Savior's "for a testimony unto them."

(a)   Elenchus 1. If, as you say, the Lord directed his teaching against the Law and the God of the Law, how could he tell his patients, I mean the leper, "Go, show thyself unto the priest?" Since he says "priest," he does not reject the priesthood of the Law.

(b)   "And offer for thy cleansing." Even if you remove the word, "gift," it will be evident, from the word, "offer," that he is speaking of a gift.

(c)   "For thy cleansing, according as Moses commanded." If he advises obedience to Moses' commandment, he does not reject or insult the God of the Law, but admits that both he and God, his Father, have given the Law to Moses.

(d)   You twisted the wording, Marcion, by saying "testimony unto you" instead of "testimony unto them." In this too you plainly lied against your own head. If he said, "testimony unto you," he called himself to witness that "I came not to destroy the Law or the prophets, but to fulfil."[155]

Scholion 2. "But that ye may know that the Son of Man hath power to forgive sins upon earth."

Elenchus 2. If he calls himself "Son of Man," the Only-begotten does not deny his incarnation, and there is nothing to your cant of his manifestation in appearance. And if he has authority on earth, the earth is not foreign to his creations and his Father's.

Scholion 3. "The Son of Man is lord also of the Sabbath."

Elenchus 3. The Savior acknowledges two things at once by teaching that he is both Son of Man and Lord of the Sabbath, to prevent the Sabbath from being considered foreign to this creation, <and himself foreign to the Father's Godhead>—even though, finally, he is called Son of Man because of the incarnation.

Scholion 4. "Judas Iscariot, which was a betrayer." Instead of, "He came down with them," he has, "He came down among them."

(a)   Elenchus 4. Judas Iscariot, "which was a betrayer." Betrayer of whom, pray? Surely of the One who was arrested—yes, and who has

---

[155] Matt. 5:17.

been crucified and has suffered many things. (b) But if, as you claim, Marcion, he is not tangible, how can he be arrested and crucified? You say he is a phantom! (c) But your opinion will be refuted by the ascription of betrayal to Judas; for he betrayed his own master and delivered him into the hands of men. (d) And it does you no good to say, "He came down among them," instead of, "with them." You cannot declare a man a phantom when you later show, even though unintentionally, that he is tangible.

Scholion 5. "And the whole multitude sought to touch him. And he lifted up his eyes," and so forth.

Elenchus 5. Again, how could the multitude have touched him if he was intangible? And what sort of eyes did he raise to heaven, if his members were not flesh? But he did this to show that the mediator between God and man is a man, Christ Jesus, and that he is possessed of both—flesh from men, and an invisible essence from God the Father.

Scholion 6. "In the like manner did your fathers unto the prophets."

Elenchus 6. If he has mentioned prophets he does not deny prophets. If he avenges the murder of the prophets and reproaches their murderers and persecutors, he is not foreign to prophets. Rather, he is their god, who establishes their authenticity.

Scholion 7. "I say unto you, I have not found so great faith, no, not in Israel."

Elenchus 7. If "*even* in Israel" he did not find "such faith" as he did in the gentile centurion, he does not censure Israel's faith. For if it were faith in a strange God and not faith in his Father himself, he would not speak in praise of it.

Scholion 8. "Blessed is he who shall not be offended in me," is altered. For he had it as though with reference to John.

(a)   Whether this refers to John or to the Savior himself, he still says "blessed" of those who are not offended at him or John, so that they will not fabricate their own doctrines, which they do not learn from him.

(b)   But there is a more important consideration here, the real reason the Savior spoke. Lest it be thought that John, whom he had ranked as the greatest of those born of woman, was greater even than the Savior himself—since he too was born of woman—he says as a safeguard, "And blessed is whoso shall not be offended in me."

(c)   Hence he says, "He that is less in the kingdom is greater than he." Chronologically, counting from his birth in the flesh, he was six months "less" than John; but as John's God he was clearly "greater" in the kingdom. (d) For the Only-begotten did not come to say anything in secret, or to lie against his own message. He says, "I have not spoken in secret, but openly."[156] For he is truth, as he says, "I am the way and the truth."[157] The way, then, contains no imposture; nor does the truth conceal itself and say what is untrue.

Scholion 9. "He it is of whom it is written, Behold, I send my messenger before thy face."

(a) Elenchus 9. If God's only-begotten Son recognizes John and foreknows him, and because he foreknows him tells those who are willing to know the truth that this is he of whom it is written, "I send my messenger before thy face," (b) the one who wrote, "I send my messenger before thy face," and said it, the eternal God who spoke in the prophets and Law, was not foreign to his own Son, Jesus Christ. (c) For he sends his messenger before his face—the face of an honored Son of a Father. He was not sending his messenger to serve a foreigner of whom, as you say, Marcion, he was even the opposite.

Scholion 10. "And entering into the Pharisee's house he reclined at table. And the woman which was a sinner, standing at his feet behind him, washed his feet with her tears, and wiped and kissed them."

Elenchus 10. "Entering," is indicative of a body, for it indicates a house and the dimensions of a body. And "reclining" can be said only of a person <with> a solid body, which is lying down. And as to the woman's washing his feet with her tears, she did not wash the feet of an apparition or phantom; she wiped, washed and kissed them because she felt the touch of the body.

Scholion 11. And again, "She hath washed my feet with her tears, and wiped and kissed them."

Elenchus 11. Lest you think, Marcion, that the sinful woman's washing, anointing and kissing of the Savior's feet was merely something people supposed, the Savior himself confirms it and teaches that it happened in reality, not appearance, to confound the Pharisees, you yourself, Marcion, and people like you. He affirms with confidence, "She hath washed my feet and kissed them." But what sort of feet? Feet made of flesh and bones and the rest!

Scholion 12. He did not have, "His mother and his brethren," but simply "Thy mother and thy brethren."

(a) Elenchus 12. Even though you falsify the Gospel's wording earlier, Marcion, to make the evangelist disagree with the words certain persons said, "thy mother and thy brethren," you cannot get round the truth. (b) Why did he not call many women Christ's mothers? Why did he not say that he had many countries? How many persons say any

---

[156] Cf. John 18:20.
[157] John 14:6.

number of things of Homer? Some claim he was Egyptian—others, that he was from Chios; others, from Colophon; others, a Phrygian. Others, Meletus and Critheidus, say that he came from Smyrna. Aristarchus declared him an Athenian, others a Lydian from Maeon, others, a Cypriote from Propoetis,* a district near Salamis. Yet Homer was a man, surely! But because of his visits to many countries, he has impelled many to give different descriptions of him.

(c)   But here, though they were speaking of God and Christ, they did not suppose that he had many mothers—just the one who has actually borne him. Or many brothers—only Joseph's sons by his actual other wife. And you cannot take up arms against the truth.

(d)   And do not let the Lord's words, "Who are my mother and brethren?" mislead you. He did not say this to deny his mother, but to check the importunity of the person who spoke when such a large crowd surrounded him, when his saving teaching was pouring forth, and when he was busy with healings and preaching. For the speaker to halt him with the words, "Behold thy mother and thy brethren," was a manifest distraction. (e) And if it was not because he heard the words with joy—not that he did not know they had come before he heard of it, but because he foreknew that they were standing outside—then he would have said this to check the speaker's untimely utterance with a rebuke, as he once told Peter, "Away from me, Satan, for thou intendest not the things that be of God, but the things that be of man."[158]

Scholion 13.   "As they sailed he fell asleep. Then he arose and rebuked the wind and the sea."

(a)   Elenchus 13.   Who fell asleep, pray? You will not dare to say this of the Godhead—or even if you do, you madman, you will be blaspheming against your own head. But anyone can see that the truly incarnate One was in need of sleep, and fell asleep because he had a body. (b) For those who woke him did not see a phantom, but a truly incarnate person. They surely testify that they roused him by shaking and calling him! (c) For the God made flesh who was asleep "arose," it says, the one who had descended from heaven and donned flesh for us. As man he "arose from sleep," but as God he "rebuked" the sea and produced <a calm>.

Scholion 14.   "And it came to pass as they went the people thronged him, and a woman touched him, and was healed of her blood. And the Lord said, Who touched me?" And again, "Somebody hath touched me; for I perceive that virtue hath gone out of me."

---

158 Mark 8:33.

(a)   Elenchus 14.   "As they went." It did not say, "as he went," so
as not to represent him as "going" in a way different from the one usual
for travellers. But as to, "The people thronged him," the people could
not have thronged a spirit. And if a woman touched him and was healed,
she made contact with a human body, not with air. (b) For to show that
the woman's touch of his body was not mere appearance, he teaches (the
contrary) by saying, "Who touched me? For I perceive that virtue hath
gone out of me."

Scholion 15.   "Looking up to heaven he pronounced a blessing upon
them."

Elenchus 15.   If he looked up to heaven and pronounced a blessing
upon them, it was not in mere appearance that he had the forms of eyes,
and the other members.

Scholion 16.   "Saying, The Son of Man must suffer many things,
and be slain, and be raised after three days."

(a) Elenchus 16.   If God's only-begotten Son acknowledged that he
was the Son of Man, and <would> suffer and be put to death, this is
an axe against you, Marcion, and it grubs your whole root up—you scion
of thorns, you cloud with no water, you barren tree with dead leaves! (b)
For he says, in turn, "and be raised again after three days." But what
was it that was raised, except the very things that had suffered and been
buried in the sepulchre? There could be no funeral and interment of a
phantom, a wind, a spirit, or an illusion, and no resurrection of them.

Scholion 17.   "And behold, there talked with him two men, Elijah
and Moses in glory."

(a) Elenchus 17.   In my opinion, Marcion, these words represent the
holy Zechariah's pruninghook against you, and it cuts away all the lies
you have invented against the Law and the prophets. (b) For since you
would deny the Law and the prophets, and call them foreign to the Savior
and his glory and inspired teaching, he brought both Elijah and Moses
with him in his own glory, and showed them to his disciples. And the
disciples showed them to us and the world—that is to everyone who
desires life—to chop your roots with the first as with an axe, but to trim
your branches off with the second, as with the pruninghook of the utterance of the truth. Branches that secrete the hemlock and deadly poison
for men, the oily sap of blasphemy!

(c)   For if Moses, to whom Christ anciently entrusted the Law, were
a stranger to him, and if the prophets were strangers, he would not reveal
them with him in his own glory.

(d)   For see the wonder! He did not show them to us in the tomb, or
beside the cross. But when he revealed the portion of his glory to us as
though for a pledge, then he brought the saints, I mean Moses and Elijah, with him, to show that these were fellow-heirs of his kingdom.

Scholion 18. "Out of the cloud a voice, This is my beloved Son."

(a) Elenchus 18. Anyone can see that the cloud from which the voice came to the Savior is not in the remote heights or above the heavens, but is in the created world around us. (b) Hence, even though the Father spoke from a cloud to indicate his Son to the disciples, the demiurge is not someone different, but the same One who bore witness to his Son from a cloud. And he does not rule the realms above heaven alone, as you claim.

Scholion 19. "I besought thy disciples." But in addition to, "And they could not cast it out," he had, "And he said to them, O faithless generation, how long shall I suffer you?"

Elenchus 19. "How long" means that there is a length of time to Christ's incarnate life. An "O faithless generation" is said because the prophets worked miracles in his name and believed, as we find Elijah doing, and Elisha and the others.

Scholion 20. "For the Son of Man shall be delivered into the hands of men."

Elenchus 20. The appearance of a "Son of Man," and of one who will be "delivered into the hands of men," is not the appearance of a phantom or apparition, but the sight of a body and limbs.

Scholion 21. "Have ye not read so much as this, what David did: he went into the house of God."

Elenchus 21. If he calls the house of the tabernacle which Moses erected a "house of God," he does not deny the Law, or the God who spoke in the Law. For he says that the person who is his father is "God," <and the Father spoke in the Law through the Son and the Holy Ghost>, or the Only-begotten spoke in it himself. For a Trinity, Father, Son and Holy Spirit, is at work at all times in the Law, the prophets, the Gospels and the apostles.

Scholion 22. "I thank thee, Lord of heaven." But he did not have "and earth" or "Father." He is exposed, however; for further on he had, "Even so, Father."

(a) Elenchus 22. He gives thanks to the "Lord of heaven," Marcion, even if you take away " <and> earth"—and <even> if you remove "Father" so as not to show that Christ calls the demiurge his father. For the truth's limbs remain alive. (b) Just as you forgot, Marcion, and retained "Even so, Father" as a leftover, <so the heaven whose Lord you admit the Father is, is part of the created world around us>. Hence it is altogether proven that Christ gives thanks to his own Father and calls him "Lord of heaven." And your madness is great since it does not see where the truth is going.

Scholion 23. "He said to the lawyer, What is written in the Law?" And after the lawyer's answer he replied, "Thou hast answered right. This do, and thou shalt live."

(a) Elenchus 23. The Son of God is truth, and misled no one who asked about life; he has come for man's life. Life is in his keeping, then, and he indicates that the Law is life to him who keeps it, and told the man who answered in terms of the Law that he was right, and "This do and thou shalt live." (b) Who can be so mad as to believe Marcion, then, who insults the God who has granted men both the Law and the grace of the Gospel, and to be carried away with him, when none of his teaching comes from the Law or the Holy Ghost?

Scholion 24. And he said, "Which of you shall have a friend, and shall go unto him at midnight, asking three loaves?" And then, "Ask, and it shall be given. If a son shall ask a fish of any of you that is a father, will he for a fish give him a serpent, or a scorpion for an egg? If ye then, being evil, know of good gifts, how much more the Father?"

(a) Elenchus 24. The wilfulness of the swindler's way of life is exposed by this text. His way of life is not for continence' sake, or for a good reward and the hope of a contest, but for impiety and the badness of a bad opinion. (b) For he teaches that it is wrong to eat meat, and claims that those who eat flesh are liable to the judgment, as they would be for eating souls.

(c) But this is altogether foolish. The flesh is not the soul; the soul is in the flesh. And we do not say that the soul in animals is as precious as men's, but that a soul is simply to keep the animal alive. But the pitiable wretch, together with those who share this opinion, believes that the same soul is in men and animals.

(d) This futile conjecture is made by many misguided sects. Valentinus and Colorbasus, and all Gnostics and Manichaeans, claim that there is a reincarnation of souls, and that there are transmigrations of the soul of ignorant persons—as they themselves call them—in accordance with some invention of mythology. They say that the soul returns and is reembodied in each of the animals until it recognizes (the truth), and is thus cleansed and set free, and departs to the heavens.

(e) And in the first place, the whole futile making of the myth itself stands exposed. No one else can know the exact truth of this better than our Lord Jesus Christ, who came for "the sheep that was lost"—that is, for the souls of men. (f) Since men were in his charge he healed them in body and soul, <as> Lord of body and soul, and giver of the life here and the life to come. And he did not raise the dead to do them harm—I mean Lazarus, the ruler's son, and the daughter of the ruler of the synagogue—as in the Marcionites' doctrine that the body is a prison. He raised them to do them good, and with the knowledge that both our service here in the flesh, and the coming resurrection of flesh and soul, are his decree.

(g)   And again, if he knew that the soul in men and animals is one soul, and he came for the salvation of souls, then, after he had cleansed one demoniac—I mean the one who came out of the tombs—he should not have told the demons to go and kill two thousand swine! Not if the souls of the men and the swine were just alike! Why would he destroy two thousand in order to care for one?

(h)   But again, if Marcion twists like a serpent and craftily replies that Christ freed the swine's souls from their bodies to let them make their ascent—then he should not have returned Lazarus to his body, once he was set free from it! Or rather, he should have set the demoniac free from the chain of the body as well! But he did not do that. Rather, he made this provision for the body, knowing what was to its advantage.

(i)   Your argument about the soul has crumpled, Marcion—and your followers', and the other sectarians'. And yet I shall speak once more of your bogus way of life, since you claim it is wicked and unlawful to eat meat. (j) But the Savior refutes you, since he knows more than you, and teaches better with a text like the following. For he says, "Which of you, whose son shall ask for a fish, will give him a serpent, or, for an egg, a scorpion?" And further on, "If ye then, being evil, know how to give good gifts unto your children, how much more shall your heavenly Father?"[159] (k) Hence, if he has called a fish and an egg "good gifts," nothing God grants is evil if it is eaten with thanksgiving. And your wickedness is altogether exposed.

Scholion 25.   The saying about Jonah the prophet has been falsified; Marcion had, "This generation, no sign shall be given it." But he did not have the passages about Nineveh, the queen of the south, and Solomon.

(a) Elenchus 25.   Even in the very places you choose to falsify, Marcion, you cannot avoid the truth. Even if you remove the <part> about the prophet Jonah—which signifies the Savior's dispensation—and the material about the queen of the south and Solomon, and the saving subject of Nineveh, and the preaching of Jonah, the very thing the Savior says first refutes <you>. (b) For he says, "This generation asketh a sign, and there shall no sign be given it,"[160] implying that those who preceded this generation were vouchsafed signs from heaven by God. (c) Thus Elijah worked a miracle with the fire which came down from

---

[159] Luke 11:11-13.
[160] Luke 11:29.

heaven and took his sacrifice. Moses divided the sea, pierced the rock and water flowed forth, brought manna from heaven. Joshua the son of Nun stopped the sun and moon. And even if you conceal what is written in scripture, swindler, nothing will harm the truth in any way; it estranges itself from the truth instead.

Scholion 26.   Instead of, "Ye pass over the judgment of God," he had, "Ye pass over the calling of God."

(a) Elenchus 26.   Where is there not refutation for you? Where can one < not > get evidence against you? The earlier sources agree with the latter to expose your tampering. (b) If he says, "Ye hold the traditions of your elders and pass over the mercy and judgment of God," find out how long he accuses them of doing this, and when they got the tradition of the elders! (c) You will discover that the tradition of Adda came to them after the return from Babylon, but that the tradition of Aqiba had come into being even before the Babylonian captivities, and that of the sons of Hasmonaeus at the time of Alexander and Antiochus, 190 years before Christ's incarnation. (d) As early as that, then, judgment was by the Law and mercy was by the prophets, and your trashy argument is a total failure.

Scholion 27.   "Woe unto you, for ye build the sepulchres of the prophets, and your fathers killed them."

(a) Elenchus 27.   If he expresses his concern for the prophets by reproaching those who killed them, the prophets were not strange to him. They were his servants, and sent before him by himself, the Father, and the Holy Ghost, to prepare for his coming in the flesh.

They witnessed to the New Testament as well. (b) Moses, who said, "The Lord God will raise up unto you a prophet of your brethren, like unto me."[161] Jacob before him, who said, "Thou hast come up, my son Judah, from a young plant; falling down thou didst sleep. There shall not fail a ruler from Judah"[162]—and shortly after that, "till he come for whom are the things prepared, and he is the expectation of the gentiles, and in him shall the gentiles hope."[163]

(c) Isaiah: "Behold, the Virgin shall conceive;"[164] Jeremiah: "And he is a man, and who shall know him?"[165] Micah: "And thou, Bethlehem," some other material, and, "out of thee shall come for me a governor,"[166] and so on. Malachi: "The Lord shall suddenly come to

---

[161] Deut. 18:15.
[162] Gen. 49:9-10.
[163] Gen. 49:10.
[164] Isa. 7:14.
[165] Jerem. 17:9.
[166] Micah 5:2.

the temple.''[167] David: "The Lord said unto my Lord, sit thou on my right hand,''[168] and so on. And much could be said; the Savior himself says, "Had ye believed Moses ye would have believed me also, for he wrote of me.''[169]

Scholion 28.   He did not have, "Therefore said the wisdom of God, I send unto them prophets," and the statement that the blood of Zacharias. Abel and the prophets will be required of this generation.

Elenchus 28.   This too is seriously embarrassing for you, Marcion. The standard of the truth is preserved, and your removal of the texts you have stolen can be discovered from the authentic copy of Luke. For the places for them are still there, and your excisions are exposed.

Scholion 29.   "I say unto my friends, Be not afraid of them that kill the body. Fear him which, after he hath killed, hath authority to cast into hell.'' But he did not have, "Are not five sparrows sold for two farthings, and not one of them is forgotten before God.''

(a) Elenchus 29.   Marcion, the sentence, "I say unto my friends, be not afraid of them that kill the body; fear him which, after he hath killed the body, hath power to cast the soul into hell,'' forces you to admit to the consequences of the parable as well. For nothing happens without God, even if you remove the part about the sparrows.

(b)   Defend yourself then, Marcion, about the words you have left in the text, and tell us what you mean by the one who has "authority.'' For if you should say that he is Christ's Father, your so-called "good God''—then, though you may make a bad distinction, you have granted that he is a judge and, having "authority,'' gives each what he deserves. (c) If, however, you say that he is not the judge, but that the demiurge is the one whom you call the actual "judge,'' tell me who has given the authority to the demiurge! If he has it of himself, he is supreme and has authority—but if he has authority to judge, he also has it to save! For he who can judge, can also pardon.

(d)   And from another viewpoint: If the good God does not rescue the souls when the judge consigns them to hell—though he is in full charge of these souls—how can he be "good''? Either the judge is more powerful than he, and he cannot save them from him. Or he can, but does not want to—and where is his goodness?

(e)   But if, since the judge created the souls himself, he also has the right to judge them, why does your mythical God on high do things part-way and save (only) certain ones? If he saves them by taking them from someone else's domain, he is covetous, since he has a desire for someone

---

[167] Mal. 3:1.
[168] Ps. 109:1.
[169] John 5:46.

else's souls. But if you deny that this is covetousness, since what he does is for a good and saving purpose, you make him a respecter of persons who does good in part, rather than equally to all.

Scholion 30.   Instead of, ''He shall confess before the angels of God,'' Marcion says, ''before God.''

Elenchus 30.   You are altogether exposed as not travelling in God's way if you alter the truth even in its least important phrase. No one who ventures to change anything in scripture is in the way of the truth to begin with.

Scholion 31.   He does not have, ''God doth clothe the grass.''

Elenchus 31.   Even though you do not leave the written phrases as the Savior worded them, their places are still preserved in the Gospel of the holy church—even if you deny the God who has created all and cares for all, even the grass, by his word; and who is confessed by the Savior.

Scholion 32.   ''And your Father knoweth that ye have need of these things,'' meaning physical things.

Elenchus 32.   The Father knows that the disciples have material needs, and he provides for persons in that position. But he provides, not in another world but here; and he makes the provision for his own servants with his own creatures, not with someone else's.

Scholion 33.   ''But seek ye the kingdom of God, and all these things shall be added unto you.''

(a) Elenchus 33.   If we draw our sustenance from the creatures of one God, while another God is the God of the kingdom of heaven, how can the saying be self-consistent? Either what is here is his and the kingdom is his, and he accordingly ''adds'' all that is here—which is his—because of the burdensomeness of our longing for his kingdom. (b) Or the kingdom and the world there are his, while what is here belongs to the demiurge, and the demiurge still consents to the kingdom of the God on high, by rendering aid to those who seek the righteousness and kingdom of the God on high. (c) But as consent is one and is not at variance, there cannot be two first principles, or three. For God, in fact, is one and made all things, but he made them well, not the reverse. Sin and error, however, belong to us, in that we will them and do not will them.

Scholion 34.   Instead of, ''Your Father,'' Marcion had, ''Father.''

Elenchus 34.   Even here you will do us no harm, but lend us further confirmation. For you have admitted that the Savior said his Father provides for those who are here.

Scholion 35.   Instead, ''in the second or third watch,' he had, ''in the evening watch.''

Elenchus 35.   The oaf stands convicted of stupidly distorting the sacred words to suit his own opinion. Watches are not kept in the daytime but at night, and extend from evening till the first hour—not from dawn till evening, the false entry he is guilty of making.

Scholion 36. "The Lord of that servant will come and will cut him in sunder, and will appoint him his portion with the unbelievers."

(a) Elenchus 36. Who cuts the servant in two, pray? If it is the demiurge and judge whom you call God who will do this, then he owns the believers. For to punish the servant who has not done well, he assigns his portion with the unbelievers.

(b) But if it is Christ's Father, or Christ himself, who will do this, then you plainly retain the witness as a witness against yourself. For in admitting that either Christ or his Father will do this, you have acknowledged without ambiguity that the judge and the good God are the same, and that <he> who provides for those who are here, and for those who are there, is one.

Scholion 37. 'Lest he hale thee to the judge, and the judge deliver thee to the officer."

(a) Elenchus 37. You say that the demiurge is a judge and that each of his angels is an officer, since they will call the sinners to account for their deeds. But what sort of deeds, other than the errors and sins which Jesus also detests, and you say you too forbid? (b) Now if the demiurge and judge detests the same deeds that the good God detests, by that fact and by their one consent he is shown to be one and the same.

Scholion 38. There was falsification of "There came some that told him of the Galilaeans whose blood Pilate had mingled with their sacrifices" till the mention of the eighteen who died in the tower at Siloam, and of "Except ye repent" <and so forth>, till the parable of the fig tree of which the cultivator said, "I am digging about it and dunging it, and if it bear no fruit, cut it down."

(a) Elenchus 38. The robber removed all this to conceal the truth from himself, because of the Lord's agreement with Pilate, who had rightly condemned such persons; and because the men at Siloam died rightly, since they were sinners and this is the way God punished them. (b) But when people tamper with imperial decrees, the copies with certified texts are produced from the archives to expose the fools. And similarly, when the Gospel is produced from the king's palace, that is, from God's holy church, it exposes the flies that spot the king's fine robes.

Scholion 39. "This woman, being a daughter of Abraham, whom Satan hath bound."

Elenchus 39. If the Lord tends to Abraham's daughter at his coming, Abraham is no stranger to him. For by showing pity for his daughter he acknowledges that he approves of Abraham.

Scholion 40.   Again, he falsified, "Then shall ye see Abraham, and Isaac, and Jacob and all the prophets in the kingdom of God." In place of this he put, "When ye see all the righteous in the kingdom of God, and yourselves thrust"—but he put "kept"—"out." There shall be weeping and gnashing of teeth.'"

(a) Elenchus 40.   How plain the tracks of the truth are! No one can hide a road. He can lead men off it, and hide it from those who do not know it, but it is impossible to hide it from those who are familiar with it. (b) For he cannot make the ground where the road was invisible. And even if he makes it hard to see, the road's location surely* remains, and he who tampered with the road is exposed by those who know it.

(c) Now, observe the tracks of the logic. To whom did he say this but the Jews? And if he said it to the Jews, he proved by the same token that they were in the kingdom, and were cast out by the righteous. (d) Now who can <these> be but the forefathers of the Jews, Abraham, Isaac, Jacob, and the prophets? He did not say, "Ye shall see the righteous entering and yourselves not entering," but, "Ye shall see the righteous in the kingdom and yourselves cast out." (e) And he gave an anticipatory ruling regarding "the ones cast out;" but he showed that those who were already righteous were not unrelated to them by birth or calling, but had been called with them, and justified already before his incarnation. (f) And though <he meant that the Jews> remain outside, <he surely did not mean all of them>, since the patriarchs are within.

And how can there be gnashing of teeth at the judgment, you fool, if there is no resurrection of bodies?

Scholion 41.   Again, he falsified, "They shall come from the east and from the west, and shall sit down in the kingdom," "The last shall be first," "The Pharisees came saying, Get thee out and depart, for Herod will kill thee." Also, "He said, Go ye and tell that fox," till the words, "It cannot be that a prophet perish out of Jerusalem" and, "Jerusalem, Jerusalem, which killest the prophets and stonest them that are sent," "Often would I have gathered, as a hen, thy children," "Your house is left unto you desolate," and, "Ye shall not see me until ye shall say, Blessed."

Elenchus 41.   See how brash he is! How much of the Gospel will he amputate? It is as though someone were to take an animal, chop half of its body off, and try to convince the ignorant with the (remaining) half, by saying that the animal looked like that, and nothing had been removed from it.

Scholion 42.   Again, he falsified the entire parable of the two sons, the one who took his share of the property and spent it on dissipation, and the other.

Elenchus 42. The results of his villainy (here) will be no different from his earlier attempts. He is making himself the poorer, while God's truth remains.

Scholion 43. "The Law and the prophets were until John, and every man presseth into it."

Elenchus 43. If he designates a Law and names prophets, and does not expose the Law as lawlessness or call the prophets false, this is a plain admission that the Savior has testified to the prophets; and it is established that they prophesied of him.

Scholion 44. The material about the rich man, and Lazarus the beggar's being carried by the angels into Abraham's bosom.

(a) Elenchus 44. Observe! The Lord included Abraham among the living and blessed, and in the inheritance of repose, and has vouchsafed Lazarus a place in his bosom! (b) Never insult Abraham again, Marcion—he recognised his own Master, and addressed him as "Lord, the judge of all the earth."[170] Observe, it was testified by the Lord himself that Abrahm is righteous, and no stranger to the life which the Savior praises.

Scholion 45. "But now he is comforted," again meaning Lazarus.

Elenchus 45. If Lazarus is comforted in the bosom of Abraham, Abraham is not excluded from the comfort of life.

Scholion 46. Abraham said, "They have Moses and the prophets, let them hear them, for neither will they hear him who is risen from the dead."

(a) Elenchus 46. It is not as though Abraham were still in the world and mistaken when he testifies to the Law of Moses and the prophets, or that he does not know what comes of these; it is after he has experienced the repose there. (b) For it is testified by the Savior in the parable that Abraham attained salvation after death by the teachings of Law and prophets—and by practicing them before the Law was given! (c) And likewise, that those who kept the Law after that, and obeyed the prophets, are in his bosom and depart to life with him. One of these was Lazarus, who was vouchsafed the blessedness of Abraham's life-giving bosom through the Law and the prophets.

Scholion 47. He falsified, "Say, we are unprofitable servants; we have done that which was our duty to do."

Elenchus 47. He does not even accept the safeguard of the Lord's teaching! As a safeguard for his own disciples, lest they lose the reward of their labor through arrogance, he counselled humility. But Marcion does not accept this; in everything he was inspired by pride, not truth.

---

170 Gen. 18:25.

Scholion 48.   When the ten lepers met him. Marcion excised a great deal and wrote, "He sent them away, saying, Show yourselves unto the priests," and yet he made a substitution and said, "Many lepers were in the days of Elisha the prophet, and none was cleansed, saving Naaman the Syrian."

Elenchus 48.   Even here the Lord calls Elisha a prophet, and says he performs the deeds which Elisha, equally, had done before him—in refutation of Marcion and all who make light of God's prophets.

Scholion 49.   "The days will come when ye shall desire to see one of the days of the Son of Man."

Elenchus 49.   If he counts days, designates a time, and calls himself Son of Man, he indicated both a limit to his life, and † a term for the days of his preaching. The Word is not fleshless then, but has chosen to have a body.

Scholion 50.   "One said unto him, Good master, what shall I do to inherit eternal life? He replied, "Call not thou me good. One is good, God." Marcion added, "the Father," and instead of, "Thou knowest the commandments" says, "I know the commandments."

Elenchus 50.   To avoid showing that the commandments have already been written, he says, "I know the commandments." But the whole point is plain from what follows. And if he says that a "Father" is "good" and calls him God, he gives good instruction, from his Father's Law, to the seeker for the inheritance of life, and does not belittle or reject him. Instead he bears witness that those who lived under the Law, both Moses and the other prophets, have inherited eternal life.

Scholion 51.   "And it came to pass that as he was come nigh unto Jericho, a blind man cried, Jesus, thou Son of David, have mercy on me. And when he was healed, he said, Thy faith hath saved thee."

Elenchus 51.   There can be no lie in faith; if it lies, it is not faith. Now he who confessed the name says, "Son of David," and is commended and granted his request. He was not reproved as a liar, but congratulated as a believer. (b) Hence the One who granted sight to the blind at the invocation of the name was not fleshless. He was real, not an apparition, and had been born in the flesh of David's seed, of the holy Virgin Mary and through the Holy Spirit.

Scholion 52.   Marcion falsified, "He took unto him the twelve and said, Behold, we go up to Jerusalem, and all things that are written in the prophets concerning the Son of Man shall be accomplished. For he shall be delivered and killed, and the third day he shall rise again." He falsified this in its entirety,

Elenchus 52.   to make sure that he would nowhere walk erect, and would be altogether exposed for his tampering because he does not. To deny what is said of the passion, if you please, he concealed the texts. But his work of tampering will go for nothing, since he later admits that Christ has been crucified.

Scholion 53. He falsified the section about the ass and Bethphage—and the one about the city and temple, because of the scripture, "My house shall be called an house of prayer, but ye make it a den of thieves."

(a) Elenchus 53. Wickedness cannot see its own refutation; it is blind. Marcion thinks he can hide the road of the truth, but this is an impossibility. (b) He started right up, and omitted these sections in their entirety, because of the testimony that the temple site was Christ's own property and had been built in his name. (c) He also omitted the whole course of the journey from Jericho which brought him to Bethphage. For there actually was an ancient highway to Jerusalem by way of the Mount of Olives, and it was not unknown to those who describe the temple site as well.

(d) But to ensure his refutation from his own mouth, Marcion says, "It came to pass on one of those days, as he taught in the temple, they sought to lay hands on him and were afraid,"[171] as in point fifty-four following. (e) How he got from Jericho to the temple will be learned from the journey itself and the length of the road. But this will show that the villain concealed what happened on the road, and what the Savior himself said in the temple before the line just quoted, I mean, "My house shall be called an house of prayer"[172] and so on, as the prophecy runs.

Scholion 54. "And they sought to lay hands on him and they were afraid."

Elenchus 54. This was considered and expounded, with the appropriately brief explanation, in the elenchus preceding.

Scholion 55. Again, he excised the material about the vineyard which was let out to husbandmen, and the verse, "What is this, then, The stone which the builders rejected?"

Elenchus 55. This will do us no harm. Even if he cut it out he did not cut if off from us, but penalized himself and his followers. For he is amply refuted by more texts (than this).

Scholion 56. He excised, "Now that the dead are raised, even Moses showed at the bush, in calling the Lord the God of Abraham and Isaac and Jacob. But he is a God of the living, not of the dead."

(a) Elenchus 56. The lame-brain is amazingly stupid not to see that this testimony is equivalent to Lazarus the beggar's, and the parable of those who are not allowed to enter the kingdom. He kept the remains of

---

[171] Cf. Luke 20:19.
[172] Matt. 21:13.

these parables and did not falsify them; moreover, he has kept "There
shall be weeping and gnashing of teeth,"[173] to his own embarrassment.
(b) If a finger is dipped in water after death, and a tongue is cooled with
water—as the rich man said to Abraham on Lazarus' account—and
there is gnashing of teeth and wailing, this is a sign of a resurrection of
bodies, even if the oaf falsifies the Lord's true sayings about the resurrection of the dead.

Scholion 57.   He did not have the following: "Now that the dead are
raised, even Moses showed, saying that the God of Abraham, the God
of Isaac, and the God of Jacob is God of the living."

Elenchus 57.   Since the Savior repeated the parable I insert it twice,
not to be like the scum, Marcion, and omit anything that has been written. <But> the rejoinder to his tampering has been given already, in
the elenchus preceding.

Scholion 58.   Again, he falsified, "There shall not an hair of your
head perish" ... (Elenchus 58 is missing.)

Scholion 59.   Again, he falsified the following: "Then let them which
are in Judaea flee to the mountains" and so on, because of the words subjoined in the text, "until all things that are written be fulfilled."

(a) Elenchus 59.   Because of his own forgetfulness he thinks that
everyone is as stupid as he, and fails to realize that even an unimportant
text which he leaves in place constitutes a rebuttal of the texts he has
falsified, though there may be many. Hence nothing will prevent
whoever wishes from comparing the material he acknowledges with these
witnesses which he has falsified. (b) For it will be shown that <the words
he left>, in which Abraham said after death, "They have Moses and the
prophets; let them hear them,"[174] agree with these words that he has
removed. What the prophets and Moses said came from God the Father,
from the Lord himself, the Son of God, and from the Holy Spirit; and
since they were written they had to be fulfilled.

Scholion 60.   "He communed with the captains how he might deliver
him unto them."

(a) Elenchus 60.   What lunacy of Marcion's! Who "communed" but
Judas? And to do what, but to "deliver" the Savior? And if the Savior
is "delivered," someone "delivered" cannot be appearance, but is
truth. If he were merely a spirit, he could not be delivered to men of
flesh. As man, however, he had become tangible. <And> since he had
put on flesh, he willingly delivered himself to man.

(b)   But they contradict themselves from stupidity. I was arguing with
some of his disciples once, some Marcionite or other, and remarking how

---

[173] Luke 13:28.
[174] Luke 16:29.

the Gospel says that the Spirit took Jesus into the wilderness to be tempted by the devil. And he asked me, "How could Satan have tempted the true God, who is both greater than he and, as you say, his Lord—his master, Jesus?"

(c) By the help of God I received understanding in a flash, and answered, "Do you not believe that Christ was crucified?"

He said, "Yes," and did not deny it.

"Who crucified him, then?"

"Men," he said.

(d) Then I said to him, "Who is more powerful—men, or the devil?"

"The devil," he said.

But after he said this, I replied, "If the devil is more powerful than men, and yet men, who are weaker, crucified Christ, no wonder he was tempted by the devil too! (e) With entire willingness and under no necessity Christ has given himself for us and truly suffered—not from weakness, but by choice—to set us an example, and <pay> the devil's claim for our salvation by his suffering of the cross, for the condemnation of sin and the abolition of death."

Scholion 61. "And he said unto Peter and the rest, Go and prepare that we may eat the Passover."

Elenchus 61. Marcion, the text contains a cloud of arows against you in one testimony. If he orders them to prepare for him to eat the Passover, but Christ kept the Passover before suffering, it was surely because of its institution by the Law. (b) But if Christ lived by the Law, it was plainly because he did not come to destroy the Law, but fulfil it. But if a king does not destroy a law, the commandment in the Law is neither profane nor forbidden by the king. (c) But if, though the Law is sacred and its commandment acknowledged, a king adds to its commandment for a greater gift, the splendor of the addition appears by right. Since, however, the legislation and the added gift belong to one and the same king, it is clear to everyone, and plain, that the king who made the addition is not opposed to the Law.

(d) Hence it is shown that the Old Testament is in no way contrary to the Gospel or the succession of the prophets. But you supplied your own refutation, Marcion, in all sorts of ways—or rather, you were forced to by the truth itself. (e) The ancient Passover was nothing but the slaughter of a lamb and the eating of meat, and the partaking of flesh with unleavened bread. And who but the truth itself—as I said—has kept you from suppressing your refutation altogether? To keep the Passover as prescribed in the Law, the Lord Jesus has eaten these meat-dishes that you abhor, with his disciples.

(f) And do not tell me that, in saying, "I desire to eat the Passover with you,"[175] he was naming in advance the mystery he intended to celebrate. To shame you completely the truth does not put the mystery at the beginning, or you might deny the truth. It says, "After supper he took certain things and said, This is such and such,"[176] and left † no room for tampering. For it made it plain that he proceeded with the mystery after eating the Jewish Passover, that is, "after supper."

Scholion 62. "And he sat down, and the twelve apostles with him, and he said, With desire I have desired to eat the Passover with you before I suffer."

(a) Elenchus 62. The Savior sat down, Marcion, and the twelve apostles sat down with him. If he "sat down" and they "sat down" with him, one expression cannot have two different meanings, even if it can be differentiated in its dignity and manner. For you must either admit that the twelve apostles have also sat down in appearance, or that he has actually sat down because he has actual flesh.

(b) And (he said), "With desire I have desired to eat this Passover with you before I suffer," to show that the Passover is already pictured in the Law before his passion and becomes the guarantee of his passion and the call for something more perfect. And he intimated <that>, as the holy apostle also said, "The Law was our schoolmaster to bring us unto Christ."[177] But if the Law was a schoolmaster to bring us to Christ, the Law was not unrelated to Christ.

Scholion 63. He falsified, "I say unto you, I will not any more eat thereof until it be fulfilled in the kingdom of God."

Elenchus 63. Marcion excised this and tampered with it to avoid putting food or drink in the Kingdom of God, if you please. The oaf was unaware that spiritual, heavenly things are capable of corresponding with things on earth, and can be partaken of in ways we do not know. (b) For the Savior testifies in turn, "Ye shall sit at my table, eating and drinking in the kingdom of heaven."[178]

(c) Or again, he falsified these things, if you please, to give the Law's provisions no place in the kingdom of heaven. Then why did Elijah and Moses appear with him in glory on the mount? But no one can accomplish anything against the truth.

Scholion 64. He falsified, "When I sent you, lacked ye anything?" and so on, because of the words, "This also that is written must be accomplished, And he was numbered among the transgressors."

---

[175] Luke 22:15.
[176] Cf. Luke 22:20.
[177] Gal. 3:24.
[178] Luke 22:30.

Elenchus 64.   Even if you falsify the words, the places they belong are evident from the deed. The Law precedes it, the prophets foretell it, and the Lord fulfils it.

Scholion 65.   "He was withdrawn from them about a stone's cast, and kneeled down and prayed."

(a) Elenchus 65.   In kneeling down he knelt visibly, and did so in a perceptible manner. But if he did it perceptibly, then he performed the act of kneeling in <human> fashion. Therefore the Only-begotten did not sojourn among us without flesh. (b) For to him "every knee shall bow, of things in heaven, and things in earth, and things under the earth"[179]—the knees of heavenly beings supernaturally, of earthly beings perceptibly, of those under the earth in their own fashion. But here he does everything in truth, is visible to his disciples and can be touched by them, and does not deceive.

Scholion 66.   "And Judas drew near to kiss him, and said..."

Elenchus 66.   He drew near to a corporeal Master and a God who had taken a body, to kiss real lips, not apparent, deceptive ones.

Scholion 67.   He falsified what Peter did when he struck the servant of the high priest and cut off his ear.

(a) Elenchus 67.   The cheat concealed what had actually happened; his intent was to hide it in deference to Peter, but he excised what was said to the Savior's glorification. (b) But it will do no good; even though you excise them, we know the miracles of God. After the ear was cut off the Lord took it again and healed it, in proof that he is God and did God's work.

Scholion 68.   "They that held him mocked him, smiting and striking him and saying, Prophesy, who is it that smote thee?"

Elenchus 68.   because "they that held," "mocked," "smite," "strike," and "Prophesy, who is it that smote thee," was not appearance, but was indicative of bodily touch and physical reality. And this is plain to everyone, even if you have gone blind, Marcion, and will not acknowledge God's plain truth.

Scholion 69.   After "We found this fellow perverting the nation," Marcion added, "and destroying the Law and the prophets."

(a) Elenchus 69.   How can you not be detected? How can you not be exposed as perverting the way of the Lord? Since to inform on yourself—I would rather not say, "on the Lord"—you add something here that is not written <and> say, "We found him destroying the Law and the prophets," its opposite will refute you despite your wasted effort. The Savior himself says, "I came not to destroy the Law and the proph-

179 Phil. 2:10.

ets, but to fulfil.''[180] (b) Now the same person <who> says, ''I came not to destroy,'' cannot be accused of destroying. For the text did not say this, but, ''We found him perverting the nation, saying that he himself is Christ, a king.''

Scholion 70.   An addition after, ''forbidding to give tribute,'' is, ''and turning away their wives and children.''

(a)   Elenchus 70. Who will get out onto a cliff, fulfilling scripture's, ''He that is evil to himself, to whom will he be good?''[181] To falsify what is written but add something that is not is an example of the utmost rashness, wickedness, and unsafe travel—especially in the Gospel, which is forever indestructible.

(b)   And the additions themselves have no place in the Gospel and contain no hidden meaning. Jesus did not turn wives or children away; he himself said, ''Honor thy father and mother,''[182] and, ''What God hath joined together, let no man put asunder.''[183]

(c)   But even if he did say, ''Except a man leave father, and mother, and brethren, and wife, and children and the rest, he is not my disciple,''[184] this was not to make us hate our parents. It was to prevent our being led <to follow the teaching> of another faith at our fathers' and mothers' command, or behavior contrary to the Savior's teaching.

Scholion 71.   ''And when they were come unto a place called Place of a Skull, they crucified him and parted his raiment, and the sun was darkened.''

(a) Elenchus 71.   Glory to the merciful God, who fastened your chariots together, Marcion, you Pharaoh, and though you hoped to escape, sank them in the sea! Though you make all possible excuses you will have none here. If one has no flesh, he cannot be crucified either.

(b) Why did you not evade this great text? Why did you not try to conceal this crucial matter, which undoes all the evil you have devised from the beginning? (c) If he was really crucified, why can you not see that the Crucified is tangible, and his hands and feet are fastened with nails? This could not be a phantom or apparition, as you say, but was a true body which the Lord has taken from Mary—our actual flesh, bones, and the rest. For even you admit that the Lord was nailed to a cross!

Scholion 72.   Marcion falsified the words, ''Today thou shalt be with me in paradise.''

---

[180] Matt. 5:17.
[181] Sir. 14:5.
[182] Matt. 15:4.
[183] Matt. 19:6.
[184] Cf. Luke 14:26.

(a) Elenchus 72.   This was a good and suitable thing for you to falsify, Marcion, since you have taken your own entry into paradise away. You will not enter yourself, or allow your companions to. For by nature those who lead astray, and those who are led astray, actually hate the good.

Scholion 73.   "And when he had cried with a loud voice he gave up the ghost."

Elenchus 73.   If he expired with the loud cry, Marcion, why did he expire, or what was it that was expired? But it is obvious, even if you deny it. It was his soul, which issued from the body with the divine nature while the body remained lifeless, as the truth is.

Scholion 74.   "And, lo, a man named Joseph took the body down, wrapped it in linen and laid it in a sepulchre that was hewn in stone."

Elenchus 74.   If the removal, the wrapping, and the deposit in a rock-hewn tomb do not convince you, Marcion, who is more of a fool? What else that was plainer could scripture show, when, to demonstrate the entire truth, it exhibited the tomb, its location, its type, the deposit of the body for three days, and the wrapper of the shroud?

Scholion 75.   "And the women returned and rested the sabbath day according to the Law."

(a) Elenchus 75.   Why did the women return? And why does scripture mention their rest, Marcion, if not to give their witness which exposes your stupidity? (b) See here, women testify, apostles, Jews, angels—and Joseph, who took a real, tangible body down and wrapped it! As scripture says, if a man has perverted himself to his own condemnation, who can put him to rights?[185]

Scholion 76.   "The men in shining garments said, Why seek ye the living among the dead? He is risen; remember all that he spake when he was yet with you, that the Son of Man must suffer and be delivered."

(a) Elenchus 76.   Not even these holy angels convince you, Marcion, though they confess that Christ has spent three days among the dead, and after that is alive, and dead no longer. (In divine nature he is always alive, and was not put to death at all; but physically he had been put to death for the three days, and was alive again.) (b) They tell the women, "He is risen; he is not here." And what does "He is risen" mean but that he also fell asleep? For they make it clearer: "Remember that while he was yet with you he told you these things, that the Son of Man must suffer."

Scholion 77.   He falsified what Christ said to Cleopas and the other disciples when he met them, "O fools, and slow to believe all that the prophets have spoken. Ought not he to have suffered these things?" And

---

[185] Cf. Eccles. 1:15 and Tit. 3:11.

instead of "what the prophets have spoken," he put, "what I have said unto you." But he is exposed, since "When he broke the bread their eyes were opened and they knew him."

(a) Elenchus 77.   Tell me, Marcion, how was the bread broken? By an apparition, or an actual solid body at work? For when he arose from the dead he really arose, in his actual sacred body.

(b)   But you have replaced, "Is not this what the prophets have spoken?" Marcion, with, "Is this not what I said unto you?" (c) If he had told them, "I said unto you," they would surely have recognized him from the phrase, "I said." Then why is it that, at the breaking of the bread, scripture says, "Their eyes were opened and they knew him and he vanished?"

(d)   It was fitting for Christ, who was God and was changing his body to a spiritual one, to show that it was a true body—but that it vanished when he chose, since all things are possible to him. (e) Even Elisha, in fact, who was a prophet and had received the grace from God, prayed God to smite his pursuers with blindness, and they were smitten and could not see him as he was. (f) Moreover, the angels concealed Lot's door in Sodom, and the Sodomites could not see it. Was Lot's door an appearance too, Marcion? But you are left with no reply, for it is plain that he broke the bread and distributed it to his disciples.

Scholion 78.   "Why are ye troubled? Behold my hands and my feet, for a spirit hath not bones as ye see me have."

(a) Elenchus 78.   Who can fail to laugh at the driveller who foolishly dragged himself and the souls of others down to hell? If he had not acknowledged these words his imposture would have been plausible, and his dupes pardonable. (b) But now, since he acknowledged these texts without excising them, and his followers read them as well, his sin and theirs remains. The fire is inescapable for him and them, since there is no excuse for them. For the Savior has clearly taught that < even after > resurrection he has bones and flesh, as he testified himself with the words, "as ye see me have."

12,1   This is the case against Marcion based on the remains of the Gospel that he preserves, in the treatise I have composed on his account. I surely believe that, contrary to his deceit, it is adequate. (2) But I shall also proceed to the next part, the texts from the apostle which he still preserves, and which I have again selected in the same way. I have put < the > ones from the Epistle to the Galatians first, and keep that order throughout, since Galatians stands first in Marcion's canon. (3) At the time I did not make my selection < in > his < order > but in the order of the Apostolic Canon, and put Romans first. But here I cite in accordance with Marcion's canon.

12   < From the Epistle to the Galatians >

Scholion 1.   "Learn that the just shall live by faith. For as many as are under the Law are under a curse; but, The man that doeth them shall live by them."

(a) Elenchus 1.   The words, "Learn that the just shall live by faith," are proof that there is ancient scripture in the things the apostle said—things the apostle < took one by one > from the Law and prophets for our salvation, said of a new covenant and allied with our hope. (b) And he says, "They are under a curse," because there was a threat in the Law against Adam's disobedience, until he who had come from above, and had donned a body taken from Adam's lump, arrived and changed the curse into a blessing.

Scholion 2.   "Cursed is everyone that hangeth upon a tree; but he that is of the promise is by the freewoman."

Elenchus 2.   Again, by showing that the provision of the incarnation and cross was for the lifting of the curse, but that it had already been written in the Law and prophesied, and that it was then fulfilled in the Savior, the holy apostle gave plain indication that the Law is not alien to the Savior. For it prophesied and witnessed to the things he would do.

Scholion 3.   "I testify that a man that is circumcised is a debtor to do the whole Law."

Elenchus 3.   He cannot be saying "he is debtor" of something that is forbidden; he must mean a heavier burden which is capable of being lightened. For the Master is one, and he is able both to burden and—of his free choice—to lighten the burden of those who did not refuse to accept salvation by his grace, when he came in the flesh.

Scholion 4.   In place of, "A little leaven leaveneth the whole lump," he put, "corrupteth the whole lump."

Elenchus 4.   To leave nothing true in his writings, he has hardly ever dealt with the scriptures without tampering. But the clarification of the matter is furnished by the analogy itself. Leaven, by its nature, is the product of a lump, and leavening is caused by a lump; and no one drawing the analogy of the riddle intelligently would begin by doing away with the nature (of leaven).

Scholion 5.   "For all the Law is fulfilled by you; thou shalt love thy neighbor as thyself."

Elenchus 5.   What use does the holy apostle have for the Law if the New Testament had been separated from the ancient legislation? But to show that the two Testaments belong to the one God, and that their agreement that love of neighbor fulfils the Law is made known in both Testaments alike—since love of neighbor does perfect good—he called love the fulfilment of the Law.

Scholion 6.   "Now the works of the flesh are manifest, which are these: Adultery, fornication, uncleanness, lasciviousness, idolatry, witch-craft, hatred, variance, emulations, wrath, strife, seditions, factions, en-vyings, drunkenness, revellings—of the which I tell you before, as I have also told you in time past, that they which do such things shall not inherit the kingdom of God."

(a) Elenchus 6.   What marvellous mysteries of God's <apostle>, and what a contrast between his examples and <the scum's imposture>! For Paul attributed everything dreadful to the flesh! But the flesh did not always exist; the flesh <came into being> on the sixth day of creation, with the fashioning of Adam. It had its origin from that time, I mean the time of its fashioning, to confound those who say that evil is everlasting and primordial.

(b)   Nor, in fact, did the flesh sin from the time of its fashioning, or its Fashioner might be held responsible for sin, because of fashioning flesh as a sinful thing. Nor did evil pre-exist the thing God fashioned. Adam fell into disobedience later by choice because of his free agency, and of himself committed the sin against himself, I mean the sin of break-ing faith with his Master through disobedience. (c) Where was evil then, before there was flesh? And why did the flesh not do evil as soon as it was fashioned, but later in time? And that disposes of what is said about the origin of evil! Evil cannot be primordial, since whether it arises or not depends on the flesh, which is of later origin. Nor, in turn, is the flesh without an inheritance in the heavens.

(d)   And let no one seize hold of the holy apostle's words, "Flesh and blood shall not inherit the kingdom of God;"[186] he is not censuring all flesh. How can we censure flesh which has not done the things we have mentioned? (e) But let me prove the point with other demonstrations as well. Paul says, "Who shall lay anything to the charge of God's elect?"[187] Why will the holy Mary not inherit the kingdom of heaven flesh and all, when she did not commit fornication or uncleanness or adultery or do any of the intolerable deeds of the flesh, but remained undefiled? (f) Therefore Paul does not mean that flesh cannot inherit the kingdom of heaven, but means carnal men who do evil with the flesh— fornication, idolatry and the like. (g) Your villainy is exposed altogether, you misguided Marcion, since the truth has fully anticipated you, and it safeguards the reliability of the message of salvation.

Scholion 7.   "They that are Christ's have crucified the flesh with the affections and lusts."

---

[186] 1 Cor. 15:50.
[187] Rom. 8:33.

(a) Elenchus 7.   If they that are Christ's have crucified the flesh too, Marcion, it is plainly in imitation of Christ that Christ's servants have purified the flesh with its affections and lusts—showing that he himself has crucified flesh. Therefore they too have crucified the flesh, with the same intent as their Master. (b) And if they have crucified the flesh, it is inconceivable that flesh which has suffered for Christ does not reign with Christ, as the holy apostle indicates elsewhere, "As ye are partakers of the sufferings of Christ, so shall ye be also of the glory."[188]

Scholion 8.   "For neither do they themselves who are circumcised (now) keep the Law."

(a) Elenchus 8.   Thus the former circumcision had not been forbidden in its own day, if it kept the Law. But Law announced that Christ would come to provide a law of liberty, and that, in the time of Christ, physical circumcision would no longer serve. For the true circumcision through Christ, of which the former was a type, has come.

(b)   And even if those still marked by the earlier circumcision keep the whole Law, this will no longer count for them as observance of the Law. For the Law said of Christ that "The Lord God will raise up unto you a prophet, of my brethren, like unto me; unto him ye shall hearken."[189] But since they have not hearkened to Christ "Circumcision is made uncircumcision unto them"[190] and their observance of the Law is no longer observance.

(c)   The Law is good, then, and circumcision is good, since from the Law and circumcision we have come to know Christ, his more perfect Law, and his more perfect circumcision.

From the < First > Epistle to the Corinthians, for this is their second Epistle and ours.

Scholion 1 and 9.   "For it is written, I will destroy the wisdom of the wise, and will bring to naught the understanding of the prudent."

Elenchus 1 and 9.   If the apostle culls evidence from the prophets' writings in proof of truth and good doctrine, the prophets are not foreign to the truth, the good God, and his good doctrine.

Scholion 2 and 10.   "That, according as it is written, He that glorieth, let him glory in the Lord."

(a) Elenchus 2 and 10.   If someone who glories in the Lord is called praiseworthy by the prophet, and yet the prophet knows the God of the Law as Lord—whom you call judge, Marcion, and demiurge, and just—then this God is none other than the Father of Christ, whose disciple Paul is. (b) For Paul, whom Christ appointed to instruct the gentiles

---

[188] Cf. 2 Cor. 1:7.
[189] Deut. 18:15.
[190] Rom. 2:25.

from the prophet's teaching, drew pure water, as it were, from teachings like these and these very teachings, and watered the church entrusted to him.

Scholion 3 and 11. "of the first beings of this world, that come to naught."

(a) Elenchus 3 and 11. If there are many "first beings" (ἄρχοντες) of this world, Marcion, and if such beings are coming to naught, you will have to stop looking for the roots of three first principles (ἀρχαί) and seek out another myth, with many principles, many roots, and lots of melodrama. (b) And when you construct one out of quibbles—you cannot find one (ready-made)—you will be confronted with the words, 'that come to naught." And your imaginary root of the first principles without any first principle of its own, will be demolished by the words of the author who said, "that come to naught."

For whatever has an end is not eternal; if it had a beginning, it will also have an end. (c) Nothing with a beginning can last forever, except by the will of the Existent, the Cause of that which once had no existence, but which began to be. Now the Existent is Father, Son and Holy Spirit; the non-existent is the whole creation, which has a beginning. Creation includes the thing which is called "evil" and is evil, for this began with men, who have come to be but once did not exist. But since evil began at the same time man <began>, though man was once non-existent, <there will also be a time> when evil will exist no longer. (d) Without doubt it will be eliminated, since He Who Is is not pleased with anyone who has had a beginning, and yet has constituted himself an evil thing.

For after the resurrection evil will be ended. And not only then. It has also been ended since the proclamation of the Law—and even before the Law, by many who have lived by the law of nature. And still more, surely, since Christ's incarnation.

(e) But it will be ended entirely after the resurrection of the dead, since "They are sown in corruption, they are reaised in incorruption,"[191] no longer to do evil, no longer to die. (f) And the same saying of the apostle, "The first beings of this world that come to naught," will testify to the coming end of evil. And that disposes of your subject, Marcion, since it is imaginary, false, shaky and irrational.

Scholion 4 and 12. "For it is written, He taketh the wise in their own craftiness. And again, The Lord knoweth the thoughts of men, that they are vain."

Elenchus 4 and 12. "It is written," which is put before a citation, and "The Lord knoweth," which corresponds with it, are not strange to

---

[191] 1 Cor. 15:42.

the person who chose the words of the saying—I mean the holy apostle, in whose writings the citation is found. And from this citation it will be evident that the character of the apostle's preaching does not differ from the Old Testament, which supplied him with the testimony.

Scholion 5 and 13. "For even Christ our Passover is sacrificed."

(a) Elenchus 5 and 13. If the apostle acknowledges the Passover and does not deny that Christ was sacrificed, the Passover is not foreign to Christ, who truly, not in appearance, sacrifices a lamb for a Passover, as the Law prescribes. Christ was a type of this lamb, since he was not sacrificed in appearance and did not suffer without flesh. (b) For how could a spirit be sacrificed? Obviously, it could not.

But since he could not have been sacrificed without flesh, and yet—as the apostle's unambiguous testimony acknowledges—he was truly sacrificed, <it is plain that he had donned flesh>. (c) Therefore it is plainly proven on all counts that the Law was not foreign to him. The Law was in force temporarily as a type till the coming of Christ, the more perfect and manifest Lamb, who was sacrificed in truth—of whom the literal lamb anciently sacrificed was an anticipation. But for "our Passover, Christ was sacrificed."

Scholion 6 and 14. "Know ye not that he which is joined to an harlot is one body? For two, saith he, shall be one flesh."

Elenchus 6 and 14. If the Law is not true, why do truthful persons take the testimonies from the Law? One such person is God's holy apostle Paul, who took this testimony, together with many others, in manifest proof of the good God's truthfulness and proclamation.

Scholion 7 and 15. Given in an altered form. In place of, "in the Law," he says, "in the Law of Moses." But before this he says, "Or saith not the Law the same also?"

(a) Elenchus 7 and 15. Even if you change the form in the second pronouncement, Marcion, and think that in writing, "in the Law of Moses," you have separated the Law from God by saying "Moses," their binding together earlier exposes your foolishness: "Or saith not the Law the same also? For it is written in the Law, Thou shalt not muzzle the mouth of the ox that treadeth out the corn." (b) Even if you add Moses' name you have helped us, not hurt us, but you have tied the evidence together to your own disadvantage, and unwittingly made the full admission that the Law of Moses is the Law of God, with the words, "in the Law of Moses," and, "the Law saith."

(c) For the apostle concurs by combining them, since he said next, "Doth God take care for oxen? Or saith he it altogether for our sakes?"[192] But if the Law has spoken for the apostles' sakes, then the God

---

[192] 1 Cor. 9:9-10.

who spoke in the Law is likewise taking care of Christ's apostles by forbidding them to be "muzzled"—either so that they can give the teaching
of Christ himself, or to ensure their adequate support by the people. He
therefore does not know the apostles as foreign to his own Godhead; and
the apostles do not regard God himself as foreign to them.

(d)   By the inspiration of this Godhead the holy apostle has testified
for all creatures in saying, "Doth God take care for oxen? But for the
apostles hath he spoken." And if God has spoken for the apostles' sakes,
and yet he is the creator of man and beast, including oxen and sparrows,
reptiles and insects, fish and the rest—then he is concerned for all, each
in proportion.

(e)   And he shows concern for all when he says, "Thou, Lord, shalt
save both man and beast;"[193] "Who provideth for the raven his food?
The young of the ravens cry to the Lord, seeking their meat;"[194] and,
"Thou shalt give to all their meat in due season."[195] But he did not forbid the muzzling of a threshing ox while the oxen are in the act of
threshing, since this would show that God cannot feed his creature otherwise than with the fodder men provide for their cattle. (f) The holy apostle has shown that it was not for lack of food that God made provision
for oxen through the thresher by forbidding him to muzzle them, but that
the riddle's meaning is the correspondence of the apostles (with the
oxen).

(g)   For God does † indeed literally provide for all, and is concerned
for all alike. The holy apostle was not writing in contradiction of the
Savior, to give the rabble an excuse of that sort. (h) Sparrows are less
important than oxen, and of them the Savior said, "Five sparrows are
sold for two farthings,"[196] and again, "Are not two sparrows sold for one
farthing?"[197] Therefore, if two sparrows are sold for one farthing, and
one will not fall into a snare without your heavenly Father, he provides
for all alike, but cares for his more important creatures by the more important mode, that of spiritual analogy. (i) Hence there is entire agreement that the Maker, Demiurge, and Law-giver in Old and New
Testaments is the same, a good God and a just, and Lord of all.

Scholion 8 and 16.   I have already dealt with this fully, and explained
it in detail, in the statement before it. Hence I see no need to speak of
it again, and am content with what I have said.

---

[193] Ps. 35:7.
[194] Job 38:41.
[195] Ps. 144:15.
[196] Luke 12:6.
[197] Matt. 10:29.

Scholion 9 and 17. "Moreover, brethren, I would not that ye should be ignorant how that all our fathers were under the cloud and all passed through the sea, and did all eat the same spiritual meat, and did all drink the same spiritual drink. For they drank of a spiritual rock that followed them, and that rock was Christ. But with many of them God was not well pleased. Now these things were our examples, to the intent we should not lust after evil things, as they also lusted. Neither be ye idolaters as were some of them; as it is written, The people sat down to eat and drink, and rose up to play. Neither let us tempt Christ," until the words, "These things happened unto them for examples, and they were written for us," and so on.

(a) Elenchus 9 and 17.   What lunacy! Who will cheat himself of the light of the rising sun, if he has eyes? If the holy apostle says that the men of those days were his fathers, that they were under a cloud and have passed through the sea, that there is both a spiritual meat and a spiritual drink, and that they have eaten, and drunk from a spiritual rock that followed them, but the rock was Christ—(b) (if that is what he says), who will believe Marcion's stupidity? He befogs his own mind and his followers' minds with his claim that Christ is foreign to the incidents in the Law, which the apostle admits occurred in actuality, not appearance.

(c)   But the apostle says that Christ was displeased with most of them, surely because of their lawless behavior. But if he was displeased with those who did things the Law calls lawless, then he was angry with such people because he himself had given the Law! And he teaches that the Law is his own Law, was given as a temporary measure, and served a legitimate purpose till his incarnation. For it is right for a master, at any given time, to give the orders appropriate for that time to his own household.

(d)   But he immediately adds, "These things were our examples, that we might not lust after evil things as they also lusted. Neither be ye idolaters, as were some of them"—not extending the sentence to all of them. (e) And how do you know this, Paul? He replies by saying, "As it is written, The people sat down to eat and drink and rose up to play." Therefore the scripture from which the apostle takes the condemnation of the lawless, is a truthful one.

(f)   Then again, "Neither let us tempt the Lord." In place of "Lord" Marcion put "Christ." But "Lord" and "Christ" are the same even if Marcion disagrees, since Christ's name has already been used at the words, "The rock was Christ, yet with many of them he was not well pleased."

(g)   But again, to give the whole purpose of the passage the holy apostle says, "These things happened unto them for examples, and were written for our admonition.'' Now if the things that happened to them as examples were written for our admonition, the one who wrote what happened then was seeing to it that we, the persons he was admonishing, should not become desirous of evil things. (h) But if he does not want us desirous of evil, then he is good, not evil. For he urges us to occupy ourselves with the things that occupy him—this same good God, who is likewise just. He is God of those who were recorded first, and of those who are admonished later. He is Creator of all, Demiurge and Legislator, Giver of the Gospels and Guide of the apostles.

Scholion 10 and 18. ''What say I, then? That sacrificial meat is anything, or that that which was offered in sacrifice to idols is anything? But the things which they sacrifice, they sacrifice to devils and not to God.'' But Marcion added, ''sacrificial meat.''

(a) Elenchus 10 and 18. ''What say I, then? That that which is offered in sacrifice to idols is anything? But the things which they sacrifice, they sacrifice to devils and not to God.'' In saying that those who sacrifice to idols sacrifice to devils, not God, the apostle did not disown the ancient time of the fathers up to his own day, while there was a Jerusalem. (b) He therefore did not condemn those who sacrificed to God while there was a need for sacrifices. But he does condemn those who sacrifice to idols—not for sacrificing, but for sacrificing to idols instead of God. (Nor are their sacrifices to prepare the food God has granted them. They sacrifice to demons, and <render service> to nonsense.)

(c) But you added ''sacrificial meat'' (ἱερόθυτον), Marcion, thinking that the correspondence of the two kinds of sacirfice would be established by mixing up the two terms, ''sacred'' (ἱερόν) and ''idol''. (d) If sacrifice were offered specifically to Christ after the new covenant came, and animals were sacrificed in his name, the lie of your quibbling might appear persuasive. Those who sacrifice to God now would be sacrificing to Christ, but those who sacrificed then in the temple at Jerusalem, and those who sacrifice to idols, would belong together and be sacrificing to demons, not God. But as no one has sacrificed animals to Christ since the coming of Christ and the new covenant, the addition in your text is evident.

(e) But even if the phrase about sacrificial meat and meat offered to idols actually stood in the apostle, persons of sound reason would take these as one and the same. The phrase would be an incorrect usage by the apostle, due to the habit of people who always call the idol ''sacred.''

(f) And your false notion collapses completely once the truth is established. Those who sacrifice to idols—or sacrifice ''sacred meat,'' as they say—make what they did or do a lie and sacrifice to demons, not God.* But not those who once quite rightly made the sacrifices the Law prescribed.

(g)   Now, however, by God's will this is no longer done, as he said even from the first through the prophet Jeremiah, "To what purpose dost thou bring to me incense from Sheba and sweet cane from a far country?" And again, "Thy sacrifices are not sweet unto me."[198] And elsewhere, "Take away thy sacrifices, O Israel, and eat flesh. For I gave your fathers no commandment concerning sacrifices in the day that I took them by the hand to bring them out of the land of Egypt, but this thing I commanded them, that every man deal justly with his neighbor."[199]

(h)   But the same God who said, "I gave no such commandment," also told Moses, in the Law, "If any man of the children of Israel shall offer a sacrifice of the beeves or of the sheep, let him offer a male without blemish."[200] And again, "If any sin and be overcome by a transgression, let him offer a sheep." And again, "If the people sin, let them offer a calf."[201] He showed that he willingly accepted the sacrifices which once were offered for the people's salvation, not because he needed or wanted them, but in deference to the people's weakness and humanity's preconceived notion, to win their hearts from polytheism to the knowledge of the one God. (i) Their hearts had been firmly set on the sacrifice they offered to idols in all piety, as sin offerings for themselves and their salvation. And to spare them any annoyance because of their custom he was willing to divert their accustomed worship to himself, < and so > wean < them > away from it < by permitting > this practice in his name for a time, rather than in an imaginary pantheon's. Thus, at last reaching a knowledge of the one God and a secure faith in the One, they could be told, "Do I eat bulls' flesh or drink the blood of goats?"[202] and, "Did ye offer unto me sacrifice in the wilderness forty years, O house of Israel?"[203]

Though in fact many sacrifices were offered then. (k) (This was said) to show that they never offered them to him, though he surely accepted them, and they offered in his name. But he accepted them because of their inherited usage in such matters, till he could undermine it by drawing them from their customary worship of many gods to the One, and they would then learn from the One that he did not need sacrifices, and does not need them. (l) And he would at last remove the entire reason for the sacrifices through the incarnation of Christ himself, when the one

---

[198] Jerem. 6:20.
[199] Jerem. 7:21-23.
[200] Cf. Lev. 22:18-19.
[201] Cf. Lev. 5:17-18 and 4:13-14.
[202] Ps. 49:13.
[203] Amos 5:25.

sacrifice, the sacrifice of Christ, had fulfilled all the previous ones. For "As our Passover, Christ is sacrificed,"[204] as scripture says. For this Sacrifice, Passover and teaching the Law served as paedagogue; for by its typification it guided and restored them to the more perfect teaching.

Scholion 11 and 19.   "A man ought not to have long hair, forasmuch as he is the image and glory of God."

Elenchus 11 and 19.   The apostle not only declares man God's image, but God's glory as well. And by representing the hair as physical—for it grows specifically on the body, not on the soul—he declares that this creature is therefore not alien to the good God, (and does so) by acknowledging things from the Old Testament which are fulfilled in the New.

Scholion 12 and 20.   "But God hath mixed the body."

Elenchus 12 and 20.   If "God" has mixed the body, the apostle is preaching no other God than the actual one. And if he confesses that "God" has mixed the body with its members, he knows no other "God" than the Demiurge, who is himself good, creator and just, the maker of all. One of all these works of his is man, who has been well mixed by him with his members.

Scholion 13 and 21.   Marcion has erroneously added the words, "on the Law's account," < after > "Yet in the church I had rather speak five words with my understanding."

(a) Elenchus 13 and 21.   Thus the languages too are a favor bestowed by the Spirit. But what sort of languages does the apostle mean? < He says, "languages in the church," > to show < those who > preened themselves on the sounds of Hebrew, which are well and wisely diversified in every expression, in various complex ways—on the pretentious kind of Greek, moreover, the speaking of Attic, Aeolic and Doric— < that God does not allow merely one language in the church. That was the assumption > of some of those responsible for the alarms and factions among the Corinthians, to whom the Epistle was sent.

(b)   And yet Paul agreed that to speak Hebrew and teach the Law is < a favor > of the Spirit. Moreover, to put down the other, pretentious forms of Greek, he said he spoke with tongues more than all of them because he was an Hebrew of Hebrews and had been brought up at the feet of Gamaliel; and he regards the learning of these Hebrews as praiseworthy, and < suggests > that it is a favor bestowed by the Spirit. Thus, in writing of it to Timothy, he said, "For from thy youth thou hast known the sacred learning."[205]

---

[204] 1 Cor. 5:7.
[205] 2 Tim. 3:15.

(c) But in addition he claimed the same <as against> the pupils of the Greek poets and orators, and he also said, "I speak with tongues more than ye all,"[206] to show that he was better versed in the Greek education as well. (d) Even his style shows that he was educated, since Epicureans and Stoics could not withstand him <when he preached the Gospel with wisdom at Athens.> They were defeated by his learned reading of the inscription on the altar, "To the unknown God," which he read in its literal form, and immediately gave in paraphrase as, "Whom ye ignorantly worship, him declare I unto you."[207] (e) And again, he said, "A prophet of their own hath said, Cretans are always liars, evil beasts, slow bellies."[208] He meant Epimenides, an ancient philosopher who erected the idol in Crete. Callimachus the Libyan also applied this testimony to himself by quoting Callimachus and falsely saying of Zeus:

> The men of Crete are liars alway, Lord;
> 'Twas men of Crete that built thy tomb, yet thou
> Didst never die—thy life is everlasting!

(f) And yet you see how the holy apostle says of languages, "Yet in the church I had rather explain five words with my understanding," that is, "with the translation." A prophet, says Paul, benefits his hearers with the prophecy when he brings to light what he has already been taught in the Holy Spirit. And I <wish> to speak (he says) so that the church may hear and be edified, and not to edify myself with the boast of Greek and Hebrew which I know, instead of edifying the church with the language which it understands.

(g) But you added, "on the Law's account," Marcion, as though the apostle meant, "I wish <to speak> (no more than) five words in church on the Law's account." Shame on you, you second Babylon and new rabble of Sodom! How long will you confound the languages? How long will you attack persons you cannot harm? You are trying to violate angelic powers by expelling the words of the truth from the church and telling the holy Lot, "Bring the men out!"[209]

(h) And yet your assault is an assault on yourself. You will not expel the words of the truth, but you will strike yourself blind and pass your life in utter darkness—fumbling for the door and not finding it, till the sun rises and you see the day of judgment, on which the fire will confront your falsehood also. For this is waiting for you, when you see. (i) "On

---

[206] 1 Cor. 14:18.
[207] Acts 17:23.
[208] Tit. 1:12.
[209] Gen. 19:5.

the Law's account'' is not in the apostle, and this is a fiction of your own. But even were the apostle to say, ''on the Law's account,'' he would say it, with his own Lord, not to destroy the Law but to fulfil it.

Scholion 14 and 22. ''In the Law it is written, With men of other tongues and other lips will I speak unto this people.''

(a) Elenchus 14 and 22. ''If the Lord had not fulfilled the things that had been said earlier in the Law, what need would there be for the apostle to mention things from the Law which are fulfilled in the New Testament? Thus the Savior showed that it was he himself who had spoken in the Law even then, and had threatened them with separation by saying, ''Therefore was I grieved with this generation and said, They do always err in their hearts, and I sware that they shall not enter into my rest.''[210] For the same reason he promised to speak to them through men of other tongues—as he indeed did, and they would not enter. (b) For we find him telling his disciples, ''Unto you are given the mysteries of the kingdom, but unto them in parables, that seeing they may not see,''[211] and so on. Hence the Old Testament sayings everywhere fulfilled in the New are enough to show anyone that the two Testaments are not compositions of two different Gods, but of the same God.

Scholion 15 and 23. ''Let your women keep silence in the church; For it is not permitted unto them to speak, but they are commanded to be under obedience, as also saith the Law.''

(a) Elenchus 15 and 23. If God's holy apostle enjoins good order on God's holy church on the Law's authority, then the Law from which he took the good order is not disorderly or foreign to God when it subordinates wife to husband. For this also commended itself to Paul when he legislated for the church, as he says, ''as also saith the Law.''

(b) And where did the Law say so, but when God said to Eve directly, ''Thy resort shall be to thy husband, and he shall rule over thee?''[212] For even though it said so in other passages as well, that was the first. (c) Now if the wife was subordinated to the husband by God's ordinance from then on—and if the apostle subordinates her accordingly, and not in contradiction to the God who made husband and wife—by giving the same commandment the apostle shows decisively that he is the lawgiver of the same God to whom both the Law and the whole Old Testament belongs. He shows that the New Testament is this God's as well—that is, the two Testaments, which then and now subordinated wife to husband for the sake of a godly order equivalent (in both).

---

[210] Ps. 94:10-11.
[211] Mark 4:11-12.
[212] Gen. 3:16.

Scholion 16 and 24. On resurrection of the dead: "Brethren, I make known unto you the Gospel which I preached unto you." Also, "If Christ be not raised, it is vain," and so on. "So we preach, and so ye believed... that Christ died, and was buried, and rose again on the third day... When this mortal shall have put on immortality, then shall be brought to pass the saying that is written, Death is swallowed up in victory."

(a) Elenchus 16 and 24. "Brethren, I make known unto you the Gospel which I preached unto you." If he has preached it and is making it known again, it is not a different Gospel or a different knowledge, subsequent to the one knowledge and the one Gospel. This is one throughout the four Gospels and the apostles—to shame Marcion who has come so many years later, after the time of Hyginus, the ninth bishop of Rome following the perfecting of the apostles Peter and Paul.[213] (b) Hence, since he knew by the Holy Spirit that Marcion and his kind would bend the road in spite of its good foundation, the same holy apostle shored it up by saying, "Though we, or an angel, preach any other Gospel unto you than that which ye have received, let him be accursed."[214] (c) This is why he no longer said, "I am preaching the Gospel to you," but, "I am making the Gospel known to you"—a Gospel which is not different but is the one I have preached to you already, and of which I now remind you. "I am making it known to you for the same reason that I preached it to you, if you hold fast to it, unless you have believed in vain." For unless you hold it fast as I preached it to you, you have become believers in vain without it."

(d) "For I preached to you that Christ died for our sins according to the scriptures." Not according to a myth, or according to the teaching of those who will take it upon themselves to say what is not in scripture. For of themselves the Jews say he has not risen; and Marcion and the rest, that he suffered and was buried in appearance. But I assure you of (Christ's resurrection) in accordance with the scriptures.

(e) For he adds immediately, "So we preached, and so ye believed, that Christ died, and was buried, and rose the third day;" and in the same breath, "If the dead rise not, then is not Christ raised. And if Christ be not risen, then is our preaching vain." (f) And after all this, "For this mortal must put on immortality, and this corruptible must put on incorruption."[215] And he did not say that this mortal contains immortality, or that this corruptible contains incorruption, but that the mortal

---

[213] Cf. Iren. III.4.2-3.
[214] Gal. 1:8.
[215] 1 Cor. 15:53.

and corruptible put on immortality and incorruption. (g) But what is
"mortal," if not the body, which does not merely contain immortality,
but is fit for immortality and will put in on? And this, not by the discar-
ding of the body and the assumption of immortality by the soul which
does not die, but by the donning of immortality by the mortal and of incorruption by the corruptible, that is by the body.

For death and temporary decay are the body's lot because of the
dissolution inflicted on it by Adam's disobedience. (h) But since Paul is
speaking of the good offices to be performed for the body, he points to
their coming fulfilment with his promise and says, "Then shall be
brought to pass the saying that is written, Death is swallowed up in victory." This means the resurrection of the dead which will take place at
that time. For death was partly swallowed up by the resurrection of
Christ and those who arose with him—"For many bodies of the saints
arose and went into the holy city,"[216] as the Gospel says. But when it
disappears altogether from everyone, then it will be swallowed up in
victory.

From the Second Epistle to the Corinthians. This stands third in Marcion but third in a different way, since in his canon Galatians is placed
first.

Scholion 1 and 25.   "For all the promises of God have their Yea in
him; therefore through him we utter the Amen to God."

(a) Elenchus 1 and 25.   Open your eyes, Marcion, and be saved! But
if you no longer can—you are dead, after all—let your dupes open their
eyes and escape from you as from a dreadful serpent which injures any
who come near it. (b) For if "All the promises of God have their Yea in
him," but the apostle knows God's promises through the Law and the
prophets, then the Yea of the promises' fulfilment was surely confirmed
in Christ. (c) Hence Christ is not foreign to the ancient Law and the
prophets, or to the God who spoke in the Law and has fulfilled his promises in Christ!

Nor is Christ opposed to the God who has given the Law and the
prophets. (d) For since the promises which were given become Yea in
him, says Paul, God also secures his Amen through him for the same
reason. For it is God the Father who promised but Christ who confirms,
and the Amen † proper is secured by him in those who are confirmed by
his promise, and who have recognized his Father as the God who spoke
in the Law and has given deliverance, in the Gospel, to those who
believe. It is they who say, through Christ who himself says it, "Yea,
Father, for so it seemed good in thy sight."[217]

---

[216] Matt. 27:52-53.
[217] Matt. 11:26.

Scholion 2 and 26.   "For we preach not ourselves, but Christ Jesus the Lord, and ourselves your servants through Jesus. For it is God who said, Out of darkness shall light shine."

(a) Elenchus 2 and 26.   The apostles do not preach themselves, but Christ Jesus, as Lord. Therefore there can be no sect or church named for the apostles. We have never heard of Petrians, Paulians, Bartholomaeans, or Thaddaeans; from the first we have heard one message, of all the apostles, (b) which proclaims not themselves but Christ Jesus as Lord. This is why they all gave one name to the church—not their own name but the name of their Lord Jesus Christ, since they were first called Christians at Antioch. This is the sole catholic church, with no < name > but Christ's. It is a church of Christians—not Christs but Christians, since Christ is one, and they are named Christians after the one Christ.

(c)   But all < the sects grew up > subsequently to this church and its messengers. They < are > no longer of the same character, < but > from their descriptive names of Manichaeans, Simonians, Valentinians and Ebionites, it is plain that they are < foreign to it >. You are one of these too, Marcion, and your dupes are given your name because you preached yourself, not Christ.

(d)   He says next, "For God who said, Out of darkness light shall shine." But which "God" if not the One, who brought light out of darkness in the prophet? That is, instead of human unbelief and ignorance he caused light and knowledge to shine in our hearts in Christ. We were once gentile idolaters but < have > now < come to know > the God who promised to shine his light in the world in the prophet, for he is not foreign to the Old and New Testaments. I keep trying to convince you of this, Marcion, from the written remains of the Gospel which you have in your possession, and not let you fool me.

Scholion 3 and 27.   "We, having the same Spirit of faith, also believe and therefore speak." But he excised "according as it is written."

(a) Elenchus 3 and 27.   Whatever you try, you will get no opening. Even if you excise "according as it is written," the conformity of the expression previously written (with what we find here) is evident. (b) After, "I believed, and therefore have I spoken," the apostle promptly added something just like it and said, "We, having the same Spirit of faith, likewise believe and therefore speak." (c) But it is plain to everyone that the line beginning, "I believed < and therefore have I spoken >"* is written in the Hundred Fifteenth Psalm, which has the Alleluia superscription, and is part of David's roll and one of his prophecies. (d) So the apostle took the wording of this and, because he was one of the apostles, said likewise, "Therefore we also believe and speak." (He said, not "Therefore *I* believed and spoke," but, "*We* believe, therefore we speak," to associate himself with the other apostles.)

(e)   And he says "having the same Spirit" to show that the Spirit which spoke in David is the same Spirit which is in the apostles. David in his day prophesied by this Spirit's inspiration and believed. The apostles too believe and speak in this Spirit.

(f)   But the injustice and, so to say, the greed of <the scum's> sick fancies is great. For when Paul maintains that the Spirit is one and the same, how can Marcion's stupidity venture to say that there was one Spirit then and another in the apostles, if it admits that the holy apostle has said this!

Scholion 1 and 28.   "As many as have sinned without law shall also perish without law; and as many as have sinned in the Law shall be judged by the Law. For not the hearers of the Law are just before God, but the doers of the Law shall be justified."

(a) Elenchus 1 and 28.   If any who sinned without law will also perish without law, then the Law contributes to one's salvation if it is kept, and does not permit those who keep it to perish. And if those who sinned by law will be judged by law, then the Law is judge of the transgressors. It is not a Law of destruction but of righteous judgment, since its judgment of the transgressors is holy.

(b)   "For not the hearers of the Law are just before God, but the doers of the Law shall be justified." If, when the Law is kept, it justifies the keeper, then the Law because of which the law-abiding are pronounced righteous, is not unjust or evil.

(c)   The Law is also the source of the faith in Christ which it prophesies. Without him no one will be justified. And again, no one can be justified in him by believing contrary to the Law's prophetic testimony. For Christ is the fulfillment of the Law—as the apostle says, "Christ is the fulfillment of the Law for righteousness,"[218] showing that there can be no righteousness without the Law and Christ. (d) For Jews, who have not received Christ, will not be justified without Christ. Neither will you, Marcion, since you deny the Law.

Scholion 2 and 29.   "Circumcision verily profiteth, if thou keep the Law; but if thou be a breaker of the Law, thy circumcision is made uncircumcision."

Elenchus 2 and 29.   If the holy apostle declares that circumcision will be useful, who can cast blame on what is useful without becoming like the serpent? For you are like the serpent, Marcion; it too reversed what God had said and misled Eve by saying, "Ye shall not surely die."[219]

(b)   For Paul linked Law with circumcision, demonstrated circumcision's appropriateness to the Law, and declared it to be the ordinance of

---

[218] Cf. Rom. 10:4.
[219] Gen. 3:4.

the same God who had once given circumcision and the Law for our assistance. And when Christ is believed on its authority, he enables the believers to say and do what is perfect.

Scholion 3 and 30. "Which hast the form of knowledge and of the truth in the Law."

Elenchus 3 and 30. If knowledge has a form, if a thing's nature is apparent from its form, and if the apostles and their disciples, who have the knowledge and the truth, know from the form of the Law that they have its nature—that is, knowledge and truth—then the Law is not foreign to the knowledge and the truth. For the messengers of the truth came to know the knowledge and truth through their form in the Law.

Scholion 4 and 31. "For when we were yet without strength, in due time Christ died for the ungodly.

(a) Elenchus 4 and 31. "Yet" and "died" are not significant of appearance but of truth. What need to say "yet," if Christ were an appearance? Christ could have appeared in semblance at any time, then and now, and "while we were yet without strength" need not be said. (b) From "yet" his death then <is evident>, (a death) <by which he paid the price for us> and justified us by dying, so that he has no further need to die. For he died once for sinners, and need not die any more on his own account.

Scholion 5 and 32. "Wherefore the Law is holy, and the commandment holy, and just, and good."

Elenchus 5 and 32. Paul assents to the holiness of the Law and to the commandment in it. And by calling this commandment holy, and just, and good, he has certified it with three witnesses—to expose you, Marcion, and teach us that it is the Law of the holy One whose commandment is also holy, and who is himself the holy and good (God). (b) Therefore, since the commandment is a good God's commandment, it is called good. Since it is a holy God's, it is called holy. Since it is a just God's, it is called a just commandment. For he who <proclaims it> then and now—he who is holy, just and good—is one. Therefore his commandment then and now, in the Law and the New Testament, is also holy, just, and good.

Scholion 6 and 33. "That the requirement of the Law might be fulfilled in us."

Elenchus 6 and 33. If the requirement of the Law is fulfilled in the apostles and in us, Marcion, how dare you call the Law foreign to God's apostles, who are justified because of their fulfilment of the Law?

Scholion 7 and 34. "For Christ is the end of the Law for righteousness to everyone that believeth."

(a) Elenchus 7 and 34.   If Christ has come for righteousness to all who believe, you Jews will not be perfected through standing by the Law, unless you believe and accept the Christ who has come to sojourn with us. The Law cannot be fulfilled unless Christ fulfils it by his coming. (b) But neither can you be saved in Christ, Marcion, since you reject the first principle and root of the proclamation, which is the Law. For Christ is known from it, and perfects him who does not despise the Law as foreign to Christ.

Scholion 8 and 35.   "He that loveth his neighbor hath fulfilled the Law."

Elenchus 8 and 35.   If the Law is fulfilled by the love of our neighbors, then the Law, which commands the love of our neighbors, is not foreign to Christ, and to God the Father of our Lord and God Jesus Christ. For God is love, and all that he proclaims is always proclaimed alike, both then and now, in the Old Testament and the New.

Since Marcion has everything from the fifth Epistle, <First> Thessalonians, in a distorted form—it stands fifth in Marcion, but is the eighth Epistle in The Apostle—I cite nothing from it.

Since Second Thessalonians, the sixth Epistle in Marcion but the ninth in The Apostle, was similarly distorted by Marcion himself, again I cite nothing from it.

(I cite) the following passages of Ephesians, the seventh Epistle in Marcion, but the fifth in The Apostle:

Scholion 1 and 36.   "Remember that ye, being in time past gentiles, who are called uncircumcision by that which is called the circumcision in the flesh made by hands; that at that time ye were without Christ, being aliens from the commonwealth of Israel, and strangers from the covenants of promise, having no hope, and without God in the world. But now in Christ Jesus, ye who sometimes were far off are made nigh by the blood of him. For he is our peace, who hath made of both one," and so on.

(a) Elenchus 1 and 36.   "Remembering" indicates time. "They who are called by that which is called" indicates the types of the real things. "In the flesh" is said of the type that waits in the flesh for the time of the Spirit, which will manifest the more perfect things instead of the type. (b) For without Christ the uncircumcised had been alienated from the commonwealth of Israel, and were strangers to covenant and promise. Their people had no hope but were without God in the world, as is shown by the words of the apostle.

(c)   But you can neither see nor hear, Marcion, or you would realize how many good things the holy apostle says the Law helped secure for those who had lived by the Law at that time. "For in Christ Jesus ye who were once afar off <have> now <been made> nigh through his blood. For he is our peace, who hath made of both one." (d) But if he made both one, and if he did not destroy the one and establish the other, then that which came first is not foreign to him and he did not separate the second from the first. He gathered them both into one, not loosely or in (mere) appearance, but visibly by his blood, as the apostle's sound teaching suggests.

Scholion 2 and 37. "Wherefore he saith, Awake thou that sleepest, and arise from the dead, and Christ shall give thee light."

(a) Elenchus 2 and 37. Where did the apostle get "Wherefore he saith" but, obviously, from the Old Testament? This is in the story of Elijah. But where did Elijah come from? Surely, he was one of the prophets who lived by the Law, and he comes from the Law and the Prophets. (b) Now if "Awake thou that sleepest and arise from the dead, and Christ shall give thee light" was a prophecy of Christ, it had been fulfilled in the first instance through Lazarus and the others—though they themselves were doubtful of it. (Mary and Martha said, "Already he stinketh, for he hath been dead four days;"[220] and the friends of the ruler of the synagogue said, "Trouble not the master any further,"[221] and the Master himself said, "Fear not; she is not dead, but sleepeth.")[222]

(c) For from that time on the Gospel said plainly that resurrection would come through Christ, and to show his capability (of this), showed the power of the ease (with which he brings it). For as it is easy for a man to raise, not a dead person but a sleeper, with a call, so Christ can say, "Lazarus, come forth!"[223] with the utmost readiness, or "Qumi, qumi, talitha," "Get up, child!"[224] (d) From these <plain> and palpable demonstrations (one can see that) his words meant the call of us former sleepers from our dead works and heavy slumber; <and> that it is Christ who raises us, and gives us light by his call. This made the second correspondence (with the prophecy). (e) But the final and universal expectation (will be fulfilled) when the same Christ who says, "I am the resurrection,"[225] calls all men, raises them body and soul, and enlightens them at his coming advent.

Scholion 3 and 38. "For this cause shall a man leave his father and mother, and shall be joined unto his wife, and they two shall be one flesh," minus the phrase, "unto his wife."

---

[220] John 11:39.
[221] Luke 8:49.
[222] Luke 8:52.
[223] John 11:43.
[224] Mark 5:41.
[225] John 11:25.

Elenchus 3 and 38. Even if you falsify the phrase "<unto his> wife,"
Marcion, it has been shown many times that what is in the Law is not
foreign to the teachings of the apostle. For the whole of your knavery will
be apparent from the words, "They shall be one flesh."

From the Epistle to the Colossians, the eighth Epistle in Marcion but
the seventh in The Apostle

Scholion 1 and 39. "Let no man therefore judge you in meat, or in
drink, or in respect of an holyday, or of the new moon and sabbath days,
which are a shadow of things to come."

(a) Elenchus 1 and 39.   A shadow is cast only by a body, Marcion,
and nothing can be a body if it casts no shadow. (b) Therefore, by the
remains of the truth of the sacred scriptures which you still preserve, your
dupes should be convinced that the ordinances of those times were not
foreign to the good things to be revealed. They were temporary provisions about food and drink, and were concerned with festivals, new
moons and sabbaths. (c) These were the shadows of those good things.
And by these shadows we have apprehended the body of the good things
now present, which were foreshadowed in the Law but fulfilled in Christ.

The Epistle to Philemon, number nine,

(a)   for this is its placement in Marcion; but in The Apostle it comes
last. In some copies, however, it comes thirteenth before Hebrews, which
is fourteenth. Other copies have the Epistle to the Hebrews tenth, before
the two Epistles to Timothy, the Epistle to Titus, and the Epistle to
Philemon. (b) But all sound, accurate copies have Romans first, Marcion, and do not place Galatians first as you do. In any case I cite nothing
from this Epistle, Philemon, since Marcion has it in a completely
distorted form.

The Epistle to the Philippians, number ten,
for this is its position in Marcion, tenth and last. But in the Apostle
it stands sixth. I likewise make no selections from it, since in Marcion
it is distorted.

This concludes Marcion's arrangement <of the> remains of the sayings and subject which he preserves from Luke's Gospel and The Apostle. From it I have selected the parts of the material he retains which are
against him, and placed the refutations next to them. But in his own
Apostolic Canon, as he called it, he also added Scholion 1 and 40 of the
so-called Epistle to the Laodiceans: "(There is) one Lord, one faith, one
baptism, one God and Father of all, who is above all, and through all,
and in all."

(a) Elenchus 1 and 40. You have also gathered these witnesses against
yourself, Marcion, in agreement with Ephesians, from the so-called Epistle to the Laodiceans. We may thus understand your own scripture by

reading it at the end of the book, and, by finding out about you, see through your strange conceptions, the three first principles with no beginnings which are different from each other. (b) For the holy apostle's subject and authenticated preaching are not of that sort, but are different from your fabrication. (c) He clearly meant, "(There is) one Lord, one faith, one baptism, one God, the same Father of all, the same above all, the same through all and in all"—through the Law and the prophets, and in all the apostles and their successors.

13,1 This is my <arrangement> (of the material). I preface it in the passages above, which were selected from the scripture that is still preserved in Marcion's own Bible. Anyone considering the selection of it must be awestruck at the dispensations of <the> bountiful God! (2) If every matter is attested and established by three witnesses, how has God granted me here, by his dispensation, to put a sheer seventy-eight witnesses from the Gospel together, as I said, and forty from The Apostle? (3) And these are preserved in Marcion to this day and are <not> disputed, so that there are 118 altogether, and all disputing Marcion's own view—as though they disputed it in the person of the Lord's name with the eighteen, and in the name of the blessing on its right with the hundred.[226] (4) And in addition <he is refuted> in another, extra testimony, <the one> outside of the Gospel and The Apostle. For the utterly wretched Marcion did not see fit to quote this one from Ephesians, but from Laodiceans which is not in The Apostle. (5) Since among his many failures the oaf foolishly does not read these testimonies, he pathetically does not see his overthrow, though it is acknowledged every day.

13,6 And no one need be surprised at this. Since he professed to have some of the Gospel and Apostle, how could he help preserving at least a few words of scripture? (7) Since sacred scripture's whole body, as it were, is alive, what dead limb could he find in agreement with his opinion, to represent as a falsehood against the truth? (8) He amputated many of the limbs, as it were, and mutilated and falsified them, but retained a few. But the very limbs he retained are still alive, and cannot be killed. They have the life of their meaning, even if, in his canon, they have been cut off in innumerable small pieces.

14,1 But after all this I recall further that some of these Marcionites, who have blundered into an abyss of blasphemy and been driven entirely mad by their own devilish teaching, are even prepared to give a bad name to the heavenly generation of the Lord whom they barely saw fit

---

[226] ιη, or 18 = Jesus. ἀμήν = 99, but if the additional text from Laodiceans is added to this, we arrive at 100.

to mention by name—and that in an impudent way, by expressing a different objection to his divinity. (2) For some have ventured to do that, as I said, and are not ashamed to call the Lord himself the son of the evil one. Others disagree, but call him the son of the judge and demiurge. (3) <But> since he has more compassion and is good, he has abandoned his father below—the demiurge, say some, others say the evil one—and has taken refuge on high with the good God in realms ineffable, and come over to his side. (4) But Christ has been sent into the world by the good God, and has come as his own father's adversary to annul all the legislation of his real father—whether this is the God who spoke in the Law, or the God of evil whom they rank as the third principle. (For they explain him variously, as I said, one calling him the demiurge, another the evil one.)

15,1   But to anyone with sense this is plainly the thought and teaching of an evil spirit. There is no need to defend ourselves on this subject or provide an argument against Marcion, who has completely forgotten his own salvation. (2) Any intelligent person can detect his blasphemous nonsense and impudent work of destruction. (3) But as it is not my custom to leave room for thorns, but to hew them out with God's sword—which scripture calls '' <sharper> than any two-edged sword, piercing even to the dividing asunder of soul and spirit, of joints and marrow''[227]—I do not mind saying a few things even to this.

16,1   In the first place, if an evil person has produced a good one, the Marcionite reckoning of the first principles cannot be maintained. If Christ's father is evil—perish the thought, he is good!—but if he is evil, he is just as capable as his son of a change of heart.

16,2   But otherwise. Suppose that the Only-begotten really came to save mankind, and bring a thief to Paradise, call a publican from a tax office to repentance, cure a whore of fornication for anointing his feet. And suppose further that, because of his goodness, compassion and mercy, he does <other> good things as well. (3) Far more should he have taken this pity on his own father and made him well first, to give a perfect demonstration of perfect goodness by converting his father first, from pity for his father. As scripture says, ''to do good first unto them who are of the household of faith''[228]—how much more, have mercy on our own fathers!

16,4   But to the explanation, and in rebuttal of Marcion, I add yet another point. If Christ is the son of the one God and yet took refuge with the other, the other will not accept him as trustworthy. (5) If he did not

---

[227] Heb. 4:12.
[228] Gal. 6:10.

keep faith with his own father, on the basis of past performance he will not be believed by the other either.

16,6 But again, otherwise. Will you accuse the good God once more, Marcion—of sending Christ in desperation, because he could not save those whom he meant to save, and on whom he had mercy through Christ? (7) For if Christ had not taken refuge with the God on high as Marcion tells it, the good God would have had no one to send—if Christ's father had not come into conflict with his own son, as Marcion says.

16,8 But also, otherwise. If Christ is the son of the demiurge, and yet is opposed to the creation and his father's work, as the opponent of his father's disposition he could have destroyed mankind as soon as he came into the world, to get rid of his own father's work. (9) Or again, once he had received the power to cure, heal and save, he should have shown the work of mercy on his own father before all, and begun by persuading his father to become like him. Thus, after he had been good to himself and his father both, one and the same goodness would have become <the cause> of men's salvation.

16,10 But there is no truth in Marcion's absurd, fictitious reckoning. There are no three first principles, there is no different father of Christ, there is no offspring of wickedness—perish the thought! (11) He says, "I am in the Father, and the Father in me."[229] And if his claim to have a father is fictitious, his falsely alleged father cannot be in him or he in the father. (12) He, however, who truthfully teaches that his actual Father is always good, that he is always God and the creator of all, and that he is in him and with him, gives the whole threat against Marcion with the words, "He that honoreth not the Son as he honoreth the Father, the wrath of God abideth on him."[230] (13) But I have shown already by many testimonies that the one true God, the Father of our Lord Jesus Christ, is good and the begetter of good, love and the begetter of love, fount of life and the begetter of a fount of life—"With thee is the well of life,"[231] says the scripture. He is truth and the begetter of truth, light and the begetter of light, life and the begetter of life—without beginning, eternally, and not in time. And Marcion's imposture is entirely refuted.

16,14 Since this is the case, and since by God's inspiration I have accomplished the cheat's downfall though much authentic proof, let us move to the rest in turn—since this sect has been trodden underfoot like a big asp, through the truthful teaching of the Savior who said, "I have

---

[229] John 14:10.
[230] Cf. John 5:23; 3:36.
[231] Ps. 35:10.

given you power to tread on serpents and scorpions, and over all the power of the adversary.''[232] And let us set ourselves to investigate the futilities of the others and refute them, calling on God for aid in all things.

43.

Against Lucianists.[1] *Number twenty-three, but forty-three of the series*

1,1 Lucian is one of the ancients—not the modern one born during Constantine's old age, whom the Arians, if you please, reckon a martyr. There was also such a Lucian, the recent one I mean, and he was Arian. I shall speak of him later, in my refutation of the Arians; now I am discussing the ancient Lucian. (2) For he was a companion of Marcion's, formed his own society by detaching it from Marcion, and headed a sect. Ancient Lucianists, as they were called, derived from him.[2]

1,3 His doctrines are just like Marcion's; but I have been told, and my impression of him is that < he has only the New Testament. I do not know, however, whether he tampers with the Gospel like Marcion. > For to be honest, as these people were ancient and were snuffed out in short order, it has been difficult for me to track them down. What I do know, in part, of Lucian's doctrines is this:

1,4 After establishing that the demiurge, judge and just God is one God, if you please, that the good God likewise is another, and that the evil God is another, Lucian, like Marcion, cites certain witnesses from the prophets in support of his opinion. The ones I mean are, ''Vain is he that serveth the Lord,''[3] and ''They withstood God and were delivered.''[4]

1,5 Contrary to his master's teaching he rejects matrimony altogether and practices celibacy, not for celibacy's sake but to repudiate the works of the demiurge. He teaches that people should refrain from marriage to oppose the prospering of the demiurge and creator through human procreation—''Because matrimony,'' he says, ''is a source of prosperity for the demiurge, through human procreation.''[5]

---

[232] Luke 10:19.

[1] With this Sect. cf. Hippol. Haer. VII.11; Ps.-Tert. 6.3; Orig. C. Cels. II.27; Tert. De Res. Carn. 2.

[2] Cf. Hippol. Haer. VII.11; Ps.-Tert. 6.3.

[3] Mal. 3:14.

[4] Mal. 3:15.

[5] There is a comparable polemic against marriage at Test. Tr. 29,26-30,17; Man. Ps. 179,18.

1,6 But he will be detected for the sort he is, and refuted, by the opposition I have already offered his master, whose rebuttal and refutation I have given with many arguments. The kinds and numbers of passages in which the Gospel agrees with the Old Testament. (7) How our Lord himself acknowledges that the making of the world is his work too, and that the creation belongs to his Father. As St. John says especially—to give a kind of crowning argument in a word—"In the beginning was the Word, and the Word was with God, and the Word was God. All things were made by him, and without him was not anything made that was made,"[6] and the rest.

2,1 But surely his sort of person will be demolished at once. For though he may say that he rejects marriage to avoid cooperation with the demiurge, to oppose and eliminate the things he has made here, and so avoids the work of the demiurge altogether, how can his opinion be other than irrational, easy to detect, and refutable at once? (2) For observe, the scummy charlatan solicits the loan of things to drink and eat from creation and the demiurge's handiwork of food and clothing, and simply* cannot escape these things and refrain from their use!

2,3 For since God, the Master and Creator of all, cares for all, he makes his sun rise on evil and good, he sends his rain on those who blaspheme and those who glorify him, and he nourishes all, but not by some irrational, blind decree. (4) He is patient because of his decree of vengeance at the coming judgment. And he orders all things by his own decrees and wisdom—as befits his solicitude for all—so that the repentant may receive his pardon and obtain salvation. (5) But if they persist in their blasphemous opinions and the futile beliefs God never gave them, then, after their departure when they have no more free agency, <he will punish them justly>—not, however, pass the sentence they will then receive from wrath, or inflict their coming <punishments> as though in anger. (6) He foretold all this because of his divinity, which has no emotions! It will be because of the <wickedness> with which each <unrighteous person>, who has done something to his own harm, has become accessory to his own <condemnation>. God is not to blame for our defection, and the judgment against us which will result.

2,7 So at all points Lucian too will be detected as part and parcel of the sects before and after him, and as one of the sons of perdition. The truth will show this, and the light of the Gospel which brightly illumines the whole world, and in truth saves the sons of the true faith.

2,8 Therefore—as though we had killed a snake quickly with a short cudgel as it peeped † from its hole, <and> left it dead—let us go on to the rest as promised, with God's help for the establishment of his truth.

---

[6] John 1:1;3.

44.

Against Apelleans.[1] *Number twenty-four, but forty-four of the series*

1,1   After this Lucian comes Apelles—not the saint whom the holy apostle[2] commends but a different person, the founder of the Apelleans. He too was Lucian's own fellow-student and Marcion's disciple—like a thick growth of offshoots from one root of many thorns!

1,2   Apelles' doctrines are different from the others'.[3] In rebellion against his own teacher and the truth, to gather his own school of misguided followers, he propounds doctrines like the following. (3) He claims that this is not how it has been, and Marcion is wrong—to make it evident that stupidity altogether refutes itself, and wickedness is shattered within itself and invites its own refutation. But the truth is always steadfast and needs no assistance. It is self-authenticating, and always established in the sight of the true God.

1,4[4]   Now this Apelles and his school claim that there are not three first principles or two, as Lucian and Marcion thought. He says there is one good God, one first principle, and one power that cannot be named. Nothing here in this world is of any concern to this one God—or first principle, if you prefer. (5) However, this same holy and good God on high made one other God.[5] And the God who was created as another God created all things—heaven, earth, and everything in the world. (6) But he proved not to be good, and his creatures not to be well made. Because of his inferior intelligence, his <creatures> have been <badly> created.

1,7   But who will accept such statements instead of laughing at such wasted effort? By holding an opinion of this sort he will prove to be doubly inconsistent. (8) And so I shall say to him, as though he were here, "Tell me, Mister! You will either admit, Apelles, that God was unaware of the future when he created a God who, you claim, has made his handiwork badly—or else he foreknew that the God he was creating would turn out like that, and he made him for this reason, to avoid being the one responsible for his bad creations. (9) In any case the God on high must be the demiurge himself, since he made the one God who has made everything. The God who has made the creatures cannot be the cause of

[1] With this Sect Cf. Hippol. Haer. VII.38; Ps.-Tert. 6.4-6; Eus. H. E. V.13.2; Tert. De Anima 23.3; 36.3; De Carn. Chr. I.6-8; Adv. Marc. III.11; IV.17; Praescr. 30; 33; 34; De Res. Carn. 2; 5.
[2] Cf. Rom. 16:10.
[3] Cf. Orig. C. Cels. II.2; Tert. De Carn. Chr. 1; Adv. Marc. IV.17.11.
[4] With 1,4-6 cf. Hippol. Haer. VII.38.3; Ps.-Tert. 6.4; Tert. De Carn. Chr. 1; 6; 8.
[5] Cf. Tert. Praescr. 34; Corp. Herm. X.10; Ascl. 16.

them; this must be the God on high who made the creator, and is himself the demiurge of all.

2,1 But he says that the son of the good God on high, Christ, has come in the last time, as has his Holy Spirit, for the salvation of those who come to the knowledge of him. (2) And he has not appeared in semblance at his coming, but has really taken flesh. Not from Mary the Virgin, but he has real flesh and a body— <though> not from a man's seed or a virgin woman. (3) He did get real flesh, <but> in the following way. On his way from heaven he came to earth, says Apelles, and assembled his own body from the four elements.[6]

2,4 And why is he not pressed further too, till it is seen that his wickedness agrees with what the ancient Greek poets thought about this nonsense? For he claims, as they did, and even more foolishly, that the Savior framed his own body. (5) <He took> the dry parts of it from the dry element, the warm ones from the warm element, the wet ones from the wet and the cool from the cool, and so fashioning his own body he has appeared in the world in reality, and taught us the knowledge on high, (6) to despise the demiurge and disown his works. And he showed us which sayings are actually his and in which scripture, and which come from the demiurge.[7] "Thus," Apelles tells us, "he said in the Gospel, Be ye trusty money-changers.[8] For from all of scripture I select what is helpful and use it."[9]

2,7 Then, says Apelles, Christ allowed himself to suffer in that very body, was truly crucified and truly buried and truly arose, and showed that very flesh to his own disciples.[10] (8) And he dissolved that very humanity of his, apportioned its own property to each element and gave it back, warm to warm, cool to cool, dry to dry, wet to wet. And thus, after again separating the body of flesh from himself, he soared away to the heaven from which he had come.[11]

3,1 How melodramatic of people who say such things! Rather than any promises of life or kind of understanding, anyone must see that they own a mimes' workshop. (2) If Christ really destroyed the body he had taken, why would he prepare it for himself in the first place? (3) If, however, he prepared it for some use but had finished using it, he should have left it in the ground—especially since, in your view, the hope of the

---

[6] Sophia builds houses for the "fellow workers" of the Son of Light "from the elements below" at Gr. Seth 51,4-7.

[7] Cf. Hippol. Haer. VII.38; X.20; Ps.-Tert. 6.6; Ambrose De Paradiso V.28; VI.30-32; VII.38-39; Eus. H. E. V.13.2; Orig. C. Cels. V.54; In Gen. Hom. II.2.

[8] A version of this saying appears at PS 348.

[9] Cf. Hippol.Haer. VII.38.4.

[10] Cf. Hippol. Haer. VII.38.4.

[11] Cf. Apocry. Jas. 2,23-25.

resurrection of the flesh need not be realized visibly. (4) But to give himself more trouble for nothing he raised it again—framing it and yet laying it in a tomb, dissolving it and yet, like a conscientious debtor, apportioning what he had taken from it to each element!

3,5 And if he really gave each one back <what belonged to it>—that is, the cool parts to the cool and the warm parts to the warm, (and so on)—his apostles could not have seen these. Certainly not the body, which is dry! (6) For "the dry" is surely a body, flesh and bones, and "the wet' is its humors surely, and flesh dissolving into wetness. He surely showed these things to the apostles, as plainly as could be, when he discarded them.

3,7 Thus right away, when his body was buried Joseph of Arimathaea was privileged to wrap it in a shroud and lay it in a tomb. (8) And meanwhile the women could also see where the remains had been left, so that they could honor them with perfumes and fragrant oils, as (he had been honored) at the first. (9) But your lie is nowhere mentioned by one of the holy apostles, you Apelleans—it is not so. The apostles saw the two invisible men in visible form, and himself ascending to heaven and received by a shining cloud, but they did not see his remains left anywhere—there was no need for that, and it was not possible. And Apelles, and his school of Apelleans, are lying.

4,1 His doctrines concerning the rest of the flesh and so on were like his master Marcion's. He claimed that there is no resurrection of the dead; and he similarly saw fit to hold all the other doctrines that <Marcion used to teach to disparage> earthly <creatures>.[12]

4,2 But because it is silly and entirely in error, his reasoning will be demolished. Darkness will not prevail where the light is glimpsed; nor will falsehood be established when the truth is <visible>. (3) If you really have the scriptures, Apelles and your Apellean namesakes, you will find yourselves refuted from these very scriptures.

4,4 In the first place, God made man in the image of God; and the Maker of man said, "Let us make man in our image and after our likeness."[13] This is as though one turned from your erring sect to the truth—like escaping darkness and getting up when night is past—and found the light of the knowledge of God dawning on him like the sun and brighter. (5) For to anyone in his right mind it will be evident that he who said, "Let us make man," is God the Father of all. But to join him he summons the divine Word, the only-begotten Son who is ever with him, who was begotten of him without beginning and not in time—and

---

[12] Cf. Hippol. Haer. X.20.2; Ps.-Tert. 6.4; Tert. De Anima 32.3; De Carn. Chr. 8.
[13] Gen. 1:26.

his Holy Spirit at the same time, who is no stranger to him or his own Son. (6) For if the God who fashioned man—that is, who also created the world—were one God and the good God on high from whom Christ came were another, Christ would not have take a body for himself and fashioned it, thus patterning himself after the demiurge. (7) But it is plain that he himself, to whom the Father said, "Let us make man in our image and after our likeness," is man's demiurge and the world's. (8) And since the workman is identified from the one work, it will be proved that it is he who made the man then, by fashioning Adam's body from earth and making it a living soul.

4,9   Thus St. John testified in the holy Gospel, "In the beginning was the Word, and the Word was with God, and the Word was God. The same was in the beginning with God. All things were made by him, and apart from him was not anything made,"[14] and the rest. (10) But if < all things > were made in him, and were made by him, he himself fashioned Adam then. And he, again, refashioned the body from the Virgin Mary, on his own model, and at last united his whole humanity, which he had fashioned then, and which was now united in him.

4,11   But suppose he took another person's work, belonging to the God who had fashioned the clay badly and who, in your teaching, is bad. And suppose he really used the bad products that your bad maker produced. Then by his use of them, his benefit to them, and his own image, he was involved in their maker's badness. (12) This cannot be. For if he was incarnate, he has taken not merely flesh, but a soul as well. This will be evident. If not, why did he say, "I have power to take my soul and power to lay it down?"[15] Thus, by assuming the entire work that the demiurge had termed his "image," the Word assumed † humanity in its entirety and came with body and soul, and all that makes a man. (14) Now since this was the way of it your poison has altogether lost its power and your edifice with no foundation has toppled, lacking the firmness of the truth's support.

5,1   But if, besides, you take what you choose from sacred scripture and leave what you choose, you are surely presiding as its judge. You do not sit as an interpreter of the laws, but as a collector of words which were not written as you would like—true ones, but you have altered them falsely to suit your deceit, and your dupes' deceit.

5,2   But if a bad maker had really produced what is here, I mean the world, why did the good Father's emissary enter this world? And if it was to save men, then he cared for his own, and their demiurge can be none

---

14 John 1:1-3.
15 John 10:18.

other (than himself). (3) If he was not providing for his own, however, but instead encroaches on other persons' domains and saves what does not belong to him, then he is a parasite hovering about someone else's possessions. Or he is a conceited person, who wants things that are not his in order to appear better than their creator in the other persons' possessions which he tries to save. And thus he cannot be trustworthy.

5,4   Or from what you say, scum, he is an incompetent, and lacking his own creation he covets the possessions of others, and he tries to seize them by helping himself, from someone else's stock, to souls which do not belong to him and his Father.

5,5   If the souls are his, however, and if it is evident that they have come from above, then they were sent into a good world—not a world poorly made—by your good God on high. (6) But if they were sent to serve some purpose, of which you probably give a mythological account, and were diverted to another one on their arrival—if, in other words, they were sent to do something right but accomplished something wrong—it will be evident that the God who sent them had no foreknowledge. He sent them for one purpose, and it turned out that they did something else. (7) Or again, if you say that they have not come by his will, but by the tyranny of the God who seizes them, then the inferior demiurge whom the good God created is more powerful than the good God—since he snatched the good God's property from him and put it to his own use.

5,8   How can you avoid refutation when the Savior himself says, "I have power to lay my soul down and to take it"[16]—meaning that after he took a soul he both laid it down and took it again, so that the soul is not foreign to him, and not the work of another creator? (9) And again, it will be evident that the Savior's body is good. No one good can be induced to make use of evil work. Otherwise, from partaking of the evil, he will be contaminated too, by the ill effect of the intermixture.

5,10   And tell me, what was the point of his abandoning it again after resurrection, even though he had raised it, and of apportioning it to the four elements, warm to warm, cool to cool, dry to dry, wet to wet? (11) If he raised it to destroy it again, this is surely stage business, not an honest act. But our Lord Jesus Christ raised the very thing which he had fashioned in his own image and took it with him, body with soul, and all the manhood in its entirety. (12) For he sat down with God as in the apostle's saying, "God raised him and made him sit with him in heavenly places"[17]—as the two testify who appeared to the apostles in shining

---

[16] John 10:18.
[17] Eph. 2:6.

garments, "Ye men of Galilee, why stand ye gazing up into heaven? This same Jesus, which is taken up from you into heaven, shall so come *in like manner* as ye have seen him being taken up."[18]

6,1   And long after our Savior's ascension—to deprive you of another excuse for mischief against the truth—when the Jews were stoning God's holy martyr Stephen he answered and said, "Behold, I see heaven opened, and the Son of Man standing at the right hand of the Father."[19] (2) This was to show that the body itself had truly risen with the Godhead of the Only-begotten, was wholly united with the spiritual, and was one with Godhead. (3) The sacred body itself is on high with the Godhead—altogether God, one Son, the Holy One of God seated at the Father's right hand. As the Gospels of Mark and the other evangelists put it, "And he ascended up to heaven and sat on the right hand of the Father."[20] And your trashy account, and the account of your dupes, will prove altogether worthless.

6,4   And hear the apostle say, of resurrection of the dead, "This corruptible must put on incorruption, and this mortal must put on immortality."[21] (5) For if the mortal body were not to put on immortality and the corruptible body incorruption, the Immortal would not have come to die. (But he came to) suffer in the mortal body, rise in it after the three-day sleep, and take it up in himself, united with his divinity and glory, so that his good sojourn with us would truly give us all we had hoped. He thus showed himself the pattern for us, and the pledge which allows us to hope for the full reality of life.

7,1   Since this is the case and since we have said so, why waste my time further, for refutation or any other purpose, on this wasp whose sting smarts despite his insignificance? He has broken his own sting, and the false doctrine of his imposture has been proved † untenable and trashy.

7,2   For they say that the wasp with a painful sting, which some have called a "smarting wasp," has a short poisoned sting that cannot cause great pain but is as poisonous as is possible for it to be. (3) And whenever someone goes through (the weeds) and destroys its den or house—it makes hives of a sort, like a honeycomb, in bushy weeds, and deposits its seed and begets its offspring in these. But if someone on his way through breaks into the honeycomb with a staff or club and knocks it down, as I said, the wasp, which is formidable but feeble, comes out in a rage. (4) And if it finds a rock or tree nearby, from the rage which has

---

[18] Acts 1:11.
[19] Acts 7:56.
[20] Mark 16:19.
[21] 1 Cor. 15:53.

filled it, it flies at it buzzing, darts at it and stings it. And yet it cannot harm the rock or the tree; and certainly not the man even if it bites him, except to the extent of a little pain. (5) And least of all can it hurt the rock; it breaks its sting and dies, but the rock cannot be harmed by the likes of it. (6) Thus this wasp-like creature too like a smarting wasp, which can cause a little pain, will be demolished by colliding with the rock, that is, with the truth, and breaking its sting.

7,7   But now that I have finished with this sect I proceed to the others in turn, trusting, as my hope is in God, that by God's inspiration my promise will be kept.

45.

Against Severians.[1] *Number twenty-five, but forty-five of the series*

1,1   After these comes <Severus>, who was either their contemporary or <born> about <their> time. I cannot speak of his time for certain, but they were quite close to each other. At all events, I shall give what information I have.

1,2   One Severus, the founder of the so-called Severians, arose next after Apelles. His mythological descriptions are these which I shall (now) give. (3) He too ascribes the creation about us to principalities and authorities, and says that there is a good God in some unnameable, very high heaven and world. (4) But he claims that the devil is the son of the chief archon[2] in the authorities' retinue, whom he sometimes terms Ialdabaoth and sometimes Sabaoth. This son whom he has begotten is a serpent. (5) But he was cast to earth by the power on high. After descending in the form of a serpent he went wild and lay with the earth as with a woman, and as he ejaculated the seed of its generation, the vine was begotten[3] of him.

1,6   Hence, for mythological proof of their nonsense, <he> represent<s> the roundness of the vine as its likeness to a snake, and he says that the vine is like a snake because it is rough. And the white vine is like a snake, but the black one is like a dragon. (7) And the vine's grapes are also like drops or flecks of poison, because of the globular or tapered, and entirely different, shape of each grape's curvature. (8) And for this reason it is wine that confuses men's minds, and sometimes makes them amorous,[4] sometimes drives them wild; or again, renders

---

[1] Eus. H. E. IV.29,4-5 (cf. Jer. Vir. Ill.29) makes Severus a follower of Valentinus, but reports no Severian mythology.

[2] For "first archon" see, e.g., Apocry. Jn. 10,19-20; Nat. Arc. 90,19. For Ialdabaoth see Index NHL.

[3] Cf. Orig. Wld. 109,26-29; Plutarch De Iside et Osiride 6,353B.

[4] Cf. Orig. Wld. 109,26-29.

them angry, since the body grows dim-witted from the power of the wine and the poison of this dragon. Persons of this persuasion therefore abstain from wine altogether.

2,1   They also claim, as the Archontics have, that woman is the work of Satan. Hence they say that those who have marital intercourse are doing Satan's work. (2) And moreover, one half of a man is God's, but half is the devil's. From the navel up, says Severus, man is the handiwork of God's power, but from the navel down he is the handiwork of the evil authority. (3) And this, he says, is why anything involving pleasure, madness and lust takes place below the navel. But the other sects have also made this claim.[5]

3,1   Hence Serverus is in all respects guilty of concurring with the other scum who have prepared their poisons for men. For he will be refuted easily; his rebuttal will require no very great effort. (2) The entire body is mixed with the desires that God has rightly implanted in it. I mean the desires that God has given, not for a wrong purpose but for a good use and as urgent necessity prescribes. (I am speaking of men's desire for sleep, drink, clothing, and all the other desires that come to us at their own pleasure and God's.) Thus I can prove that not even sexual desire is wrong. (3) It has been solemnly given for procreation and the glory of the maker of all, as seeds were given to the soil for an outpouring of an abundance of the good produce which God has created, I mean <greenery> and fruit-trees. So seeds were given to man, for the fulfilment of the commandment, "Increase, and multiply and fill the earth."[6]

4,1   Severians have certain apocrypha, I have heard, as well as the canonical books in part. They comb them just for those things that they can handle differently by combining them to suit their purpose.[7]

4,2   For anyone can see that the vine was neither engendered by a devil nor sown by a snake. How could it be, when the Lord himself testifies for it with the words, "I shall not drink of the fruit of this vine until I drink it new with you in kingdom of heaven?"[8] (3) And since—as God foreknew the evils to come—the truth, which forever sheds its beams, has already framed its words in refutation, sacred scripture everywhere foretold the rout of those who would rise against the truth. (4) Thus, in refutation of the pathetic, misguided Severus, the Lord somewhere expressly calls himself the vine and says, "I am the true

---

[5] A polemic against sexual intercourse is found passim in Th. Cont. and at Test. Tr. 29,22-30,17.

[6] Gen. 1:28.

[7] Cf. Eus. H. E. IV.29.5.

[8] Matt. 26:29.

vine.''[9] If the vine really had a bad name he would not make a comparison of the name with himself.

4,5 Moreover, in the work called the Constitution the apostles say, ''The catholic church is God's plantation and vineyard.''[10] (6) Again moreover, in giving the parable of the vineyard in the Gospel, the Lord himself says, ''A certain man that was an householder, having a vineyard, let it out to husbandmen and sent seeking fruit, and they did not give it.''[11] (7) And again moreover, ''A man that was an householder, having a vineyard, went out seeking laborers for his vineyard, both about the third hour, and the sixth, and the ninth, and the eleventh.''[12] (8) In conclusion, then, the knavery of this cheat's practice too is altogether vulnerable to a word of the truth. For even if the darkness appears in the absence of light, its disappearance will be caused by a tiny spark of its refutation.

4,9 But I have dealt summarily with this sect, since its cure is easy as I stated already, and not much effort is needed to establish the truth against it. But most of all, I also believe that it has no more adherents, except for a very few in the far north. (10) Now that I have crushed it all at once like a horrid scorpion, let me move on from this sect and investigate the rest—calling God's power to my aid that I may speak the truth and escape harm myself, particularly as I shall be giving a glimpse of such dreadful, deadly badness of doctrine.

46.

Against Tatianists.[1] Number twenty-six, but forty-six of the series

1,1 A Tatian arose after these in turn. He was either their contemporary or, again, presented the teaching of his nonsense after them. (2) At first, since he had a Greek background and education,[2] he throve in the company of Justin[3] the philosopher, a holy man dear to God, who had been converted from Samaritanism to faith in Christ. (3) This Justin was Samaritan, <but> after his conversion to Christ, a rigorous asceticism, and the exhibition of a virtuous life, he finally suffered mar-

---

[9] John 15:1.
[10] Didascalia 1.1.
[11] Matt. 21:33-35 par.
[12] Matt. 20:1-6.

[1] Sect 46 seems to be based on Iren. I.28.1. For other presentations see Hippol. Haer. VIII.16; Ps.-Tert. Haer. 7; Clem. Alex. Strom. II.232.22-24; III.81.1-3. Epiphanius may have read Tatian's *Oratio Ad Graecos*, but this is not certain.
[2] Cf. Tat. Or. 42.
[3] Cf. Iren. I.28.1.

tyrdom for Christ's sake in mature manhood at the age of thirty, and was vouchsafed a perfect crown at Rome during the prefecture of Rusticus and the reign of Hadrian.

1,4 Since Tatian had flourished with Justin he was all right at first and sound in the faith, so long as he was with St. Justin Martyr. (5) But when St. Justin died[4] it was as though a blind man in need of a guide, <who> had been abandoned by his escort, got onto a precipice in his blindness, and because of his abandonment kept falling with no one to stop him until he fell to his death. So it was with Tatian.

1,6 From what I have learned he was Syrian.[5] But originally he set up his school in Mesopotamia, about the twelfth year of Antonius, the Caesar surnamed Pius.[6] (7) For after the perfecting of St. Justin he went from Rome to the east, and while living there he fell into an evil way of thinking and introduced certain aeons of his own as in Valentinus'[7] myths, and certain first principles and emanations. (8) He did the greater part of his preaching from Antioch by Daphne to as far away as Cilicia, but, to a greater extent, in Pisidia; for the so-called Encratites have his poison and are his successors. (9) He is said to be the author of the Diatessaron,[8] which some call the Gospel According to the Hebrews.

2,1 His doctrines are the same as the ancient sects'. And in the first place, he claims that Adam cannot be saved.[9] And he preaches continence, regards matrimony as fornication and seduction,[10] and claims that marriage is no different from fornication but is the same. (2) He thus adopted his tricky mode of conduct under the pretense of continence and the continent way, like a ravening wolf putting a sheep's fleece on and misleading its dupes with the temporary disguise. (3) He has mysteries too in imitation of the holy church, but in these mysteries he uses only water.[11]

2,4 He too will fail altogether, since his preaching is without proof. (Indeed, I believe that he has been snuffed out and come to an end already, and his school as well.) For where is there not evidence to refute

---

[4] Cf. Iren. I.28.1; Ps.-Tert. Haer. 7.

[5] Cf. Clem. Alex. Strom. III.81.1; Tat. Or. 42.

[6] This is apparently a mistake for Marcus Aurelius, in whose twelfth year Eus. Chron. 206,13 (Helm) puts the recognition of Tatian's heresy.

[7] Iren. I.28.1; Hippol. Haer. VIII.16; Ps.-Tert. Haer. 7; Clem. Alex. Strom. II.238.22; III.92.1 make Tatian a Valentinian.

[8] Tatian's composition of the Diatessaron is noted at Eus. H. E. IV.28.6; Theodoret Haeret. Fab. I.20. Holl suggests that Epiphanius might have called the Diatessaron "According to the Hebrews" because it was written in Syriac.

[9] Cf. Iren. I.28.1; III.23.8; Hippol. Haer. VIII.16; Ps.-Tert. Haer. 7.

[10] Cf. Iren. I.28.1; Hippol. Haer. VIII.16; Theodoret Haeret. Fab. I.20; Jer. Adv. Jov. I.3; II.16.

[11] Cf. Theodoret Haeret. Fab. I.20.

such a man? (5) First < it must be said to him too > —as I have indicated already, and < said > to the sects which make such claims—that there cannot be many first principles giving rise to the successive products of generation. (6) Though there actually are many, it will turn out that †each of them originates from the one—from the actual < first > cause of all of them.* And there cannot be many first principles. There must be one which has been the cause of these, and everything must be referred back to the one governing principle. And the plausible-sounding speech of a person like Tatian is no good, < since it is falsehood >, not truth, and can have no plausibility. For everything that he preaches is foolish.

2,7   And if Adam cannot be saved when he is the lump, neither can any < product of > the lump be saved. For if the man who was fashioned first and came from virgin soil can have no salvation, how can the things begotten of him have salvation?

3,1   For Tatian will prove to be speaking against himself in two ways. He claims that matrimony is not of God but is fornication and uncleanness—and yet he thinks that he, a child of matrimony and born of a woman and a man's seed, can be saved! (2) In turn, then, he has demolished his own blasphemy of marriage. For if he, a child of marriage, will have salvation, then marriage is no abomination whatever he may choose to say, since it produces those who have salvation.

3,3   But if his argument that marriage is unlawful can be sustained, then all the more will Adam be saved. He is no product of marriage; he has been fashioned by the hand of the Father, Son and Holy Spirit, as was said to the Son by the holy Father himself, "Let us make man in our image and after our likeness."[12] (4) And why can Adam, whom you despair of, not be saved when, on coming into the world, our Lord Jesus Christ himself raised the dead, body and all, after their deaths—like Lazarus, and the widow's son, and the daughter of the ruler of the synagogue? (5) And if it was not he himself who fashioned Adam from earth at the beginning, why did he spit on the ground, make clay, anoint the eyes of the man born blind, and make him see—(6) to prove that he himself was his fashioner, with the Father and the Holy Spirit? And why did he use the clay to add the part that was missing from the man born blind, to the place which did not have it? He has plainly done this to repair the defective part.

3,7   But again, Tatian, if it is the Lord who both has fashioned Adam, and destroys the man he fashioned first while saving the others, how empty-headed of you! (8) If the Lord's first-fashioned was expelled from Paradise for one transgression and was subject to no little

---

[12] Gen. 1:26.

discipline—spending his life in sweat and toil, and living opposite
Paradise as a reminder of his good <life there>—then you are ascribing
powerlessness to the Lord with all your might, if he is powerless to save
the first-fashioned through his repentance at the memory.

3,9   Or if he had the power to save him but showed no mercy, <you
are ascribing cruelty to the Lord>. Why did Christ descend even to the
underworld—why did he sleep for three days after he suffered, and rise?
Where is the fulfilment of "that he might be Lord both of the dead and
living?"[13] Lord of what "living and dead" but those who require his aid,
above and below? (10) And how can the products of the lump be holy
if the lump is not holy itself, as the holy apostle says? For even of Eve
the same apostle says, "She shall be saved through childbearing, if they
continue in faith and righteousness."[14]

4,1   And much can be said about this, since anyone with wisdom can
see the obvious blasphemy, and the giddy reason, of Tatian and his Ta-
tianist namesakes. (2) I have discussed them briefly, and with the Lord's
truth and power have cured their bites, like mosquito bites, by applying
a salve of the oil of the Lord's teaching to those who have been bitten by
Tatian's arguments. For the Lord himself says, "I am not come but for
the lost sheep of the house of Israel."[15]

4,3   This is why he said in parables that a man went down from
Jerusalem to Jericho, the man he also said fell among thieves—meaning
the sheep, the one gone down from Jerusalem, fallen from the greater
glory to diminution, lured away from the one commandment of his own
shepherd, and gone astray. (4) Hence we believe that the holy Adam,
<our> father, is among the living. For his sake, and for the sake of all
of us, his descendants, Christ came to grant pardon to those who had
always known him and had not strayed from his divinity, but who were
detained in Hades for lapses into sin—pardon through repentance to
those who were still in the world, pardon through mercy and salvation
to those who were in Hades.

5,1   Strange about Tatian, when he knows—as I too have found in
the literature—that our Lord Jesus Christ was crucified on Golgotha, the
very place where Adam's body lay buried. (2) For after leaving Paradise,
living opposite it for a long while and growing old, Adam later came and
died in this place, I mean Jerusalem, and was buried there, on the site
of Golgotha. (3) This is likely how the place, which translates, "Place of
a Skull," got the name—since the shape of the place shows no likeness
to the name. (4) It is not on a peak, so that this can be interpreted as a

---

[13] Rom. 14:9.
[14] 1 Tim. 2:15.
[15] Matt. 15:24.

skull like <the> place of a head on a body. Nor is it <on> a height. (5) Nor, in fact, is it higher than the other "places". Opposite it is the Mount of Olives, which is higher; and Gabaon, eight mile-stones off, is highest of all. Even the height which was once in Zion though it has been levelled now, was taller than Golgotha.

5,6   Why the name "Skull," then, unless it had been named "Place of a Skull" because the skull of the first-formed man was there, and his remains laid to rest? (7) By being crucified above it our Lord Jesus Christ mysteriously indicated our salvation, with the water and blood that flowed from him out of his pierced side. For he sprinkled our forefather's remains first, starting from the first of the lump, to show us the sprinkling of his blood to cleanse our defilement and the defilement of any repentant soul. (8) And for an example of leavening, and of the cleansing of the spot our sins have left, (he first sprinkled) the water shed (from his side) on the one who lay buried on the site, for his hope and the hope of us, his descendants.

5,9   Thus the prophecy, "Awake thou that sleepest, and arise from the dead, and Christ shall give thee light,"[16] was fulfilled here. For even though it speaks of us, who are dead in our works and sleep a deep sleep of ignorance, this was surely where the riddle originated; <for> it contains the manner of <the resurrection>. (10) And in no loose or idle fashion; it says, "Many bodies of the saints arose"—as the Gospel puts it—"and went with him into the holy city."[17] And it did not say, "souls of the saints" arose; the actual bodies of the saints arose and went into the holy city with him, and so on.

5,11   And now that we have entirely rid ourselves of this mosquito's bites, with the oil of God's lovingkindness, with our Lord's sojourn, and with the light of the Gospel of the truth, let us do what we always do and hasten, by the power of God, to go to the rest.

---

[16] Eph. 5:14.
[17] Matt. 27:52-53.

SUBJECT INDEX

(References to sects and sectarian leaders are generally to mentions which occur outside of the principal discussions. For the principal discussions, consult the Table of Contents and the Anacephalaeoses.)

Abel 17, 31, 252-3, 256, 267
Abiram 209, 250, 275
Abraham 9, 18, 24-5, 27, 121, 143-4, 303, 304, 305; apocalypse 258
Abrasax 55, 74
abstinence from meat and wine 135
Achamoth 182; creates through the demiurge 172-3; passion and restoration 169-72, 180, 181-2; salvation 177; sows seed in the demiurge's breath 174; world created from her passion 170-2
Acts of the Apostles in Hebrew 122, 124; apocryphal *acta* 132
acts, progress through all human 55-6, 100-3, 249
Adam, animated from on high 64-5, 244; apocalypses 88; buried on Golgotha 351-2; a Christian 15; is Christ 56, 121, 151; created by angels 64; created by demiurge 174; created by sons of Ialdabaoth 244; finished with difficulty 64-5, 244; gives divine oracle 205-6; married his own daughter 259; name 13-14; not begun on the fifth day 13; not saved 349; offspring of powers 250; a prophet 15; recognizes the Father 244; repentance 350-1; two first men 65, 256; uncircumcised 15
Adda(n) 38, 300
aeon(s) 80-1, 181, 182-3, 188, 220-1, 229, 233, 237, 243; arithmetical explanation 222-4; Colorbasian account 233-4; erring aeon 188, 190, 192, 223; first aeon 162; in pairs 153, 154, 155, 158-9, 163 (see also, syzygy); Marcosian account 214-16, 217-18, 219-20, 222-4; produce Jesus 166; Ptolemaean account 197-8; restoration 166, 217, 223-4; Secundian account 191-2, 195-6, 196-7; Valentinian accounts 153-4, 156-9, 162-3
alphabet, = body of Truth 216; = Jesus 220; = the thirty aeons 214-15, 216; everything constituted of 209, 216
amen 215, 223, 328, 335; = 99 223
angel(s) 19, 33, 36, 39, 249, 264-5; divide the world by lot 71; existence denied 36;

give the Law 107; = God of the Jews 71; human acts offered through 249; in each heaven 58, 70-1, 263; made the heavens 70-1; made man 58, 64, 66-7, 71, 105, 106; made the world 55, 56, 58, 60, 62, 64, 70, 71, 100, 103, 106, 107; = "officer" 103, 303; place Ham in ark 257; produced by Womb 80; rebelled 64, 100, 186; retinue 263; Savior's bodyguard 166, 171-2, 174; seduced 58-9, 78; = soul 238; = sounds of the alphabet 215; war on each other 58-9, 71-2, 256
Anna 182
anonymous Valentinian work 156-9
Apelles 210, 340, 346
apocalypse of Abraham 258
apocalypses of Adam 88
Apollinarius 143
apostles 53; books in their names 139; inferior to Gnostic teachers 101, 213; witnesses of the resurrection 342
Apostolic Constitution 348
Aqiba 38, 300
Aquila 91
archon(s) 79, 87, 89, 90, 98, 209, 250, 263, 318; acts offered to 89; children of 94; dragon-like 90; in each heaven 60, 79, 263; feed on souls 90-1, 263; flesh belongs to 89; of lust 87, 90; made the world 60, 83, 110, 209
Archontics 347
Ascension of Isaiah 263
Ascension of Paul 250
astrology 39-40, 42
Athena 59-60
atoms 22
Azura, wife of Cain 259

baptism 32-3, 41-2, 52-3, 274; administered by women 210, 275; daily 41-2, 56, 120, 131; for the dead 110, 210; Ebionite 131; of Jesus 130; of the Jewish patriarch 122-4; preliminary to "redemption" 230; repeated 210, 274; repudiated 263-4